Kangnikoé Bado

The Court of Justice of the Economic Community of West African States as a Constitutional Court

Member States obligations resulting from the Court's rulings

Nomos

Open Access funding provided by Max Planck Society.

The Deutsche Nationalbibliothek lists this publication in the Deutsche Nationalbibliografie; detailed bibliographic data are available on the Internet at http://dnb.d-nb.de

ISBN 978-3-8487-6051-0 (Print)
978-3-7489-0180-8 (ePDF)

British Library Cataloguing-in-Publication Data
A catalogue record for this book is available from the British Library.

ISBN 978-3-8487-6051-0 (Print)
978-3-7489-0180-8 (ePDF)

Library of Congress Cataloging-in-Publication Data
Bado, Kangnikoé
The Court of Justice of the Economic Community of West African States as a Constitutional Court
Member States obligations resulting from the Court's rulings
Kangnikoé Bado
353 pp.
Includes bibliographic references.

ISBN 978-3-8487-6051-0 (Print)
978-3-7489-0180-8 (ePDF)

1st Edition 2019

Published by
Nomos Verlagsgesellschaft mbH & Co. KG
Waldseestraße 3-5 | 76530 Baden-Baden
www.nomos.de

Total Print Production:
Nomos Verlagsgesellschaft mbH & Co. KG
Waldseestraße 3-5 | 76530 Baden-Baden

Printed and bound in Germany.

ISBN (Print): 978-3-8487-6051-0
ISBN (ePDF): 978-3-7489-0180-8

DOI: https://doi.org/10.5771/9783748901808

To my parents with gratitude

Preface

Almost two years after the publication of the first edition in German, I am delighted to be able to present this English edition which aims at meeting the need to reach broader audience. In this respect, I owe my particular gratitude to Birgit Böttner, Leonie Spangenberger und Prof. Dr. André Thomashausen who were entrusted with the translation.

Substantially the topical issue remains, in my view, relevant and pertinent as it did in 2015 when I have completed the researches, since the court is always confronted by the problematic at the centre of this reflection and its jurisprudential practice has not really changed until now. The examination at hand broaches the subject of a supra-constitutional function of the Court of Justice of the Economic Community of West African States (ECOWAS). . A particular source of inspiration for this book has been the research project "Constitutional Jurisdiction and Democratisation in West Africa" financed by the German Research Foundation (DFG). Although I became a Member of the project team rather late, the work within the project inspired me to think about the role of the ECOWAS Court of Justice. For example, I refer to the decision in Ameganvi et al vs. Togo and its relevance for the relationship between the regional courts and the courts of the Member States, in particular, the Constitutional Courts. I especially wanted to show the development of human rights jurisdiction since the inception of the additional protocol in 2005 and on this basis the possible individual complaints before the Court of Justice. based on recent developments in international law, my main objective is to clarify all the legal consequences arising from this extension of competence of the Court, in particular with regard to the international responsibility of member states in the event of human rights violations. Moreover, this paper aims to examine the constitutional implications of this reform and the guarded use by the court of its own competence.

Finally, I would also like to contribute to the reduction of the deficit of legal protection within the Economic Community of West African States by strengthening the constitutional role of the ECOWAS Court of Justice. According to my thesis, the declaratory judgments by the Court of Justice should be able to unfold their legal force in the signatory-countries to their fullest extent.

During the preparation of this research, which was completed in December 2015 and accepted by the Justus-Liebig-University of Gießen's Faculty of Law as a dissertation, I have received support from numerous persons and institutions.

Firstly, I would like to thank my mentor Prof. Dr. Thilo Marauhn for his mentorship during this dissertation. I am endlessly grateful for his steadfast trust and patience. The exchange of ideas with him was always effective and constantly resulted in new findings. These exchanges belong to my fondest memories. I would like to thank Prof. Dr. Rainer Grote for contributing a second opinion and for his valuable further inspirations. Furthermore, I would like to thank Prof. Dr. Dres. h.c. Herbert Kronke for his constant support and for being a willing partner for discussion.

I would like to particularly thank Vera Strobel for her support regarding the editorial revision of the German edition.

I would like to thank Prof. Dr. Sven Simon for his tremendous support. I owe my special gratitude to the numerous discussions and professional suggestions. I would further like to extend my sincere thanks to Dr. Ignaz Stegmiller for his critical review of the completed version before the paper went to print.

I would like to sincerely thank professors Adama Kpodar, Joèl Aivo, Babakar Kanté and Akuété Santos for their valuable advice during my research trip in West Africa.

Moreover, I would like to thank Dr. Daniel Behailu as well as Katharina Bielka, Dr. Prosper Simbarashe Maguchu, Dr. Wisdom Momodu, Dr. Collins Mbuayang and Dr. Asmin Franziska for the constant exchange of ideas. Similarly, I would like to thank my colleagues Dr. Ayşe-Martina Böhringer, Judith Thorn, Joscha Müller, Marie-Christin Stenzel, Dr.Lisa Hemann, Dr. Anne Winter and Chadischa Schöpffer for their collegiality and support. I would like to sincerely thank Ms Ulrike Rein and Ms Susanne Seitz for the friendly environment and their helpfulness within the team of the professorship.

Furthermore, my circle of friends in Germany has contributed considerably to the realisation of this paper. I would like to thank my friends Fabian Kiehlmann, Edem Atsiatorme, Juliane and Cornelia Glinz as well as Vera Bense, Fanny Raisch, Robin Azinovic, Gabriel Noll, the Degbè family (Brussels), the Doglo family and the Tèko family.

This work presented thrilling scientific challenges for me. The handling of these would not have been possible without the support of my family. In particular, I owe my brothers Ékoé Richard and Messanh Nicolas as well as my sisters Marie Povi and Ayélévi endless gratitude for giving me strength through their continued support and encouraging words.

Amongst various instutitions which I would like to thank, I owe my thanks first and foremost to the Konrad-Adenauer Foundation which not only financed significant part of my researches in Germany but also covered the costs of translation and publication of the English edition of the manuscript. I must acknowledge my sincere thank to Dr. Arne Wulff who has been available to coordinate the English translation and publication of this work. Moreover, I am genuinely grateful to Ms Anja Berretta's and Mr. Berthold Gees' for their understanding during my scholarship period at the Konrad-Adenauer foundation. In the same manner, I owe gratitude to the Max Planck Institute for Social Law and Social Policy and the Max Planck Society for making the Open Access publication of this Book possible. Furthermore, I am also grateful for the German Research Foundation's (DFG) interest in the legal developments in Africa and for their funding.

I would also like to thank the Max-Planck Institute for Comparative Public Law and International Law (Heidelberg) for making their library available to me. Besides, I would like to thank Mr. Albrecht Günther of the branch library for Law and Economy for his assistance in trying to locate documents that were not available in Gießen. My sincere thanks go to the library manager, Mr. Vincente Mendes Correia, for giving me access to the ECOWAS-Court of Justice Library and for making numerous official documents by the ECOWAS Community.

This dissertation is dedicated to my sisters Kayi and Tsotso.

Kangnikoé Bado Munich, in the spring of 2019

Abstract

Whereas the Court of the Economic Community of West African States (ECOWAS) had originally been established to address matters of regional integration only, it has been tasked to rule on human rights violations since 2005. This has led to jurisdictional conflicts between national (constitutional) courts of ECOWAS member states and the Court itself. This study analyses the relationship between the national and the regional level, and develops proposals on how to overcome such jurisdictional conflicts. This thesis is based on the ruling of the Constitutional Court of Togo N °E-018/10 of 22 November 2010 and the position of the ECOWAS Community Court of Justice, N°ECW/CCJ/JUG/09/11 of 7 October 2011 and N °ECW/CCJ/JUG/06/12 of 13 March 2012, concerning the aforementioned ruling of the Constitutional Court of Togo. The thesis is an attempt at finding an answer to the question as to whether the judgments of the Court carry a binding effect within the Member States and particularly on judgments of constitutional courts.

This work explores real and potential tensions within the ECOWAS legal order. The tensions stem from the legal force of judgments of constitutional courts of Member States and the admissibility of individual petitions before the Court according to Art. 9.4 and 10.d of Supplementary Protocol A/SP.1/01/05 Amending the Protocol A/P.1/7/91 Relating to the Community Court of Justice. Since the binding effect of the rulings of the Court is not clearly defined, Member States resist implementing the Court's decisions particularly in constitutional matters. Pursuant to article 9.4 of the aforementioned supplementary protocol the Court has authority to examine the conformity of the actions of Member States' institutions with the African Charter on Human and Peoples' Rights whether the organ exercises legislative, executive, and judicial or any other similar functions. However, it is interesting to note that the decisions of Constitutional Courts or Supreme Courts of ECOWAS Member States are final and not subject to further appeal. It is true that a Constitution and decisions of Constitutional Courts express the sovereignty of a state. Nevertheless Art. 27 of the Vienna Convention on the Law of Treaties forbids the states to invoke their national law to hinder the implementation of their international obligations. To that extent the *res judicata* is not a valid argument to hinder the implementation of the Court's rulings. Then a state party endorses the obligation of restitution in integrum according to international customary law and judicial precedents of the International Court of Justice. Moreover, according to international customary law, all organs of the state involved in a case are bound by the rulings of the Court. Constitutional Courts are state organs. Hence, they are also bound by the findings of the ECOWAS-Court.

This work also identifies some deficiencies in the current regime of the human rights mandate of the Court. Gaps exist not only at the level of the Member States constitutional order but also at the community level. At the national level, there are no legal provisions in ECOWAS Member States about the legal force and how the rulings of the Court should be domesticated. At the community level, the binding effect of the rulings of the Court is not adapted to its human rights mandate. With regard to its human rights mandate, the Court plays a role of supranational constitutional court. For instance, the Court is empowered to decide on individual petitions and its rulings are final and binding. For a better compliance with the judgments of the Court, this thesis suggests innovative remedies to render national legislation adequate to the human rights mandate of the ECOWAS Community Court of Justice. Some of the key remedies proposed in the thesis include the following: the Court should be empowered to order concrete measures about how its rulings should be implemented. Art. 15 par. 4 of the Revised Treaty should be adapted to extend the jurisdiction of the Court; a Committee should be created to work with the Court about the implementation of its rulings; Member States should provide exceptional provisions that permit a new enrolling of a case after the rulings of the Court, as available in many Member States of the European Council, and particularly kindred to Art. 122 of the Constitutional Process Law of Switzerland.

Table of Contents

List of Abbreviations

ANC	Alliance Nationale pour le Changement
AU	African Union
BVerfGE	Decisions by the Federal Constitutional Court of the Federal Republic of Germany
CDRF	Centre de Recherche pour les Droits Fondamentaux
CEDEAO	Communauté Economique des Etats de l'Afrique de l'Ouest
CEDH	Cour Européenne des Droits de l'Homme
CHARTA	African Charta for Human Rights and Peoples' Rights
CIJ	Cour Internationale de Justice
CJ CEDEAO	Cour de Justice de la CEDEAO
CJEU	Cour de Justice de l'Union Européenne
CPJI	Cour Permanente de Justice Internationale
ders.	By the same author
DÖV	Die Öffentliche Verwaltung (Legal Journal)
EAC	East African Community
EACJ	East African Court of Justice
ECCJ	ECOWAS Community Court of Justice
ECOWAS	Economic Community Of West African States
ECtHR	European Court of Human Rights
ECHR	European Convention on Human Rights
EuGH	European Court of Justice
EuGRZ	European Magazine on Fundamental Rights
EuR	Journal on European Law
FS	Commemoratice Publication
ICJ	International Court of Justice
ILC	International Law Commission
OAU	Organisation of African Unity
PCIJ	Permanent Court of International Justice
R.Q.D.I	Revue Québécoise de Droit International
SADC	Southern African Development Community
UFC	Union des Forces du Changement
VRÜ	The Journal "Law and Politics in Africa, Asia and Latin America"
ZaöRV	Journal for Foreign Public Law and International Law

Introduction

This paper is concerned with the conflict of jurisdiction within the ECOWAS Community and the function of the ECOWAS Court of Justice resulting from it's nature as a supranational Constitutional Court.[1] In order to explain the term "conflict of jurisdiction", it is necessary to define the term "jurisdiction" in greater detail. Jurisdiction can be understood in a formal and material sense.[2] In a formal sense, jurisdiction means the competence of a court to decide on a legal dispute.[3] In this sense, the term "jurisdiction" is understood as the competence of the court in a judicial instance. In contrast, jurisdiction in a material sense describes the material manifestations of these responsibilities, i.e. the contents of the decision.[4]Since the conflict relates to the term "jurisdiction", the term of "conflict" is also to be understood from both points of view.[5] Formal conflicts arise when two or more courts claim jurisdiction as only one claim can be fulfilled at a time.[6]A divergence in the content of decisions taken by different courts on the other hand refers to a conflict in a material sense.[7]

Finally, regarding the conflict of laws, the term of conflict of jurisdiction has another, very different meaning. It insofar concerns the conflict of competence between courts of different countries as these have not necessarily signed an international treaty. This conflict of jurisdiction is two-dimensional. A positive conflict arises in cases where multiple courts, according to the relevant collisionregulations, claim their power to adjudicate in a particular case so that, in theory, this case could be brought before numerous courts. In contrast, a negative conflict of jurisdiction arises, when

1 Cohen-Jonathan, La fonction quasi constitutionnelle de la Cour Européenne des Droits de l'Homme, in: Renouveau du Droit constitutionnel. Mélanges en l'honneur de Louis Favoreu, 1127 (1028); Wildhaber, Eine verfassungsrechtliche Zukunft für den Europäischen Gerichtshofs für Menschenrechte?, in: EuGRZ (2002), 569 (569) [A constitutional future for the European Court of Justice for Human Rights].

2 Klatt, Die praktische Konkordanz von Kompetenzen, 34. [The practical concordance of competences].

3 Klatt, Die praktische Konkordanz von Kompetenzen, 34.

4 Klatt, Die praktische Konkordanz von Kompetenzen, 58.

5 Klatt, Die praktische Konkordanz von Kompetenzen, 60.

6 Klatt, Die praktische Konkordanz von Kompetenzen, 60.

7 Klatt, Die praktische Konkordanz von Kompetenzen, 60.

none of the courts may be approached due to a conflict of law regarding the rules of competence or all approached forums reject responsibility due to the aforementioned rules. As a result, none of the courts may adjudicate.

For the purpose of this paper, the term "conflict of jurisdiction" has a more specific meaning. Whilst not necessarily, conflicts of jurisdiction are often conflicts of competence.[8] The examination presented here looks at the competing or contradictory conflicts of competence of different organs of jurisdiction in multi-level-governance systems.[9] To be specific, it is about the theoretical possibility of conflicts of jurisdiction between national Constitutional Courts or Supreme Courts of West African countries and the ECOWAS Court of Justice. In general, national constitutional courts have the competence to issue legally binding and final judgments which develop an *erga-omnes* effect on national level. The conflict and its effects[10] can, for example, be found in Art. 46 (3) of the Nigerian Constitution or in Art. 106 of the Togolese Constitution. Therefore, the conflict of jurisdiction has its origin in the juxtaposition of the finality of decisions of national courts and the possibility of legal action at the court of justice on the ECOWAS-level.[11] By challenging the final binding decisions of national Constitutional Courts[12], these conflicts of jurisdiction not only represent a theoretical paradox but are also the basis for a substantial and real risk potential, because they challenge the final binding decision of domestic constitutional courts.[13] This risk potential comes to show in such cases where courts on different levels reach contradicting verdicts.[14] It is then no

---

8 Sauer, Jurisdiktionskonflikte in Mehrebenensystemen, 59. [Conflicts of jurisdiction in multi-level-governance systems].

9 Linder, Grundrechtsschutz in Europa – System einer Kollisionsdogmatik, in: EuR (2007), 160 (161); Schilling, Deutscher Grundrechtsschutz zwischen staatlicher Souveränität und men- schenrechtlicher Europäisierung, 10. [Protection of fundamental law between state sovereignity and Europeanisation in terms of Human Rights].

10 Enabulele, International Community Law Review (2010), 111 (119); Ebobrah, A critical Ana- lysis of the human rights mandate of the ECOWAS Community Court of Justice, 14, available at: http://docs.escr-net.org/usr_doc/S_Ebobrah.pdf (last accessed on 16/05/2015); Knop, Völker- und Europarechtsfreundlichkeit als Verfassungsgrundsätze, 57. [Openness toward International and European Law].

11 Enabulele, International Community Law Review (2010), 111 (132).

12 Sauer, Jurisdiktionskonflikte in Mehrebenensystemen, 60. [Conflicts of jurisdiction in multi-level-governance systems].

13 Sauer, Jurisdiktionskonflikte in Mehrebenensystemen, 60.

14 Sauer, Jurisdiktionskonflikte in Mehrebenensystemen, 60.

longer comprehensible for the parties to the dispute which judgment is binding.[15] This state situation could lead to a loss of confidence in the validity of the law. Because of this, the risk of a conflict of jurisdiction was removed at a continental level by Art. 10 of the Protocol (2005).[16]Theoretically, the conflict arises out of the fact that the protection of human rights does not fall exclusively in the competence of national Constitutional Courts but also in the jurisdiction of the ECOWAS Court of Justice.[17] Just as in the European judicial area, the possibility of such conflicts of jurisdiction is not impossible. The conflict also arises at a European level when the European jurisdiction contradicts that of the constitutional courts of the Member States.[18] Within ECOWAS, the conflict is revived especially, if the ultimately binding decision by the national Constitutional Court is declared to be in violation of human rights by the ECOWAS Court of Justice. How can this conflict be resolved? How can a harmonious functioning between the ECOWAS Court of Justice and national constitutional courts of Member States be created? These questions form the fundamental object of this paper.

From a procedural point of view, the conflict arises when two different legal systems with contradictory judgments that are difficult to overcome in their respective procedural principles, collide. These quasi insurmountable differences concern, on one hand, the legal force and the binding effect of constitutional court-decisions (Chapter 2), and on the other hand, the possibility to the ECOWAS Court of Justice to supersede the decisions of national courts (Chapter 3).

---

15 Sauer, Jurisdiktionskonflikte in Mehrebenensystemen, 60.

16 Ebobrah, A critical analysis of the human rights mandate of the ECOWAS Community Court of Justice, 15, available at: http://docs.escr-net.org/usr_doc/S_Ebobrah.pdf (last accessed on 16/05/2015).

17 Alter/Helfer/McAllister, A new international human right court for West Africa: the ECOWAS Community Court of Justice, in: The American Journal of International Law (2013), 737 (759).

18 Benda/Klein, Verfassungsprozeßrecht, 2. edition, erstes Kap., Rn. 63 [Benda/Klein, Constitutional Process Law, 2. edition, first chapter., see recital 63].

Chapter 1 Research Question and Structure of the Study

In the following, the term "the Court of Justice" is used to describe the ECOWAS Court of Justice and "Charta" is used for the African Charta on Human and Peoples' Rights. I would like to mainly discuss in this chapter the historical background of the ECOWAS Court of Justice as an International court (A), the competences of the Court of Justice (B) and in particular its jurisdiction regarding human rights (C). Thereafter, the reason behind this paper is explained (D). The jurisdiction poses complex fundamental questions regarding the binding effect of the decisions taken by the Court of Justice and the consequences regarding the national legal system of the contracted states stemming from them. These complex questions are examined in section (E). Not all forms of jurisdiction of the Court of Justice are discussed in this study. Rather, the relationship between the Court of Justice and the highest court of the Member States (Constitutional Court or Supreme Court) with respect to the binding legal effect form the focus of this dissertation. Therefore, in order to clarify this relationship, the complex questions need to be narrowed down (F).

A. The ECOWAS Court of Justice as an International Court

It should be noted that we assume the association of the African states in the African Union constitutes a continental organisation. Therefore, the term *"regional organisation"* is used for the respective region within the African Union instead of *"sub-regional organisation"*. In West Africa, the term *„regional organisation of West African States"* is used at a continental level, as the institutions of the African Union constitute a continental organisation. Effectively, the term *ECOWAS* summarises the Economic Community of West African States.[1]It was founded in Lagos on 28/05/1975 and is an intra-regional organisation of currently 15 countries, since Mauretania's exit in 1999[2]. The starting point for the establishment of an economic

1 In the French version: La communauté des Etats de l'Afrique de L'ouest (CEDEAO).

2 Ebobrah, A critical Analysis of the human rights mandate of the ECOWAS Community Court of Justice, 6, available at: http://docs.escr-net.org/usr_doc/S_Ebobrah

association in West Africa was the Biafra War in Nigeria. Goals of the regional ECOWAS are stipulated in Art. 3 of the Amendment Agreement of Cotonou. According to this objective, ECOWAS strives to achieve accelerated and sustained economic development in West Africa[3]. According to the original objective of the association, the key-issue was step-by-step economic integration and cooperation of the Member States by forming a customs union, economic union, and currency union.[4] All this will be possible, if there is economic collaboration within the framework of eco-political coordination. For this purpose, the presidents of state may add additional objectives which seem necessary to reach the goals of the association.[5] Therefore the policies of the Member States must be harmonized and coordinated.[6] However, the question may be posed how ECOWAS has evolved from an economic association into a community of values. Before methodically demonstrating how the jurisdiction of the ECOWAS Court of Justice is a *supra-national Court of Justice*, the reasons why the Signatories granted the Court of Justice the authority to decide on questions of human rights will be briefly outlined.

B. The Jurisdiction of the Court of Justice

The assignment of the Court of Justice of responsibilities regarding questions on human rights stems from a curious history in the region. One indeed wonders why a Court of Justice, which was originally meant for economic integration, barely operates in this field.[7] The inactivity of the Court of Justice in the field of economic lawsuits, can be explained by various factors[8].Remarkably, the ECOWAS Court of Justice was turned into a

.pdf (last accessed on 16/05/2015); Hartmann, in: Freistein/Leininger (Publ.), Manual International Organisations, 86.

3 Hartmann, in: Freistein/Leininger (Publ.), Manual International Organisations, 86.

4 Art. 3 of the amendment agreement of Cotonou (23/07/1993).

5 Art. 3 Abs. 2 (0) of the amendment agreement of Cotonou (23/07/1993).

6 Ebobrah, A critical Analysis of the human rights mandate of the ECOWAS Community Court of Justice, 6, available at: http://docs.escr-net.org/usr_doc/S_Ebobrah.pdf (last accessed on 16/05/2015).

7 Alter/Helfer/McAllister, A new international human right court for West Africa: the ECOWAS Community Court of Justice, in: The American Journal of International Law (2013), 737 (738).

8 Alter/Helfer/R.McAllister, A new international human right court for West Africa: the ECOWAS Community Court of Justice, in: The American Journal of International Law (2013), 737 (756).

court for human rights in 2005. How can this shift be explained? The Member States agreed that successful economic development and integration are dependent on political stability, the adherence to human rights and the principles of the rule of law within the Community.[9] Regarding the regional integration in West Africa, politics were at first considered to be a side-issue.[10] The overwhelming attention on political stability and the monitoring of human rights by the ECOWAS Court of Justice essentially has to do with the security policy and the role of the Community as well as the consensus regarding economic integration conditional on human rights[11]. Precisely because of this, the Signatories came to the conclusion in the early stages of integration that the economic purpose can not be attained if the political stability within the Member States and the region cannot be secured. Securing political stability by observing the principles of the rule of law and human rights,is a good prerequisite for the attainment of economic growth.[12] This raises an important question: why does the question of security within the ECOWAS Community play such a significant role? How did ECOWAS become a force for peace in the region[13]? The answer to this question dates back to the exciting and difficult history

9 Saliu, Governance and development questions in West Africa, in: Bamba/Igué/Sylla (Publ.), Sortir du sous-développement, 185 (196); Ebobrah, Legitimacy and feasibility of human rights realisation through regional economic communities in Africa: the case of ECOWAS, 4; Ahadzi-Nonou, Droits de l'Homme et Développement: Théories et Réalités, in: Territoires et Liberté, Mélanges en Hommage au Doyen Yves Madiot, 107 (108); Ndiaye, Les organisations internationa- les Africaines et le maintien de la Paix: L'exemple de la CEDEAO, 37.

10 Ebobrah, Legitimacy and feasibility of human rights realisation through regional economic communities in Africa: the case of ECOWAS, 3.

11 Ebobrah, Legitimacy and feasibility of human rights realisation through regional economic communities in Africa: the case of ECOWAS, 5; Alter/Helfer/McAllis-er, A new international human right court for West Africa: The ECOWAS Community Court of Justice, in: The American Journal of International Law (2013), 737 (753); Ebobrah, Human rights developments in sub-regi onal court in Africa during 2008, in: African Human Rights Law Journal (2009), 312 (313).

12 Ebobrah, A critical Analysis of the human rights mandate of the ECOWAS Community Court of Justice, 7, available at: http://docs.escr-net.org/usr_doc/S_Ebobrah.pdf (last accessed on 16/05/2015).

13 Van den Boom, Regionale Kooperation in Westafrika, 92; Obi, Economic Community of West African States on the Ground: Comparing Peacekeeping in Liberia, Sierra Leone, Guinea Bissau, and Côte d'Ivoire, in: Söderbaum/Tavares (Publ.), Regional Organizations in African Se- curity, 51 (62); Söderbaum/Tavares, Problematizing Regional Organizations in African Security, in: Söderbaum/Tavares (Publ.), Regional Organizations in African Security, 1 (3); Dampha, Nationalism and Reparation in West Africa, 121; Mair/Peters-Berries,

of the ECOWAS Community. The association was indeed founded with the purpose of ensuring economic collaboration. However, events led to a necessary extension of the Community's objectives, e.g. in the area of security. It all began with the involvement of Nigeria in Liberian conflicts in 1990–1999. The ECOWAS Community has effectively taken on a humanitarian mandate in the region with this intervention.[14] The concern for security and peace in the region has led to a situation where the observation of human rights and the rule of law has become a main priority for the organisation. On the basis of the objectives stipulated by the Community in the Amendment Agreement, further military interventions have taken place in the region, such as in Sierra Leone (1998–2002), Guinea-Bissau (1998–1999), again in Liberia (2003) and in the Ivory Coast (2002–2004).[15] In order to find a legal framework for such interventions, an additional Protocol regarding the creation of a *Mechanisme de prévention, de règlement des conflits, de maintien de la paix et de la sécurité* was adopted in 1999. The regulations stipulated in this additional Protocol are unusual in the light of Art. 2 paragraph 7 of the Charta of the United Nations. This Protocol does not only grant ECOWAS extensive rights of intervention but also mentions extensive reasons and possibilities for the authorisation of an intervention in other Member States.[16] Among these are, besides severe humanitarian emergencies and serious human rights violations, cross-border and internal violent conflict and the prevention of coups against the constitutional order within Member States.[17] Ultimately, an intervention is justified under any circumstances which pose a severe risk to the security

Regional Integration and Cooperation in Africa south of the Sahara: EAC, ECOWAS and SADC in comp., 189.

14 Hartmann, in: Freistein/Leininger (Publ.), Manual International Organisations, 88.

15 Hartmann, in: Freistein/Leininger (Publ.), Manual International Organisations, 88.

16 See inter alia Art. 22, 25 et 26 du Protocol relatif au mécanisme de prévention, des gestions, de règlement des conflits, de maintien de la paix et de la sécurité (10/12/1999); Ebobrah, Legitimacy and feasibility of human rights realisation through regional economic communities in Africa: the case of ECOWAS, 7.

17 Edi, Globalization and Politics in the Economic Community of West African States, 105; Gambari, Political and comparative dimensions of regional integration: the Case of ECOWAS, preface, vii; Mair/Peters-Berries, Regional Integration and Cooperation in Africa south of the Sahara: EAC, ECOWAS and SADC in comp., 233.

and peace in Member States.[18] Voices in literature consider the immediate vicinity of the Signatories to be the main reason for this particular regulation of interventions within ECOWAS, namely the concern for the guarantee of security in the region.[19]

At a universal level and after the horrors of the Second World War, the issue of human rights has moved away from the complete exposure of the fundamental rights of the individual in totalitarian regimes and a purely nationalistic relationship towards an issue of supra-national and international understanding.[20] Thus, citizens are also entitled to the Universal Declaration of Human Rights, the International Covenant on Civil and Political Rights and the African Charter on Human and Peoples' Rights, besides the fundamental freedoms and constitutional individual rights of the Togolese Constitution (to name one example). The Charta is at the centre of the West African Architecture of Human Rights. It was conceived in the instruments of Community not only as a standard of review of national government action but also as the minimal standard of regional protection of human rights – as per the Protocol of Good Governance and Democracy.

This brief historical insight is important because the aforementioned acute crises in the region are the prerequisites for the involvement of the ECOWAS Community in reinforcing human rights protection within the system of the Community. In order to contain a repressive political regime and military coups stemming from it, the Signatories decided to adopt a peoples' rights pact that recognised the principles of human and peoples' rights in the rule of law as standards of the Community. Indeed, an additional Protocol for Good Governance[21] was adopted as a reaction to the instability and the endangerment of the rule of law within the Community. It codifies the significant principles of constitutional convergence, the rule of law and human rights set out in the African Charta. A number of fundamental principles of the rule of law, such as separation of powers, fair elec-

---

18 Hartmann, in: Freistein/Leininger (Publ.), Manual International Organisations, 88.

19 Ebobrah, Litigating Human Rights before Sub-Regional Court in Africa: Prospects and challenges, in: African Journal of International and Comparative Law (2009), 79 (87).

20 Rohleder, Protection of Constitutional Rights in the European Multi-level-System, 29.

21 Protocole A/SP.1/12/.01 sur la Démocratie et la Bonne gouvernance, Additionnel au Protoco le relatif au mécanisme de prévention, de gestion, de règlement des conflits, de maintien de la paix et de la sécurité (21/12/2001).

tions as the only legitimate path to power and the guarantee of political freedoms for the citizens are laid down in this Protocol as basic principles of the Community.[22] Furthermore, inclusive and political participation in political life in the country as well as free activity for political parties is guaranteed. According to the Protocol, the army must, in the secular constitutional system, play a subordinate role to the government (Art. 1 of the Protocol A/SP.1/12/01). As per this Protocol, amendments to the electoral acts without consent by the most important political actors of a Member state in the last six months before new elections are strictly prohibited (Art. 2 of the Protocol A/SP.1/12/01). Moreover, it allows for an intervention in a Member state if it is found that the democratic order of a signatory has been severely breached or the human rights situation is endangered in a fundamental manner (Art. 45 of the Protocol A/SP.1/12/01). Therefore, the defense of democratic rules of governance constitutes, as set out in this Protocol, an indispensable standard within the Community. All of these principles must be adhered to by the Member States. A contravention of the stipulated principles of the rules of law is punished with sanctions. According to a few voices in literature these requirements in the Protocol for good governance establishes a Constitution for West African states.[23] Based on the considerable threat to the constitutional state in West Africa, this opinion is justified. However, it must be stated here that despite the implementation of the Protocol in July 2005 with new instruments of ratification, there have been repeated political upheavals (Burkina Faso, October 2014) and unconstitutional transfers of power as well as military coups in the region, e.g. in Togo (February 2005), Guinea (2008), Niger (2010). This legal situation within the region clearly shows that democracy within the constitutional order of the Member States is still fragile.[24] For this very reason, an impartial and independent organ of jurisdiction at Community-level seems particularly necessary, as the disregard for constitutional principles can directly lead to such constitutional crises and consequently to political instability within the legal order of the Community. The adherence to human rights and the inherent democratic principles will therefore become the current task of the ECOWAS Court of Jus-

22 Likibi, La Charte africaine pour la démocratie, les élections et la gouvernance, 69.

23 Fall/Sall, Une constitution régionale pour l'espace CEDEAO: le protocole sur la démocratie et la bonne gouvernance, available at: http://la-constitution-en-afrique.org/article-34239380. html (last accessed on 16/05/2015).

24 Hartmann, in: Freistein/Leininger (Publ.), Manual International Organisations, 91.

tice, effectively formalizing the role of human rights in the development process[25].

The legal foundations for the ECOWAS Court of Justice are only laid out in the Founding Treaty. Art. 6 of the amendment agreement (1993) defines the institutions of the Community. The decision-making organs of the Community include the Conference of the Heads of State, the Council of Ministers, the Parliament, the Economic and Social Committee, the executive administration and the ECOWAS Court of Justice.

The ECOWAS Court of Justice can look back on 23 years of history as the judicial pillar of the Community. Effectively, the Protocol A/P1/7/91[26]on the Court of Justice for the Community was adopted on 6 July 1991. This Protocol, however, is a firm component of the Founding Treaty (28/05/1975) and later of the amendment agreement, the so-called Cotonou-Agreement, of 23 July 1993.[27] Therefore, its date of inception was 05/11/1996. According to Art. 6 (e) of the amendment agreement, the ECOWAS Court of Justice embodies the supra-national core of the Community.

Concerning its factual competences, the Court of Justice disposes of a broad competence in comparison to other intra-regional judiciary bodies. According to Art. 9 of the Protocol A/P1/7/91 (1991), the Court of Justice is responsible for the decision on legal disputes regarding the interpretation of the ECOWAS founding Treaty as well as the inherent Protocols and Conventions.[28] Therefore, the Court of Justice may adjudicate on the breaches of the treaty by a Member state and decide on disputes regarding the interpretation and implementation of the treaty. Disagreements between the institutions of the Community and the civil servants also fall within the Court's sphere of responsibility. It is important to point out that there are still many inconsistencies regarding individual complaints against breaches of the Community's economic laws.[29] The ECOWAS Court of Justice should also be called a hybrid court. In fact, the court is *mutatis mutandis* a combination of ECJ (European Court of Justice) and ECtHR (European Court of Human Rights).

---

25 Bryde, Überseeische Verfassungsvergleichung nach 30 Jahren [Overseas Comparison of Constitutions after 30 years], in: VRÜ (1997), 452 (460).

26 Protocole A/P1/7/91 (06/07/1991), relatif à la Cour de Justice de la Communauté.

27 Art. 34 Abs. 3, Protocole A/P1/7/91 (06/07/1991), relatif à la Cour de Justice de la Communauté.

28 In addition Art. 15 of the Amendment Agreement.

29 Hartmann, in: Freistein/Leininger (Publ.), Manual on International Organisations, 89.

Indeed, the ECOWAS Court of Justice can in many respects be compared to the ECJ. It is the court in the first and last instance[30] for legal disputes regarding the interpretation and application of the founding Treaty of the Community and the inherent additional protocols.

The factual competences of the Court of Justice are set down in Art. 3 of the additional Protocol.[31] According to Art. 3 of the additional Protocol A/SP.1/01/05 (19/01/2005), the court is responsible for the adjudication of every legal dispute regarding the following areas:

> « 1. La Cour a compétence sur tous les différends qui lui sont soumis et qui ont pour objet:
> a)L'interprétation et l'application du traité, des Conventions et protocoles de la Commu- nauté; b) l'interprétation et l'application du Traité, des règlements, des directives, des déci- sions et de tous autres instruments juridiques subsidiaires adoptés dans le cadre de la CEDEAO; c) l'appréciation de légalité des règlements, des directives, des décisions et de tous autres instruments juridiques subsidiaires adoptés dans le cadre de la CEDEAO; d) l'examen des manquements des Etats membres aux obligations qui leur incombent en vertu du Traité, des Conventions, Protocoles et Règlements, des décisions et directives; e) l'application des dispositions du Traité, Conventions et Protocoles, des règlements, des directives ou décisions de la CEDEAO; f) l'examen des litiges entre la Communauté et ses agents; g) les actions en réparation des dommages causés par une institution de la Communauté ou un agent de celle- ci pour tout acte commis ou toute omission dans l'exercice de ses fonctions. 2. La Cour est compétente pour déclarer engagée la responsabilité non contractuelle et condamne la Com- munauté à la réparation du préjudice causé, soit par des agissements matériels, soit par des actes normatifs des Institutions de la Communauté ou de ses agents dans l'exercice ou à l'occasion de l'exercice de leurs fonctions. 3. L'action en responsabilité contre la Communauté ou celle de la Communauté contre des tiers ou ses agents. Ces actions se prescrivent par trois (3) ans à compter de la réalisation des dommages. 4. *La Cour est compétente pour connaitre des cas de violation des droits de l'Homme dans tout Etat membre.* 5. En attendant la mise en place du Tribunal Arbitral, prévu par l'Article 16 du Traité Révisé, la Cour remplit également

30 Art. 19 Parag. 2 du Protocole A/P1/7/91 (06/07/1991), relatif à la Cour de Justice de la Communauté.

31 Protocole Additionnel A/SP.1/01/05 (19/01/2005) Portant Amendement du Protocole (A/P.1/ 7/91) Relatif à la Cour de Justice de la Communauté.

des fonctions d'arbitre. 6. La Cour peut avoir compétence sur toutes les questions prévues dans tout accord que les Etats membres pourraient conclure entre eux, ou avec la CEDEAO et qui lui donne compétence. 7. La Cour a toutes les compétences que les dispositions du présent Protocole lui confèrent ainsi que toutes autres compétences que pourraient lui confier des Protocoles et Décisions ultérieures de la Communauté. 8. La Conférence des Chefs d'Etat et de Gouvernement a le pouvoir de saisir la Cour pour connaitre des litiges autres que ceux visés dans le présent article ».

"1. The Court has the competence to adjudicate on any dispute relating to the following:
a) the interpretation and application of the Treaty, Conventions and Protocols of the Com- munity; b) the interpretation and application of regulations, directives, decisions and other subsidiary legal instruments adopted by ECOWAS; c) the legality of regulations, directives, decisions and other subsidiary legal instruments adopted by ECOWAS; d) the failure by Member States to honour their obligations under the Treaty, Conventions and Protocols, reg- ulations, directives or decisions of ECOWAS Members States; f) the Community and officials, and g) the actions for damages against a Community institution or an official of the Community for any action or omission in the exercise of official functions. 2. The Court shall have the power to determine any non-contractual liability of the Community and may order the Community to pay damages or make reparation for official acts or omissions of any Com- munity institution or Community officials in the performance of official duties or functions.
3. Any action by or against a Community Institutions or any Member of the Community shall be statute-barred after three (3) years from the date when the right of action arose. 4. The Court has jurisdiction to determine cases of violation of human rights that occur in any Member State. 5. Pending the establishment of Arbitration Tribunal provide for under Article 16 of the Treaty, the Court shall have the power to act as arbitrator for the purpose of Article 16 of the Treaty
6. The Court shall have jurisdiction over any matter provided for in any agreement where the parties provide that the Court shall settle disputes arising from the agreement.
7. The Court shall have all the power conferred upon it by the provisions of the Protocol as well as any other powers that may be conferred by subsequent Protocols and Decisions of the Community. 8. The Authority of Heads of State and Government shall have the power to

grant the Court the power to adjudicate on any specific dispute that it may refer to the Courtother than those specified in this Article".[32]

Except for paragraph 4, the rules of competence for the ECOWAS Court of Justice are *mutatis mutandis* comparable to the ECJ. Essentially, the decision-making competences of both courts extend to safeguarding the laws of the European Union regarding the interpretation and application of the agreements (Art. 19 EUV). It is the task of the Union's jurisdiction to ensure the adherence to the community legislation when it comes to the interpretation and application of the instruments of the Community. This includes compliance control regarding the legal acts of the Executive and the Legislature.[33] The organs of the Union are bound by the lawfulness of their actions. Thereby, the area of competence for both Courts of Justice encompasses the damages caused by the unlawful conduct of organs of the Community and civil servants. Moreover, the ECOWAS Court of Justice and the ECJ deal with official liability claims According to Art. 3 paragr. 1.g of the Additional Protocol A/SP.1/01/05 and Art. 268 TFEU. The permitted official liability claims, According to Art. 3 paragr. 1.g of the Additional Protocol A/SP.1/01/05 and Art. 268 TFEU fall within the exclusive competence of both courts.[34] The extra-contractual liability regulation of the respective area of competence can also be compared (Art. 3 Abs. 2 of the Additional Protocol A/SP.1/01/05 and Art. 340 TFEU). By way of preliminary rulings, collaboration can be noted in the ECOWAS-court system as well as the ECJ. Because for the guarantee of the unified validity of the fundamental norms of the ECOWAS Community and the European Union, national courts are obligated, According to Art. 10.f of the Additional Protocol A/SP.1/01/05 and Art. 267 TFEU, to submit to the respective Court a legally relevant question concerning the interpretation of the agreements or Protocols of the respective community to the respective Court of Justice.

Those entitled to file a suit are also similar at both courts. These include the signatory states, the organs of the respective Union as well as natural and legal persons. In addition, the individual courts ofthe Member States, by way of preliminary ruling, as well as the parties to the disputes are both directly entitled to approach the intra-regional court. As only the courts of

32 Emphasis by the author.

33 Pache, in: Vedder/Heintschel von Heinegg (Publ.), Europäisches Unionsrecht[European Union Law], commentary, 1. edition, Art. 19 EUV, Rn. 5.

34 Pache, in: Vedder/Heintschel von Heinegg (Publ.), Europäisches Unionsrecht[European Union Law], commentary, 1. edition, Art. 268 TFEU, Rn. 4.

the member states are directly entitled to litigate in this regard, the possibility of the parties to indirectly act by inducing the filing of a suit is of great importance. The parties to the initial proceedings are, however, not entitled to submit.[35] Moreover, there are differences between the system of the ECJ and the ECOWAS Court of Justice regarding the question of submission. Indeed, there is a difference between the entitlement to submit and the duty to submit. Entitled to submit are, according to the stipulations in Art. 267 paragr. 2 TFEU only the courts of the Member States.[36] However, Art. 267 paragr. 3 TFEU prescribes a duty to submit to the court in the last instance for the Member States of the European Union.[37] Obligated to submit are therefore all courts against whose decision, in a particular case, no legal remedies are available. This does not only include court of cassation but also the Constitutional Courts of Member States.[38] This second scenario, the duty to submit, does not exist in the system of the ECOWAS Court of Justice. As in Art. 10 a) of the Additional Protocol A/SP.1/01/05, the ECOWAS Court of Justice, just like ECJ, is responsible for bringing legal action in cases of a breach of the agreement (comparable to Art. 258 and 259 TFEU).[39] With regard to the action of annulment, both systems show similarities regarding the right to bring proceedings. Natural and legal persons actively have *locus standi* before both courts regarding an action of annulment.[40] Subsequently, there are no substantial differences in both systems regarding the object of dispute. Effectively all legally adverse actions caused by an organ of the Community constitute an object of dispute.[41]

---

35 Pache, in: Vedder/Heintschel von Heinegg (Publ.), Europäisches Unionsrecht [European Union Law], commentary, 1. edition., Art. 267 TFEU, Rn. 22; also see Art. 10 f) Protocole Additionnel A/SP.1/01/05 (19/01/2005) Portant Amendement du Protocole (A/P.1/7/91) Relatif à la Cour de Justice de la Communauté.

36 Pache, in: Vedder/Heintschel von Heinegg (Publ.), Europäisches Unionsrecht[European Union Law], commentary, 1. edition, Art. 267 TFEU, Rn. 21.

37 Pache, in: Vedder/Heintschel von Heinegg (Publ.), Europäisches Unionsrecht[European Union Law], commentary, 1. edition, Art. 267 TFEU, Rn. 21.

38 Pache, in: Vedder/Heintschel von Heinegg (Publ.), Europäisches Unionsrecht[European Union Law], commentary, 1. edition, Art. 267 TFEU, Rn. 28.

39 Tsikrikas, Die Wirkungen der Urteile des Europäischen Gerichtshofs im Vertragsverlet- zungsverfahren. [The Effects of Judgments by the Court of Justice of the European Union in Proceedings due to Breach of Agreement], 82.

40 Art. 10 c) Protocole Additionnel A/SP.1/01/05 (19/01/2005) Portant Amendement du Proto-cole (A/P.1/7/91) Relatif à la Cour de Justice de la Communauté (Comp. with Article. 263 paragr. 4 TFEU).

41 Art. 10 c) Protocole Additionnel A/SP.1/01/05 (19/01/2005) Portant Amendement du Proto- cole (A/P.1/7/91) Relatif à la Cour de Justice de la Communauté

.Furthermore, both courts show similarities when it comes to the monitoring of the lawfulness of the legislative procedure of the Community as well as the actions of organs of the Community (Art. 10 b of the Additional Protocol A/SP.1/01/05 and Art. 263 TFEU).

However, the sequence of competences of the ECOWAS Court of Justice is significantly longer in comparison to the otherwise – as shown – rather similar ECJ. In fact, since 2005 the ECOWAS Court of Justice has been given jurisdiction in questions of human rights. As the Protocol for Good Governance of 2001 clarifies, ECOWAS is not only an economic community but also and particularly so, a community of values. Therefore, principles of the rule of law and human rights are seen as an important pillar of the Community. This particular status of human rights can already be observed in the ratification of the Agreement of Cotonou.[42] The strengthening of the competence of the court was the best solution to enforce these goals. In contrast to other intra-African, intra-regional courts of law, ECOWAS was given jurisdiction with regards to human rights not by its own interpretation of the legal norms of the Community but, and this is significant, by an explicit decision by the Member States.[43] This concession of jurisdiction in human rights questions to the ECOWAS Court of Justice took place by way of the Additional Protocol A/SP.1/01/05, signed in Accra in January 2005. The jurisdiction in human rights questions by the ECOWAS Court of Justice was set out in Art. 4 of this Additional Protocol A/SP.1/01/05. This, on the other hand, shows how highly the Member States rate the compliance with human rights and the rule of law within the territory of the Community.[44]

However, a significant question regarding the liability of the Member States with regard to a breach of the order within the Community has not yet been clarified. The question is whether individuals are entitled to bring proceedings against a Member State for actions which are inconsistent

---

und Art. 263 paragr. 4; also Pache, in: Vedder/Heintschel von Heinegg (Publ.), Europäisches Unionsrecht [European Union Law], Handkommentar, 1. edition, Art. 263 TFEU, Rn. 32.

42 Fourth section of the preamble and Art. 4 (g) of the Amendment Agreement of Cotonou (23/07/1993).

43 Ebobrah, Litigating Human Rights before Sub-Regional Court in Africa: Prospects and challenges, in: African Journal of International and Comparative Law (2009), 79 (86).

44 Ebobrah, Litigating Human Rights before Sub-Regional Court in Africa: Prospects and challenges, in: African Journal of International and Comparative Law (2009), 79 (88).

with Community law. This question can be affirmed in the ECJ-system.[45] It can thus be deduced that the ECOWAS-Community, like the European Union, constitutesa legal order of peoples' rights in whose favour the states have limited their sovereignty on a narrow basis. Legal entities within this new legal order are not only the states but also individuals.[46] However, one can clearly deduct from the wording of Art. 10 c) of the Additional Protocol A/SP.1/01/05 (19/01/2005) that the individual has a legal remedy against unlawful action or inaction by a Member State with the ECOWAS Court of Justice.The Court of Justice saw itself confronted with this question in its first decision in 2004.

I would first like to briefly present the main facts. A Nigerian lodged a complaint with the ECOWAS Court of Justice against the Republic of Nigeria and Benin. The object of the dispute was the fact that the plaintiff was supposed to have had an important appointment in the Republic of Benin regarding his trade activities. Unfortunately, the border between Nigeria and Benin was closed on the said day from the Nigerian side and due to this, the plaintiff suffered considerable economic losses. For this reason, he lodged a complaint against the Republics of Nigeria and Benin. His complaint was dismissed with the reason that the ECOWAS Court of Justice does not have a mandate for individual complaints. Moreover, the court clarified that the only possibility for private persons to bring proceedings was for a Member State to take the reins in the legal matter and bring proceedings on behalf of the private person.[47] The judgment caused enormous attention and triggered a campaign in the region to allow complaints by individuals before the ECOWAS Court of Justice.[48] Even if the question of *locus standi* was eventually clarified after this judgment by the Protocol A/SP.1/01/05, it is still unclear whether the Member States are also liable for their unlawful actions within the Community in favour of natural or legal persons. The question still remains unanswered whether or not natural and legal persons have a declaratory claim regarding the breach of the fundamental rights of free traffic of goods and capital as well as the

45 Pache, in: Vedder/Heintschel von Heinegg (Publ.), Europäisches Unionsrecht [European Union Law], commentary, 1. edition, Art. 340 TFEU, Rn. 16.

46 ECJ, 26/62, Van Gend & Loos (5/02/1963), 25.

47 CCJECOWAS, Afolabi v. Nigeria, N°ECW/CCJ/JUD/01/04 (27/04/2004), in: Community Court of Justice, Law Report (2004–2009), 1 (12); Sall, La Justice d'Intégration, 273 (274).

48 Alter/Helfer/McAllister, A new international human right court for West Africa: the ECOWAS Community Court of Justice, in: The American Journal of International Law (2013), 737 (738).

freedom of movement within the territory of the Community. There is also currently no clear answer to the question, whether natural and legal persons are entitled to bring legal proceedings if they lodge a complaint against the breach of their basic rights by organs of the Community. Until 2005, only Signatories were privileged to bring proceedings. Since then. the situation has, however, changed significantly.

C. *In particular: the Jurisdiction of the Court with regards to Human Rights since the Inception of the Additional Protocol of 2005*

The Additional Protocol A/SP.1/01/05 from 2005 brought institutional changes regarding the competences of the Court of Justice. Following the inception of the Additional Protocol A/ SP.1/01/05 of 2005 the Court received jurisdiction over human rights disputes. The turning point in that year can be explained by the objective by the Community discussed above. ECOWAS represents a unique linking of human rights jurisdiction and economic litigation on the African continent.[49] There are many reasons in favour of such an exception and stance with regards to general Peoples' Rights. The changes in the policy of the rule of law and human rights in the Community included the extension of factual responsibilities of the Court of Justice. The court was supposed to make a significant contribution to the implementation of the human rights entrenched in the African Charta for Human Rights and the accepted Principles of Good Governance in the Protocol for Good Governance. The last step toward human rights jurisdiction by ECOWAS was eventually triggered by the case Afolabi which was briefly presented above.[50] Therefore, one can speak of a double face of the ECOWAS Court of Justice since the inception of the Additional Protocol (ratified in Accra on 19 January 2005).

The mentioned Protocol on Good Governance and Democracy was indeed signed in 2001 in the course of regional integration. In order to enforce the requirements of this Protocol on Democratic Principles and Good Governance the court received a special, corresponding, competence. The Signatories also extended the decision-making authority of the

---

49 CCJECOWAS, Afolabi v. Nigeria, N°ECW/CCJ/JUD/01/04 (27/04/2004), in: Community Court of Justice, Law Report (2004–2009), 1 (12).

50 CCJECOWAS, Afolabi v. Nigeria, N°ECW/CCJ/JUD/01/04 (27/04/2004), in: Community Court of Justice, Law Report (2004–2009).

Court of Justice. According to Art. 10 of the Additional Protocol of 2005[51], the Court of Justice decides on violations of human rights in the territory of the Member States. Consequently, the Protocol on the Court of Justice of 1991 was improved in many places by the Additional Protocol A/SP.1/01/05 on 19/01/2005 in Accra. According to this, individual complaints with regards to human rights violations are permissible before the Court of Justice. This is a judicial guarantee to regard the human rights laid out in the African Charta of Human Rights and Peoples' Rights (Art. 7 of the Charta).

Through its human rights mandate, the ECOWAS Court of Justice resembles the ECtHR in many ways because, just like the ECtHR, the ECOWAS Court of Justice now adjudges on human rights violations in Member States. The protection of human rights by the ECOWAS Court of Justice is therefore equal to the ECtHR in various ways (Art. 10 d of the Additional Protocol A/SP.1/01/05 in comparison to Art. 34 ECHR). However, there is a significant difference between the wording of Art. 10 d of the Additional Protocol (A/SP.1/01/05) and Art. 34 ECHR (this will be enlarged upon in the 2. chapter.)

However, the attribution to the court of special competences regarding human rights and democratic principles entails legal problems. As a result, there is no clearly defined relationship between the Court of Justice and the constitutional organs of the Member States. Indeed, the results of the changes to the Protocol A/P1/7/91 (06/07/1991), concern the admissibility requirements and the entitlement to lodge a complaint. The great difference between the two intra-regional human rights instances lies in the fact that complaints before the ECOWAS Court of Justice are admissible without the prior exhaustion of other legal remedies. Here, the access requirements to the ECOWAS Court of Justice differentiate from those of the ECtHR (Art. 35 paragr. 1 ECHR). Since the recognition of the human rights jurisdiction of the court through the Additional Protocol A/SP.1/01/05 of Accra (2005), the jurisdiction of the ECOWAS Court of Justice is marked by four significant features: it differs from other sub-regional Economic courts of law because of the direct access for individual complaints, there is no requirement of prior exhaustion of legal remedies, it has unlimited factual competence regarding human rights and has a relatively broad adjudication on human rights and barely noticeable jurisdiction regarding com-

51 Protocole Additionnel A/SP.1/01/05 (19/01/2005) Portant Amendement du Protocole (A/P.1/7/91) Relatif à la Cour de Justice de la Communauté.

plaints of a legal economic-integrational nature. [52] Through its jurisdiction and institutional form, the ECOWAS Court of Justice is qualified as being *sui generis*.[53]

However, there is still no clarity which human rights fall within the sphere of the court's responsibility.[54] In fact, the teachings agree that the African Charta for Human Rights and Peoples' Rights of 1981 constitutes the material basis for human rights jurisdiction of the Court of Justice. Nevertheless, the question remains whether, over and above this, the violation of other human rights instruments may function as an object of litigation. However, it is indisputable that the court itself refers to the African Charta for Human Rights and Peoples' Rights as a core element of the community of values of West African states in its judgments.[55] Therefore, we must assume that the ECOWAS Court of Justice is supposed to monitor the adherence to the Charta by the Member States. In order to overcome possible conflicts with the African Court for Human and People's Rights, all complaints that have already been adjudicated by other international court are admissible, According to Art. 4 d) of the Additional Protocol A/SP.1/01/05 (19/01/2005). This finally confirms the status of the ECOWAS Court of Justice as an international court of law. In its latest judgment, the court emphasised its international character with the following words:

> « Dans leurs écritures, les requérants se sont en effet référés aussi bien à la Constitution na tionale [...] qu'à la Charte de la Transition [...] La Cour doit considérer de telles références comme inappropriées dans son prétoire. Juridiction internationale, elle n'a vocation à sanc-tionner

52 Alter/Helfer/R.McAllister, A new international Human Rights Court for West Africa: The ECOWAS Community Court of Justice, in: The American Journal of International Law (2013), 737 (753 ff.).

53 Ebobrah, Legitimacy and feasibility of human rights realisation through regional economic communities in Africa: the case of ECOWAS (200), 10.

54 Ebobrah, A critical Analysis of the human rights mandate of the ECOWAS Community Court of Justice, 8, available at: http://docs.escr-net.org/usr_doc/S_Ebobra h.pdf (last accessed on 16/05/2015).

55 CJ CEDEAO, Affaire Ameganvi et al. c. Etat du Togo, N°ECW/CCJ/JUD/06/12 (13.03.2012), par. 11, available at: www.courtecowas.org (last accessed on 16/07/2015); CJ CEDEAO, Af- faire Congrès pour la démocratie et le Progrès (CDP) & Autres c. Etat Burkina, N°ECW/CCJ/ JUD/16/15 (13/07/2015).

que la méconnaissance d'obligations résultant de textes internationaux opposables aux Etats ».[56]

The system does, however, show weaknesses resulting in the emergence of an extensive range of topics which definitely require clarification. Since the concession of the jurisdiction on human rights to the ECOWAS Court of Justice. One of the main problems in the ECOWAS system of protection is that there are no set of rules concerning the implementation of declaratory judgments under international law. There is a lack of regulation on Member State level for the reception and intra-national effectiveness of ECOWAS declaratory judgments. Especially the question of implementation requires clarification, because the effective legal protection in favour of the individual plaintiff logically assumes that the elimination of breaches of the convention, as ascertained by the ECOWAS Court of Justice, can also be implemented at intra-national level. In this respect, the awarding of damages does currently not constitute full compensation.[57]

D. *Reason for the Study: The Case of Ameganvi et al vs. Togo*

The ECOWAS Court of Justice has in the past already reached four significant verdicts[58] which are especially important for the present paper. Addi-

56 CJ CEDEAO, Affaire Congrès pour la démocratie et le Progrès (CDP) & Autres c. Etat Bur- kina, N°ECW/CCJ/JUD/16/15 (13/07/2015), par. 26.

57 Polakiewicz, Die Verpflichtung der Staaten aus den Urteilen des Europäischen Gerichtshofs für Menschenrechte (2012), 4.[The Obligation of States resulting from Judgments by the European Court of Human Rights (2012), 4.].

58 Adeloui, L'autorité de la chose jugée par les juridictions constitutionnelles en Afrique, in: Revue Togolaise des Sciences Juridiques 54 (74); Olinga, Les Droits de l'Homme peuvent-ils sous- traire un ex-dictateur à la justice? L'affaire Hissène Habré devant la Cour de justice de la CEDEAO, in: Revue Trimestrielle des Droits de l'Homme (2011), 735 (736); Sall, L'affaire Hissène Habré, Aspects judiciaires nationaux et internationaux, 16; CC CEDEAO, Mamadou Tandja c. République du Niger, Arrêt, N°ECW/CCJ/JUD/05/10 (08/11/2010), available at: www.courtecowas.org (last accessed on 16/07/2015); CC CEDEAO, Hissein Habré c. République du Sénégal, Arrêt, N°ECW/CCJ/JUD/06/10 (18/11/2010), available at: www.courtecowas.org (last accessed on 16/07/2015); CJ CEDEAO, Affaire Ameganvi et al. c. Etat du Togo, N°ECW/CCJ/JUD/09/11 (07/10/2011), par. 66, available at: www.courtecowas.org (last accessed on 16/07/2015); CJ CEDEAO, Affaire Gbagbo c. République de la Côte d'Ivoire, N°ECW/CCJ/JUD/03/13 (22/02/2013), accesible at: www.courtecowas.org (last accessed on 16/07/2015); Ebobrah, Human rights development in African sub-regional econo-

tionally, the latest decision by the ECOWAS Court of Justice against the Republic of Burkina Faso, in which the court considered an electoral act as a breach of the principles of the rule of law anchored in the Protocol on Good Governance of 2001 in Art. 1.g) and 2.3, is of great importance.[59] With regard to these judgments, the question is justified, whether the ECOWAS Court of Justice can be considered to be a supra-national Constitutional Court[60] as the ECOWAS Court of Justice hereby demonstrates that the last word no longer belongs to the Constitutional Court or Supreme Court of the Member States.[61] Due to their constitutional references these Court of Justice judgments trigger a tense relationship between the Court of Justice and the Constitutional jurisdictions of the Member States.

The present study concerns itself primarily with the question of the relationship between constitutional jurisdiction of Member States and the ECOWAS-jurisdiction on human rights. In this respect, the case of Ameganvi against the State of Togo is a prime example where the Court of Justice arrived at a groundbreaking judgment following the examination of a decision by the Togolese Constitutional Court. The Togolese Constitutional Court decision and the resulting declaratory judgment by the ECOWAS Court of Justice represent the main subject matter of the present study.

I. Decision by the Togolese Constitutional Court

Nine parliamentarians of the opposition party UFC left the party and founded a new party, the ANC. On 18 November 2010, the President of the Parliament submitted a list of these parliamentarians to the Constitutional Court with the request to find successors for them. With the decision N° N°E018/10 of 22 November 2010, the Togolese Constitutional Court gave notification of substitutes for these parliamentarians in court.

---

mic communities during 2010, in: African Human Rights Law Journal (2011), 216 (236).

59 CJ CEDEAO, Affaire Congrès pour la démocratie et le Progrès (CDP) & Autres c. Etat Bur- kina, N°ECW/CCJ/JUD/16/15 (13/07/2015), par. 31.

60 Bolle, La Cour de Justice de la CEDEAO: une cour (supra)constitutionnelle?, available at: http://la-constitution-en-afrique.org/article-la-cour-de-justice-cedeao-une-cour-supra-constitutionnelle-87092524.html (last accessed on 09/07/2015).

61 Adeloui, L'autorité de la chose jugée par les juridictions constitutionnelles en Afrique, in: Revue Togolaise des Sciences Juridiques (2012), 54 (75).

This happened without consulting the concerned parliamentarians (detailed presentation of the facts in chapter 1).

II. Declaratory Judgment by the ECOWAS Court of Justice

The nine parliamentarians lodged an individual complaint with the ECOWAS Court of Justice against this decision by the Togolese Constitutional Court. The Court of Justice was thus confronted with two questions. The first is of a procedural nature and the second represents a material legal question. The ECOWAS Court of Justice summarises these two questions in the following words:

> « Les questions soumises à l'appréciation de la Cour, à savoir la transmission par le Président de l'Assemblée Nationale à la Cour Constitutionnelle de lettres de démission attribuées aux requérants et contestées par ceux-ci, et la décision n°E18/10 du 22 novembre 2010 de la Cour constitutionnelle prise à la suite de cette transmission, relèvent-elles de la compétence de laCour comme étant susceptible de constituer des violations de droits de l'homme des requé rants comme ils le soutiennent? »[62]

In its decision of 07 October 2011, the ECOWAS Court of Justice found an obvious breach of Art. 1 and 33 of the Protocol on Democracy and Good Governance, ratified by Togo in 2001, and of Art. 7/1, 7/1c and 10 of the African Charta for Human Rights. According to Art. 7 paragr. 1 of the Charta, everybody is entitled to a legal hearing. This includes the right to legal protection before the responsible national court against all actions that violate ones fundamental rights under agreements, laws, regulations and customary law. Furthermore, everybody is entitled to be considered innocent until ones guilt has been proven by a responsible court. This procedural guarantee also entails the right of defense. This includes the right to be defended by a defense attorney of one's choice. Lastly, this guarantee gives the individual the right to a judgment within an appropriate period of time and by an impartial court.

---

62 CJ CEDEAO, Affaire Ameganvi et al. c. Etat du Togo, N°ECW/CCJ/JUD/09/11 (07/10/2011), par. 53, available at: www.courtecowas.org (last accessed on 16/07/2015).

The Court of Justice further pointed out that the constitutional judgment also represents a breach of Art. 10 of the United Nations Universal Declaration of Human Rights of 1948.

After the declaration of the breach of the relevant regulations in the Charta (Art. 7 paragr. 1 of the African Charta) as well as the United Nations Universal Declaration of Human Rights (Art. 10), the plaintiffs expected to be automatically reinstated in parliament but the Togolese state rejected their application of reinstatement.

A detailed presentation of the facts until the judgment was rendered by the ECOWAS Court of Justice on 7 October 2011 and can be found in chapter 2 of the present paper.

III. Interpretation of the Declaratory Judgment by the ECOWAS Court of Justice

There is a possibility to initiate interpretation proceedings after a declaratory judgment. Such a process means that a judgment has been rendered on a particular object of dispute. However, various points of the decision are obviously unclear. Therefore, an application for clarification of the open points is admissible before the Court of Justice. Consequently, the plaintiffs initiated such interpretative proceedings with the Court of Justice. These proceedings are admissible According to Art. 64 of the rules of procedure of the Court of Justice. Therefore, the Togolese relevant parliamentarians again turned to the Court of Justice on 16 November 2011 within the framework of this process. The Court of Justice declared this application admissible.[63]

The question the Court of Justice had to answer was whether the declaration of this breach also constituted an annulment of the decision by the Togolese Constitutional Court[64], which would constitute a violation of human rights.

After extensive examination, the ECOWAS Court of Justice was however not in favour of this. The purpose of the first decision, According to

63 CJ CEDEAO, Affaire Ameganvi et al. c. Etat du Togo, N°ECW/CCJ/JUD/06/12 (13/03/2012), par. 11, available at: www.courtecowas.org (last accessed on 16/07/2015).

64 Cour constitutionnelle du Togo, Entscheidung N°E-018/2010 vom 22. November 2010, available at : http://www.courconstitutionnelle.tg/ (last accessed on 22/06/2015).

the Court of Justice, was to declare a breach of Art. 7 of the Charta. The Court of Justice however does not have the power to go over and above that and order a reinstatement of the plaintiffs. This would constitute an underestimation or annulment of the decision by the Togolese Constitutional Court. The ECOWAS Court of Justice does not possess such a competence. This decision is to be criticised in many respects (for this purpose, a detailed criticism in chapter 5).

Indeed, it is understandable when the Court of Justice states that it does not have the competence to set aside a binding constitutional decision. However, the opinion of the Court of Justice regarding the legal consequences of the declaration of the breach is to be criticised.

With its findings of 7 October 2011, the ECOWAS Court of Justice declared that the decision by the Togolese Constitutional Court, which led to the loss of mandate by the parliamentarians in the Togolese parliament, constitutes a breach of Art. 7 paragr. 1 of the African Charta for Human Rights and Peoples' Rights.[65] This declaratory judgment by the ECOWAS Court of Justice entails a number of consequences. Insofar as the Court of Justice qualified the proceedings that led to the loss of mandate in parliament by the plaintiffs, as being in violation of human rights, the logical consequence would have been to reinstate the status prior to that. This is the application of the principle *Restitutio in Integro. Restitutio in Integro* is a legal principle recognised in international law and by international courts. According to this principle, countries are bound to meet their obligations stemming from judgments by international courts. Therefore, the countries are obligated to withdraw the legal action that caused the breach once it has been declared to be a violation of human rights by the international court.

Based on the principle of *Restitutio in Integro*, countries are also obligated to grant the victim of the violation appropriate damages.The reference to the principle of *Restitutio in Integro* is important because the ECOWAS Court of Justice neglected significant aspects of this principle in its interpretation judgment of 13 March 2012.[66]

---

65 CJ CEDEAO, Affaire Ameganvi et al. c. Etat du Togo, N°ECW/CCJ/JUD/09/11 (07/10/2011), par. 66, available at: www.courtecowas.org (last accessed on 16/07/2015).

66 CJ CEDEAO, Affaire Ameganvi et al. c. Etat du Togo, N°ECW/CCJ/JUD/06/12 (13/03/2012), available at: www.courtecowas.org (last accessed on 16/07/2015).

This declaratory judgment of 7 October 2011 by the ECOWAS Court of Justice, should invoke a number of consequences regarding the national judgment (this will be discussed in more detail in chapter 3).

Until the Case Ameganvi was submitted to the ECOWAS Court of Justice, the relationship between the ECOWAS Court of Justice and national constitutional courts was not viewed as a possible institutional source of conflict within the ECOWAS Community. However, a scientific study of this relationship seems obligatory after the judgment by the ECOWAS Court of Justice and the hesitation of the national court in this conflict scenario.

E. Binding Force of the Decision by the ECOWAS Court of Justice

The system introduced in Protocol A/SP.1/01/05 (19/01/2005) can be compared to constitutional complaints in Benin because the system allows for an individual complaint to be submitted directly to the ECOWAS Court of Justice. Moreover, attention must be drawn to the fact that the protection system allows for ECOWAS to be more lenient with admissibility requirements. In fact, an individual complaint before the Court of Justice is permissible without the prior exhaustion of legal remedies. This special feature is protected by many reasons (this will be discussed in more detail in chapter 3). However, the protection system, provided by the Protocol, presents a certain predictable danger. Due to the existence of the protection of human rights on several levels with different effects, one must reckon with different, even contradictory judgments.[67] How to resolve this actual and potential problem is the object of the present study.

In contrast to Benin, a direct complaint by an individual against the state is foreign to the Togolese constitutional process. For this very reason, the admissibility of individual complaints causes difficulties regarding the constitutional process for many of the Member States from a constitutional point of view. Therefore, they are struggling to give the judgment of the ECOWAS Court of Justice national validity.

---

67 Lindner, Grundrechtschutz in Europa – System einer Kollisionsdogmatik [Protection of Constitutional Rights in Europe – a System of Collision-Dogmatism], in: EuR (2007), 160 (161); Rohleder, Grundrechtsschutz im europäischen Mehrebenensystem [Protection of Constitutional Rights in the European Multilevel System], 30.

This Protocol A/SP.1/01/05 (19/01/2005) enhances the territorial scope of application of the Charta by supporting the effectiveness of the Charta in the Community system by allowing individual complaints before the ECOWAS Court of Justice.

I. Contractual Foundations

According to Art. 15 paragr. 4 of the Amendment Agreement:

> « Les arrèts de la Cour de Justice ont force obligatoire à l'égard des Etats Membres, des Institutions de la Communauté, et des personnes physiques et morales ».
>
> "Judgments of the Court of Justice shall be binding on the Member States, the Institutions of the Community and on individuals and corporate bodies".

Due to the lack of a precise definition of the scope of the legal force of this regulation, the development of the law through case law is particularly called upon. In this sense, the famous quote by a British Tribunal is particularly relevant:

> "International law, as well as domestic law, may not contain, and generally does not contain express rules decisive of particular cases but the function of jurisprudence is to resolve the conflict of opposing rights and interests by applying, in default of any specific provision of law, the corollaries of general principles and so to find – exactly as in the mathematical science – the solution of the problem. This is the method of jurisprudence; it is the method by which the law has been gradually evolved in every country resulting in the definition and settlement of legal relations as well as between States as between private individuals".[68]

II. Teleological Interpretation

The wording of the text of the agreement clearly does not allow for an easy understanding of the binding effect of the decisions within the national legal systems of the Signatories. Without determining the scope of the bind-

68 Cassesse, International Law, 2nd éd, 188.

ing effect, the national implementation of the declaratory judgments by the Court of Justice is difficult. It is therefore necessary to interpret the agreement by the ratio of the norms.According to this method of interpretation, the terms in an international treaty are to be interpreted in regard to their object and purpose, thereby giving the agreement the greatest possible effectiveness. However, with the proviso that the object and purpose can be deduced from the treaty text itself.[69]

III. The Problem of National Implementation

Which role does the ECOWAS Court of Justice play according to the two Additional Protocols?[70] In the reticence of the texts, the rules of interpretation of the Vienna Convention on the Law of Treaties is methodically pointed out. This question will find particular attention in the present study. It is necessary to clarify this question because the consequences are legally relevant to the implementation of the declaratory judgments of the ECOWAS Court of Justice. Even if the ECOWAS Court of Justice were to receive the authority to decide on individual human rights complaints through Protocol A/SP.1/01/05, it is still dependent on the national court regarding the implementation of its decision. Precisely because of this there should be a dual relationship, namely, in a legally institutional respect, regarding a hierarchical relationship in favour of the ECOWAS Court of Justice and, in a legally material respect, regarding a cooperative relationship. In view of this, the question of enforceability of the African Charta as well as the decisions by the ECOWAS Court of Justice within the order of the Community must be posed.[71] It may be true that a separate meaning is reserved in the constitutional orders of the Member States

69 Ipsen, Völkerrecht [International Law], 6. edition., § 12, Rn. 10.

70 Protocole A/P1/7/91 (06/07/1991), relatif à la Cour de Justice de la Communauté; Protocole Additionnel A/SP.1/01/05 (19/01/2005) Portant Amendement du Protocole (A/P.1/7/91) Relatif à la Cour de Justice de la Communauté.

71 Kilian, Die Bindungswirkung der Entscheidungen des Europäischen Gerichtshofs für Men- schenrechte auf die nationalen Gerichte der Mitgliedstaaten der Konvention zum Schutze der Men- schenrechte und Grundfreiheiten vom 4. November 1950, 68. [The Binding Effect of Decisions taken by the European Court of Law for Human Rights with regards to the National Court of the Member States regarding the Convention on the Protection of Human Rights and Constitutional Freedoms of 4 November 1950, 68].

for the African Charta for Human Rights and Peoples' Rights.[72] However, various court instances are assigned to the Constitutions at national, transnational and international level, so that scholars in Europe tend to speak of a constitutional "Multi-level System" in Europe.[73] This reality is transferable to the African continent and in particular to ECOWAS Community.

In order to realise the African Charta on a national level, ECOWAS Member States have formally acknowledged the Charta as a binding legal instrument in their respective constitutional systems. Apart from this theoretical incorporation of the Charta into the national constitutional system of the respective Member State, the question may be posed whether and to what extent the judicial institutions of Member States view the ECOWAS Court of Justice as the authentic interpreter of the Charta, based on its human rights mandate. The national constitutional courts primarily watch over the compliance with the human rights set out in the Charta. Knowing that the state governed by the rule of law through the actions of state organs can be questioned by the judiciary[74] the signatories have provided ECOWAS legal remedies at a regional level. This primarily involves the guarantee for citizens in the region of an impartial and independent instance at international level.[75] The regulation of the relationship between the regional organ of ECOWAS and the national constitutional courts must still be clarified.

Hence, the task of the ECOWAS Court of Justice is particularly important for the full compliance with the guarantees of the Charta. Especially with regards to its task, the question arises of how the enforceability of the Charta and the corresponding declaratory judgments by the Court of Justice can be guaranteed. Once the ECOWAS Court of Justice has adjudicated in a concrete case, how should the decision be implemented in the national legal system of the concerned Member State? In order to effectively implement the declaratory judgment in the national legal system, the issued declaratory judgment would have to activate a standard of implemen-

---

72 Kamto, Charte africaine, instruments internationaux de protection des droits de l'homme, constitutions nationales: Articulation respectives, in: Flauss/Lambert-Abdelgawad (Publ.), L'application nationale de la Charte africaine des droits de l'homme et des peuples, 11 (30).

73 Rohleder, Grundrechtsschutz im europäischen Mehrebenensystem, 30. [Protection of Constitutional Rights in the European Multi-level System, 30].

74 Adeloui, L'autorité de la chose jugée par les juridictions constitutionnelles en Afrique, in: Revue Togolaise des Sciences Juridiques (2012), 54 (73).

75 Adeloui, L'autorité de la chose jugée par les juridictions constitutionnelles en Afrique, in: Revue Togolaise des Sciences Juridiques (2012), 54 (73).

tation for the individual plaintiff. This primarily means that a conflicting judgment by the national constitutional court or another exercise of public power would have to be set aside. The question which constitutional principles would allow for an action of annulment to be lodged thus arises here. These are all questions that concern the enforceability of the declaratory judgment in the national legal system of the convicted Member State. In this respect, the question concerning which legal action should be taken must also be posed in order to effectively enforce the declaratory judgment. Are legal remedies against the concerned Member State available in the case that it fails to implement?

These problems of the "Multi-level human rights protection"[76] entail dogmatic questions.[77] Following a precise examination of the regulations as well as the Amendment Agreement and the Additional Protocols, a need for regulation regarding these questions becomes apparent. To date, clear rules concerning the implementation of declaratory judgments neither exist at Community-level nor at national level of the Member States.

F. Limitation of Question and Structure

The Protocol on Good Governance, contains substantive and procedural constitutional elements. The countries do not disagree on the substantive constitutional elements, i.e. the factual competence of the Court of justice with regards to interpreting the Charta which establishes and justifies the basis of the decision-making authority of the court. However, they are divided when it comes to the resulting consequences for the national constitutional courts. The human rights mandate of the ECOWAS Court of Justice relates explicitly to the African Charta for Human Rights and Peoples' Rights. Therefore, the present study mainly concerns itself with the scope of the judgments by the Court of justice in relation to the interpretation of the Charta. This excludes the reference to the Protocol on Good Governance as a supra-national Constitution, even if the Court of justice usually refers to this Protocol. The observations in this paper focus fundamentally

76 Lindner, Grundrechtsschutz in Europa – System einer Kollisionsdogmatik [Protection of Constitutional Rights in Europe System of Collision Dogmatics...], in: EuR (2007), 160, (161).

77 Lindner, Grundrechtsschutz in Europa – System einer Kollisionsdogmatik [Protection of Constitutional Rights in Europe System of Collision Dogmatics...], in: EuR (2007), 160, (160).

on the human rights mandate of the Court of justice . This work limits itself primarily to the relationship between the jurisdiction of a constitutional court in the signatory states and the human rights jurisdiction of the ECOWAS Court of Justice. This is basically about the task of the Court of justice with regards to the upholding of the joint constitutional system and the resulting possible conflicts of jurisdiction with the constitutional courts of Member States.

In order to avoid the risk of confusions in this thesis a further differentiation is necessary. The jurisdiction of the Court of justice regarding proceedings following after a breach of contract[78] and the annulment proceedings[79] brought by a Member State, the Council or an executive secretary, are not dealt with here. The jurisdiction regarding the preliminary ruling procedure is also not taken into consideration.[80] The excluded areas of competence may be referred to insofar as the jurisdiction on such serves the purpose of this paper.

The following problems represent the main questions in the present study: based on its characterisation as a Constitutional Court: what is the binding force that decisions by the ECOWAS Court of Justice unfold in the Member States and, in particular, for the constitutional courts of the Member States? Which consequences arise from differing verdicts of the national constitutionals court and the ECOWAS Court of Justice concerning, from a substantive law viewpoint, the concurrent human rights? What are the obligations of the signatories derive out of the judgments by the Court of Justice? In particular, the question whether the Court of justice represents a supra-national constitutional court will be dealt with.[81]

In addition to these main questions, accessory, yet no less significant questions will also be covered. How far should the obligation of a convicted Member State extend to a payment of damages or how can it be justified with regards to international law? This will be discussed with respective arguments. With the ratification of Protocol A/SP.1/01/05, the ECOWAS Member States, and therefore their sovereign acts, have unconditionally submitted themselves to the jurisdiction of the ECOWAS Court of Justice for review of the conformity of the exercising of state authority in con-

---

78 Art. 10 a) in c. w. Art. 9 d) of the Protocol.

79 Art. 9 c) in c. w. Art. 10 b) of the Protocol.

80 Art. 10 f) of the Protocol.

81 Vgl. Wildhaber, Eine verfassungsrechtliche Zukunft für den Europäischen Gerichtshof für Menschenrechte? [A constitutional future for the European Court of Law for Human Rights?...], in: EuGRZ (2002), 569 (570).

formity with the Charta. Can an individual deduce a claim from a declaratory judgment to recognize a ECOWAS Court of Justice judgment in the national legal system? The present paper concerns itself moreover with the question, whether and to what extent, the decisions by the ECOWAS Court of Justice should be legally binding especially for the constitutional courts in the area of their human rights jurisdiction. Should there a legal obligation arise for the constitutional courts? If yes, what does this obligation entail? In other words: which substantive and procedural obligations arise for the constitutional courts regarding the implementation of the decisions by the ECOWAS.Court of Justice?[82] Furthermore, the question must be answered, whether the individual plaintiff is entitled to legal remedy in case such an obligation to implement, deriving from the declaratory judgment by ECOWAS, is breached. Finally, the question on how the various competences of the ECOWAS Court of Justice and the constitutional jurisdictions of the Member States can be meaningfully coordinated so that they can be made fruitful for one another, must be answered.[83] It can be particularly noted that the network of relationships of national, regional and continental human rights jurisdiction is barely regulated. Due to the admissibility of the individual complaints' procedure without prior exhaustion of other legal remedies the further question of whether the Member States want to withdraw the primary competence of the application and interpretation of the Charta from the national constitutional courts, arises.

It is thus clear that there is a need for regulation within the ECOWAS system of justice. Scholars have unanimously recognized and agreed to the need for such regulation.[84] Yet, nobody has shown the way on how to close this gap within the legal order of the Community.

The aim of the present study is to draw attention to the problem area of actual and potential tension within the ECOWAS legal order regarding the human rights mandate of the ECOWAS Court of Justice. The African Charta for Human Rights and Peoples' Rights is part of the constitutions of the Member States and the national constitutional courts must guarantee the human rights set out in the Charta to the persons subject to the re-

---

82 Oppong/Niro, Enforcing Judgment of International Court in National Court, in: Journal of International Dispute Settlement (2014), 1 (4).

83 Rohleder, Grundrechtsschutz im europäischen Mehrebenensystem[Protection of Constitutional Rights in the European Multi-level System], 31.

84 Oppong/Niro, Enforcing Judgment of International Court in National Court, in: Journal of International Dispute Settlement (2014), 1 (5).

spective sovereign power. From a constitutional law point of view, there is a mixture of normative frames of reference for the constitutional review of sovereign acts in the light of the Charta. This is due to the fact that from the perspective of the national constitutional law, the constitutional courts act under the constitution and, at the same time, under the Charta (international law). As a servant of two masters, the constitutional court must always take care to protect the individual human rights and constitutional freedoms according to the standards of the Charta in its decisions. From an international point of reference, the competence of the ECOWAS Court of Justice includes the review of the compatibility of sovereign acts by the Member States with the Charta through the means of individual claims. Hence, there are two levels of judicial guarantees of human rights: the national level and the ECOWAS-level. This results in a tense relationship between the two, due to a divergence in the jurisdiction.[85] After closer inspection, it is a confrontation of *res iudicata* and *restitutio in integrum*. It is the goal of this study, to find internationally acceptable possibilities which can close a gap within the joint protective system of the ECOWAS legal system. The current reticence of the texts does not offer a good basis for effective legal protection for the individual plaintiff. It is in fact a matter of the actual and the potential conflict of jurisdiction between the ECOWAS Court of Justice and the constitutional courts and Supreme Courts as well as the constitutional regulations of the Member States. It is regrettable that the ECOWAS Court of Justice currently contents itself solely with the payment of damages after a violation has been determined. The restrictive interpretation of its judicial authority should be overhauled with acceptable arguments under international law.

There may be voices that do not necessarily agree with these proposed solutions or who remain skeptical about them. Perhaps the proposed solutions seem unenforceable in the region or unrealistic, especially since there is already, according to the current legal situation, resistance against the implementation of the declaratory ECOWAS-judgments.[86] This possible objection would be understandable: however, one should not forget that it

85 Mückl, Kooperation oder Konfrontation? – Das Verhältnis zwischen Bundesverfassungsge- richt und europäischem Gerichtshof für Menschenrechte, in: Der Staat 44 (2005), 403 (405). [Cooperation or Confrontation? – The Relationship between the Federal Constitutional Court and the Court of Law for Human Rights, in: The State 44...].

86 Alter/Helfer/McAllister, A new international human right court for West Africa: the ECOWAS Community Court of Justice, in: The American Journal of International Law (2013), 737 (739); nach Austausch mit den Justizbeamten des Gericht-

is the task of scientific consideration to identify problems and to raise questions. Therefore, solutions should be proposed. Whether these will be successful in reality is then a question of practice. The proposed solutions in the present study may appear unrealistic in the near future but theory and practice may meet at a future point in time.

There are two theoretical contributions in this study: for one thing, this work does not aspire to resolve all problems regarding the relationship between the ECOWAS Court of Justice and Constitutional Courts of Member States. It only has the goal of comprehensibly examining the divergence of jurisdiction on both levels, i.e. national and ECOWAS-level. This thesis should contribute tothe resolution of this conflict by means of international legal requirements and the practice by a comparable regional court, such as the ECtHR. Therefore, it will be referred to the decision-taking practice by the ECtHR and the legal practice of European Member States regarding the resumption as a source of inspiration in order to close the regulations-gap in the ECOWAS Community. Moreover, further remedies will be shown, which are supposed to simplify the execution of the judgment by the ECOWAS Court of Justice at a national level. However, the proposed solutions are based on agreements within the ECOWAS Community. On the other hand, the study serves to remove a supposed collision[87] between the national legal systems of the signatory states and that of the ECOWAS at community level.According to Art. 15 paragr. 4 of the Amendment Agreement, the Member States are bound by the decisions of the ECOWAS Court of Justice and due to the fact that constitutional courts represent the organs of the Member States, they too are bound by the judgments of the ECOWAS Court of Justice. Therefore, the question whether and to what extent the national organs and, in particular, the Constitutional Courts are bound by decisions of the ECOWAS Court of Justice will be answered in the present study. According to

---

shofs, lässt sich folgender Umsetzungs- stand feststellen: Niger, Senegal und Liberia haben die gegen sie ergangenen Urteile umgesetzt. Dagegen haben die Republik Togo, Burkina Faso, Gambia, Nigeria und Ghana ihre Urteile immer noch nicht vollumfangreich umgesetzt. [After the exchange with the Judicial Officers of the Court of Law, the follwing Status of Implementation may be noted: Niger, Senegal and Liberia have implemented the judgments against them. On the other hand, The Republic of Togo, Burkina Faso, Gambia, Nigeria and Ghana still have not implemented their Judgments to their full Extent.].

87 Lindner, Grundrechtsschutz in Europa – System einer Kollisionsdogmatik, EuR (2007), 160 (160). [Protection of Constitutional Rights in Europe – a System of Collision-Dogmatism...]

Art. 19 paragr. 1 of the Protocol A/P1/7/91, the general principles of law recognized by civilized nations, as stipulated in Art. 38 of the IGH-statute can be applied to the modus operandi of the ECOWAS Court of Justice. Based on this reference, the present paper expressly refers to the general rules of International Law and jurisdiction of the IGH.

Moreover, in order to justify some of the following opinions, reference will be made to the jurisdiction of the ECtHR. There is a reason for this: The ECOWAS Court of Justice itself often refers to the jurisdiction of the ECtHR.[88] This approach by the ECOWAS Court of Justice is justified because most human rights as inherent to the African Charta are essentially the same as those of the ECHR. The Inter-American Court of Law also mainly refers to thejurisdiction of the ECtHR because of the long-time experience of the ECtHR.[89]

The present study is the result of a comparative analysis. Regarding the methodology, the study primarily uses the regulations of the Founding Treaty and the Additional Protocols pertaining to it. Furthermore, the analysis of the jurisdiction of the ECOWAS Court of Law, the IGH, the ECtHR and other comparable regional courts of law plays a significant role. Thereby, the study often refers to the current practice of the EACJ and SADC Tribunal in the area of human rights jurisdiction. Not least, the constitutional regulations of the ECOWAS Member States are used from a comparative legal perspective. Furthermore, the study uses official legal determinations of ECOWAS-institutions. Finally, a personal visit to the ECOWAS Court of Justice, informal discussions with staff members as well as judges at the Court of Law was very useful. This involved inter-

88 CJ CEDEAO, Koraou c. Republique du Niger, N°ECW/CCJ/JUD/06/08 (27/10/2010), par. 85, available at: www.courtecowas.org (last accessed on 24/07/2015); CC CEDEAO, Mamadou Tandja c. République du Niger, Arrêt, N °ECW/CCJ/JUD/05/10 (08.11.2010), available at: www. courtecowas.org (last accessed on 16/07/2015); CC CEDEAO, Hissein Habré c. République du Sénégal, Arrêt, N°ECW/CCJ/JUD/06/10 (18/11/2010), available at: www.courtecowas.org (last accessed on 16/07/2015); CJ CEDEAO, Affaire Ameganvi et al. c. Etat du Togo, N°ECW/CCJ/ JUD/09/11 (07/10/2011), par. 66, available at: www.courtecowa s.org (last accessed on 16/07/2015); CJ CEDEAO, Affaire Gbagbo c. République de la Côte d'Ivoire, N°ECW/CCJ/ JUD/03/13 (22/02/2013), available at: www.cou rtecowas.org (last accessed on 16/07/2015); CC CEDEAO, Manneh c. République de la Gambie, Arrêt, N°ECW/CCJ/JUD/3/08 (05/06/2008), par. 21, available at: www.courtecowas.org (last accessed on 16/07/2015).

89 Neuman, Import, Export, and Regional Consent in the Inter-American Court of Human Rights, in: European Journal of International Law (2008), 101 (104, 111, 114 und 116).

views being conducted in the form of questionnaires. Further meetings with representatives of the Member States during regional conferences represented a considerable contribution as the present study orientates itself on the actual implementation problems and the mentality of the highest instance of the signatories regarding the jurisdiction of the Court of justice . With regards to the ECtHR, a personal visit to the Court of Justice and an informal discussion with staff members and a judge was a noteworthy contribution.

Further justification for the reference to the ECtHR case law lies in the jurisdiction of the ECtHR and the practice of implementation by the Member States of the European Council that serves as a model for deeper analysis and resolution of the tension between *res judicata* and *restitutio in integrum*. Because of the significant influence the judicature of the ECtHR has on the jurisdiction of the ECOWAS Court of Justice, the jurisdiction of the ECtHR is referred to for the purpose of supporting the arguments of this examination.

In the second chapter of the present study, the impact of rulings by the national Constitutional Court will be demonstrated. In the third chapter of the study, the supra-national overcoming of national legal force will also be addressed. This is followed by the reception of the legal force through the national rule of law in the fourth chapter. Finally, the result of the study will be presented in chapter five.

Chapter 2 The Legal Effect of Rulings by National Constitutional Courts

In all of the constitutions of the ECOWAS Member States which were created in the course of the third *vague de démocratisation (The third wave*[1]*)*, the respective Constitutional Court has its own chapter dedicated to it.[2] Therefore, the Constitutional Court is separate from the various stages of court proceedings. Also, from a systematic viewpoint, Togo's Constitution confirms the highest weighting of the Constitutional Court by rendering respective regulations, (Titel VI: De la Cour Constitutionnelle) even before the regulations regarding the Judiciary (Titel VIII: Du Pouvoir Judiciaire). Therefore, the Constitutional Court is placed above the Judiciary.[3] This marks the special constitutional role that is assigned to the Constitutional Court within this novel process of democratisation. With regard to the substantive jurisdiction of the Constitutional Court, the Constitutional Court of Togo exercises, for example, both an advisory and a judicial competence. The judicial competence of the Constitutional Court essentially includes the examination of the constitutionality of laws, the delimitation

---

1 Huntington, The Third Wave. Democratization in the late twentieth century, 41.

2 Art. 152 Constitution of Burkina Faso of 02 June 1991; Art. 99 Constitution of Togo of 14 Oc- tober 1992; Art. 114 Constitution of Benin of 11 December 1991; Art. 88 Constitution of Ivory Coast of 23 July 2000; Art. 93 Constitution of Guinea of 07 May 2010; Art. 120 Constitution of Niger of 25 November 2010; Art. 85 Constitution of Mali of 25 February 1992.

3 Please see: § 129 paragr. 2 Constitution of Ghana of 1992; Art. 106 Constitution of Togo of 14. October 1992; Art. 124 Constitution of Benin of 11 December 1991; Art. 94 Constitution of Mali of February 1992; Art. 134 Constitution of Niger of 25 November 2010; Art. 99 Constitution of Guinea of 07 May 2010, Art. 98 Constitution of Ivory Coast of 23 July 2000; Art. 159 Constitution of Burkina Faso of 02 June 1991; Art. 92 paragr. 2 Constitution of Senegal of 22 January 2001; Sect. 230, 232, 233, 235 Constitution of Nigeria of 29 May 1999; Art. 65 Constitution of Liberia of 06. January 1984; Art. 92 Constitution of Bissau Guinea of 16 January 1984; Sect. 126, 127 Constitution of Gambia of 16. January 1997; Art. 229 paragr. 1 Constitution of Cape Verde of 23 November 1999; Art. 122 paragr. 1 Constitution of Sierra Leone of 03 September 1991; Bado, Constitutional Jurisdiction and Democratisation in francophone West Africa, Study of countries/Benin, 18, available at: http:// intlaw-sgiessen.de/fileadmin/user_upload/bilder_und_dokumente/forschung/westafrikaprojekt/ workingpapers/Draft_WP_2014_benin.pdf (last accessed on 02/07/ 2015).

of competences of constitutional state organs and the amendment of the constitution. In general, the respective Constitutional or Supreme Court, as guardian of the Constitution, watches over the constitutional interpretation of any state acts.[4]

According to the constitutions of the ECOWAS Member States, the Constitutional Court or the Supreme Court represents the highest judicial power in the respective Member State. As such, a special binding force is attributed to the decisions of the Constitutional Courts or the Supreme Courts [5]. Therefore, this chapter will primarily address the question of judicial power in its various forms (B). Meanwhile, the case which partially forms the grounds for this study will be preemptively presented (A). Subsequently, a few opinions by Constitutional Courts will be critically examined (C). Lastly, the reasoned positions will be correlated to the initial case (D).

A. *The Initial Case under Municipal Law*

The predominant initial case regarding municipal (national) law is the decision N° N°E018/10 of 22. November 2010 by the Constitutional Court of Togo and resulting from it, the dispute over imperative of a parliamentarian mandate (as opposed to a free mandate of parliamentarians). Before the question of the effect of the decision can be dealt with at a deeper level it

4 Art. 104 Constitution of Togo of 14 October 1992; Art. 114, 117, 118 Constitution of Benin of 11 December 1991; Art. 152 Constitution of Burkina Faso of 02 June 1991; Art. 88, 94, 95 Constitution of Ivory Coast of 23 July 2000; Art. 94 Constitution of Guinea of 07 May 2010; Art. 120 Constitution of Niger of 25. November 2010; Art. 85, 86, 87, Constitution of Mali of 25 February 1992; Art. 92 Constitution of Senegal of 22 January 2001; Art. 237 Constitution of Cape Verde of 23. November 1999); Art. 124 Sierra Leone Constitution of Sierra Leone of 03 September 1991.

5 See also: § 129 paragr. 2 Constitution of Ghana of 1992; Art. 106 Constitution of Togo of 14 October 1992; Art. 124 Constitution of Benin of 11 December 1991; Art. 94 Constitution of Mali of February 1992; Art. 134 Constitution of Niger of 25 November 2010; Art. 99 Constitution of Guinea of 07. May 2010; Art. 98 Constitution of Ivory Coast of 23 July 2000; Art. 159 Constitution of Burkina Faso of 02 June 1991; Art. 92 Abs. 2 Constitution of Senegal of 22. January 2001; Sect. 230, 232, 233, 235 Constitution of Nigeria of 29 May 1999; Art. 65 Constitution of Liberia of 06 January 1984; Art. 92 Constitution of Guinea-Bissau of 16 January 1984; Sect. 126, 127 Constitution of Gambia of 16 January 1997; Art. 229 paragr. 1 Constitution of Cape Verde of 23 November 1999; Art. 122 paragr. 1 Constitution of Sierra Leone of 03 September 1991.

seems recommendable, from a methodical point of view, to summarily describe the decision by the Constitutional Court of Togo[6] which is the object of this study.

Nine parliamentarians of the opposition party UFC left the party and founded a new party, the ANC. On 18 November 2010, the President of the Parliament submitted a list of these members of parliament to the Constitutional Court with the request to find successors or substitutes for them. However, the concerned parliamentarians had already informed the Constitutional Court on 17 November 2010 that they did not intend to resign from Parliament.[7] Notwithstanding this irregularity, the Constitutional Court implemented the substitution of the parliamentarians.[8] They, in turn, brought a complaint before the Constitutional Court. At the centre of the discussion were the letters of resignation that the parliamentarians had signed as candidates during the legislative election campaign in 2007. The content of these letters read: "I commit myself to the party.

Should I deviate from the orientation of the party, I resign as a member of parliament." Such disclaimers are fundamentally unconstitutional. In effect, such a promise contravenes Art. 52 of the Constitution, which expressly emphasises that Members of Parliament are representatives of the entire people. Despite this, the Constitutional Court rejected the complaint and replaced the parliamentarians respectively with their substitutes.[9]

For a deeper insight into the presented decision, a detailed description of all of the elements in the Constitutional Court judgment is required. On closer inspection, three basic elements can be determined from the external division of the judgment transcript: the facts of the case, the main reasons for the decision and the verdict. Not least, a legal judgment generally also consists of non-abstract elements: These are the counterpart to the external division of the decision. However, the decision of the Constitutional Court must, before it can be called such, become *res judicata*. Last but not least, the decision has a binding effect. After all these questions, an analysis now follows.

---

6 Cour constitutionnelle du Togo, Decision N°E-018/2010 of 22 November 2010, available at: http://www.courconstitutionnelle.tg/ (last accessed on 22/06/2015).

7 CJ CEDEAO, Affaire Isabelle Ameganvi v. Republique Togo, N°ECW/CCJ/JUD/09/11 (07/10/2011), par. 65.

8 Cour constitutionnelle du Togo, Decision N°E-018/2010 of 22 November 2010, available at: http://www.courconstitutionnelle.tg/ (last accessed on 22/06/2015).

9 Cour constitutionnelle du Togo, Decision N°E-018/2010 of 22 November 2010, available at: http://www.courconstitutionnelle.tg/ (last accessed on 22/06/2015).

B. The Legal Force of Decisions by National Constitutional Courts

Object of the present study is the comparison of the Togolese Constitutional Court with the ECOWAS Court of Justice. For this reason, the effects of procedural law regarding the judicial review proceedings according to Art. 104 of the Constitution of Togo, which concerns solely national law, will not be included in the examination. Instead, the constitutional complaint against a breach of a constitutional right by the state as the object of dispute will be mainly analysed. The decisions by the Constitutional Court in this regard and their legal consequences will be presented to their full extent.

The legal force has a date of effect (formal legal force), a subject matter(material legal force), Addressees, a scope(key-reasons for decisions and tenor) as well as a limit.

I. Formal Legal Force

The legal force has two fundamental directions of effect. On one hand, it has an inwards effect (irrevocability), and on the other hand, an outward effect (non-appealability). Before the effect concerning the outward legal force is explained (2) the binding of the court itself will be discussed (1).

1. The Binding Force of Internal Proceedings of the Constitutional Court

The inward effect of the decision means the internal procedural self-commitment of the Constitutional Court to the content of its own decision.

a. Irrevocability of the Decision in Principle

It must be noted upfront that the institute of legal force, in a constitutional-procedural sense, is rarely regulated or mentioned. Is this a legislative error? The question cannot be conclusively answered here. In almost all constitutions there is, however, a separate regulation regarding the binding effect res judicata of constitutional decisions. The internal procedural effect results directly out of the decisions entry into force. Therefore, out of the rule of legal certainty results the prohibition of a revocation of that which was already decided upon.[10] It is thus clear that the formal legal force is constitutional plays a significant role for the Constitutional Court in that it must observe the rule of irrevocability. The risk of endlessly pursued proceedings is thus resolved.[11] Due to the formal legal force for the Constitutional Court a judgment can no longer be randomly amended once it has been issued. All these consequences are not expressly regulated in the constitution but result out of the principle of the rule of law.[12] In this sense, the principle of the rule of law is understood, in an African context, as the self-limiting authority of the state through ones own legislation.[13] This means that the state is obligated to comply with the regulations that itself has stipulated.[14]

Furthermore, the legal force of a Constitutional Court judgment expresses the authority of the Constitution.[15] Therefore, the sovereignty of the Constitution is linked to the sovereignty of the decision by the Constitutional Court.[16] This, The Constitutional Court of Benin has recently emphasised this irrevocability and finality of its legal decision with the following words:

> « Qu'en conséquence, en application des dispositions de l'article 124 [...] de la Constitution, il y a autorité de chose jugée; que, dès lors, la requête [...] doit être déclarée irrecevable».[17]

Art. 106 of Togo's Constitution follows the same principle and ascribes the decision of the Constitutional Court the highest possible effect that a court

---

10 Diop, La justice constitutionnelle au Sénégal. Éssai sur l'evolution, les enjeux et les réformes d'un contre pouvoir juridictionnel, 162.

11 Yebisi, The constitutional power of review of Supreme Court of Ghana: Lesson for Nigeria, in: International Journal of Humanities and Social Science (2014), 39 (40).

12 Detterbeck, Streitgegenstand und Entscheidungswirkungen im öffentlichen Recht, 328. [Object of Dispute and Legal Effects in Public Law, 328].

13 Cabanis/Martin, Les constitutions d'Afrique francophone. Évolutions récentes, 64.

14 Cabanis/Martin, Les constitutions d'Afrique francophone. Évolutions récentes, 65.

15 Renoux, Autorité de la chose jugée ou autorité de la Constitution? A propos de l'effet des décisions du conseil constitutionnel, 817 (834); Adeloui, L'autorité de la chose jugée par les juri- dictions constitutionnelles en Afrique, in: Revue Togolaise des Sciences Juridiques (2012), 54 (56).

16 Adeloui, L'autorité de la chose jugée par les juridictions constitutionnelles en Afrique, in: Revue Togolaise des Sciences Juridiques (2012), 54 (59).

17 Décision DCC 15–027 (12/02/2015), p. 6, available at: www.cour-constitutionnell e-benin. org (last accessed on 25/04/2015).

decision can have. Therefore, the decisions of the Constitutional Court have at first the effect that is generally attributed to court decisions.[18] However, the face that the Constitutional Court is itself bound not only affirms the prohibition of amendment but also of deviation.[19]

b. Interdiction of deviation

The substantive res judicata does not oppose the admissibility of the object of dispute from a new point of view.[20] Therefore, the irrevocability is to be seen separately from the interdiction of deviation. The irrevocability has already been mentioned. [21]The interdiction of deviation also prohibits the Constitutional Court to distance itself from its previous legal opinion when deciding on a case involving different aspects of the same subject. The admissibility of an application with new factual and legal aspects is an exception of the *ne bis in idem* principle. However, because of the intent and purpose of the substantive res judicata, the decision must be left untouched. It serves to ensure legal certainty and legal order. In the case that new factual and legal circumstances which give rise to new causes of action exist, the application should be declared admissible. Intent and purpose of the legal force prohibit, in such a case, a renewed examination, yet allow for a renewed decision.[22] A deviation from the previous decision by the Constitutional Court would only be justified if the new facts represent a radical change of the object of the dispute.[23]

---

18 Benda/Klein, Verfassungsprozeßrecht, 2. edition, § 38, Rn. 1289.

19 Kpodar, Commentaire des grands avis et décisions de la Cour constitutionnelle togolaise, 102.

20 Kpodar, Commentaire des grands avis et décisions de la Cour constitutionnelle togolaise, 105.

21 See irrevocability in principle of the decision on page 38.

22 Detterbeck, Streitgegenstand und Entscheidungswirkungen im öffentlichen Recht, 343. [Object of Dispute and Effects of Decisions in Public Law, 343].

23 Detterbeck, Streitgegenstand und Entscheidungswirkungen im öffentlichen Recht, 344.
[Object of Dispute and Effects of Decisions in Public Law, 344].

c. Possibility of a Rectification of Material Errors

The legal force neither opposes a rectification of errors in drafting nor a mere supplementation. According to Art. 27 and 28 of the rules of procedure of the Constitutional Court of Togo, the Constitutional Court may rectify factual errors in its decision.[24] This includes typing errors, confusions and drafting errors. The fact that these factual mistakes represent an acceptable reason regarding the relativisation of the legal force is recognised amongst academics as well as in case law.[25] Such legally flawed judgments by the Constitutional Court are based on a mistake that does not lead to consequences relevant to the decision.In other words, actual errors are not grave mistakes which are able to significantly change the content of decision of the Constitutional Court.[26] The Constitutional Court of Benin defines these material errors as follows:

> « Considérant que, selon une jurisprudence constante de la Cour, l'erreur matérielle se définit comme une simple erreur de plume ou de dactylographie, d'orthographe d'un nom, de termi nologie ou d'une omission dans la décision ».[27]

Moreover, the rectification of the facts of the case is permissible. This would be the case if the court pointed out a fact in the tenor of its judgment that does not appear at all in the facts of the case.[28]

Even additions to a ruling are permissible, if the court simply by mistake did not decide on an application ascertained in the facts. In this case, there is the possibility to adjudicate on this application in hindsight to its full

---

24 Also see the Rules of Procedure of the ECtHR (Art. 81 Rules of Procedure ECtHR).

25 Adeloui, L'autorité de la chose jugée par les juridictions constitutionnelles en Afrique, in: Revue Togolaise des Sciences Juridiques (2012), 54 (68); Yebisi, The constitutional power of review of Supreme Court of Ghana: Lesson for Nigeria, in: International Journal of Humanities and Social Science (2014), 39 (39); Décision DCC 96–010 du 24 janvier 1996 de la Cour constitutionnel- le du Bénin; Décisions DCC 03–166 du 11 novembre 2003 de la Cour constitutionnelle du Bénin; Benda/Klein, Verfassungsprozeßrecht[Constitutional Process Law]., 2. edition, § 16, Rn. 331.

26 Adeloui, L'autorité de la chose jugée par les juridictions constitutionnelles en Afrique, in: Revue Togolaise des Sciences Juridiques (2012), 54 (68).

27 Cour constitutionnelle du Bénin, Décision DCC 03–166 (11.11.2003), available at: www. cour-constitutionnelle-benin.org (last accessed on 25/04/2015).

28 Benda/Klein, Verfassungsprozeßrecht [Constitutional Process Law], 2. edition, § 16, Rn. 331.

extent without intervention of the legal force. This would be possible through supplementing the decision.[29] However, the legal force prohibits a rectification of the decision at a later date. This means that the possibility of an addition depends on the modus operandi of the Constitutional Court. In case that the Constitutional Court would like to retract a wrong decision under the pretext of an addition, the principle of non-appealability would oppose such an approach.[30] It can no longer deviate from the original decision during the same proceedings. This means that the legal consequences, resulting from the originally rendered judgment, must be considered in the further course of the same object of dispute.[31]

Concerning the prerequisites for approaching the Constitutional Court with regards to the material errors, Art. 27 and 28 of the rules of procedure of the Constitutional Court of Togo stipulate:

> « Toute personne intéressée peut saisir la Cour d'une demande en rectification d'erreur maté rielle d'une de ses décisions. La Cour peut rectifier d'office une erreur matérielle dûment constatée par elle-même. »[32]

Contrary to the rectification of the factual error, the possibility of resumption or the amendment of the legal assessment on the grounds of gross procedural errors represent a special scenario.

d. Resumption due to gross miscarriage of justice

The question must be asked whether a misjudgment by the Constitutional Court, because of its legal force, will be untouchable or if it can be changed by rectifying the legal assessment of the misjudgment?[33] In principle, the reexamination of its own legal assessment is not possible under the

29 Benda/Klein, Verfassungsprozeßrecht [Constitutional Process Law], 2. edition, § 16, Rn. 331.

30 Benda/Klein, Verfassungsprozeßrecht[Constitutional Process Law], 2. edition, § 16, Rn. 331.

31 Benda/Klein, Verfassungsprozeßrecht[Constitutional Process Law], 2. edition, § 38, Rn. 1291.

32 Art. 27 und 28 der Geschäftsordnung des Verfassungsgerichts Togo: Reglement intérieur du
26.01.2005. [Rules of Procedure of the Constitutional Court of Togo...].

33 Adeloui, L'autorité de la chose jugée par les juridictions constitutionnelles en Afrique, in: Revue Togolaise des Sciences Juridiques (2012), 54 (57).

principle of irrevocability. Therefore, this is a rather rare case. Nevertheless, the constitutional system of Ghana, for example,. provides the possibility of a reexamination of the legal assessment. According to § 133 paragr. 1 of the Constitution (Ghana):

> "The Supreme Court may review any decision made or given by it on such grounds and sub-ject to such conditions as may be prescribed by rules of the Court".[34]

At first glance, this regulation seems to contradict the principle of non-appealability of a Supreme Court decision which has acquired the status of *res judicata*. However, the revision is not made automatically and is not unconditional. There must be special circumstances in order for the judgment to be brought before the Supreme Court again. This regulation takes the principle of the assumption of truth into account. The reasons for a possible examination of the judgment are listed in detail in Art. 54 of the rules of procedure of the Supreme Court of Ghana:

> "The Court may review any decision made or given by it on the following grounds –
> (a) exceptional circumstances which have resulted in miscarriage of justice;
> (b) the discovery of new and important matter or evidence which, after the exercise of due diligence, was not within the applicant's knowledge or could not be produced by him at the time when the decision was given."[35]

It is in the interest of the judiciary, in case of a gross miscarriage of justice[36] that the court amends the decision that is already entered into force[37]. In this exceptional procedure, the composition of the Supreme Court is, According to § 133 section 2 of the Constitution, different compared to normal circumstances:

34 § 133 section 1 Constitution of Ghana of 1992.

35 Ghana's Supreme Court Rules, 1996 (C.I 16), Art. 54.

36 See also erreur de droit bei Adeloui, L'autorité de la chose jugée par les juridictions cons- titutionnelles en Afrique, in: Revue Togolaise des Sciences Juridiques (2012), 54 (68).

37 Yebisi, The constitutional power of review of Supreme Court of Ghana: Lesson for Nigeria, in: International Journal of Humanities and Social Science (2014), 39 (44).

> "The Supreme Court, when reviewing its decisions under this article, shall be constituted by not less than seven Justices of the Supreme Court".

The signifigance of the exceptional review of a decision already in force accounts for this raised number of judges according to stipulations in § 133 section 2.The resumption of the judgment already in force has the advantage of granting better legal protection to persons seeking justice. Under exceptional circumstances, especially if there is an obvious factual error or mistake in the assessment of the relevant prerequisites for admissibility, an application[38]already declared inadmissible can be declared as partially admissible.[39] The Supreme Court also points out that the applicant has to prove the violation of his fundamental rights.[40] It is also not in the interest of legal certainty that a miscarriage of justice remains non-appealable within a legal order. In particular because a miscarriage of justice causes, in some cases, further injustice which in turn is not in the interest of legal certainty.[41] Therefore, it should be recommended that the Constitutional Court quickly rectifies, within a reasonable period of time, its own error by resuming its consideration of the object of dispute.[42] An error-free, constitutional decision has priority over legal force and takes the idea of the principle of fairness into account.[43] However, the question must be asked what the meaning of "exceptional circumstances" in Art. 54 of the rules of procedure (Supreme Court Ghana) is. Neither voices in literature nor case law can offer well-established criteria.[44] According to some authors, however, an error in law seems to be considered a special circumstance in the

38 CEDH, Nr. 61603/00, Arrêt (16/06/2005), Affaire Storck c. Allemagne, par. 4.

39 CEDH, Nr. 61603/00, Arrêt (16/06/2005), Affaire Storck c. Allemagne, par. 7.

40 Bimpong-Buta, The role of the Supreme Court in the development of constitutional law in Ghana, 70.

41 Yebisi, The constitutional power of review of Supreme Court of Ghana: Lesson for Nigeria, in: International Journal of Humanities and Social Science (2014), 39 (49).

42 Yebisi, The constitutional power of review of Supreme Court of Ghana: Lesson for Nigeria, in: International Journal of Humanities and Social Science (2014), 39 (49).

43 Yebisi, The constitutional power of review of Supreme Court of Ghana: Lesson for Nigeria, in: International Journal of Humanities and Social Science (2014), 39 (40); Bimpong-Buta, The role of the Supreme Court in the development of constitutional law in Ghana, 355.

44 Yebisi, The constitutional power of review of Supreme Court of Ghana: Lesson for Nigeria, in: International Journal of Humanities and Social Science (2014), 39 (43).

adjudication of the object of dispute.[45] It therefore concerns a severe legal error in the assessment of the facts of the case. [46]

There is no exclusive list of facts under the current Supreme Court case law that constitute grounds for an exceptional revision of an already decided case.[47] In particular, legal force may be deviated from if a gross mistake has been made regarding an already taken decision. In such a case the Constitutional Court would not be prevented from revisiting the same object of dispute as long as an application is made.[48] It is predominantly assumed amongst scholars that if gross procedural injustice has been committed, an exception of non-appealability can be made.[49] However, a new assessment is only done if new causes of action exist under the German Constitutional Court.[50] The Federal Supreme Court of Germany recognised that it can never be completely ruled out that objectively wrong judgments are made because of the natural limitations of human ability.[51] In view of the relevance of this point, it is recommended to quote the following statement:

> „Die rechtsprechende Gewalt, die den Richtern anvertraut ist, hat zum Inhalt, im Rahmen des dem Gericht unterbreiteten Sachverhalts einen bestimmten Lebenstatbestand festzustellen, den Tatbestand unter Gesetz und Recht zu subsumieren und die sich danach aus diesem Tatbestand ergebenden Rechtsfolgen verbindlich auszusprechen. Dass hierbei auch objektiv unrichtige Richtersprüche ergehen können, ist niemals völlig auszuschließen, da *dem menschlichen Erkenntnisvermögen von der Natur her Grenzen gesetzt sind*".[52]

45 Adeloui, L'autorité de la chose jugée par les juridictions constitutionnelles en Afrique, in: Revue Togolaise des Sciences Juridiques (2012), 54 (62); Yebisi, The constitutional power of re- view of Supreme Court of Ghana: Lesson for Nigeria, in: International Journal of Humanities and Social Science (2014), 39 (43).

46 Adeloui, L'autorité de la chose jugée par les juridictions constitutionnelles en Afrique, in: Revue Togolaise des Sciences Juridiques (2012), 54 (67).

47 Bimpong-Buta, The role of the Supreme Court in the development of constitutional law in Ghana, 71.

48 Yebisi, The constitutional power of review of Supreme Court of Ghana: Lesson for Nigeria, in: International Journal of Humanities and Social Science (2014), 39 (43); Benda/Klein, Verfas- sungsprozeßrecht[Constitutional Process Law...], 2. edition, § 16, Rn. 332.

49 Benda/Klein, Verfassungsprozeßrecht [Constitutional Process Law...], 2. edition, § 16, Rn. 332; dazu BVerfGE 72, 84 (84).

50 BVerfGE 72, 84 (91); vgl. Bimpong-Buta, The role of the Supreme Court in the development of constitutional law in Ghana, 71.

51 BGHZ 36, 379 (393).

52 BGHZ 36, 379 (393), (emphasis added by author).

There is no regulation comparable to § 133 (Constitution of Ghana) in the Benin constitution. Indeed, Art. 23 of the rules of procedure of the Constitutional Court of Benin allows the rectification of constitutional judgments which are already in force. However, this rectification of actual errors does not represent a breach of the legal force. Hence, the Constitutional Court decided in 2002 that the legal force is not opposed to the rectification of the actual error in the judgment draft.[53] In contrast to the rectification of actual errors, the review of the legal grounds of the decision represents a breach of the legal force. Despite the fact that there is no constitutional regulation regarding this scenario, the Constitutional Court allowed the review of legal errors through case law.[54] In this manner, the Constitutional Court of Benin decided in one of its first judgments that the arrest and containment of a plaintiff (Loko M. Maurice) by police for more than 48 hours as constitutional.[55] However, the Court found in a new assessment of the same case that this was unconstitutional.[56] Therefore, the second decision nullifies the legal force of the first judgment. It is questionable which effect a resumption of the proceedings will have on the legal force. One can assume this will result in a suspension of the legal effect. At the very least, the resumption of the proceedings should have a *suspensory effect*[57] on the first judgment, because on resuming the proceedings, the result is not predictable. Therefore, the execution of the judgment should be postponed until the court has made its judgment.

As a result, it is certain that the perpetuation of a misjudgement by the Constitutional Court would forcibly harm legal certainty even more than the breaching of the legal force.[58] Therefore, the institution of legal force is not absolute but may be breached under justified circumstances, such as misjudgements, by a renewed assessment of the case. It is recommended

53 Cour constitutionnelle du Bénin, Décision DCC 02–134 (18/12/2002), available at: www. cour-constitutionnelle-benin.org (last accessed on 25/04/2015).

54 Adeloui, L'autorité de la chose jugée par les juridictions constitutionnelles en Afrique, in: Revue Togolaise des Sciences Juridiques (2012), 54 (68).

55 Cour constitutionnelle du Bénin, Décision DCC 98–24 (12/03/1998), available at: www. cour-constitutionnelle-benin.org (last accessed on 25/04/2015); Kommentar dazu bei Adeloui, L'autorité de la chose jugée par les juridictions constitutionnelles en Afrique, in: Revue Togolaise des Sciences Juridiques (2012), 54 (68).

56 Cour constitutionnelle du Bénin, Décision DCC 98–098 (11/12/1998), available at: www. cour-constitutionnelle-benin.org (last accessed on 25/04/2015).

57 Benda/Klein, Verfassungsprozeßrecht [Constitutional Process Law...], 2. edition, § 36, Rn. 1234.

58 Adeloui, L'autorité de la chose jugée par les juridictions constitutionnelles en Afrique, in: Revue Togolaise des Sciences Juridiques (2012), 54 (57).

that the procedure of a renewed assessment of the judgment, if obvious miscarriages of justice are present, should be included in a constitutional code of procedure of West African states.[59]This would contribute to an effective implementation of judgments by Constitutional Courts and at the same time enforce the confidence in the rule of law. Overall, the possibility of a later, revision of the object of dispute displays the double nature of the legal force.[60] It is absolute if there are no special circumstances. It is, however, relative if special and relevant circumstances were not taken sufficiently into consideration when the case was first assessed.

e. Delimitation with regard to future disputes

The internal procedural commitment of the Constitutional Court precludes a renewed opinion by the court regarding the same object of dispute. This follows, as shown, from the principles of the rule of law and serves legal certainty. However, the legal force of decisions by the Constitutional Court is limited in time (see also below: limits of legal force). The temporary element in the legal force allows for a new decision to be based on reasons if new facts arise after the decision has been made. New facts are, in this sense, actual changes.[61] Primarily, a new fact can be understood as a fundamental change of the life circumstance.[62] These actual changes include, amongst others, amendments to the law and the general legal opinion.[63] The relevance of this change is measured by the core elements of the legal force. At this point, it is important to note that new facts must relate to the object of dispute and the same parties to the dispute. Without an identity of the object of the dispute and the parties to the dispute, there is no legal force.[64]Whether a legal force is ascribed to the decision by Con-

59 Adeloui, L'autorité de la chose jugée par les juridictions constitutionnelles en Afrique, in: Revue Togolaise des Sciences Juridiques (2012), 54 (75).

60 Kpodar, Commentaire des grands avis et décisions de la Cour constitutionnelle togolaise, 103.

61 Pestalozza, Verfassungsprozeßrecht. [Constitutional Process Law...], 3. edition, § 20, Rn. 69.

62 Benda/Klein, Verfassungsprozeßrecht [Constitutional Process Law...], 2. edition, § 13, Rn. 245.

63 Pestalozza, Verfassungsprozeßrecht [Constitutional Process Law...], 3. edition, § 20, Rn. 69; Benda/Klein, Verfassungspro- zeßrecht, 2. edition, § 13, Rn. 245.

64 Adeloui, L'autorité de la chose jugée par les juridictions constitutionnelles en Afrique, in: Revue Togolaise des Sciences Juridiques (2012), 54 (54); Pestalozza, Verfassungsrozeßrecht [Constitutional Process Law...], 3. edition, § 20, Rn. 69.

stitutional Court[65], According to Art. 106 of the Togolese Constitution is insignificant with regard to the judgment of the legal force of such future changes in legal opinion. A prerequisite for this remains the fundamental change of the object of the dispute. The possibility of future changes in legal opinion of the Constitutional Court is expressly stipulated in the Ghanaian Constitution. With this in mind, § 129 section 3 of the Constitution of Ghana stipulates as follows:

> "(3) The Supreme Court may, while treating its own previous decisions as normally binding, depart from a previous decision when it appears to it right to do so; and all other courts shall be bound to follow the decisions of the Supreme Court on questions of law."[66]

This regulation clearly shows that some degree of development of the Constitutional Court jurisdiction should be possible. It is solely questionable who can kick-start this change in legal reasoning. According to the literal interpretation of § 129 section 3, the change in legal reasoning happens at the discretion of the Supreme Court itself. It is also left to the discretion of the court whether it should deviate from its previous opinion.[67] This regulation cannot be interpreted in the sense that the legal force of previous decisions by the court is principally no longer binding. Rather, the creator of the Constitution does not wish to exclude future changes of the legal force just by having the above criteria present.[68] This represents a reasonable stance by the creator of the Constitution to prevent rigidity of the legal force. It is, however, difficult to imagine that the court will change its legal opinion ex officio without an application to do so because, as it is commonly known, parties to the dispute drive the proceedings and are therefore able to influence the decision by the Constitutional Court in many ways. Consequently, one must assume that the change in legal opinion can also take place at the request of the parties to the dispute through due process.

---

65 According to the expression on the website of the Constitutional Court of Togo: „*Lex est quod notamus*“, available at: http://www.courconstitutionnelle.tg/ (last accessed on 22/06/2015).

66 See also sect.126 paragr. 2 Constitution of Gambia of 16 January 1997; Art. 122 paragr. 2 Constitution of Sierra Leone of 03 September 1991.

67 Yebisi, The constitutional power of review of Supreme Court of Ghana: Lesson for Nigeria, in: International Journal of Humanities and Social Science (2014), 39 (43).

68 Benda/Klein, Verfassungsprozeßrecht [Constitutional Process Law...], 2. edition, § 38, Rn. 1334.

As a result, a renewed complaint before the Constitutional Court or Supreme Court may be permitted if there are significant changes in life circumstances. Nevertheless, the resumption of the proceedings represents a special exception. Apart from this case the judgment may not be appealed by the parties to the dispute. It is not at their disposal.

2. The Non-appealability of the Decision

The formal legal force, excluding its irrevocability, follows the principle of non-appealability of the decision. This means that the decision by the court is neither subject of negotiation by the Constitutional Court nor by the parties to the dispute. It is final and binding. This principle of non-appealability (a) can be justified (b) in such a manner that the judgment of a Constitutional Court isdeterminant for all participants. However, an exception to the principle of non-appealability exists (c).

a. The principle of non-appealability

The decision by the Constitutional Court, according to the judgment, facilitates an assumption of truth according to the principle: *„res judicata pro veritate habetur"*. This legal assumption of truth prevents the participants to the proceedings from questioning the judgment by the Constitutional Court again.[69] The principle of non-appealability does justice to the fundamental principle of *interest republicae ut sit finis litium* because it is not in the interest of the public that proceedings before the Constitutional Court are endlessly continued. Hence, the non-appealability of the judgment develops its effect, first and foremost, for the benefit of the parties to the dispute. More than anything, this has practical reasons because the proceedings must ultimately reach an end. This can be seen as a direct result from the requirement for legal certainty. On the one hand, the non-appealability of the Constitutional Court decision is therefore addressed to the parties to the proceedings. They may not question the authority of the decision and therefore that of the Constitutional Court. On the other hand, non-appealability means that there are no legal remedies against decisions by the Con-

69 Kpodar, Commentaire des grands avis et décisions de la Cour constitutionnelle togolaise, 100; Adeloui, L'autorité de la chose jugée par les juridictions constitutionnelles en Afrique, in: Revue Togolaise des Sciences Juridiques (2012), 54 (54).

stitutional Court. As the judgment has been delivered, it cannot be appealed. Therefore, the formal legal force confirms the nature of the decision-making authority of the Constitutional Court as a last instance. There are no other higher-ranking instances above the Constitutional Court. Especially for this reason, its decisions immediately develops formal legal force with it's delivery or notification.[70] In terms of external legal effect, the formal legal force expresses the authority of the constitutional court (s. a.). Jurisdiction and doctrine also unanimously assume that the function of the substantive res judicata, with regard to the decision by the constitutional court, is indispensable.[71]

b. Justification of non-appealability

There are many reasons that speak for the non-appealability of a Constitutional Court decision. There is simply no higher instance above the Constitutional Court that is responsible for the review of Constitutional Court decisions. Moreover, the Constitutional Court represents the only legitimate interpreter of the Constitution. With this in mind, it can be assumed that it avails of the monopoly to interpret the Constitution. Especially since the legally effective decision has been given by the Constitutional Court itself, there is no reason why its decision should be appealed before it. Seeing as the object of dispute and the parties to the dispute are identical, the Constitutional Court would not take a different point of view when interpreting the constitutional regulations.[72] Furthermore, it can be observed that the respective Member State's Constitutions express its outward and internal sovereignty and authority. Therefore, the jurisdiction of the Constitutional Court also represents the judicial confirmation of this national sovereignty.

---

70 Benda/Klein, Verfassungsprozeßrecht[Constitutional process law], 2. edition, § 38, Rn. 1291.

71 Cour constitutionnelle du Togo, Décision N°E-002/2011 vom 22 June 2011, available at: http://www.courconstitutionnelle.tg/ (last accessed on 22/06/2015); Décision DCC 15–027 (12/02/2015), available at: www.cour-constitutionnelle-benin.org (last accessed on 25/04/2015); Kpodar, Commentaire des grands avis et décisions de la Cour constitutionnelle togolaise, 105.

72 Kpodar, Commentaire des grands avis et décisions de la Cour constitutionnelle togolaise, 101.

c. Need for legal protection as an exception

It cannot, however, be underestimated that reasons may exist in exceptional cases that could challenge the legal force. There is consensus amongst scholars that the legal force represents a negative prerequisite for proceedings. Nevertheless, there is a possibility to modify the sanctity of the legal force to a certain degree. This is because there are factors that, in exceptional circumstances, can allow a breach of the legal force. E.g., the legal force can be breached if there is a particular need for legal protection.[73] Should there be a particular interest in legal protection, a complaint with regard to the same object of dispute would be admissible.[74]This should not be seen as a violation against the *ne bis in idem* doctrine but as a special case regarding the generally valid non-appealability of the legal force. The latter scenario addresses a different level (see chapter 3: Derogation of Legal Force). For example, in case of a sustained human rights complaint before the ECOWAS Court of Justice, one should come to the conclusion that there is a need for legal protection, which should be reason for aresumption of proceedings regarding a constitutional complaint.[75]Whether the plaintiff has a legally protected need in an individual case after the legal force takes effect depends on the intensity of the Unconstitutionality of the violation and the risk of its repetition.[76] It does not matter whether the violation took place in the past or not.[77] This aspect of the exceptional overriding of the principle was unfortunately overlooked by the Constitutional Court of Togo as it proclaimed without differentiation an *erga-omnes-effect* of its decisions without pointing out the possibility of an individual complaint at an international level. Thus, the Constitutional Court proclaimed the following words:

> « Qu'aucune autorité civile ou militaire, qu'aucune institution, fut-elle internationale, ne peut s'opposer à une décision de la Cour».[78]

---

73 Hillgruber/Goos, Verfassungssprozeßrecht[Constitutional Process Law...], 4. edition, § 5, Rn. 469.

74 Koussoulis, Beiträge zur modernen Rechtskraftlehre[Contributions to modern doctrine of legal force], 209.

75 See also the resumption of the proceedings (page 227).

76 Hillgruber/Goos, Verfassungsprozeßrecht [Constitutional Process Law...], 4. edition, § 5, Rn. 475.

77 Hillgruber/Goos, Verfassungsprozeßrecht [Constitutional Process Law...], 4. edition, § 5, Rn. 475.

78 Cour constitutionnelle du Togo, Décision N°E-002/2011 vom 22 June 2011, available at: http://www.courconstitutionnelle.tg/ (last accessed on 22/06/2015).

The difference between the renewed proceedings due to a special need of legal protection and the rectification due to gross miscarriages of justice includes the fact that the former is launched by a complaint of the concerned party after the declaratory judgment by an international instance[79], while the latter is supposed to be executed after the declaration by the judiciary body itself (compare § 133 of the Constitution of Ghana).

A need for legal protection also exists, if a fact becomes known after the judgment which would have been suitable for exercising a significant influence on the result of an already decided dispute. Therefore, the Constitutional Court of Togo could have decided differently once it had realised that the parliamentarians, who were excluded from parliament, had not submitted a proper waiver.[80] Unfortunately, the Constitutional Court overlooked this aspect in its legal assessment.[81] In this case, it would have been plausible to assume an exceptional breach of the legal force, based on the need for legal protection. Thus, Art. 80 of the rules of procedure of the ECtHR, for example, allow under certain circumstances a resumption of proceedings with regard a judgment that is already in legal force.[82]

II. Substantive Res Judicata

The practical significance of the differentiation between the formal and substantive res judicata lies in the face that the substantive res judicata has effect in a second trial. The formal legal force, on the other hand, binds the court irrespective of a second trial.[83] As already mentioned, the formal legal force is the basis for the substantive res judicata.[84] In the following, the individual elements (1), the exact object (2) and the legal consequences (3) of the substantive res judicata will be discussed.

---

79 See also the declaratory judgment ECOWAS: CJ CEDEAO, Affaire Isabelle Ameganvi v. Republique Togo, N°ECW/CCJ/JUD/09/11 (07/10/2011), par. 66.

80 CJ CEDEAO, Affaire Isabelle Ameganvi v. Republique Togo, N°ECW/CCJ/JUD/09/11 (07/10/2011), par. 61, 62.

81 Cour constitutionnelle du Togo, decision N°E-018/2010 of 22 November 2010, available at: http://www.courconstitutionnelle.tg/ (last accessed on 22/06/2015).

82 Art. 80 paragr. 1 of the Verfahrensordnung des EGMR [Rules of Procedure of ECtHR].

83 Pestalozza, Verfassungsprozeßrecht. [Constitutional Process Law...], 3. edition, § 20, Rn. 49.

84 Benda/Klein, Verfassungsprozeßrecht, 2nd edition, § 38, Rn. 1295. [Constitutional Process Law...].

1. Object of Substantive res judicata

Substantive res judicata means that a claim, raised in a complaint or counter-complaint, has been decided upon.[85] The substantive res judicata therefore includes the decision regarding the disputed claim. With this in mind, there is no difference between the object of the dispute and the object of the decision, because what is being litigated during the trial by the parties must also be decided on by the court.[86]The substantive res judicata fixates the factual and temporal elements of the object of the decision. It means that the decision by the Constitutional Court is significant for the Constitutional Court as well as for those participants in the dispute seeking adjudication. As such, the purpose of the substantive res judicata is to ensure the content of a formal final judgment for a possible second trial.[87]

2. Elements of Substantive res judicata

Not everything contained in a decision by the Constitutional Court, is to be included in the substantive res judicata. The substantive res judicata has a specific scope (a) and has certain limits (b).

a. Extent of legal force

First of all, the question must be answered whether the tenor and the key reasons for the decision make up the respective elements of the substantive res judicata.[88] In response, the French Conseil Constitutionnel has taken the following position:

> « Considérant, d'une part, qu'aux termes de l'article 62 in fine de la Constitution les décisions du Conseil constitutionnel s'imposent aux pouvoirs publics et à toutes les autorités adminis tratives et juridiction-

85 Adeloui, L'autorité de la chose jugée par les juridictions constitutionnelles en Afrique, in: Revue Togolaise des Sciences Juridiques (2012), 54 (54).

86 Rosenberg/Schwab/Gottwald, Zivilprozessrecht [Rules of Civil Procedure], 13 th edition, § 153, Rn. 2.

87 Lechner/Zuck, Bundesverfassungsgesetz [Federal Constitutional Law...], § 31, Rn. 11.

88 Adeloui, L'autorité de la chose jugée par les juridictions constitutionnelles en Afrique, in: Revue Togolaise des Sciences Juridiques (2012), 54 (55).

> nelles; que l'autorité des décisions visées par cette disposition s'attache non seulement à leur *dispositif* mais aussi aux *motifs* qui en sont le soutien nécessaire et en constituent le fondement même».[89]

This suggests that the substantive res judicata fixates the content of the decision. In this regard, the elements of the tenor are decisive. As a result, the substantive res judicata in principle does not include the key reasons for the decision. However, these key reasons for the decision help with the interpretation of the verdict.[90] They describe in more detail the grounds for the verdict. In other words, the reasons for the decision are all those statements from which the court comes to the answer of the claim by way of logical conclusion.[91] To this extent, the reasons for the decision partake in the legal force[92] and influence its effects. Moreover, the key reasons for the decision are closely linked to the extent of the procedural claim, which forms the basis for the object of the dispute. Especially when a claim is rejected or dismissed a recourse to the key reasons of the decision is essential [93]because the Constitutional Court does not explain the rejection of the claim in the formula of the judgment but solely in the key reasons for the decision. In the formula of the judgment the Constitutional Court gives an answer only to the pertinent legal issue raised regarding a certain constitutional regulation. Thereby, the preliminary and incidentally dealt with question by the Constitutional Court does not share the legal nature of the material legal question.[94]

Furthermore, the substantive res judicata does not develop an unlimited effect.

---

89 Conseil constitutionnel francais, Décision n°62–18 L (16/01/1962), available at: www.conseil-constitutionnel.fr (last accessed on 08/07/2015).

90 Conseil constitutionnel francais, Décision n°62–18 L (16/01/1962), available at: www.conseil-constitutionnel.fr (last accessed on 08/07/2015).

91 Zeuner, Die objektiven Grenzen der Rechtskraft im Rahmen rechtlicher Sinnzusammenhän- ge, 5. [The objective limits of legal force within the framework of legal contexts...].

92 Zeuner, Die objektiven Grenzen der Rechtskraft im Rahmen rechtlicher Sinnzusammenhän- ge, 6. [The objective limits of legal force within the framework of legal contexts...].

93 Detterbeck, Streitgegenstand und Entscheidungswirkungen im öffentlichen Recht [Object of dispute and effects of decisions in public law...], 333; Ben- da/ Klein, Verfassungssprozeßrecht, 2. edition, § 38, Rn. 1298. [Constitutional Process Law...].

94 Detterbeck, Streitgegenstand und Entscheidungswirkungen im öffentlichen Recht, 332. [Object of dispute and effects of decisions in public law...].

b. Limits of legal force

First of all, it should be mentioned that the question of the objective scope of the substantive res judicata is hardly regulated in the Constitutions of the ECOWAS. For this very reason, the question regarding the limits of the legal force of decisions by the Constitutional Court is especially difficult. Due to the lack of legal remedies against decisions by the Constitutional Courts, the decisions initially have an unlimited effect. However, there are opinions in literature that allege an objective limit to the substantive res judicata.[95] These opinions are supported by the rule of law. The general effect of the decisions can, According to Art. 106 (Constitution of Togo), not take effect absolutely because there are constitutional obligations of the state at international level which may question the legal force of the decisions by the Constitutional Court. This may be the case within the ECOWAS legal order, where individual complaints are admissible at the ECOWAS Court of Justice (discussed in detail in chapter 3). The admissibility of such complaint proceedings against the decision of national Constitutional Courts represents, from a procedural viewpoint, an *objective limit of the legal force* of the judgment by the national Constitutional Courts.

The legal force of the decision by the Constitutional Court is also limited in time. This means that the substantive res judicata only refers to the circumstances that occurred before the judgment was rendered. The element of time represents, according to prevailing opinion within the doctrine, a barrier to the substantive res judicata.[96] The point in time at which the legal force takes effect plays an important role in its preclusive effect. This means that actual and legal circumstances which were present before the legal force took effect and which refer to the object of the dispute are precluded regarding the same object of dispute.[97] For the assessment of the decisiveness of this point in time, the formal legal force should be applied. There are two exceptions that should be paid attention to when it comes to the preclusive effect. Firstly, circumstances that were not included in the initial assessment by the Constitutional Court are not affected. Because of

95 Kpodar, Commentaire des grands avis et décisions de la Cour constitutionnelle togolaise, 105 f.

96 Detterbeck, Streitgegenstand und Entscheidungswirkungen im öffentlichen Recht, 338. [Object of dispute and effects of decisions in public law…].

97 Detterbeck, Streitgegenstand und Entscheidungswirkungen im öffentlichen Recht, 338. [Object of dispute and effects of decisions in public law…].

the objective function of the constitutional jurisdiction, these circumstances would require a different object of dispute.[98] Secondly, the actual and legal circumstances that occurred before the legal force took effect are not included in the preclusive effect. A transformation of the views and values prevailing in the population, e.g. is seen as a circumstance of an actual nature that is opposed to the preclusive effect of the legal force.[99]

Regarding the addressees of the effects of the legal force, it is established in general procedural law that the substantive res judicata only concerns the parties directly involved in the dispute.[100] However, the constitutional procedural law has a special nature which justifies a general *erga-omnes-effect* (also see C below).

3. Consequences of Substantive res judicata

The substantive res judicata must be strictly separated from the substantive legal effects of the judgment. As shown, *substantive res judicata* concerns the core elements of the decision. In contrast, the substantive legal effects of the judgment concern the legal consequences which are caused by the decision of the Constitutional Court. In this regard, the *substantive res judicata* represents an obstacle to proceedings (a). Meanwhile, there is the possibility of the admissibility of a new complaint despite the enforcement of *substantive res judicata*. This situation is possible, if there are new reasons for a complaint (b).

a. Substantive res judicata as an obstacle to proceedings

One of the most important consequences of substantive res judicata from a procedural-legal viewpoint is the possible inadmissibility of further law suits. Therefore, the legal force serves as an obstacle to proceedings. The

98 Detterbeck, Streitgegenstand und Entscheidungswirkungen im öffentlichen Recht, 339. [Object of dispute and effects of decisions in public law...].

99 Detterbeck, Streitgegenstand und Entscheidungswirkungen im öffentlichen Recht, 339.

100 Koussoulis, Beiträge zur modernen Rechtskraftlehre, 22f. [Object of dispute and effects of decisions in public law...].

doctrine therefore rightfully qualifies the *substantive res judicata* as a negative prerequisite for a decision in the matter.[101]

In general, the finality of the legal force takes effect, once all possible legal remedies have been exhausted.[102] Since there are no legal remedies available against the decisions by the Constitutional Court, the finality of decisions by the Constitutional Court take immediate effect once the judgment is announced.[103]Therefore, the judgment by the Constitutional Court is also immediately enforceable.[104]

Since most of the proceedings at the Constitutional Court do not involve disputes between parties, the effect is usually enforced for the overall constitutional order. In case of disputes between parties, there are specifics regarding the effect of the decision. In this case, the substantive res judicata presents an obstacle to proceedings that interferes if there is the same object of dispute between the same parties in a two-party case.[105] This is logical, because a renewed assessment of the same case would contravene the principle of *ne bis in idem*. The Constitutional Court of Togo has just referred to exactly this principle in order to reject the application of the parliamentarians of the Togolese parliament in the initial case. In this regard, the court said the following:

> « Considérant par ailleurs que par décision n°E-018 du 22 novembre 2010, la Cour a constaté la vacance des sièges occupés par le requérant et huit (08) autres personnes, précédemment députés inscrits de l'Union des Forces de Changement (UFC) à l'Assemblée nationale, et a procédé à leur remplacement conformément aux dispositions du Code électoral; [...] qu'ainsi les décisions de a Cour constitutionnelle ont un

101 Kpodar, Commentaire des grands avis et décisions de la Cour constitutionnelle togolaise, 100; Benda/Klein, Verfassungsprozeßrech t[Constitutional Process Law...], 2. edition, § 38, Rn. 1296.

102 Kpodar, Commentaire des grands avis et décisions de la Cour constitutionnelle togolaise, 100.

103 Kpodar, Commentaire des grands avis et décisions de la Cour constitutionnelle togolaise, 100.

104 Kpodar, Commentaire des grands avis et décisions de la Cour constitutionnelle togolaise, 100.

105 Kpodar, Commentaire des grands avis et décisions de la Cour constitutionnelle togolaise, 100; Benda/Klein, Verfassungsprozeßrecht [Constitutional Process Law...], 2. edition, § 38, Rn. 242.

caractère impératif; qu'il en résulte qu'une obéissance absolue est due aux décisions de la Cour [...]».[106]

With this statement, the Constitutional Court clearly confirms the scope of substantive res judicata as a negative prerequisite for a decision. However, substantive res judicata does not oppose a new application with regards to the same object of dispute if it is based on other causes of action.

b. Admissibility in the presence of new causes of action

First of all, it must be pointed out that the legal force does not have an absolute effect on the object of dispute. Rather, the effect of the legal force is essentially enforced with regard to the non-appealability of the causes of action, because with regards to the same dispute, different reasons could still justify another action regarding the same object of dispute.

This would be admissible from a constitutional-procedural point of view.[107]At first glance, this opinion seems difficult to justify but on closer inspection it becomes clear that the admissibility of a renewed application with regards to the same legal dispute does not violate the principle of *ne bis in idem*. In this context, the French Conseil Constitutionnel has rejected the opinion that the legal force conflicts with a law already declared unconstitutional by the Conseil, if the Parliament resubmits the disputed law to the Constitutional Court under new aspects. Based on the significance of this judgment, the respective opinion by the Conseil Constitutionnel is herewith repeated:

> « Considérant que l'autorité de chose jugée attachée à la décision du Conseil constitutionnel du 22 octobre 1982 est limitée à la déclaration d'inconstitutionnalité visant certaines disposi- tions de la loi qui lui était alors soumise; qu'elle ne peut être utilement invoquée à l'encontre d'une autre loi conçue, d'ailleurs, en termes différents ».[108]

---

106 Cour constitutionnelle du Togo, Décision N°E-002/2011 of 22 June 2011, available at: http://www.courconstitutionnelle.tg/ (last accessed on 22/06/2015).

107 Kpodar, Commentaire des grands avis et décisions de la Cour constitutionnelle togolaise, 105.

108 Conseil constitutionnel français, Décision n°88–244 DC (20/07/1988), 18ème Considérant, available at: www.conseil-constitutionnel.fr (last accessed on 08/07/2015).

This point of view by the French Conseil Constitutionnel expresses that the legal force only then develops a relative binding effect if the Constitutional Court is presented with the same object of dispute with different reasons for legal action for review.[109] The admissibility of new reasons for legal action regarding the same object of dispute contributes to the development of the Constitutional Courts' case law and must be welcomed for this reason.[110]

A further important argument in support of this view is that the Constitutional Court gives an answer in its tenor specifically to questions posed in the reasons for legal action. This means that the opinion by the court in its tenor does not necessarily refer to the object of dispute but instead to the legal issues raised.[111]

In conclusion, the legal force and the associated principle of non-appealability do not conflict in every case with a subsequent application regarding the same object of dispute. There are exceptions when the reasons for legal action, on which the new application is based, give rise to a different legal assessment of the object of dispute.[112]Over and above the legal force of the decision, decisions by the Constitutional Court develop further particular effects.

C. *The Binding Effect of the Decision*

Generally, the decisions by the Constitutional Court have an *erga-omnes*-effect (I). However, there are in exceptional cases also some decisions that only develop an *inter-omnes*-effect (II).

I. Erga-omnes-Effect

The decisions by the Constitutional Court result in final legal force not only in a formal and material respect but also have a binding effect with re-

109 Kpodar, Commentaire des grands avis et décisions de la Cour constitutionnelle togolaise, 104.

110 Kpodar, Commentaire des grands avis et décisions de la Cour constitutionnelle togolaise, 106.

111 Kpodar, Commentaire des grands avis et décisions de la Cour constitutionnelle togolaise, 106.

112 Kpodar, Commentaire des grands avis et décisions de la Cour constitutionnelle togolaise, 105.

gard to all state powers. Procedural principles of the *erga-omnes*-effect[113] are constitutionally entrenched in Art. 106 of the Constitution of Togo,[114] which in turn expands the circle of the target group the binding effect applies to. The civil and military authorities as well as the judiciary are bound to the decisions by the Constitutional Court.[115] Thereby, it must be noted that the legal force develops a binding effect not only externally but also internally because the Constitutional Court itself is, like the mentioned target group, also bound by its decision.[116] The decision may, therefore, not be arbitrarily changed, as long as there is no circumstantial change.[117]

It is correct that, in the interest of legal certainty, all actors are subject to the binding effect of decisions by the Constitutional Court.[118] Logically, the Constitutions of ECOWAS Member States do not provide legal reme-

---

113 Kpodar, Commentaire des grands avis et décisions de la Cour constitutionnelle togolaise, 103.

114 See also: § 129 section 2 Constitution of Ghana of 1992; Art. 124 Constitution of Benin of 11 December 1991; Art. 94 Constitution of Mali of 25 February 1992; Art. 134 Constitution of Niger of 25 November 2010; Art. 99 Constitution of Guinea of 07 May 2010; Art. 98 Constitution of Ivory Coast of 23 July 2000; Art. 159 Constitution of Burkina Faso of 02 June 1991; Art. 92 Abs. 2 Constitution of Senegal of 22 January 2001; Sect. 230, 232, 233, 235 Constitution of Nigeria of 29 May 1999; Art. 65 Constitution of Liberia of 06 January 1984; Art. 92 Constitution of Guinea-Bissau of 16 January 1984; Sect. 126, 127 Constitution of Gambia of 16 January 1997; Art. 229 Abs. 1 Constitution of Cape Verde of 23 November 1999; Art. 122 Abs. 1 Constitution of Sierra Leone of 03 September 1991.

115 Bado, Verfassungsrechtliche Gerichtsbarkeit und Demokratisierung im frankophonen Westafrika, Länderstudie/Benin [Constitutional Jurisdiction and democratisation in Francophone West Africa], 14, available at: http://intlaw-sgiessen.de/fileadmin/user_upload/bilder_ und_dokumente/forschung/westafrikaprojekt/workingpapers/Draft_WP_2014_benin.pdf (last accessed on 02/07/2015).

116 Kpodar, Commentaire des grands avis et décisions de la Cour constitutionnelle togolaise, 102.

117 Kpodar, Commentaire des grands avis et décisions de la Cour constitutionnelle togolaise, 103.

118 Jeze, De la vérité de la force légale attachée par la loi à l'acte juridictionnel, in: RDP 1913, 439 (440); Adeloui, L'autorité de la chose jugée par les juridictions constitutionnelles en Afrique, in: Revue Togolaise des Sciences Juridiques (2012), 54 (54).

dies against the jurisdiction of the court.[119] The Constitutional Courts within the region emphasise repeatedly the *erga-omnes*-effect of their decisions and declare all complaints regarding their previous decisions as inadmissible.[120]In this regard, the legal force of decisions by Constitutional Courts are to be differentiated from decisions by specialised courts. Regarding the courts of general jurisdiction, only the parties to the dispute in the proceedings are bound to its decision.[121] The proceedings before the Constitutional Court, however, are usually objective proceedings.[122] They usually do not comprise of two-party proceedings. Even though the possibility of individual constitutional complaints exists, these mainly serve the interpretation of the Constitution. As a result, the legal force of decisions by the Constitutional Court has the same legal nature as this objective type of legal action. A violation of the legal force of decisions by the Constitutional Court thereby represents a violation of the Constitution.[123] This is an expression of the significance of the jurisdiction of the Constitutional Court. The *erga-omnes*-effect also demands that the authorities, as well as

---

119 Siehe dazu: § 129 Abs. 2 Constitution of Ghana of 1992; Art. 106 Constitution of Togo of 14 October 1992; Art. 124 Constitution of Benin of 11 December 1991; Art. 94 Constitution of Mali of 25 February 1992; Art. 134 Constitution of Niger of 25 November 2010; Art. 99 Constitution of Guinea of 07 May 2010; Art. 98 Constitution of Ivory Coast of 23 July 2000; Art. 159 Constitution of Burkina Faso of 02 June 1991; Art. 92 Abs. 2 Constitution of Senegal of 22 January 2001; Sect. 230, 232, 233, 235 Constitution of Nigeria of 29 May 1999; Art. 65 Constitution of Liberia of 06 January 1984; Art. 92 Constitution of Guinea-Bissau of 16 January 1984; Sect. 126, 127 Constitution of Gambia of 16 January 1997; Art. 229 Abs. 1 Constitution of Cape Verde of 23 November 1999; Art. 122 Abs. 1 Constitution of Sierra Leone of 0. September 1991.

120 Décision de la Cour constitutionnelle du Bénin DCC 15–027 (12/02/2015), available at: www.cour-constitutionnelle-benin.org (last accessed on 25/04/2015); Décision de la Cour cons- titutionnelle du Bénin N°DCC 14–038 of 20 February 2014, available at: www.cour-constitutionnelle-benin.org (last accessed on 25/04/2015); Cour constitutionnelle du Togo, Décision N °E-002/2011 of 22 June 2011, available at: http://www.courconstitutionnelle.tg/ (last accessed on 22/06/2015); see also Yebisi, The constitutional power of review of Supreme Court of Ghana: Lesson for Nigeria, in: International Journal and Social Science Invention (2014), 39 (42).

121 Adeloui, L'autorité de la chose jugée par les juridictions constitutionnelles en Afrique, in: Revue Togolaise des Sciences Juridiques (2012), 54 (55).

122 Detterbeck, Streitgegenstand und Entscheidungswirkungen im öffentlichen Recht [object of Dispute and the Effect of Legal Decisions in Public Law], 333.

123 Adeloui, L'autorité de la chose jugée par les juridictions constitutionnelles en Afrique, in: Revue Togolaise des Sciences Juridiques (2012), 54 (55).

other courts, participate in the implementation of Constitutional Court's judgments. [124]

Thereby, one must pay attention to two characteristics of the binding effect. The binding effect results in a duty of omission as well as a positive obligation. With this in mind, the Constitutional Court of Benin states:

> « Selon une jurisprudence constante de la Cour, l'autorité de chose jugée ainsi attachée à ses décisions impose à l'Administration une double obligation à savoir d'une part, l'obligation de prendre toutes les mesures pour exécuter la décision juridictionnelle et d'autre part, l'obligation de ne rien faire qui soit en contradiction avec ladite décision». [125]

The binding effect demands that the addressees of the judgment, mainly the state organs, must refrain from doing anything that could impede the effectivity of the binding judgment by the Constitutional Court. [126] On the other hand, the binding effect causes a positive obligation, whereby the recipients of the binding decision must take all necessary steps to ensure the effective impact of the judgment. [127]

Moreover, the binding effect of the judgments by the Constitutional Court has an *ex-tunc*-effect. Accordingly, all sovereign measures declared as unconstitutional by the Constitutional Court are null and void from the outset. For this reason, the Constitutional Court of Benin stipulates that the refusal of the demand by the Constitutional Court to the Minister of Justice to reinstate the candidates to their former status represents a violation against the legal force of its first decision. [128] With this judgment, the Constitutional Court implicitly refers to the *ex-tunc*-effect of its first judgment of 12 July 2005. [129] The Constitutional Court of Benin demands that the unconstitutional measures taken by the administration before the judg-

---

124 Yebisi, The constitutional power of review of Supreme Court of Ghana: Lesson for Nigeria, in: International Journal of Humanities and Social Science (2014), 39 (40).

125 Cour constitutionnelle du Bénin, Décision DCC 06–016 (31/01/2006), available at: www. cour-constitutionnelle-benin.org (last accessed on 25/04/2015).

126 Ould Bouboutt, Les Juridictions constitutionnelles en Afrique, évolutions et Enjeux, in: Annuaire international de justice constitutionnelle (1997), 38 (45).

127 Adeloui, L'autorité de la chose jugée par les juridictions constitutionnelles en Afrique, in: Revue Togolaise des Sciences Juridiques (2012), 54 (65).

128 Cour constitutionnelle du Bénin, Décision DCC 06–016 (31/01/2006), available at: www. cour-constitutionnelle-benin.org (last accessed on 25/04/2015).

129 Cour constitutionnelle du Bénin, Décision DCC 05–067 (12/07/2005), available at: www. cour-constitutionnelle-benin.org (last accessed on 25/04/2015).

ment was made,[130] should be regarded as null and void from the beginning.[131] Overall, the measures declared as unconstitutional by the Constitutional Court, may not be applied at all.

The legal ineffectiveness[132] of the measure demands that the possible consequences must be removed.

II. Inter-omnes-Effect

As shown, the formal legal force constitutes the basis for *substantive res judicata*. The formal legal force gives rise to an *inter-omnes*-effect in special types of proceedings and especially in proceedings regarding parties, as in the initial case. This *inter-omnes*-effect in turn results in a binding effect regarding the facts of the case (1) as well as a direct effect (2).[133]

1. The impact of the decision on the facts of the case

The impact of the facts of the case usually occurs when an authority is bound by law to facts established by the court and to the subsequent consequences.[134]In case of a Constitutional Court decision, the impact of the facts comes to bear, when legal norms are linked to the decisions. The court links its decision to the legal norms and subsequently established facts. This consists of substantive legal effects of the decision. A typical example is the loss of a mandate in parliament as a result of the finding of the unconstitutionality of the corresponding political party.[135] In the initial case, the ANC members of parliament gave up their mandates in the Togolese Parliament. The Constitutional Court established this as fact. This determination by the court causes a so-called determination-impact.

---

130 Cour constitutionnelle du Bénin, Décision DCC 05–067 (12/07/2005), available at: www. cour-constitutionnelle-benin.org (last accessed 25/04/2015).

131 Cour constitutionnelle du Bénin, Décision DCC 06–016 (31/01/2006), available at: www. cour-constitutionnelle-benin.org (last accessed on 25/04/2015).

132 Schlaich/Korioth, Das Bundesverfassungsgericht [The Federal Constitutional Court], 8. edition, Rn. 379.

133 Benda/Klein, Verfassungsprozeßrecht [Constitutional Process Law...], 2. edition, § 38, Rn. 1295.

134 Creifelds, Rechtswörterbuch [Legal Dictionary], 19. edition, 1138.

135 Benda/Klein, Verfassungsprozeßrecht [Constitutional Process Law...] available at, 2. edition, § 38, Rn. 1295.

The declaration of renunciation According to Art. 192 of the Togolese electoral law and the substitution of the members of parliament by the Constitutional Court of Togo therefore represents results in a binding effect regarding the facts of the case. Accordingly, the Constitutional Court stated in the tenor:

> « La Cour *constate* la vacance des sièges préalablement occupés ».[136]

Based on the use of the word *"constate"*, one can speak of the impact of the facts of the case. Equally, the determination of the unconstitutionality of a political party by the Constitutional Court and its legal consequences represent an impact of the facts of the case. The direct effect of the substantive res judicata is closely linked to the binding force concerning the facts of the case. The decision by the court actually creates a new situation for the new members of parliament[137] and at the same time determines the loss of the seats in parliament for the members of parliament who stepped down.[138] This double effect is a special feature of subjective decisions by the Constitutional Court.

2. The material impact of the decision

Scholars understand the impact that the design will have, as an intended change of the substantive res judicata which is attained by the inter omnes effective decision. It can be said that the decision by the Constitutional Court realises this effect.[139] In the subjective litigation of constitutional proceedings, it may occur that the decision by the Constitutional Court causes such design impacts. This scenario occurs when the Constitutional Court renders a positive judgment and, from the plaintiffs viewpoint, positive effects follow. Through the effective judgment, the legal situation is di-

---

136 Cour constitutionnelle du Togo, Decision N°E-018/2010 of 22 November 2010, available at: http://www.courconstitutionnelle.tg/ (last accessed on 22/06/2015), Hervorhebung durch den Verfasser [emphasis by the author].

137 Cour constitutionnelle du Togo, Decision N°E-018/2010 of 22 November 2010, available at: http://www.courconstitutionnelle.tg/ (last accessed on 22/06/2015).

138 Cour constitutionnelle du Togo, Decision N°E-018/2010 of 22 November 2010, available at : http://www.courconstitutionnelle.tg/ (last accessed on 22/06/2015).

139 Pestalozza, Verfassungsprozeßrecht [Constitutional Process Law...], 3. edition, § 20, Rn. 71.

rectly altered according to the decision.[140] In the tenor of the decision in the initial case in this examination, the Constitutional Court clarifies this as the impact of the design and the effect of the determination. The Togolese Court stated in particular:

> « La Cour constate la vacance des sièges préalablement occupés; dit que les sièges devenus vacants doivent être occupés [...] »[141]

In this tenor, the Constitutional Court determined not only the loss of the mandate by the allegedly resigned members of parliament but designs at the same time a new legal situation for the new appointment of Members of Parliament.[142]

D. Appreciation and Criticism of the Decision in the Initial Case

In the initial case in this thesis,[143] the Constitutional Court was approached mainly in order to decide on the substitution of the parliamentarians. However, before the main question could be fully clarified, the loss of mandate for the parliamentarians who had resigned, had to be assessed as a preliminary question (I). The primary discussion of this question alone can make it possible for the Constitutional Court to discover a possible violation against the substantive res judicata as well as constitutional regulations with regard to the loss of mandate and the declaration of renunciation (II).

---

140 Benda/Klein, Verfassungsprozeßrecht [Constitutional Process Law...], 2. edition, § 37, Rn. 1243.

141 Cour constitutionnelle du Togo, Decision N°E-018/2010 of 22 November 2010, available at : http://www.courconstitutionnelle.tg/ (last accessed on 22/06/2015).

142 Cour constitutionnelle du Togo, Decision N°E-018/2010 of 22 November 2010, available at : http://www.courconstitutionnelle.tg/ (last accessed on 22/06/2015).

143 Cour constitutionnelle du Togo, Decision N°E-018/2010 vom 22 November 2010, available at : http://www.courconstitutionnelle.tg/ (last accessed on 22/06/2015).

I. Preliminary Question regarding the Object of the Dispute

The content of the preliminary question is defined as follows:

> « Question que le juge doit examiner pour vérifier si certaines des conditions requises pour l'existence de la question principale sont réunies.»[144]

A preliminary question therefore represents a prejudicial legal relationship. The impact of the facts of the case, triggered by the substantive res judicata, raises the question whether during the decision-making process regarding the substitution of the resigned parliamentarians the Constitutional Court of Togo should have examined the constitutional aspect of the resignation beforehand. Could the fear of the constitutional court regarding a violation against the principle of *ne ultra petita* justify the silence of the constitutional court? All this concerns the question of prejudicial legal relationships in Constitutional Procedural Law. Accordingly, the constitutional court must first decide on the constitutionality of the resignations by the previous parliamentarians, before it can decide on the application by the president of the Togolese National Assembly.[145]

This decisive question must be clarified before the main question in the main proceedings is addressed. In contrast to the scenario of the proceedings for preliminary decisions in the European judicial area,[146] a transfer to another instance is not required. Rather, the preliminary question must be decided on by the constitutional court itself. In the initial case, the constitutional court was approached, in order to decide on the substitution of the resigned parliamentarians. This was the main question. It is questionable, whether the question of the constitutionality of the resignation must be assessed before the assessment of this main question. This question is justified, because the answer to the main question of the substitution of the parliamentarians depends on the constitutionality of this resignation. In other words, the question of the legality of the resignation poses a preliminary question of significant importance, which needs to be answered before the main question can be assessed. Therefore, the answer to the preliminary question has a resounding effect on the main question.

---

144 Guinchard/Debard, Lexique des termes juridiques, 18 éd., 660.

145 Cour constitutionnelle du Togo, Decision N°E-018/2010 of 22 November 2010, available at: http://www.courconstitutionnelle.tg/ (last accessed on 22/06/2015).

146 Hillgruber/Goos, Verfassungsprozeßrecht [Constitutional Process Law...], 4. edition, § 13, Rn. 963d.

However, the question, whether the court should be approached in independent proceedings in order to decide on this preliminary question, seems problematic. From a constitutional point of view, the question arises whether the preliminary question should be linked independently or dependently to the main question. This question is legally significant regarding the prerequisites for the admissibility, especially since there are restrictions in the Togolese constitutional system for approaching the Constitutional Court. This concerns the locus standi which must be primarily considered here as a prerequisite to admissibility. With regard to these restrictions, a dependent connection would be, from a procedural point of view, advantageous to the concerned parties Especially, since the parties to the dispute are confronted with the legal effect of the decision regarding the main question. This is consistent: No objection may be brought against the legal effect of the decision by the Constitutional Court. As the decision by the Constitutional Court of Togo demonstrates in the initial case, the application of review of the constitutionality was rejected with the argument that the plaintiffs were not entitled to bring a complaint.[147] Over and above its influence on the participants to the proceedings the preliminary question also raises questions of competence. The question must be asked, whether the Constitutional Court must, of its own accord, ask this preliminary question in order to be able to better assess the main question as the principle that the Constitutional Court may only decide within the framework of the application applies. The ex officio rule found in the constitutional system of Benin is not customary in all Constitutional Procedural Laws of the region. Indeed the Constitutional Court of Benin may decide on its own initiative, i.e. *ex officio,* on the proper proceedings of the presidential elections (Art. 117 VerfB). This article is an appropriation of the *ex officio principle* in Benin's constitution.[148] Moreover, it may, on its own initiative, decide on human rights violations which it has determined without a prior complaint. Furthermore, the court established a *„procedure de saisine d'office"*. This type of proceedings represents a creation of the judiciary and is, at the same time, an expression of the principle of constitutionality. This relates to a situation where the court declares an application as inad-

147 Cour constitutionnelle du Togo, Décision N°E-002/2011 of 22 June 2011, available at: http://www.courconstitutionnelle.tg/ (last accessed on 22/06/2015).

148 See comparison with German public law: ex officio access, official principle of ex proprio motu investigation, inquisitorial principle; Leibholz/Rupprecht, Federal Constitutional Court Act, § 90, Rn. 6; Pestalozza, Verfassungsprozeßrecht [Constitutional Process Law...], 3. edition, § 23, Rn. 21.

missible but, at the same time, assesses the constitutionality of the law in question. The assumption of a violation of the human rights rooted in the Constitution is a requirement.[149]

Even if the Togolese constitutional system is not aware of the proceedings of the *ex-officio-* access, the dependent linkage of the preliminary question still simplifies the assessment of the main question. Therefore, the Constitutional Court may, in my opinion, assess the preliminary question as a dependent matter without being afraid of acting outside of its competence. This primary special treatment of the preliminary question triggers the intervention[150] of third parties in the proceedings. French law defines this so-called accession as:

> « Introduction volontaire ou forcée d'un tiers dans un procès déjà ouvert. »[151]

As it will be shown, the parties to the preliminary question are not always identical to those in the proceedings regarding the main question. There is an accession if at first parties, who are not concerned in the initial proceedings, join the current proceedings based on an own concern.[152] Moreover, the accession is admissible, if the answer to the main question is decisive for the parties with the intention to accede. This aspect clarifies our initial case: the substitution of the parliamentarians in the Togolese parliament has significant meaning to the resigned parliamentarians. Lastly, the decision by the Constitutional Court has the same importance for the parties to the dispute in the main proceedings as for those willing to join the assessment of the preliminary question.

In conclusion, it is established that the non-assessment of the preliminary question in the initial proceedings represents a severe mistake by the Constitutional Court of Togo because this question was legally decisive to the resigned parliamentarians. It is therefore not comprehensible why the

---

149 Kangnikoé Bado, Constitutional Jurisdiction and Democratiation in francophone West Africa, country study/Benin, 18, available at: http://intlaw-sgiessen.de/fileadmin/user_ upload/bilder_und_dokumente/forschung/westafrikaprojekt/workingpapers/Draft_WP_2014_ benin.pdf (last accessed on 02.07.2015).

150 Benda/Klein, Verfassungsprozeßrecht [Constitutional Process Law...], 2. edition, § 23, Rn. 852.

151 Guinchard/Debard, Lexique des termes juridiques, 18 éd., 452; Abebe/Vijoen, Amicus Cu- riae Participation Before Regional Human Rights Bodies in Africa, in: Journal of African Law (2014), 22 (25).

152 Hillgruber/Goos, Verfassungsprozeßrecht [Constitutional Process Law...], 4. edition, § 4, Rn. 353.

Constitutional Court of Togo did not observe this decisive feature of procedural law. In this regard, the decision by the Constitutional Court thus represents a violation of procedural guarantees. Even the ECOWAS Court of Justice confirmed this opinion[153] (explained in detail in chapter 3).

A further aspect that should have been given special attention in the initial proceedings of the legal assessment of the Constitutional Court of Togo was the question of the imperative mandate.

II. The prohibition of the imperative mandate and declaration of renunciation

Two fundamental aspects were misjudged in the case Ameganvi et al. in the initial proceedings by the Constitutional Court of Togo. In the parliamentarian system, the imperative mandate differs from the free mandate. An imperatives mandate means that the parliamentarian is bound by instructions of his party as well as his voters. In other words, a legal bond exists between parliamentarians and the will of the voters as well as instructions by his party.[154] Such a mandate is prohibited under Art. 52 of the Togolese Constitution. According to Art. 52 paragraph. 1 clause 2 of the Togolese Constitution:

> « Chaque député est le représentant de la Nation tout entière. Tout mandat impératif est nul.»

Thereby, the principle of the free mandate is entrenched in the constitution. The invalidity of the imperative mandate in Art. 52 prescribed in the Constitution of Togo aims at ensuring the independence of the parliamentarians. Voices in literature see this as a protective regulation.[155] It is surprising that the Constitutional Court confirmed the exclusion of the parliamentarians and their substitution, despite this constitutional guarantee of the free mandate and express prohibition of the imperative mandate as

153 CJ CEDEAO, Affaire Isabelle Ameganvi v. Republique Togo, N °ECW/CCJ/JUD/09/11 (07/10/2011).

154 Marsch/Vilain/Wendel (Publ.), Französisches und Deutsches Verfassungsrecht [French and German Constitutional Law], 139.

155 Cabanis/Martin, Les constitutions d'Afrique francophone. Évolutions récentes, 126; Kou pokpa, La perte du mandat par un parlementaire pour cause de démission ou d'exclusion de son parti en cours de législature en Afrique noire francophone, in: Revue Togolaise des Sciences Juri diques (2013), 65 (75).

in the initial event.[156] Indeed, the prohibition of a bond with a party is questionable in this context as the political parties are mainly conduits of decision-making for the people.On the other hand, the parliamentarian is a representative of the entire population and not the mere representative of his party in parliament.[157] Based on the tense relationship resulting from this double-status, the parliamentarians are, as representatives of the entire people in parliament, solely amenable to their conscience. The constitutional status of the parliamentarian as a representative of the entire people with a free mandate grants him a number of rights and obligations. He exercises a right to speak and his right to vote.[158] He may participate in the parliament's right to question and information. Furthermore, he may take parliamentary initiatives. He for example has the possibility to join together with other parliamentarians to form a parliamentary group.[159] Exercising these competences contributes to the realisation of the legislative task given to parliament. The representatives of the people thus fulfill their official obligations.[160] This results in additional consequences for the status of the member of parliament. He is neither accountable to his party nor the voter.[161] His political accountability only bears relevance at the end of his current mandate and a subsequent electoral campaign. The highest priority is the principle that the party may not unlimitedly influence the parliamentarian. There are clear limits whereby one must differentiate between party discipline and line whip. Every time a measure by the parliamentary group threatens the direct freedom of choice of a representative of the people, one can assume an unlawful transgression. Such influences are

156 See also the Criticism Koupokpa, La perte du mandat par un parlementaire pour cause de démission ou d'exclusion de son parti en cours de législature en Afrique noire francophone, in: Revue Togolaise des Sciences Juridiques (2013), 65 (75).

157 Marsch/Vilain/Wendel (Publ.), Französisches und Deutsches Verfassungsrecht [French and German Constitutional Law], 139.

158 Koupokpa, La perte du mandat par un parlementaire pour cause de démission ou d'exclusion de son parti en cours de législature en Afrique noire francophone, in: Revue Togolaise des Scien- ces Juridiques (2013), 65 (65).

159 The parliamentarians, who resigned, exercised this right in the Togolese Parliament: CJ CEDEAO, Affaire Isabelle Ameganvi v. Republique Togo, N °ECW/CCJ/JUD/09/11 (07/10/2011), par. 63.

160 Marsch/Vilain/Wendel (Publ.), Französisches und Deutsches Verfassungsrecht [French and German Constitutional Law], 140;BVerfGE 80, 188 (218).

161 . Koupokpa, La perte du mandat par un parlementaire pour cause de démission ou d'exclusion de son parti en cours de législature en Afrique noire francophone, in: Revue Togolaise des Scien- ces Juridiques (2013), 65 (66).

fundamentally prohibited. In addition, there is the important rule that the parliamentarian will keep his mandate even if he resigns from the party.[162] This reflects a confirmation of the high priority of the freedom of opinion in a liberal democracy.[163] The ECtHR therefore rightfully rated the dissolution of the DEP, a Turkish political party, as a violation of human rights.[164] Based on his status as a representative of the whole people, every parliamentarian is, in this respect, untouchable. [165]

The only possibilities of a forced discharge from office are therefore death, incompatibility [166], resignation and forfeiture.[167] These barriers to a free mandate serve to ensure the functionality of the parliament in a free democracy.[168]

Except in the aforementioned cases, neither the Constitution nor the supplementary laws provide for further ways to lose a parliamentary mandate. Especially for this reason it is inconceivable why the Constitutional Court was unable to prevent such a serious infringement of the constitution. With its decision, the Constitutional Court deprives Art. 52 paragr. 1 clause 2 of the Constitution of Togo of its essence.[169] Luckily, the legal dispute did not end before the national Constitutional Court. The case was later submitted to the ECOWAS Court of Justice in Abuja for assessment. The ECOWAS Court of Justice rightfully assumed a serious infringement of principles of the rule of law (more in detail in chapter 3).

Although several voices in literature consider the prohibition to resign from one's party to be a certain "therapy" of the phenomenon of "*transhu-*

---

162 Marsch/Vilain/Wendel (Publ.), Französisches und Deutsches Verfassungsrecht [French and German Constitutional Law], 140.

163 Hillgruber, Parteienfreiheit, in: Handbuch der Grundrechte [Manual of Fundamental Rights](HGR) V, § 118, Rn. 108.

164 CEDH, Nr. 25.144/94, Arrêt (11/06/2002), Affaire Selim Sadak et.al c. Turquie, par. 38, 40.

165 Koupokpa, La perte du mandat par un parlementaire pour cause de démission ou d'exclusion de son parti en cours de législature en Afrique noire francophone, in: Revue Togolaise des Scien- ces Juridiques (2013), 65 (66).

166 Art. 211 of the Togolese electoral law N°2012–002.

167 Koupokpa, La perte du mandat par un parlementaire pour cause de démission ou d'exclusion de son parti en cours de législature en Afrique noire francophone, in: Revue Togolaise des Scien- ces Juridiques (2013), 65 (66).

168 Hillgruber/Goos, Verfassungsprozeßrecht [Constitutional Process Law...], 4. edition, § 9, Rn. 721.

169 Koupokpa, La perte du mandat par un parlementaire pour cause de démission ou d'exclusion de son parti en cours de législature en Afrique noire francophone, in: Revue Togolaise des Scien- ces Juridiques (2013), 65 (75).

mance politique“[170], the fear of a constant change of party cannot justify the assumption of an infringement of the free mandate entrenched in Art. 52.

What would the legal situation be if the Constitutional Court would assume the loss of mandate based not on a resignation from the party, but because of the unconstitutionality of a newly founded party? This question comes to mind because the determination of unconstitutionality of a party triggers the loss of mandate as a substantive effect and consequence of the decision. In this sense, the decision has a constitutive meaning.[171]

For instance, in the SRP and KPD-proceedings, the Constitutional Court of Germany recognised the loss of a mandate as a legal consequence of the banning of a party.[172] The loss of the mandate would follow from the finding that the respective party would now be considered to be unconstitutional.[173] The mandate of the concerned parliamentarian would only be lost by way of this declaration.[174]

It is primarily intended that proceedings on banning political parties should themselves also suffice substantial principles of the rule of law. National security or the safeguarding of stability are in some cases the background of possible restrictions.[175] This range of topics deserves a separate and individual assessment since the new parliamentarians in the initial case immediately founded a new party (ANC)[176] after the resignations. Even in this case, a loss of mandate would have been a possibility due to the unconstitutionality of the newly founded party because the parliamentarians were entrusted with their parliamentary mandate as members of a constitutional and recognised political party. A declaratory judgment

170 Koupokpa, La perte du mandat par un parlementaire pour cause de démission ou d’exclusion de son parti en cours de législature en Afrique noire francophone, in: Revue Togolaise des Scien- ces Juridiques (2013), 65 (67); Boumakani, La prohibition de la « transhumance politique » des parlementaires. Étude de cas africains, in: Revue française de Droit constitutionnel, (2008), 499- 512.

171 Hillgruber/Goos, Verfassungsprozeßrecht [Constitutional Process Law...], 4. edition, § 9, Rn. 715.

172 Hillgruber/Goos, Verfassungsprozeßrecht [Constitutional Process Law...], 4. edition, § 9, Rn. 721.

173 Benda/Klein, Verfassungsprozeßrecht [Constitutional Process Law...], 2. edition, § 38, Rn. 1295.

174 Hillgruber/Goos, Verfassungsprozeßrecht [Constitutional Process Law...], 4. edition, § 9, Rn. 715.

175 Hillgruber, in: Handbuch der Grundrechte [Manual of Fundamental Rights] (HGR) V, § 118, Rn. 111.

176 CJ CEDEAO, Affaire Isabelle Ameganvi v. Republique Togo, N °ECW/CCJ/JUD/09/11 (7/10/2011), par. 63.

would, quite rightly, not develop a retrospective effect.[177] A loss of mandate on the grounds of a later finding of a partys unconstitutionality would be a non-acceptable infringement of the sovereign right of the voter, who gave the parliamentarians their parliamentary assignment.[178] Nevertheless, the ECtHR has, in similar cases, decided that an automatic loss of mandate due to the banning of a party represented a disproportionate infringement of the guaranteed right to free elections as per Art. 3 of the 1st Additional Protocol.[179] It explained in detail:

« La Cour conclut que la sanction infligée aux requérants par la Cour constitutionnelle ne saurait passer pour proportionnée à tout but légitime invoqué par le Gouvernement. Dès lors, la Cour considère que la mesure litigieuse était incompatible avec la substance même du droit d'être élus et d'exercer leur mandat, reconnu aux requérants par l'article 3 du Protocole no 1, et a porté atteinte au pouvoir souverain de l'électorat qui les a élus députés. Il s'ensuit que l'article 3 du Protocole no 1 a été violé en l'espèce».[180]The decision by the Constitutional Court regarding the validity of the declaration of renunciation does not seem justified. Regarding the facts of the initial case, it follows that the plaintiffs, the rejected parliamentarians, submitted a declaration of renunciation before their election. In this declaration of renunciation, they committed to relinquish their seat in parliament in case of resignation from their party. Such blank declarations of renunciation or agreements regarding the exercising of the mandate are null and void because they are directed against the freedom of expression of the will of the parliamentarian.[181] The nullity of the general declaration of renunciation can also be justified by the fact that the parliamentarians were ordinary citizens when the signing of such blank declarations of renunciation took place.[182] Only after their election did they receive their

177 Hillgruber/Goos, Verfassungsprozeßrecht [Constitutional Process Law...], 4. edition, § 9, Rn. 715.

178 CEDH, Nr. 25.144/94, Arrêt (11.06.2002), Affaire Selim Sadak et al. c. Turquie, par. 40.

179 CEDH, Nr. 25.144/94, Arrêt (11.06.2002), Affaire Selim Sadak et al. c. Turquie, par. 37; vgl. Hillgruber, in: Handbuch der Grundrechte[Manual of Fundamental Rights] (HGR) V, § 118, Rn. 114.

180 CEDH, Nr. 25.144/94, Arrêt (11/06/2002), Affaire Selim Sadak et al. c. Turquie, par. 40.

181 Marsch/Vilain/Wendel (Publ.), Französisches und Deutsches Verfassungsrecht [French and German Constitutional Law], 140.

182 CJ CEDEAO, Affaire Isabelle Ameganvi v. Republique Togo, N °ECW/CCJ/JUD/09/11 (07.10.2011), par. 62; Adeloui, L'autorité de la chose ju-

status as members of parliament.[183] Therefore, all obligations they agreed to before being elected as parliamentarians are legally invalid.[184]

It follows that the loss of mandate of the Togolese parliamentarians cannot be justified in any way whatsoever. Therefore, the contrary decision by the Togolese Constitutional Court must be seen as a serious miscarriage of justice. It is therefore not surprising that the ECOWAS Court of Justice regarded the loss of mandate and therefore the decision by the Togolese Constitutional Court as a serious infringement against Art. 7 paragr. 1 of the African Charta for Human Rights and Peoples' Rights.[185]

It may be concluded: legal force does not, dogmatically, represent an absolute legal concept. Many actual and legal grounds can trigger a derogation or can supersede legal force.[186] The need for legal protection is for example the typical case which triggers an exception to legal force. On closer inspection, the Togolese Constitutional Court, however, gives the impression that the legal force is an absolute institution of constitutional processes.[187] Such an understanding is, however, misguided. Consequently, the Constitutional Court rid itself of its task as the guardian of the Constitution in the present matter,[188] by not recognising explicit infringements against procedural and substantive constitutional guarantees in the present case. This can and should be addressed before the ECOWAS Court of Justice by way of an individual human rights complaint.

Moreover, a regulation such as § 133 in the Constitution of Ghana seems necessary for the constitutional jurisdiction of every ECOWAS Member State. Although Constitutional Courts are, without a doubt, faced

---

gée par les juridictions constitutionnelles en Afrique, in: Revue Togolaise des Sciences Juridiques (2012), 54 (75).

183 CJ CEDEAO, Affaire Isabelle Ameganvi v. Republique Togo, N °ECW/CCJ/JUD/09/11 (07.10.2011), par. 62.

184 Adeloui, L'autorité de la chose jugée par les juridictions constitutionnelles en Afrique, in: Revue Togolaise des Sciences Juridiques (2012), 54 (75).

185 Darauf wird ausführlich im dritten Kapitel eingegangen. Siehe dazu Adeloui, L'autorité de la chose jugée par les juridictions constitutionnelles en Afrique, in: Revue Togolaise des Sciences Juridiques (2012), 54 (74).

186 Kpodar, Commentaire des grands avis et décisions de la Cour constitutionnelle togolaise, 105.

187 Cour constitutionnelle du Togo, Décision N°E-002/2011 vom 22 June 2011, available at: http://www.courconstitutionnelle.tg/ (last accessed on 22/06/2015).

188 Tchapnga, Le juge constitutionnel, juge administratif au Bénin et au Gabon?, in: Revue française de Droit constitutionnel (2008), 551 (583).

with a dilemma regarding legally-flawed decisions with legal effect[189] either to rectify the error through a renewed assessment of the case, which would comply with a breach of the legal force, or to insist on the retention of the legal force. However, as a few voices in the literature emphasise, a correction of its own miscarriages of justice would, in the end, be better for the Constitutional Court than to insist on the retention of errors.[190]190 Last but not least, it is even in the interest of justice itself that the Constitutional Courts or Supreme Court has the opportunity to rectify misjudgements. All this justifies a derogation of the legal force at an international level.

189 Adeloui, L'autorité de la chose jugée par les juridictions constitutionnelles en Afrique, in: Revue Togolaise des Sciences Juridiques (2012), 54 (68).

190 Yebisi, The constitutional power of review of Supreme Court of Ghana: Lesson for Nigeria, in: International Journal of Humanities and Social Science (2014), 39 (41); Adeloui, L'autorité de la chose jugée par les juridictions constitutionnelles en Afrique, in: Revue Togolaise des Sciences Juridiques (2012), 54 (68).

Chapter 3 Supranational Derogation of the Legal Force in Municipal Law

A number of questions should be posed, namely: Is the res judicata decision by the national constitutional court insurmountable? Is the legal force opposed to the review competence of the international court (ECOWAS Court of Justice)? Under which circumstances can the legal force possibly be surmounted? Why should the legal force be surmountable? What should be comprised in the differentiation between conquest and breach? These questions will be discussed in this chapter.

Upfront, the use of the term "derogation" instead of "breach" should be explained. A breach of the legal force is given whenever a decision regarding the object of a res judicata judgment is to be made anew. The admissibility of a resumption of the proceedings and the respective decision triggers an automatic annulment of the judgment already in legal force. However, decisions by constitutional courts in the light of the aforementioned (in chapter 2) regulations, regarding the constitutional process by the ECOWAS Member States is non-appealable and irrevocable. There is no legal remedy available against them. Therefore, the decision of the Constitutional Courts is unchangeable. Subsequently, there is no court instance that can revoke the judgment by a Constitutional Court. Further, the breach can be defined as a legal revocation of a judgment by a higher instance. The legal revocation in a new, complete fact-finding trial by the Constitutional Court itself, does not apply here. The presented legal nature of the decision is opposed to the breach of the legal force. In terms of legal consequences, the breach of the legal force triggers the resumption of the proceedings.[1]

For these reasons, the term "derogation" is used in the present paper. To explain the term, the definition by the Federal Constitutional Court of Germany is referred to. With this in mind, the Federal Constitutional Court of Germany explained:

> „Entscheidungen des Europäischen Gerichtshofs für Menschenrechte, die neue Aspekte für die Auslegung des Grundgesetzes enthalten, ste-

1 Benda/Klein, Verfassungsprozeßrecht [Constitutional Process Law...], 2. edition, § 38, Rn. 1304 f.

> hen rechtserheblichen Änderungengleich, die zu einer *Überwindung der Rechtskraft einer Entscheidung des Bundesverfassungsgerichts* führen können".[2]

The preference of this term can be justified by the fact that the legal force is not breached by the declaratory judgment of the international court of law. It rather remains untouched because the essential nature of Constitutional Court judgments is, as shown, its non-appealability as well as its irrevocability. However, it can be derogated or surmounted based on an international verdict. Indeed, the legal force does not represent an untouchable, dogmatic legal form. The *erga-omnes*-legal effect of constitutional decisions is not opposed to the national effectivity of obligations of the convicted Member State under international law. Consequently, the creators of the constitution restricted the *erga-omnes*-legal effect, for example, in Art. 106 of the Togolese Constitution only to the national rule of law. Subsequently, the legal force does not develop its effect outwardly but only internally.

This chapter contemplates the question whether final judgments by a constitutional court represent an unassailable obstacle which might be standing in the way of the jurisdiction of the ECOWAS Court of Justice under international law. The opening of an international legal process represents the limitation of the objective legal force.[3] A human right dispute before the ECOWAS Court of Justice requires the international unlawfulness or at least the assumption of a violation against human rights by the national constitutional courts. In other words: The decisions by the national Constitutional Court could become the object of an international human rights dispute in the ECOWAS legal system. The assumption is based on the general idea that the necessity of legal control should also include the third force in a constitutional state which aims at the moderation and legal bond of all public exercise of power.[4] Is a new regulation of the relationship between the subregional Court of Law and the national constitutional courts necessary according to the concession of a human rights juris-

2 BVerfGE, 326 (326) (Hervorhebung durch den Verfasser [Emphasis by the author]); Pettiti, Le réexamen d'une déci- sion pénale française après un arrêt de la Cour Européenne des Droits de L'Homme: La loi fran- çaise du 15 juin 2000, in: Revue Trimestrielle des Droits de l'Homme (2001), 3 (12).

3 Pettiti, Le réexamen d'une décision pénale française après un arrêt de la Cour Européenne des Droits de L'Homme: La loi française du 15 juin 2000, in: Revue Trimestrielle des Droits de l'Homme (2001), 3 (12).

4 Breuer, Staatshaftung für judikatives Unrecht [Government liability for judicative injustice], 1.

diction to the ECOWAS Court of Justice? The lodging of a human rights complaint at regional level against possible decisions by the constitutional courts has direct procedural effects on the national legal force.

In order to answer these complex questions regarding the relationships between the ECOWAS Court of Justice and the highest courts of the Member States, a precedence-case before the ECOWAS Court of Justice offers a good starting point for the investigation. Following the extensive demonstration of this case (A), the primary features of the ECOWAS Court of Justice as a constitutional court will be discussed (B). Furthermore, the procedure of an individual complaint before the ECOWAS Court of Justice (C) as well as the forms of decision-making by the Court of Law (D) will be given special attention. Subsequent to this, the interpretation of Art. 15 paragr. 4 of the amendment agreement will be explained according to the rules of interpretation in the Vienna Convention on the Law of Treaties (E). For the purpose of a better understanding regarding the forms of decision-making, the expression of the effect of the legal force will be demonstrated (F). Lastly, the understanding of the concept of jurisdiction in the present work requires a justification (G).

A. The Initial Case before the ECOWAS Court of Justice

The object of dispute before the ECOWAS Court of Justice is the continuation of the national legal dispute before the Togolese Constitutional Court as demonstrated in chapter 2. For the purpose of assessing the legal dispute before the ECOWAS Court of Justice it is advisable to recall the judgment by the ECOWAS Court of Justice.

The judgment by the ECOWAS Court of Justice was issued on 7 October 2011 in French. The individual complaint N°ECW/APP/12/10 was submitted to the Court of Law on 30 November 2010. The legal dispute was based on an individual complaint N°ECW/APP/12/10 brought by Mrs Ameganvi, among others, against the Republic of Togo. She had been excluded from parliament as a plaintiff based on the decision by the Constitutional Court. This individual complaint by Mrs Ameganvi is thereby directly targeted at the Republic of Togo and indirectly against the decision N° N°E018/10 of 22 November 2010 by the Constitutional Court of Togo. The Togolese state was represented by the government. After an exchange of written pleadings between the individual plaintiff and the government, the ECOWAS Court of Justice considered the legal dispute on 7 October 2011.

It was concluded from the facts that the new parliamentarians in the Togolese Parliament had lost their mandate in parliament based on the decision by the Togolese Constitutional Court.[5] They presented the following facts before the Court of Law: They were members of the Togolese parliament until 22 November 2010, this being the date of their exclusion due to the decision by the Togolese Constitutional Court.[6] They were members of the political party UFC (Union des Forces du Changement). They resigned from this party on 12 August and 12 October 2010 respectively. They added: Before their acceptance as candidates of their party during the electoral campaign for parliamentary elections, they were presented with three documents. Among these was a confidentiality agreement (contrat de confiance de l'UFC) between the candidates and a letter of resignation for their signature. It stated the following declaration of resignation:

> « Je vous informe qu'à compter de ce jour, et pour des raisons de convenance politique, je démissionne de mes fonctions de Député à l'Assemblée Nationale».

However, these letters of resignation were supposedly a blank declaration of renunciation, because the declarations of renunciation were allegedly neither dated nor composed by the concerned candidates themselves.[7] After the elections the UFC party received 27 seats in parliament. All 27 members of parliament joined a parliamentarian faction. However, during the time of their mandate, an irreconcilable disagreement arose within the faction. This led to a resignation of 20 parliamentarians on 20 October 2010. Thereafter, they founded their own party (Alliance Nationale pour le Chan- gement, so-called ANC). The leader of their previous party nominated a new president of the UFC faction in parliament on 27 September 2010. The new president of the faction subsequently requested that the president of the parliament should undertake the substitutions for the resigned parliamentarians. On 18 November 2010, the president of the parliament submitted the list of these members of parliament to the Constitutional Court of Togo with the request to name their successors. However, the concerned parliamentarians had allegedly already announced to the

---

5 Cour constitutionnelle du Togo, Decision N°E-018/2010 vom 22 November 2010, available at: http://www.courconstitutionnelle.tg/ (last accessed on 22/06/2015).

6 Cour constitutionnelle du Togo, Decision N°E-018/2010 vom 22 November 2010, available at: http://www.courconstitutionnelle.tg/ (last accessed on 22/06/2015).

7 CJ CEDEAO, Affaire Ameganvi et al. c. Etat du Togo, N°ECW/CCJ/JUD/09/11 (07/10/2011), par. 13, available at: www.courtecowas.org (last accessed on 16/07/2015).

Constitutional Court on 17 November 2010 that they did not intend to resign from parliament.[8] Nevertheless, despite this irregularity, the Constitutional Court announced the substitution of the parliamentarians with their decision N° N°E018/10 of 22 November 2010.[9] The decision by the Constitutional Court was based on the parliamentarians' declarations of renunciation. The individual plaintiffs reminded the Court that these declarations of renunciation had been ineffective blank declarations of renunciation. They thereafter emphasised that a declaration of renunciation must be signed by the concerned parliamentarian with the date and specification of his name in order to have any legal effect. This had not been the case. Furthermore, they had not submitted any declarations of renunciation to the new president of the faction. They referred to the declaration of renunciation by Mr Lawson, who had not been elected as a member of parliament, as evidence. He confirmed that the declarations of renunciation in question had been blank declarations.

The government alleged that the dispute involves circumstances under which the plaintiffs were substituted, i.e. that the Constitutional Court of Togo decided on the resignation of the plaintiffs on application by the president of the National Assembly. According to the government, certain internal problems within the UFC party had led to the split of the party and the founding of a new party. Furthermore, it assumed that the individual plaintiffs submitted the declarations of renunciation of their own free will According to regulation in Art. 6 of the rules of procedure of the parliament. Subsequently, the Constitutional Court legally decided in a legally binding manner on the substitution of the concerned parliamentarians According to Art. 192 of the Electoral Act.

The individual plaintiffs alleged: A parliamentarian is a representative of the whole people and not only a representative of his party in parliament. Based on the tension resulting from this dual role, the parliamentarians are representatives of the whole people in parliament and as such are only bound by their own conscience. The constitutional status of the parliamentarian as a representative of the whole people based on a free mandate gives him a number of rights whereby any obligation he has towards his

8 CJ CEDEAO, Affaire Ameganvi et al. c. Etat du Togo, N°ECW/CCJ/JUD/09/11 (07/10/2011), par. 65, available at: www.courtecowas.org (last accessed on 16/07/2015).

9 Cour constitutionnelle du Togo, Entscheidung N°E-018/2010 vom 22 November 2010, available at: http://www.courconstitutionnelle.tg/ (last accessed on 22/06/2015).

party before his election as a parliamentarian is not binding. They base the admissibility of their individual complaint on Art. 9.4 and 10 d of the Protocol A/SP.1/01/05. The wording of both regulations stipulates:

> « La Cour est compétente pour connaitre des cas de violation des droits de l'homme dans tout Etat Membre; peut saisir la Cour [...] toute personne victime de violation des droits de l'homme ».

Regarding the merits of the claim the individual plaintiffs argued, in particular, that their right to fair proceedings was violated by the Togolese Parliament as well as the decision N°E018/10 of 22 November 2010 by the Constitutional Court of Togo. It therefore followed that the guaranteed right to fair court proceedings according to Art. 7 Abs. 1; Art. 7 Abs. 1.c and Art. 10 Abs. 2 of the African Charta for Human Rights and Peoples' Rights was violated. Moreover, they alleged that through the actions of the Republic of Togo, the rights guaranteed in Art. 1, Art. 1.a Abs. 2 and 33 of the Protocol for Good Governance were also violated. To further argue the merits of their complaint, they also referred to the relevant national regulations namely Art. 52 of the Constitution of Togo and Art. 6 of the rules of procedure of the Togolese Parliament. They expressly repeated the regulation in Art. 52 of the Constitution of Togo:

> « Chaque député est le représentant de la nation toute entière, tout mandat impératif est nul».

Subsequently, they referred to Art. 10 of the General Declaration of Human Rights of 10 December 1948. The government rejected this view of the plaintiffs and made the following statement: it first rejected the jurisdiction of the Court of justice on the grounds that there was no violation of human rights with regard to the proceedings that had led to the substitution of the concerned parliamentarians. According to the government, the Constitutional Court had observed all constitutional regulations when it decided on the substitution of the parliamentarians. The regulations of the Electoral Act had also been observed during the proceedings. To support their view, the government referred to a judgment by the ECOWAS Court, Decision N°ECW/CCJ/APP/05/06 of 22 May 2007. The government further stated that the declarations of renunciation had been undisputed because each of the concerned parliamentarians had personally declared their resignation before the President of the National Assembly. They were therebyno longer members of the National Assembly. The founding of a new party could not heal the resignation retroactively. In this regard, the government expressly referred to Art. 6 of the Rules of Procedure of the Parliament:

> « Tout député régulièrement élu peut démettre de ses fonctions. Les démissions sont adres- sées au Président qui en donne connaissance à l'Assemblée Nationale dans la plus prochaine séance et les notifie à La Cour constitutionnelle».

The government further alleged that, according to Art. 6 of the Rules of Procedure of the Parliaments, the president of the National Assembly had been informed of the declarations of renunciation in the course of the third legislative period in 2010 because of this, the President of the National Assembly approached the Constitutional Court in order to carry out the substitution. Subsequently, the entire proceedings regarding the substitution of the parliamentarians had been constitutional and did not represent an infringement of the individual and civil rights of the plaintiffs. Therefore, the legal dispute did not fall in the jurisdiction of the ECOWAS Court of Justice. The government thus referred to Art. 106 of the Constitution of Togo. Art. 106 of the Constitution of Togo states:

> « Les décisions de le Cour constitutionnelles ne sont pas susceptibles de recours. Elles s'im- posent aux pouvoirs publics et à toutes les autorités civiles, militaires et juridictionnelles ».

In this sense, the government referred to a judgment by the ECOWAS Court of Justice, namely the Decision N°ECW/CCJ/APP/02/05 of 7 October 2005, in which the ECOWAS Court of Justice expressly rejected its competence with regards to assessing decisions by national courts of the Member States. Moreover, the government emphasised that the plaintiffs had purposefully signed the declarations of renunciation. The declarations of renunciation give the basis of an obligation of the concerned parliamentarians toward their party which must be fulfilled. The declarations of renunciation were not to be viewed as blank declarations of renunciation as they had been signed.

Regarding the violation of Art. 33 of the Protocol for Good Governance, the government alleged that the decision, with regard to the authenticity of a declaration of renunciation, had to be evaluated at the discretion of the Constitutional Court of Togo.

Regarding the violation of the Fairness Principle, the government disputed that Art. 7 paragr. 1, Art. 7 paragr. 1.c of the African Charta for Human Rights and Peoples' Rights had been violated. According to the government, these regulations refer to court proceedings and not proceedings within a national assembly. Regarding the violation of Art. 10 of the African Charta for Human Rights and Peoples' Rights, the government highlighted that the individual plaintiffs had made use of their right to freedom of association and thus had founded a new party. Therefore, Art. 10 of the African Charta for Human Rights and Peoples' Rights had been adhered to. Consequently, the government applied before the ECOWAS Court of Justice for the assessment of the lawfulness of the parliamentarian's declarations of renunciation as well as the lawfulness of the decision of the Constitutional Court of Togo The government further asked the Court of Law to reject the application by the plaintiffs. It also asked the Court of Law to order the plaintiffs to pay the legal fees for the proceedings.The Court of justice declared the application by the plaintiffs to be admissible according to Art. 9 Abs. 4 and Art. 10 d of the Additional Protocol A/SP.1/01/05.The Court of Law rejected the plaintiffs' application for urgent proceedings with the reason that there was no requirement for urgency according to Art. 59 of the rule of procedure of the Court of justice .

Primarily, the Court of Law was not convinced that the declarations of renunciation had been lawfully submitted. The Court of justice stated:

> « Toutefois ces documents ne peuvent être considérés comme étant une lettre de démission au sens de l'Article 6 du règlement de l'Assemblée Nationale. En effet, selon cet article une lettre de démission doit être signée par le Député régulièrement élu, statut juridique que les signa- taires n'avaient pas acquis au moment de la signature par eux des dites lettres; ce qui n'est pas contesté par le Défendeur ».[10]

Regarding the alleged violation of Art. 7 of the Charta and Art. 10 of the General Declaration of Human Rights, the Court of Law was confronted by the following legal issue:

> « Les questions soumises à l'appréciation de la Cour, à savoir la transmission par le Président de l'Assemblée Nationale à la Cour Constitutionnelle de lettres de démission attribuées aux requérants et contestées par ceux-ci, et la décision n°E18/10 du 22 novembre 2010 de la Cour constitutionnelle prise à la suite de cette transmission, relèvent-elles de la compétence de la Cour comme étant susceptible de consti-

10 CJ CEDEAO, Affaire Ameganvi et al. c. Etat du Togo, N°ECW/CCJ/JUD/09/11 (07/10/2011), par. 62, available at: www.courtecowas.org (last accessed on 16/07/2015).

> tuer des violations de droits de l'homme des requé- rants comme ils le soutiennent? »[11]

After extensive assessment of the object of dispute, the Court of Law was of the opinion that the provisions of Art. 6 of the rules of procedure of the National Assembly had not been observed. The president of parliament should especially not have submitted an application for substitution of the concerned parliamentarians. This lack of observation of the provisions of Art. 6 of the rules of procedure of Parliament led to the announcement of the substitution of the plaintiffs by the Constitutional Court of Togo without a prior hearing. In the opinion of the Court of Law, such an approach by the Constitutional Court constitutes a violation of Art. 7 paragr. 1 of the African Charta for Human Rights and Peoples' Rights and Art. 10 of the Universal Declaration of Human Rights. The Court of Law further confirmed that, according to provisions of Art. 1(h) of the Protocol for Good Governance, all of these pertinent instruments of human rights are part of the standards of review by the Court of justice .

The Court of justice had to, in particular, ascertain that the requirement for fair proceedings as per Art. 7 paragr. 1 of the African Charta during the entire national proceedings had been sufficiently observed. In this context, the Court of justice called special attention to the fact that it was its task to ensure that the signatory states complied with their international legal obligations. The Court of Law further pointed out that the judgment by the Constitutional Court also represented a violation of Art. 10 of the Universal Declaration of Human Rights of the United Nations of 1948.

In the tenor, the Court of Law rejected the objection regarding its lack of competence. It declared itself competent. In light of the above explanations, the Court found that the Republic of Togo had violated the individual plaintiffs' right of a Fair Hearing. This violation at the same time represents an infringement of the provisions in Art. 7/1, 7/1c of the African Charta on Human Rights and of Art. 10 of the General Declaration of Human Rights. The Court of justice ordered the Republic of Togo to pay three million (3,000,000) FCFA to the respective individual plaintiffs. The defendant state had to bear the costs and expenses. After the determination of the infringement of pertinent regulations in the Charta (Art. 7 paragr. 1 of the African Charta) as well as the General Declaration of Human Rights

---

11 CJ CEDEAO, Affaire Ameganvi et al. c. Etat du Togo, N°ECW/CCJ/JUD/09/11 (07/10/2011), par. 53, available at: www.courtecowas.org (last accessed on 16/07/2015).

(Art. 10), the plaintiffs expected to be automatically reinstated in Parliament. The Togolese state, however, rejected their application for reinstatement.

There is, however, the possibility to initiate review proceedings following a declaratory judgment. This process means that a judgment regarding a certain object of dispute has been rendered. However, several points in the decision are unclear. Therefore, an application before the Court of Law to clarify these yet unanswered questions is admissible.

Subsequently, the plaintiffs in the above presented main proceedings.[12]submitted an application for review to the Court of Law. These proceedings are admissible according to Art. 64 of the Rules of Procedure of the Court of justice . The concerned Togolese parliamentarians therefore re-approached the Court of justice on 16 November 2011 within the framework of these proceedings.

According to the facts, the plaintiffs asked the Court of Law in the review proceedings to take a clear position regarding the consequence of its declaratory judgment, i.e. their reinstatement in the Togolese parliament. According to the reason for the complaint by the plaintiffs in this separate trial, the parliamentarians sought their reinstatement in parliament. This can be justified by the fact that their loss of mandate in parliament was based on the unfair proceedings. These proceedings were qualified by the ECOWAS Court of Justice rightfully as being in violation to human rights.[13] Therefore, they have a claim to re-obtain their seats in parliament.

The individual plaintiffs argued that the Court of justice had rendered the declaratory judgment N°ECW/CCJ/JUD/09 between them and the Republic of Togo on 7 October 2011. The Court of Law had, however, overlooked one of their causes of action. Namely: the Court of Law expressly confirmed in its declaratory judgment that they had not submitted lawful declarations of renunciation.

Object of their application for review was the explicit order of reinstatement by the Court of Law in the Togolese Parliament. In their opinion, this was the logical consequence of the first declaratory judgment. The government alleged that they had fulfilled all obligations arising out of the

12 CJ CEDEAO, Affaire Ameganvi et al. c. Etat du Togo, N°ECW/CCJ/JUD/09/11 (07/10/2011), par. 65, available at: www.courtecowas.org (last accessed on 16/07/2015).

13 CJ CEDEAO, Affaire Ameganvi et al. c. Etat du Togo, N°ECW/CCJ/JUD/09/11 (07/10/2011), par. 62, available at: www.courtecowas.org (last accessed on 16/07/2015).

declaratory judgment N°ECW/ CCJ/JUD/09 on 7 October 2011. Further, the government reiterated the fact that, according to the provisions in Art. 106 of the Constitution of Togo, the decisions by the Constitutional Court are final. There is no legal remedy available against the decision of the Constitutional Court. The individual plaintiffs could not be reinstated in Parliament because their resignation occurred by way of the decision N °018/10 of 22 November 2010 by the Constitutional Court of Togo. According to the government, this decision developed an *erga-omnes*-effect and could not be questioned in any way whatsoever.[14]

The Court of justice declared this application admissible.[15]

The question to be answered by the Court of justice was whether the finding of a violation at the same time amounted to an annulment of the decision in violation of human rights by the Togolese Constitutional Court.[16] In the key reasoning of the decision, the Court of justice failed to draw extensive conclusions in the review proceedings.[17]In its key statement, the Court of justice said: despite the Court of Laws finding of in its first decision, it could not order the reinstatement of the parliamentarians. According to settled case law, the ECOWAS Court of Justice was neither a court of appeal nor a court of cassation for judgments in Member States. It did not avail of such a competence. A reinstatement by the Court of justice of the parliamentarians in parliament would equate to an annulment or disregard of the decision by the Togolese Constitutional Court, which does not lie in the competence of the Court of Law.[18]

The Court of justice once again highlighted the fact that the reinstatement of the plaintiffs to their previous position, i.e. the reinstatement in the Togolese parliament, represented a possible consequence of a violation

---

14 CJ CEDEAO, Affaire Ameganvi et al. c. Etat du Togo, N°ECW/CCJ/JUD/06/12 (13/03/2012), par. 8, available at: www.courtecowas.org (last accessed on 16/07/2015).

15 CJ CEDEAO, Affaire Ameganvi et al. c. Etat du Togo, N°ECW/CCJ/JUD/06/12 (13/03/2012), par. 11, available at: www.courtecowas.org (last accessed on 16/07/2015).

16 Cour constitutionnelle du Togo, Entscheidung N°E-018/2010 vom 22 November 2010, ab- rufbar unter: http://www.courconstitutionnelle.tg/ (last accessed on 22/06/2015).

17 CJ CEDEAO, Affaire Ameganvi et al. c. Etat du Togo, N°ECW/CCJ/JUD/06/12 (13/03/2012), par. 18, available at: www.courtecowas.org (last accessed on 16/07/2015).

18 CJ CEDEAO, Affaire Ameganvi et al. c. Etat du Togo, N°ECW/CCJ/JUD/06/12 (13/03/2012), par. 66, available at: www.courtecowas.org (last accessed on 16/07/2015).

of human rights by the Republic of Togo.[19] The Court of justice was not authorised to order this reinstatement. Furthermore, it was not the Court of Laws responsibility to determine whether the respondent state had violated the relevant human rights. The Court of Law had thus fully fulfilled its function in its first declaratory judgment.[20] Essentially, the Court of Law stated:

> « La Cour estime que la demande en réintégration s'apparente à un recours contre la Décision N°018/10 du 22 Novembre 2010 de la Cour constitutionnelle de la République du Togo qui est une juridiction nationale d'un Etat Membre, juridiction pour laquelle la Cour, suivant sa ju- risprudence constante, n'est ni une juridiction d'appel, ni de cassation et dont la décision par conséquent ne peut être révoquée par elle. La Cour n'avait donc pas à aller au-delà de sa compétence pour se prononcer sur la demande de réintégration, qui, si elle était ordonnée, équivaudrait à l'annulation de la décision de la Cour Constitutionnelle pour laquelle la Cour de Justice de la Communauté n'a pas de compétence.»[21]

The Court of justice declared the formal admissibility of the plaintiff's application for review. The allegation that causes of action had been omitted in the main proceedings was dismissed by the Court of Law.This conjecture is true to a certain extent, because as the Court of justice indicated, it is not a super appellate court. Therefore, it does not have the competence to examine misjudgments of national institutions in a factual or legal respect. However, the determination of a violation represents an exception to the general lack of competence regarding the examination of judgments by national courts at a regional level.[22] Moreover, a number of important principles with regard to the human rights complaint should be mentioned at international law level. It must be pointed out that there are nu-

19 CJ CEDEAO, Affaire Ameganvi et al. c. Etat du Togo, N°ECW/CCJ/JUD/06/12 (13/03/2012), par. 14, available at: www.courtecowas.org (last accessed on 16/07/2015).

20 CJ CEDEAO, Affaire Ameganvi et al. c. Etat du Togo, N°ECW/CCJ/JUD/06/12 (13/03/2012), par. 16, available at: www.courtecowas.org (last accessed on 16/07/2015).

21 CJ CEDEAO, Affaire Ameganvi et al. c. Etat du Togo, N°ECW/CCJ/JUD/06/12 (13/03/2012), par. 17 et suivant, available at: www.courtecowas.org (last accessed on 16/07/2015).

22 Peukert, in: Frowein/Peukert, Europäische Menschenrechtskonvention [European Human Rights Convention]. EMRK-commentary, 3. edition, Art. 6, p. 214, Rdn. 185.

merous differences between the national and the regional legal dispute. The parties, the object of dispute, the applicable legal principles (principles in international law) and the addressee of the decision (the State and the Plaintiff) differ significantly from those of that had been seized in the constitutional procedure on the national level. With regard to the object of dispute, the parties do not seek the derogation of the national judgment. They rather move to determine the violation of the human rights, to which they are entitled.[23]

B. Role of the ECOWAS Court of Justice as a Constitutional Court

Which function does the ECOWAS Court of Justice have within the framework of its competences as an international and human rights court? In order to ensure the adherence to the community-specific obligations as well as the obligations deriving from the Charta, the high contracting parties established a Court of Law. The operating principle as well as the statute of this Court of justice resemble, in some respects, those of a Constitutional Court (Art. 15 paragr. 1 of the Amendment Agreement, 9 and 10 d of the Additional Protocol A/SP.1/01/05).[24] Hereby, the elements of the role of the Constitutional Court are discussed (I). It is however questionable whether the sovereignty of the contracting states is opposed to this perception of competence of the Court of Law (II).

I. Articulations of the Constitutional Role of the ECOWAS Court of Justice

Through the jurisdiction regarding the human rights monitoring within the rule of law of the entire Community, the question must be posed whether the Court of Law's jurisdiction extends to that of a supranational

23 CJ CEDEAO, Affaire Ameganvi et al. c. Etat du Togo, N°ECW/CCJ/JUD/09/11 (07/10/2011), par. 53, available at: www.courtecowas.org (last accessed on 16/07/2015).

24 See also regarding the ECtHR: Cohen-Jonathan, La fonction quasi constitutionnelle de la Cour Européenne des Droits de l'Homme, in: Renouveau du Droit constitutionnel. Mélanges en l'hon- neur de Louis Favoreu, 1127 (1128).

Constitutional Court.[25] In answering this question, the main features of a Constitutional Court are addressed, namely:

- the independence of a Constitutional Court in the constitutional order of the state;
- the adjudication of a last decision-making competence above all state organs;
- the binding effect of the decisions by the Constitutional Court.

The role of a Constitutional Court comprises the monitoring of the entire constitutional order and to enforce the individual and civil rights embedded in the constitution. It examines the constitutionality of the actions of all other state organs according to the constitution. The decisions of a Constitutional Court bind all state organs. Therefore, there are no legal remedies available against these decisions. They are final court orders and therefore unappealable.

Within the framework of the competences assigned to it, the Court of Law exercises its jurisdiction autonomously and independently of the Member states and the institutions of the Community (Art. 15 paragr. 3 of the Amendment Agreement of 1993). Just as a Constitutional Court, the ECOWAS Court of Justice has the function to guarantee the enforcement of human rights of the Community. The Court of Law is, so to speak, the guardian of the human rights embedded in the African Charta in favour of the citizens of the Community. Especially for this reason, the Court of justice can and should, when exercising its function, define the guaranteed human rights in more detail in favour of the individual plaintiff. In order for this goal to be reached, a last decision-making competence is conferred to the Court of Law According to Art. 19 paragr. 2 of the Protocol A/P1/7/91 (2). Before the question of the final decision-making authority of the Court of Law is discussed, the status of the Court of justice should be addressed (1).

1. Status of the ECOWAS Court of Justice, in particular, its independence

The question of the statute refers first of all to the facilities of the Court of justice and its position toward the other organs of the Community. Therefore the status of the judges, on one hand, and the status of the Court of Law, on the other hand, will be addressed. With regards to the judges, the

25 Ebobrah, Legitimacy and feasibility of human rights realisation through regional economic communities in Africa: the case of ECOWAS (200), 16.

office of the judge will also be addressed. Regarding the Court of Law, the regulations regarding the independence of the Court of Law is addressed.

The status of the judge refers to the requirements for the office, the term of office and the end to a term of office. According to Art. 3 paragr. 1 of Protocol A/P1/7/91 (06/07/1991) signatory states citizens who enjoy a high moral reputation and who avail of the prerequisites necessary to exercise a high judicial office can be elected as judges. Moreover, legal scholars who can prove special knowledge in international law may be appointed as judges. The number of judges at the Court of Law does not correspond to those of the signatories because regarding the composition of the Court of justice, it is comprised of seven judges (Art. 3 paragr. 3 of Protocol A/ P1/7/91). A candidate for the judicial office must have completed their fortieth year of age (Art. 3 paragr. 7 of Protocol A/P1/ 7/91). The question regarding the election of the judges is at the discretion of the state presidents of the Community (Art. 3 paragr. 4 of Protocol A/P1/7/91).[26] In Art. 3 paragr. 4 of Protocol A/P1/7/91 it is stated:

> « Les membres de la Cour sont nommés par la Conférence et choisis sur une liste de per- sonnes désignées par les Etats Membres. Aucun Etat Membre ne peut désigner plus de deux personnes ».

> "The member of the Court shall be appointed by the authority and selected from a list of persons nominated by Member states. No Member State nominates more than two persons."

After the Member States have drawn up a list of fourteen candidates who meet the requirements of Art. 3 paragr. 1 and 7 of Protocol A/P1/7/91 the decision falls to the Conference of Heads of State, as the judges are appointed by the heads of state during the Conference of Heads of State (Art. 3 paragr. 6 of Protocol A/P1/7/91). It may be concluded from this that, in contrast to the case of the ECtHR (Art. 22 ECHR) where they are voted into their office through an electoral process, the judges are chosen and appointed by the high heads of state. Thereby, a large responsibility by the heads of state of the ECOWAS Community must be noted. During the selectionof the judges, it is especially important to pay attention to their qualifications as the quality of the Court of Law and therefore the protection of human rights within ECOWAS closely corresponds to the quality

26 Tikonimbé, Indépendance de la Cour de Justice de la CEDEAO, Communication donnée au colloque international de Lomé organisée par le Centre de Droit public de Lomé et le Département de Droit administratif de la faculté de droit de l'Université de Gand (02/03/2012), 5.

of the judges. Furthermore, the candidates are put forward for election by every high signatory party (Art. 3 paragr. 6 of Protocol A/P1/7/91). The election procedure was strongly criticised because the candidates proposed by the signatory state, might be biased in favour of their home country, which could threaten the independence of the judges.[27] There was also no guarantee that the candidates of a signatory party met the necessary requirements, in particular, knowledge of international law.[28] Last but not least, there was no interstate public procedure with regards to the candidates. All of this did not provide good conditions for an independent Court of Law.[29]

The Conference of Heads of State has taken note of this criticism and has reacted positively to it. During the Conference of State Presidents the heads of state passed a resolution on 14 June 2006, regarding the election of judges.[30] In Art. 1 and 2 paragr. 2 of the resolution of the heads of state it is stated:

> « Il est créé un Conseil judiciaire de la Communauté pour gérer le processus de recrutement des juges de la Cour de Justice de la Communauté et les questions disciplinaires. Lorsqu'il gère le recrutement des juges de la Cour de Justice de la Communauté, le Conseil Judiciaire de la Communauté est composé des Président des juridictions suprêmes de l'ordre judiciaire ou de leurs représentants, des Etats auxquels les postes de juges n'ont pas été attribués ».[31]

Through this decision, a Conseil Judiciaire was created by the ECOWAS Community. The Conseil Judiciaire is comprised of the presidents of the

---

27 Tikonimbé, Indépendance de la Cour de Justice de la CEDEAO, Communication donnée au colloque international de Lomé organisée par le Centre de Droit public de Lomé et le Département de Droit administratif de la faculté de droit de l'Université de Gand (02/03/2012), 6.

28 Tikonimbé, Indépendance de la Cour de Justice de la CEDEAO, Communication donnée au colloque international de Lomé organisée par le Centre de Droit public de Lomé et le Département de Droit administratif de la faculté de droit de l'Université de Gand (02/03/2012), 6.

29 Tikonimbé, Indépendance de la Cour de Justice de la CEDEAO, Communication donnée au colloque international de Lomé organisée par le Centre de Droit public de Lomé et le Département de Droit administratif de la faculté de droit de l'Université de Gand (02/03/2012), 6.

30 Décision A/DEC.2/6/06 de la Conférence des Chefs d'Etat et de Gouvernement portant créa- tion du Conseil Judiciaire (14 juin 2006).

31 Art. 1 et 2 Al.1 de la Décision A/DEC.2/6/06 de la Conférence des Chefs d'Etat et de Gou- vernement portant création du Conseil Judiciaire (14 juin 2006).

highest courts of the highest signatory parties (Art. 2 paragr. 1 of Resolution A/DEC.2/6/06). Henceforth, the election of candidates into the judicial office is the responsibility of this Conseil Judiciaire (Art. 2 paragr. 1 of the Resolution A/ DEC.2/6/06). Moreover, the judges are elected for a duration of five years.

Their re-election is permitted only once (Art. 4 paragr. 1 of Protocol A/ P1/7/91). The judges remain in office until the inauguration of their successors. However, they will continue working on the disputes they were already involved in (Art. 4 paragr. 3 of Protocol A/P1/7/91).

Regarding the independence of the Court of Law, Art. 2 of Protocol A/ P1/7/91 shows that the ECOWAS Court of Justice is a permanent and independent court of justice of the Community. The independence of the Court of Law is expressly confirmed in Art. 15 paragr. 3 of the Amendment Agreement. In order to guarantee the independence of the Court of Law towards the signatory states and the other institutions of the Community,[32] the signatories decided, after the Additional Protocol A/SP.1/01/05 (19/01/2005) came into force, to underpin the regulations regarding the independence of the Court of Law. This took place with the creation of the above mentioned Conseil Judiciaire through the decision taken by the heads of state.[33] The fact that the selection of the judges was taken away from the power of the heads of state with the creation of this Conseil Judiciaire shows the first step for independence of the Court of Law.[34] Members of the Conseil Judiciaire may not come from the same signatory state as the judges to be elected (Art. 2 paragr. 2 of Decision A/DEC. 2/6/06). Moreover, Art. 1 and 2 of the Protocol A/P1/7/91 clarify that the judges of the ECOWAS Court of Justice do not belong to the signatory state for which they were elected. The judges rather belong to the ECOWAS Court of Justice in their personal capacity.

During their term of office, the judges are not allowed to carry out activities that are incompatible with their independence, their impartiality or

32 Ebobrah, Legitimacy and feasibility of human rights realisation through regional economic communities in Africa: the case of ECOWAS (200), 4 (16).

33 Décision A/DEC.2/6/06 de la Conférence des Chefs d'Etat et de Gouvernement portant créa- tion du Conseil Judiciaire (14 juin 2006).

34 Sall, La Justice d'Intégration, 53; Tikonimbé, Indépendance de la Cour de Justice de la CEDEAO, Communication donnée au colloque international de Lomé organisée par le Centre de Droit public de Lomé et le Département de Droit administratif de la faculté de droit de l'Université de Gand (02.03.2012), 7; Kane, « La Cour de Justice de la CEDEAO, à l'épreuve de la protection des droits de l'homme», Université Gaston Berger, Maitrise en Sciences Juridiques 2012, 36.

with the requirements of a full-time occupation in that position. Art. 4 paragr. 11 of Protocol A/P1/7/91 therefore prohibits the judges to carry out political, administrative or any other professional activities. This regulation takes the fact into account that the ECOWAS Court of Justice is a permanent court of law. Especially for this reason, the judges must guarantee their own independence and impartiality. In particular, the guarantee of independence represents an important element of justice for those seeking justice.[35] In orderto strengthen the independence even further, the judges enjoy the immunities and privileges recognised for diplomatic corps according to Art. 6 of Protocol A/P1/7/91. In this context, the question of independence should be separated from that of impartiality. A removal from the position as a judge during their term of office is not possible. The only possibility for a removal from office is the determination of gross misconduct, inability to carry out one's office or physical or mental inability (Art. 4 paragr. 7 and Art. 6 paragr. 2 of Protocol A/P1/7/91).[36] The competence to decide on the disciplinary question is not that of the heads of state but is allocated to a committee of independent judges.[37]While the independence of the judges concerns an institutional bond of the judges and thus of the Court of Law in relation to other organs within the Community, the impartiality of the judges represents a purely individual, even psychological element. This difference explains why the status of the Court of Law, the electoral process of the judges as well as the privileges and the immunity (Art. 6 of Protocol A/P1/7/91) of the judges are decisive when measuring the independence of the Court of justice .[38] With respect to the impartiality, carrying out political, administrative or professional activities threaten the impartiality of the judges. Due to this, the prohibition of carrying out sideline activities in Art. 4 paragr. 11 of Protocol A/P1/7/91 is justified.

---

35 Tikonimbé, Indépendance de la Cour de Justice de la CEDEAO, Communication donnée au colloque international de Lomé organisée par le Centre de Droit public de Lomé et le Département de Droit administratif de la faculté de droit de l'Université de Gand (02/03/2012), 2; Kane, « La Cour de Justice de la CEDEAO, à l'épreuve de la protection des droits de l'homme», Université Gaston Berger, Maitrise en Sciences Juridiques 2012, 67.

36 Siehe dazu auch Gans, Die ECOWAS. Wirtschaftsintegration in Westafrika, 70.

37 Art. 2 Abs. 2, Décision A/DEC.2/6/06 de la Conférence des Chefs d'Etat et de Gouvernement portant création du Conseil Judiciaire (14 juin 2006).

38 Tikonimbé, Indépendance de la Cour de Justice de la CEDEAO, Communication donnée au colloque international de Lomé organisée par le Centre de Droit public de Lomé et le Département de Droit administratif de la faculté de droit de l'Université de Gand (02/03/2012), 4.

The Court of justice itself elects its president and vice president (Art. 6 of the rules of procedure of the Court of Law). The internal organisation of the court derives from Protocol A/P1/7/91 and the rules of procedure, in the version of 2 June 2002, the Court of Law set for itself According to Art. 32 of Protocol A/P1/7/91. Regarding the composition of the Court of Law in case of a decision in a legal matter, a quorum of at least two judges and the president of the Court of Law is necessary (Art. 15 paragr. 2 of the Additional Protocol A/SP.1/01/05 and Art. 22 paragr. 2 of the rules of procedure of the Court of Law). Furthermore, According to Art. 15 paragr. 2 of the Additional Protocol A/SP.1/01/05, an uneven number of judges is necessary to make a decision in a legal matter (see also Art. 22 paragr. 3of the rules of procedure of the Court of Law). The Court of Law is based in Abuja (Nigeria). It can, however, also hold external sessions if the circumstances of a case so require (Art. 26 of Protocol A/P1/7/91 and Art. 21 paragr. 2 of the rules of procedure of the Court of Law).

2. Exclusive and ultimate power of decision-making competence

The ECOWAS Court of Justice avails of an exclusive competence regarding the legal instruments of the Community. Art. 23 paragr. 1 and 2 of the Additional Protocol A/SP.1/01/05[39] attribute to the Court of Law an exclusive competence regarding the interpretation and application of the Amendment Agreement and the associated Protocols:

> « Aucun différend relatif à l'interprétation ou à l'application des dispositions du présent Trai- té ne peut être soumis à un autre règlement que celui prévu par le Traité ou le présent Proto- cole. Lorsque la Cour est saisie d'un différent, les Etats Membres ou les Institutions de la Communauté doivent s'abstenir de toute action susceptible de l'aggraver ou d'en entraver le règlement. Les Etats Membres et les Institutions de la Communauté sont tenus de prendre sans délai toutes les mesures nécessaires de nature à assurer l'exécution de la décision. »
>
> "No dispute regarding interpretation or application of Treaty may be referred to any other form of settlement except that which is provided for by the Treaty or this Protocol. When a dispute is brought before the Court, Member States or Institutions of the Community shall re-

39 A.F of Art. 22 of Protocol (A/P1/7/91) regarding the Court of Law of the Community.

frain from any action likely to aggravate or militate against its settlement."

Furthermore, Art. 34 paragr. 3 of Protocol A/P1/7/91 clarifies that Protocol A/P1/7/91 must be seen as a fixed component of the Amendment Agreement. However, the question must be asked, whether the ECOWAS Court of Justice avails itself of an exclusive competence regarding human rights violations. Art. 10 d of Protocol A/SP.1/01/05 namely confers the right to the individual to directly submit an individual complaint to the ECOWAS Court of Justice without prior exhaustion of legal remedies. Can it be deduced from this that the ECOWAS Court of Justice has an exclusive competence regarding the interpretation and application of the African Charta within the ECOWAS Community? Is the competence to decide on human rights an exclusive competence of the ECOWAS Court of Justice? This question is important, because the competence is mainly attributed to the African Court on Human Rights and Peoples' Rights. The Member States know the last word in favour of their own national Constitutional Courts regarding the interpretation and application of their respective constitution (as shown in Chapter 2 of the present examination).

Moreover, the human rights accepted by the African Charta were incorporated in the respective constitutions of the Member States. Because of this, the Constitutional Courts of the Member States have the competence to monitor the rights of the Charta. The jurisdictions and the relationship between the ECOWAS Court of Justice and the national courts is difficult to define *ratione materiae*. Verbatim and following Art. 23 paragr. 1 and 2 of the Additional Protocol A/SP.1/01/05, one must assume an exclusive competence of the Court of Justice regarding the interpretation and application of the African Charta. However, based on the possibility to bring a claim within national law regarding the scope of competence of the Constitutional Courts, one must refer to a teleological interpretation of the regulation in Art. 23 paragr. 1 and 2 of the Additional Protocol A/SP.1/01/05. Therefore, the competence to monitor the rights of the African Charta is attributed primarily to the courts of the Member States and, in particular, the Constitutional jurisdictions . The admissibility of a direct individual complaint before the ECOWAS Court of Justice should not be evaluated as the denial of the primary obligation by the signatory states. To allow direct individual complaints without requiring the prior exhaustion of national legal remedies only corrects a certain deficit in legal protection and problems in some Member States (this will be discussed in detail below in chapter 4).

The regulation in Art. 9 paragr. 4 of the Additional Protocol A/SP.1/01/05 highlights the fact that it is the task of the ECOWAS Court of Justice to guard over the adherence to the obligations by the high contract parties embedded in the African Charta. This means that the Court of Justice neither monitors the adherence to national law nor other international instruments. It decides basically on the obligation of the signatory states regarding the African Charta on Human Rights and Peoples' Rights. In its latest declaratory judgment, the Court of Law has confirmed its rejection in principle of the competence to interpret national law of the signatory states. Here, the Court of Law states:

> « La Cour, en effet, toujours rappelé qu'elle n'était pas une instance chargée de trancher des procès dont l'enjeu est l'interprétation de la Constitution des Etats de la CEDEAO. [...] qu'il s'agisse de la Constitution du Burkina Faso, ou de normes infra-constitutionnelles quelles qu'elles soient. Dans leurs écritures, les requérants se sont en effet référés aussi bien à la Constitution nationale, qu'à la Charte de la Transition. La Cour doit considérer de telles réfé- rences comme inappropriées dans son prétoire. Juridiction internationale, elle n'a vocation à sanctionner que la méconnaisse d'obligations résultant de textes internationaux opposables aux Etats ».[40]

In the end, Art. 23 Abs. 1 and 2 of the Additional Protocol A/SP.1/01/05 does not attribute an exclusive competence to the ECOWAS Court of Justice regarding its authority to decide on human rights disputes. The ECOWAS Court of Justice is not to be seen as the only decision-making organ regarding the violation of the human rights embedded in the Charta. The individual complaints are *ratione materiae* directly admissible to the Court of Justice because structural shortcomings in several ECOWAS signatory states were known to the parties to the agreement. Even though the Court of Justice does not avail of an exclusive competence to monitor the Charta, it does have a final decision-making competence. Two elements meet and strengthen this ultimate decision-making competence of the ECOWAS Court of Justice in the area of human rights.

On one hand, the *erga-omnes* binding effect of the national constitutional judgment is restricted to the national rule of law. There is no reference whatsoever in the constitutional regulations of the Member States claim-

40 CJ CEDEAO, Affaire Congrès pour la démocratie et le Progrès (CDP) & Autres c. Etat Bur kina Faso, N°ECW/CCJ/JUD/16/15 (13.07.2015), par. 24 et 26, available at:www.courtecowas.org (last accessed on 16/07/2015).

ing an extension of the *erga-omnes* binding legal effect in an international legal system. On the other hand, the ECOWAS laws acknowledge the last decision-making competence of the Court of Justice in the area of human rights. Another justification for the ECOWAS Court of Justice's competence to review is based on the *erga-omnes* binding effect, intended by the constitutions of Member States to limit such on the national constitutional order. The binding effect of the decisions of the Constitutional Court includes, *erga omnes* effect at a national level. As the creator of the constitution purposefully did not create a binding effect of international court instances, one can draw the conclusion that the creator of the constitution did not exclude the possibility of challenging the legal force of decisions by the Constitutional Court at an international level. The creator of the constitution thus intends for an implicit supremacy of the ECOWAS Court of Justice in terms of the significance of its interpretation and application of the Charta.

On closer inspection of the legal provisions of the ECOWAS Community, a certain implicit relativisation of the final judgment by the Constitutional Court must be noted. According to Art 9.4 and Art 10 d of Protocol A/SP.1/01/05, the ECOWAS Court of Justice is authorised to decide in matters of individual human rights complaints against Member States. Both regulations include references to the possibility of controlling the actions of states by the Court of Justice. According tothis regulation, all actions of governmental authority can be the object of a complaint. In this respect, court decisions are per se actions of state authority. Therefore, it can be deduced that the possibility of relativisation of the legal force of final decisions by the Constitutional Court are also to be included according to Art. 9 paragr. 4 of Protocol A/SP.1/01/05. Consequently, the ECOWAS Court of Justice has the last decision-making competence regarding the interpretation and application of the Charta within the Member States.

Regarding the procedure, the decisions of the Court of Justice take legal effect following their notification (Art. 62 of the Rules of Procedure of the Court of Law). There are namely no legal remedies, such as appeal against or revision of the decisions of the ECOWAS Court of Justice. In this respect, Art. 19 paragr. 2 of Protocol A/P1/7/91 stipulates:

> « Les décisions de la Cour sont lues en séances publiques et doivent être motivées. Elles sont, sous réserve des dispositions du présent protocole relatives à la révision, immédiatement exécutoires et ne sont pas susceptibles d'appel ».

> "Decisions of the Court shall be read in open court and shall state the reasons on which they are based. Subject to the provisions on review contained in this Protocol, such decisions shall be final and immediately enforceable."

The regulation in Art. 19 paragr. 2 of Protocol A/P1/7/91 clearly shows that, in the framework of its jurisdiction, the ultimate decision-making competence lies with the ECOWAS Court of Justice. Furthermore, Art. 15 of the Amendment Agreement confirms that the Member States are bound by the final declaratory judgment by the Court of Justice. There is no exclusive list of actions which may fall within the scope of competence of the Court of Justice. The Member States, therefore, do not provide for an exception concerning which state organ must carry out the state action in violation of human rights in order to establish the legal competence of the Court of Justice. The Member States would have made express provision for this exception if the last and final judgment by the highest state organ, such as the Constitutional Court or the Supreme Court, should be exempted from the scope of competence of the ECOWAS Court of Law. This would, in turn, only cause astonishment. Based on this, the conclusion must be drawn that a decision by the Constitutional Courts or the Supreme Court in violation of human rights falls within the scope of competence of the ECOWAS Court of Justice. There is therefore no exception regarding the scope of application of Art. 9.4 and Art 10 d of Protocol A/SP.1/01/05. Therefore, the Member States have confirmed the supremacy of the jurisdiction with regards to human rights of the ECOWAS Court of Justice in terms of international law.

The Court of Law is supreme in comparison to the other institutions of the community. Even the Conference of Heads of State is subject to the decisions by the Court of Justice. Should it address a decision that at the same time falls within the scope of competence of the Court of Justice, the conference must leave the last decision to the Court of Justice . The competence of the Court of Justice replaces the competence of the conference in all legal matters with regards to the interpretation and application of the Amendment Agreement and the Additional Protocol. After the Court of Justice has decided in a legal matter, all Member States must comply with the decision of the Court of Law. This is not opposed by the sovereignty of the signatory states.

II. Objections with regard to sovereignty

The judiciary represents an essential component of national sovereignty. Therefore, exercising its jurisdiction expresses the sovereignty of the states. One of the basic principles under international law is the principle of sovereign equality. This basic principle of sovereign equality is codified in Art. 2 No. 1 of the Charta of the United Nations. This emphasises that the principle of sovereign equality of states is in closest relationship to the principle of sovereignty.[41] The principle of sovereign equality of all states, in turn, is one of the oldest rights because international law has always been a right among equals even though the states are not, in fact, anything but equal.[42] The sovereignty of a state also means that the state is the highest autonomous entity to its subjects on its territory and that an appeal to a higher instance against its orders and decisions is not possible.[43] To make it even clearer: The sovereignty resembles the independence of a state to issue orders.[44] Consequently, the only law which applies nationally is law which either originates there or was incorporated there by the national constitution.[45] The Constitutional Court of the State monitors the adherence to constitutional regulations. Therefore, sovereignty means „Exclusivity and Imperviousness" of the legal order of the state.[46]The exclusive competence of states can be deduced from Art. 2 clause 7 of the Charta of the United Nations,. This includes the legislative, judiciary and executive sovereignty. Consequently, the state doesn't seem to be subject to any other law but the state law.[47] Therefore, in case of a conflict between international law and national law, legal practitioners tend to prefer the latter.[48]

The judicial prerogative of a sovereign state can be organised in whichever way the state pleases because the state is free to do so.. This requires due consideration of matters that inherently belong to the national

41 Ipsen, Völkerrecht [International Law], 6. edition, § 5, Rn. 254.
42 Ipsen, Völkerrecht [International Law], 6. edition, § 5, Rn. 254.
43 Verdross/Simma, Universelles Völkerrecht [Universal International Law], 3. edition, § 35, 29.
44 Bertele, Souveränität und Verfahrensrecht [Soverignty and Procedural Law], 64.
45 Verdross/Simma, Universelles Völkerrecht [Universal International Law], 3. edition, § 35, 30.
46 Verdross/Simma, Universelles Völkerrecht [Universal International Law], 3. edition, § 35, 30.
47 Ebobrah, Legitimacy and feasibility of human rights realisation through regional economic communities in Africa: the case of ECOWAS (200), 28.
48 Oppong, Legal Aspects of Economic Integration in Africa, 192.

competence of a state. This, in turn, follows from the principle of equal sovereignty of states.[49]

However, the question must be posed whether human rights issues are „*solely within the domestic jurisdiction*".[50]From this follows that the sovereign authority of a state is in principle indivisible. International law itself guarantees this principle. However, there are possibilities to delegate this exclusive authority of a sovereign state. Indeed, states seem to comply with international law when they observe mutual goals. These can only be reached if states cooperate and thus share their sovereign authority.[51] The delegating signatory state exercises its „freedom of contract" through its delegation.[52]

Therefore, we must differentiate between two questions: whether a factual situation falls within the internal scope of competence or whether a matter shall remain within that national scope of competence. This differentiation is important because the judicial authority belongs to the fundamental rights of a state. However, the state is able to transfer, within the framework of its freedom of contract, this judicial authority to international organisations. This approach is completely comprehensible in the light of Art. 2 clause 7 of the Charta. The signatory states already agreed in the preamble of the Amendment Agreement of 1993 to relinquish their sovereignty of state step by step in favour of the Community in the areas stipulated in theagreement and the associated protocols. The goal of transferring sovereignty is to enable a collectivisation or a common autorisation of sovereign power. The wording of clause 5 in the preamble of the Amendment Agreement provides for the following obligation by the ECOWAS signatory states:

> « Convaincus que l'intégration des Etats Membres en une Communauté régionale viable peut requérir la mise en commun partielle et pro-

49 Kokott, Souveräne Gleichheit und Demokratie im Völkerrecht [Sovereign Equality and Democracy in International Law], in: ZaöRV (2004), 517 (519).

50 Ress, Supranationaler Menschenrechtsschutz und der Wandel der Staatlichkeit [Supranational Protection of Human Rights and the Change in Statehood], in: ZaöRV (2004), 621 (621); Nolte, in:Simma/Khan/Nolte/Paulus, The Charter of the United Nations. A Commentary, 3rd ed., Art. 2 (7), par. 38.

51 Ebobrah, Legitimacy and feasibility of human rights realisation through regional economic communities in Africa: the case of ECOWAS (200), 29.

52 Kelsen, Die Einheit von Völkerrecht und staatlichem Recht [The Unity of International Law and State Law], in: ZaöRV 19 (1958), 234 (237).

> gressive de leur *souveraineté nationale* au profit de la Communauté dans le cadre d'une volonté politique collective […]».[53]
>
> "Convinced that the integration of the Member States into a viable regional Community may demand the partial and gradual pooling of *national sovereignties* to the Community within the context of a collective political will […]"

The political sovereignty of a state can therefore be limited by its integration into an international Community such as the ECOWAS Community. This thought arises from clause 5 of the preamble of the Amendment Agreement. The limitation of the political sovereignty of a state goes hand in hand with the adoption of obligations under international law[54] because the ECOWAS Member States have exercised their sovereignty through the ratification of the African Charta. Moreover, all states of the Community legally confirmed their affiliation to a value system by signing the Protocol of Dakar 2001 and thereby accepted a limitation of their sovereignty.[55] The protection of these rights is guaranteed by the Court of Justice. As a result, the Member States have acknowledged the human rights competence of the ECOWAS Court of Justice and at the same time transferred onto it the corresponding sovereign power. The transfer of sovereignty is expressed through the acknowledgement of the last decision-making competence of the Court of Justice in all its areas of competence. In this regard, the protection of human rights under international law can be reconciled with state sovereignty if there is a provision that an individual complaint may be submitted against an alleged violation before an international organ such as the ECOWAS Court of Justice.[56]

The sovereignty of a state cannot be understood in such a way that an international Court of Law, established by the state within the framework of its freedom of contract, may not exercise its competence.[57]On the contrary, the signatory states are obligated to observe the competences of the

53 Emphasised by the author.

54 Schaffarzik, Europäische Menschenrechte unter der Ägide des Bundesverfassungsgerichts [European Human Rights under the Aegis of the Federal Constitutional Court], DÖV (2005), 860 (867).

55 Ebobrah, Legitimacy and feasibility of human rights realisation through regional economic communities in Africa: the case of ECOWAS (200), 107.

56 Verdross/Simma, Universelles Völkerrecht [Universal International Law], 3. edition, § 36, 31.

57 Hopkins, The effect of an African Court on the domestic legal orders of African states, in: Human Rights Law Journal (2002), 234 (235).

established international court according to the principle of good faith. Thereby, Art. 22 paragr. 2 and 3 of Protocol A/P1/7/91 stipulates:

> « 2. Lorsque la Cour est saisie d'un différend, les Etats Membres ou les Institutions de la Communauté doivent s'abstenir de toute action susceptible d'en aggraver le règlement.
> 3. Les Etats Membres et les Institutions de la Communauté sont tenus de prendre sans délai toutes les mesures nécessaires de nature à assurer l'exécution de la décision de la Cour ».

> "2. When a dispute is brought before the Court, Member States or Institutions of the Commu- nity shall refrain from any action likely to aggravate or militates against its settlement.
> 3. Member States and Institutions of the Community shall take immediately all necessary measure to ensure execution of the decision of the Court".

From the aforementioned, it is certain: There is no conflict between the Constitutional Courts of the Member States and the ECOWAS Court of Justice. Similarly, there is no conflict between international law and state law. The reason for this is clear: The national law as well as the international law are rooted in the will of the same state.[58] As the result of this section it can be summarised:

The question of the transfer of judicial competence to international courts, such as the ECOWAS Court of Justice, does not constitute a violation of the prohibition of intervention in internal affairs of states according to Art. 2 clause 7 of the Charta of the United Nations. It must rather be seen as the state exercising its freedom of contract. The prohibition of intervention therefore depends on the extent of regulation of a factual situation by international or state law. This requires examination in individual cases.[59]

C. *Individual Complaints Procedure before the ECOWAS Court of Justice*

The African Charta and the Additional Protocol A/SP.1/01/05 are agreements under international law that are binding for the signatory states af-

58 Kelsen, Die Einheit von Völkerrecht und staatlichem Recht [The unity of international and state law], in: ZaöRV 19 (1958), 234 (238).

59 Simma, Charta der Vereinten Nationen [Charta of the United Nations]. commentary, Art. 2 clause 7, Rn. 37.

ter their ratification. Both agreements directly establish the obligation of persons subject to the jurisdiction of the high parties to the agreement to ensure thehuman rights stipulated in the African Charta. These rights are created directly under international law in such a manner that an individual in the territory of the signatory states is entitled to protection under international law against the signatory states. This right is made more concrete by the possibility of a direct individual complaint before the ECOWAS Court of Justice. Therefore, the admissibility of the individual complaint before the ECOWAS Court of Justice should be addressed at this point (I). Thereafter, the aspects of procedural law, in particular the object of the complaint and those entitled to complain, will be demonstrated (II).

I. Admissibility of the Individual Complaint before the ECOWAS Court of Justice

Since the inception of the Additional Protocol A/SP.1/01/05 regarding the Court of Justice individual complaints became admissible before the Court of Justice . The prerequisites for admissibility of the individual complaint are stipulated in Art. 10. d of Additional Protocol A/ SP.1/01/05. Thereby, the Court of Justice may be approached by any person who is a victim of human rights violations. For this, the application may according to Art. 10 d Additional Protocol A/SP.1/01/05:

> « Peuvent saisis la Cour: [...] Toute personne victime de violations des droits de l'homme; la demande soumise à cet effet: i) ne sera pas anonyme; ne sera pas portée devant la Cour de Justice de la Communauté lorsqu'elle a déjà été portée devant une autre Cour internationale compétente ».

> „Access to the Court is open to the following: [...] Individuals on application for relief for violation of their human rights; the submission of application for which shall: i) not be anon- ymous; nor ii) be made when the same matter has been instituted before another international Court for the adjudication."

Should the application satisfy both requirements, the Court of Justice will declare the application admissible. Apart from these two requirements, the Protocol does not require any more criteria for admissibility. This represents a significant simplification of the legal process at the Court of Justice because in other legal systems, individual complaints before international courts are only admissible if all national legal remedies have been exhausted.[60] Art. 10 d of Additional Protocol A/SP.1/01/05 does not demand any further admissibility requirements. The abolishment of the prerequisite of a prior exhaustion of legal remedies can be justified in the ECOWAS legal order (this will be address later).

Based on the principle of subsidiarity regarding international courts, the prerequisite of prior exhaustion of the legal process represents a procedural principle generally accepted before international courts. In this context, the IGH has emphasised:

> « La règle selon laquelle les recours internes doivent être épuisés Avant qu'une procédure internationale puisse être engagée est une Règle bien établie du droit international coutumier; elle a été généralement Observée dans les cas où un Etat prend fait et cause pour son ressortissant dont les droits auraient été lésés dans un autre Etat en violation du droit international. Avant de recourir à la juridiction internationale, il a été considéré en pareil cas nécessaire que 1'Etat où la lésion a été commise puisse y remédier par ses propres moyens, dans le cadre de son ordre juridique interne ».[61]

An historical case regarding the admissibility of a complaint without the prerequisite of prior of the national legal process from the jurisdiction of the ECOWAS Court of Justice is reflected in there following:

The factual situation is as follows: In the year 1984, Ms Hadijatou Mani was born as the daughter of a female slave. When she was twelve years old, she was sold by the owner of her mother for 240 000 FCFA[62]. Mr El Hadj Souleymane Naroua, her new master, already had four wives and seven female slaves. According to the tradition of the "Wahiya" in Niger, these seven girls are generally purchased from poor circumstances and are simultaneously servants in the house of the master and fifth wife "sadaka" because the Muslim religion only permits four wives. Therefore, Mr El Hadj Souleymane Naroua raped Ms Hadijatou Mani regularly from the age of thirteen. This resulted in the birth of three children. One of these children died. The master decided in the year 2005 to set her free and therefore gave her an "exemption certificate". After the receipt of the certificate, Hadijatou Mani left the house and rejected the offer of marriage by her former master. Mr El Hadj Souleymane Naroua, however, insisted on marrying her.

60 Art. 1 paragr. 1 EMRK.

61 Art. 1 paragr. 1 EMRK.

62 Converted to Euro = 365 €.

Regarding the legal proceedings: She approached a national court in order to confirm her freedom. The court declared the marriage to be invalid due to her lack of consent.[63] Her former master was angry and took her to court at a higher instance for bigamy. The Tribunal de Grande Instance Konnis rejected the first judgment with the reason that Ms Mani was already married due to her status as a slave. The proceedings continued before the Cour Supreme. The Cour Supreme annulled the judgment of the Tribunal de Grande Instance Konnis. Unfortunately, the judgment was quashed by the Tribunal de Grande Instance Konnis in its verdict, not because of the exercise of slavery, but because of procedural errors.[64] Therefore, the matter was referred back to the Tribunal de Grande Instance Konnis for renewed assessment. In the meantime, Hadijatou Mani had married a man of her own choice. Due to the renewed assessment, the Tribunal de Grande Instance Konnis sentenced Ms Mani and her husband to a six months prison-term for bigamy. She had to serve two months before the proceedings were suspended.[65] With the help of an NGO, Ms Mani submitted an individual complaint to the ECOWAS Court of Justice against the Republic of Niger.

After giving extensive reasoning regarding the factual area of competence, the Court of Justice declared in the tenor of the judgment that there was a violation of the Charta with the following words:

> « que dame Hadijatou Mani Koraou a été victime d'esclavage et que la République du Niger en est responsable par l'inaction de ses autorités administratives et judiciaires ».

The Court of Justice requested the state to act in order to change this legal situation according to the convention. Voices in literature welcomed this order of specific corrective measures in order to stop the violation by Niger.[66] However, the question still remains unanswered whether the ECOWAS Court of Justice now represents a court of law in the first and

---

63 Arrêt N°06 du 20 mars 2006 du tribunal civil et coutumier de Konni.

64 Cour Suprême de Niamey, Chambre judiciaire, Arrêt N°06/06/du 28 décembre 2006.

65 See for greater detail on the national procedures: Badet, Commentaire de l'arrêt dame Ha- dijatou Mani Korauou contre la République du Niger, in: Revue Béninoise des Sciences Juridiques et Administratives (2010), 153 (157).

66 Hamuli-Kabumba, La répression internationale de l'esclavage. Les leçons de l'arrêt de la cour de justice de la Communauté économique des États de l'Afrique de l'ouest dans l'Affaire Hadijatou Mani Koraou c. Niger, in: Revue québécoise de droit international (2008), 25 (52).

last instance. Whereby the national Constitutional Court and the ECOWAS Court of Justice should simultaneously observe the adherence to the Charta. This possibility of direct submission of a complaint before the ECOWAS Court of Justice without prior exhaustion of legal procedures already causes tension between the national constitutional courts and the ECOWAS Court of Justice.[67] The danger of *"forum shopping"* is certainly unavoidable under such circumstances.[68]

In the proceedings described above, the plaintiff had not exhausted all of the nationally available legal remedies before submitting a human rights complaint with the Court of Justice . The government, as the respondent, was of the opinion that the plaintiff had not make use of all legal remedies available.

Furthermore, the proceedings regarding the factual situation had not been fully clarified by national courts. Based on the non-exhaustion of legal remedies, the government could not be blamed for the violation of Art. 5 of the African Charta as well as other human rights instruments ratified by Niger. Moreover, the government stated that the admissibility of an individual complaint without prior exhaustion of the legal remedies was an error in the protection system of human rights in the Community and the Court of Justice should rectify this error.

The Court of Justice did not follow this argument. The objections made in *limine litis* by the respondent were rejected with the reasoning that no higher prerequisites regarding the legal procedure may be requested than the prerequisites for admissibility provided in Art. 10 d. ii. In the reasoning for this decision, Court of Justice expressly referred to the prior case law by the ECtHR from the year 1971.[69] The Court of Law assumed that the practice of requiring the exhaustion of the legal remedies before submitting a complaint to international courts only had the purpose of avoid-

67 Etim Moses Essien v. Gambia & Anor, Judgment N° ECW/CCJ/JUD/05/07, para 27; dazu: Community Court of Justice, ECOWAS, Law Report (2004–2009), 113 (119).

68 Helfer, Forum Shopping for Human Rights, in: University of Pennsylvania Law Review (1999), 285 (289).

69 Legal matter N° ECW/CCJ/JUD/06/08- Hadijatou Mani Koraou v. Republic of Niger of 27 October 2008, clause 39. Gilles Badet sees this differently to the Court of Law. According to him, the direct accessibility of the Court of Law in terms of individual complaints without prior exhaustion of national legal procedures, may cause certain repressive measures by signatory states. See also Badet, Commentaire de l'arrêt Dame Hadijatou Mani Koraou contre la République du Niger, in: R.B.S.J.A N° 23, Année 2010, p. 153 (191).

ing parallel proceedings at the level of international law. According to the Court of Law, this practice should not jeopardise the effective legal protection of the plaintiffs. Regarding the question of effective legal protection, a recent decision by the ECtHR must be quoted. In the legal matter Sürmeli against the Federal Republic of Germany, the Federal Government raised the objection of inadmissibility due to non-exhaustion of the nationally available legal remedies. This objection was rejected by the ECtHR. In its reasoning, the court was of the opinion that the existence of a constitutional complaint does not necessarily offer effective legal protection against the extensive duration of civil proceedings. Therefore, the individual complaint was admitted for adjudication.[70] After this jurisdiction, the plaintiff is not obliged to make use of the legal remedy if it is in reality ineffective.[71]

By the way, it does not fall within the scope of competence of the Court of Justice to establish additional prerequisites besides the prerequisites given by the signatory states. [72] Therefore, the Court of Justice declared the complaint admissible.

II. Object of the complaint and those entitled to complain

Within this section, the object of the complaint represents the violation of the primary obligation by the signatory states (2). From a procedural point of view, the assessment of the party-respective requirements comes before the decision in the matter. Therefore, the right to complain before the Court of Justice will be addressed first (1).

1. Those entitled to complain

For the purpose of clarifying this difference, it is recommended to reflect on the original version of both texts. Art. 10 d of Additional Protocol A/SP.1/01/05:

---

70 ECtHR (Great Chamber), judgment of 08/06/2006–75529/01 Sürmeli/Germany.

71 Peukert, in: Frowein/Peukert, Europäische Menschenrechtskonvention [European Human Rights Convention]. EMRK commentary, 3. edition, Art. 35, p. 505, Rdn. 25.

72 Legal matter N° ECW/CCJ/JUD/06/08- Hadijatou Mani Koraou v. Republic of Niger of 27 October 2008, clause 53.

> « Peuvent saisir la Cour: [...] toute personne victime des violations de droits de l'homme».
>
> "Access to the Court is open to the following: [...] individuals on application for relief for violation of their human rights".

Art. 34 ECHR:

> « La Cour peut être saisie d'une requête par toute personne physique, toute organisation non gouvernementale ou tout groupe de particuliers qui se prétend victime d'une violation par l'une des Hautes Parties contractantes des droits reconnus dans la Convention ou ses protocoles. Les Hautes Parties contractantes s'engagent à n'entraver par aucune mesure l'exercice efficace de ce droit. »
>
> "The Court may receive applications from any person, nongovernmental organisation or group of individuals claiming to be the victim of a violation by one of the High Contracting Parties of the rights set forth in the Convention or the Protocols thereto. The High Contract- ing Parties undertake not to hinder in any way the effective exercise of this right".

The essential difference between both systems (ECtHR and ECOWAS Court of Justice) consists of the capacity to sue . Not only natural persons have the capacity to sue before the ECtHR according to Art. 34 ECHR, but also associations of persons and non-governmental organisations.[73] This regulation *expressly* specifies the persons who are entitled to appeal as individuals.In contrast, the wording of Art. 10 d of Additional Protocol A/SP.1/01/05 limits the capacity to sue and be sued for human rights complaints directly before the ECOWAS Court of Justice to *every person*. The question must be posed, whether every "Person" also includes groups of persons. Limiting it to natural persons would not be justified as the African Charta guarantees human rights that can also establish claims for legal persons and political parties. Therefore, Art. 10 d of Additional Protocol A/SP.1/01/05 requires further specification through case law. Indeed, the Court of Justice will need to address the objection of the opposing party in the legal matter CDP vs Burkina Faso, regarding the capacity to sue

73 Meyer-Ladewig, Europäische Menschenrechtskonvention [European Human Rights Convention]. Hand commentary, 2. edition, Art. 34, Rn. 7f; Frowein, in: Frowein/Peukert, Europäische Menschenrechtskonvention [European Human Rights Convention]. ECHR commen- tary, 3. edition, Art. 34, Rn. 12 f.

and be sued by the political party before the Court of Justice.[74] The government regards the complaint by the political party (CDP) as inadmissible and states:

> « Au titre de l'irrecevabilité du recours, l'Etat du Burkina Faso estime que le droit en cause, qui est la participation à la gestion des affaires publiques, est un droit individuel et subjectif et non un droit collectif. Devrait alors être déclarée irrecevable au moins la partie de la re quête présentée par des partis politiques ».[75]

The Court of Justice did, however, not follow this opinion by the government. In essence, it explained:

> « La Cour doit d'abord rappeler qu'elle n'est pas saisie que par des partis politiques, elle l'est également par des citoyens. Mais même si elle n'était saisie que par des associations de type politique, la Cour estime que rien ne l'empêcherait d'en connaitre, pour la raison qu'une restriction d'un tel droit peut parfaitement léser une formation politique, structure dont la voca- tion consiste justement à solliciter le suffrage des citoyens et à participer à la gestion des af- faires publiques. Non seulement les textes qui régissent la Cour n'excluent pas que celle-ci puisse être saisie par des *personnes morales*, à la condition qu'elles soient cependant vic- times ».[76]

From this clause, fundamental requirements regarding the party to proceedings before the ECOWAS Court of Justice can be derived. Every person may directly approach the Court of Justice . They must allege that the human and civil rights guaranteed in the African Charta have been violated. "Directly" in this sense means that the person concerned must personally be affected.

Through this requirement, the Court of Justice can prevent a collective action. Besides the right to complain of natural persons, such a right also exists for legal persons. In particular because of the specific nature of politi-

---

74 CJ CEDEAO, Affaire Congrès pour la démocratie et le Progrès (CDP) & Autres c. Etat Bur- kina Faso, N°ECW/CCJ/JUD/16/15 (13/07/2015), par. 31, available at: www.courtecowas.org (last accessed on 16/07/2015).

75 CJ CEDEAO, Affaire Congrès pour la démocratie et le Progrès (CDP) & Autres c. Etat Bur- kina Faso, N°ECW/CCJ/JUD/16/15 (13/07/2015), par. 11, available at: www.courtecowas.org (last accessed on 16/07/2015).

76 CJ CEDEAO, Affaire Congrès pour la démocratie et le Progrès (CDP) & Autres c. Etat Bur- kina Faso, N°ECW/CCJ/JUD/16/15 (13/07/2015), par. 20, available at: www.courtecowas.org (last accessed on 16/07/2015). emphasis by the author.

cal rights, natural as well as legal persons can complain. It is therefore sufficient that the individual plaintiff claims that the infringement of the party's rights will likely lead to a measure that will affect him personally.[77] It can be further derived from this judgment that the ECOWAS Court of Justice would now declare individual complaints by associations of persons but not state organisations as entitled to appeal. This is because associations of persons especially include political parties. Therefore, the Court of Justice clearly states that nothing opposes the admissibility of an appeal of an individual complaint by a political party. At any rate, the respective association of persons must claim to be impaired in their own rights by an action or omission of the signatory state.

2. Object of the complaint (breach of primary duty, compare Art. 1 ECHR)

A reason for exclusion must first be mentioned. In Art. 10. d. ii of Additional Protocol A/SP.1/01/05 a complaint is inadmissible if the legal dispute is already the object of proceedings before other international courts. The reference to "other international competent courts" is legally relevant because the individual complaint may be declared inadmissible if an international court has already decided on the matter. It would be a different constellation if the same individual complaint was the object of a *listispendens* at another international court. Otherwise, the complaint is admissible without further requirements. The consequences of this are as follows:

- The reprimanded violation may be an action of the executive power;
- or the complaint may be based on the action of the judiciary in a broader sense;
- The individual complaint may reprimand the judicial act.

In conclusion, complaints are admissible if the violation is caused by the actions of sovereign organs. This means that all actions in violation of human rights by state powers are appealable before the Court of Law. This, in turn, means that the courts decisions in violation of human rights can represent the object of anindividual complaint in terms of Art. 10. d. ii i. V. m. Art. 9 paragr. 4 of Additional Protocol regarding the Court of Law. It is irrelevant, whether the court, whose decision is reprimanded, is a Consti-

77 Meyer-Ladewig, Europäische Menschenrechtskonvention [European Human Rights Convention]. Hand commentary, 2. edition, Art. 34, Rn. 11a.

tutional Court or a specialised court. Moreover, an individual complaint can be directed at legislative acts as well as administrative measures in terms of this regulation.

The proceedings before the ECOWAS Court of Justice consider other legal questions and is not to be regarded as an extension of the national proceedings.[78] Should the Court of Justice not have competence to assess a final judgment by Constitutional Courts of Member States, this would have been included as an impediment to an appeal in the admissibility requirements under Art. 10 d ii. of the Additional Protocol. As long as the signatory states did not provide for this obstacle to proceedings, it can be assumed that the Court of Justice has the competence to review final decisions by Constitutional Courts. It is questionable, which consequences are drawn from this authority to review. In other words: Which decisions can the Court of Justice make when it declares a complaint against a final judgment by Constitutional Courts of Member States as admissible?

D. Types of Judgments by the ECOWAS Court of Justice

An overview of the extent of the binding effect requires a demonstration of the different types of decisions by the ECOWAS Court of Justice. This primarily means that the decisions that concern only the organisation of the Court of Law[79] will not be analysed in this section. Rather, the decision on merits by the Court of Law regarding the binding effect is mainly taken into account. The decision on merits by the ECOWAS Court of Justice generally includes the declaratory judgment (I) and the sentence regarding compensation in terms of remuneration (II). There is also a special form of decision by the Court of Law regarding the interpretation of its declaratory judgment: the interpretative judgment (III). According to case law, it is certain that the decisions of the Court of Law do not have an effect of cassation. This aspect must therefore be addressed (IV). According to the current legal situation, the possibility of an appeal decision already exists, which should be expanded on *de lege ferenda* (V).

---

78 Sall, La Justice de l'intégration, 322.

79 .That internal judicial decision concerns, in principle, the election of the President of the Court of Justice, the composition of the Court of Law and the power to establish the Rules of Procedure of the Court of Justice.

I. Declaratory Judgment

Within the framework of its judicial power, the Court of Justice must render a judgment after receiving an admissible individual complaint. The nature of the judgment is not expressly regulated in the text of the Convention. According to the preamble of the Additional Protocol the Court of Justice has the task to ensure that the signatory states fulfill their obligations. Moreover,the extension of competence of the Court of Justice regarding human rights aims at controlling sovereign actions by the Member States in accordance with the accepted human rights. As the previous practice by the Court of Justice shows, it will render a declaratory judgment in the case of an individual complaint. The declaratory judgment can be defined as a judgment which possesses a declaratory content. When submitting an individual complaint, the plaintiff desires the declaration of a violation of human rights. Therefore, the Court of Justice must render a declaratory judgment. This means that the plaintiff asks the Court of Justice to give a legally binding statement regarding a violation of his guaranteed human rights by a signatory state. The legal action by the plaintiff can, in this respect, be called a declaratory legal action against the respondent Member State. Whether the plaintiff seeks an annulment of the act of law causing the violation is unclear at this point. The declaratory judgment is not generally enforceable. The judgment can therefore not be enforced because it is in the prerogative of the sentenced Member State to choose the remedies by which the violation will be removed.

The big difference between the declaratory judgment and the design judgment is that, in the case of a declaratory judgment, the decision by the Court of Justice only indirectly influences the rectification of the national judgment which violates human rights. The design judgment would enable the Court of Justice to directly annul the action in violation of human rights. Whether the Court of Law has this authority will be addressed at a later stage. However, all of this is irrelevant for the sentenced Member State because sentenced state is bound by the declaratory judgment by the Court of Justice in any case. It carries the obligation under international law to implement the decision by the Court of Justice.

II. Judgment granting Reparation (Compensation)

Before a decision can become res judicata, a court must be approached. The court must, in turn, justify its decision based on legal principles.

Therefore, the legal standards of the declaratory judgment will be demonstrated first (1). Subsequently, the enforcement procedure of the judgment regarding the compensation will be addressed (2).

1. Standards of a Judgment granting Reparation

The judgment granting satisfaction in a broader sense is based on a law suit aimed at receiving future satisfaction together with the sentencing of the respondent (to do, omit or tolerate something).[80] In this context, such a law suit, if successful, will lead to a corresponding judgment granting satisfaction. Here, the judgment granting satisfaction can be understood in its own terms. This involves a demand of the Court of Law, in the tenor of the judgment, of payment of a sum of money to the individual plaintiffs.[81] After an individual complaint has been granted, the Court of Law may, indeed, sentence the respondent to pay justified damages alongside the declaration of an infringement.[82] When calculating the damages as a sum of money to be paid to the plaintiff, the Court of Law bases its decision on equity. This is due to the fact that neither the protocol regarding the Court of Law nor the rules of procedure include an established basis to calculate the incurred damage. It cannot be determined from the Amendment Agreement nor the Additional Protocol which legal basis the Court of Justice must apply regarding the question of compensation. This is because, according to Art. 9.4, the Court of Justice decides on human rights violations. It is, however, not mentioned whether the Court of Law may order compensations based on violations of human rights. Therefore, the general principles of international law regarding monetary compensation following a violation of international law must be used. Indeed, the Court of Justice may apply the principles based on international law as per Art. 38 of the IGH statute.[83] In practice, the Court of Justice's application of the *ubi jus ibi remedium* principle can be ascertained, because in almost all deci-

80 Creifelds, Rechtswörterbuch, 19. edition, 741.

81 Cohen-Jonathan, Quelques considérations sur la réparation accordée aux victimes d'une violation de la Convention Européenne des Droits de l'Homme, in: Les Droits de l'Homme au seuil du troisième millénaire. Mélanges en hommage à Pierre Lambert, 109 (116).

82 Arangio-Ruiz, Second Report on State Responsibility, UN Doc.A/CN.4/425 (09.06.1989),
§ 137.

83 Art. 19. Abs. 1 des Protocol (A/P1/7/91) über den Court of Law von 1991.

sions in which the Court of Justice determined a violation of human rights, it simultaneously ordered compensation in the form of a monetary sum in favour of the plaintiff.[84] This is consequential because, in any case, the violation of the convention represents a *conditio sine qua non* of the damages. As such, the compensation requires a certain causal link.[85] It is therefore surprising why the Court of Justice , in some cases, also grants compensation regarding the contravention of the African Charta. In any case, a contravention of the African Charta itself represents the basis of a claim for compensation for immaterial damages, at least in a symbolic amount.[86]

Subsequently, the declaratory judgment and the decision regarding the compensation usually go hand in hand with the judgment on merits. It is established that the determination of the compensation is at the reasonable discretion of the Court of Justice in respect of the special circumstances in each respective case. A sufficient satisfaction is thus granted to the plaintiff. In every trial based on an individual complaint, material as well as immaterial damages which were caused by a violation of human rights are considered.

The requirements regarding the costs of the proceedings are stipulated in Art. 66 to Art. 71 in the rules of procedure of the Court of Justice. A refund of incurred expenses during the complaints procedure is granted to the successful plaintiff according to Art. 66 paragr. 2. It is questionable whether, when calculating the incurred expenses during the procedure, the Court of Justice also considers the expenses incurred before national instances. This should be conceivable[87] because these expenses would not

84 CJ CEDEAO, Koraou c. Republique du Niger, N°ECW/CCJ/JUD/06/08 (27/10/2010), available at: www.courtecowas.org (last accessed on 24/07/2015); CC CEDEAO, Manneh c. Répu- blique de la Gambie, Arrêt, N°ECW/CCJ/JUD/ 3/08 (05/06/2008), available at: www.courteco- was.org (last accessed on 16/07/2015); CJ CEDEAO, Affaire Ameganvi et al. c. Etat du Togo, N °ECW/CCJ/JUD/09/11 (07/10/2011), available at: www.courtecowas.org (last accessed on 16/07/2015).

85 Dannemann, Schadensersatz bei Verletzung der Europäischen Menschenrechtskonvention [Compensation in Case of a Violation of the European Convention on Human Rights], 115.

86 Dannemann, Schadensersatz bei Verletzung der Europäischen Menschenrechtskonvention [Compensation in Case of a Violation of the European Convention on Human Rights], 362.

87 Peukert, in: Frowein/Peukert, Europäische Menschenrechtskonvention [European Convention on Human Rights]. ECHR commentary, 3. edition, Art. 41, Rn. 4.

have been incurred had it not been for the violation of human rights. Because of this, the inclusion of the incurred expenses during the procedure in the end calculation would be consequential.

2. Enforcement Procedure

Now the question must be asked of how the final decision of the Court of Law is enforced. At the same time, the question of the execution of the decisions by the ECOWAS Court arises. There are two regulations in this respect. The rules regarding the judgments of the Court of Justice which impose a payment obligation on the sentenced Member State are stipulated in Art. 24 of the Protocol (A/SP.1/01/05) in conjunction with Art. 15 of the Amendment Agreement. In Art. 24 of the Protocol (A/SP.1/01/05) it states:

> « Les arrêts de la Cour qui comportent à la charge des personnes ou des Etats, une obligation pécuniaire, constituent un titre exécutoire. L'exécution forcée, qui sera soumise par le Gref- fier du Tribunal de l'Etat membre concerné, est régie par les règles de procédure civile en vigueur dans ledit Etat membre. La formule exécutoire est apposée, sans autre contrôle que celui de la vérification de l'authenticité du titre, par l'autorité nationale que le Gouvernement de chacun des Etats membres désignera à cet effet. Les Etats membres désigneront l'autorité nationale compétente pour recevoir ou exécuter la décision de la Cour et notifieront cette désignation à la Cour. L'exécution forcée ne peut être suspendue qu'en vertu d'une décision de la Cour de Justice de la Communauté».

> "Judgments of the Court that have financial implications for nationals of Member States are binding. Execution of any decision of the Court shall be in the form of a writ of execution, which shall be submitted by the Registrar of the Court to the relevant Member State for exe- cution according to rules of civil procedure of that Member State. Upon the verification by appointed authority of the recipient Member State that the writ is from the Court, the writ shall be enforced. All Member States shall determine the competent national authority for the purpose of receipt and processing of execution and notify the Court accordingly. The writ of execution issued by the Community Court may be suspended only by a decision of the Com- munity Court of Justice."

Five important consequences can be deduced from this regulation:

- First of all, the judgment by the Court of Justice is per se an enforcement instrument according to paragraph 1 of this regulation (section 1).
- The enforcement is carried out according to the enforcement rule of the sued state (section 2).
- The sued state may not give a separate writ of execution, before the settlement verdict can be executed at national level (section 3).
- It is the responsibility of the Member State to decide which national instance of execution should monitor the implementation of the payment obligations (section 4).
- All measures regarding the potential suspension of the enforcement procedure are directly decided on and are possibly ordered by the ECOWAS Court of Justice itself.Art. 24 of the Protocol (A/SP.1/01/05) can be compared with Art. 244 EG (today Art. 267 TFEU) in many respects. On the one hand, both regulations enable international law to have a direct effect on the legal order in the Member States. The direct national enforceability of the obligation to pay confirms the direct legal effect of the final decision by the ECOWAS Court of Justice. In Art. 24 of the Protocol (A/ SP.1/01/05), the Member States have regulated the priority of judgments ordering payment by the Court of Justice under international law. By granting the direct national enforceability of the judgments ordering payment, the plaintiff has an enforceable claim under international law [88]which must be implemented according to the Protocol at national level.

Now the question arises of who should guarantee the implementation of the judgment. It is regrettable that no specific organ in the Community is responsible for following up on the implementation of the judgments and for informing the Court of Justice on how the sentenced state attends to its obligations as per the judgment. Only a general responsibility of all Member States and institutions of the Member State, regarding the implementation of the judgments by the Court of Justice can be deduced from Art. 22 paragr. 3 of the Protocol (A/P1/7/91). According to Art. 22 paragr. 3:

> « Les Etats membres et les Institutions de la Communauté sont tenus de prendre sans délai toutes les mesures nécessaires de nature à assurer les décisions de la Cour ».

88 Vgl. Rohleder, Grundrechtsschutz im europäischen Mehrebenen-System, 156.

> "Member States and Institutions of the Community shall take immediately all necessary measures to ensure execution of the decision of the Court".

From this, a collective responsibility regarding the monitoring of the judgments by the Court of Justice is established. Unfortunately, a regulation, such as Art. 46 paragr. 2 ECHR does not exist. With regard to judgments that grant a just compensation to the plaintiff, it is the responsibility of the plaintiff himself to inform the institutions of the Community that the sentenced state did not meet its payment obligation. Moreover, it is hard to imagine, how the Court of Justice should ensure that individual measures arising from its judgments are implemented. Here, a loophole in the execution procedure regarding the judgments by the Court of Justice can be found which can lead to a delay of the actual implementation of final decisions. Furthermore, it must be noted that the signatory states have no choice regarding the implementation of the obligation of payment. They must take measures to enable the enforcement of the claim of compensation under international law. The signatory states want to prevent manoeuvers which delay implementation (*manœuvre dilatoire*) by a sentence Member State. The regulation is to be welcomed insofar as it may occur that a possible reference regarding national law, with respect to the enforceability of the judgment, would delay the implementation of the obligation of payment. In this context, one can only recall the opinion of the Gambian government in the Manneh case. In this case, the government tried, with reference to national law, to delay their obligation of payment. However, it is regrettable that there is no monitoring body, such as the Committee of Ministers in the ECtHR protection system, within the Community which regularly informs the Court of Law on the execution of the implementation because the plaintiff is equal to the sued Member State before the ECOWAS Court of Justice during the complaint proceedings. However, the situation changes after the sentencing of the state. After the declaratory judgment, the plaintiff stands alone against the sentenced state and its enforcement organs, whereby the international attention in national law is not nearly as much as it is in cases before the ECOWAS Court of Justice. This can lead to a delayed implementation of the judgment. In order to improve the mechanisms of implementation of the judgments by the Court of Justice, the establishment of a monitoring body or transfer of such monitoring roles to already existing organs is desirable.

III. Interpretative Judgments

Art. 23 of the Protocol (A/P1/7/91) prescribes a procedure of interpreting a judgment. It is questionable, whether the interpretative judgment may affect the irrevocability of a decision. In other words: May the Court of Justice change its own decision on application by the parties to the dispute without the presentation of new facts?

The interpretation of a judgment has two fundamental requirements. Firstly, the application for interpretation of the judgment is open to every party to the dispute and the institutions of the Community. A particular interest in legal protection is required. Regarding the effect of this procedure, it should be pointed out that the admissibility of the application does not suspend the already rendered judgment in the main proceedings. Therefore, the interpretative proceedings do not represent an obstacle to its enforcement.

IV. Not a Court of Cassation

The question posed here is whether the ECOWAS Court of Justice avails of a possible direct cassatory decision-making authority. In other words: it is questionable whether the Court of Law, like the Federal Constitutional Court of Germany, may set aside the unconstitutional decisions of specialised courts within the framework of a constitutional complaint (§ 95 section 2 and 3 BVerfGG) or declare parliamentary acts null and void.[89] The cassatory authority of a court resembles the possibility for the Court of Justice to directly set aside decisions made by courts of prior instances. In the legal matter Ameganvi et. al. vs. Togo, the ECOWAS Court of Justice stated:

> « la Cour estime que la demande de réintégration s'apparente à un recours contre la Décision n° E018/10 du 22 novembre 2010 de la Cour Constitutionnelle de la République Togolaise qui est une juridiction nationale d'un Etat Membre, juridiction pour laquelle la Cour, suivant sa jurisprudence constante, n'est ni une juridiction d'appel, ni de cassa-

89 Mückl, Kooperation oder Konfrontation? – Das Verhältnis zwischen Bundesverfassungsge- richt und europäischem Court of Law für Menschenrechte, in: Der Staat 44 (2005), 403 (414) [Cooperation or Confrontation? – The Relationship between the Federal Constitutional Court and the European Court of Law for Human Rights, in: The State 44 (2005), 403 (414)].

> tion et dont la décision par conséquent ne peut être révoquée par elle ».[90]

This reasoning is partially correct as the Court of Justice does not avail of a cassatory authority for two reasons. Firstly, the signatory states did not provide for this possibility when they expanded the decision-making authority although all international courts generally move within the framework provided for by the state parties. Secondly, a cassatory authority touches on the principle of observance of the sovereignty of the state. However, in contrast to satellites which only move within their orbit, international courts can move out of their orbit if it serves the concretisation of their tasks. This occurs by way of appropriate interpretation of international law. After an appropriate interpretation the Court of Justice must be regarded as a indirect cassatory court because the Court of Justice does not have the authority to set aside court decisions by Member States that are in violation of human rights and to refer the matter back to another national court. The same goal is however reached by the obligation of the sentenced state to comply.

There is in fact no breach of state sovereignty when a Member State Constitutional Court in a legal dispute negates a human rights violation, as in the present case of the Togolese parliamentarians, and the ECOWAS Court of Justice affirms this in the same matter. There are reasons that justify the different legal opinions by both courts. These reasons are of a procedural and substantive nature. Regarding the procedural reason the object of the dispute, the cause of action and the claim differ at national, constitutional-procedural and at regional level. Moreover, the parties to the dispute are not always the same depending on the type of procedure. The ECJ has confirmed this point of view with the following words:

> « Il y a lieu de considérer cependant que la reconnaissance du principe de la responsabilité de l'État du fait de la décision d'une juridiction statuant en dernier ressort n'a pas en soi pour conséquence de remettre en cause l'autorité de la chose définitivement jugée d'une telle décision. Une procédure visant à engager la responsabilité de l'État n'a pas le même objet et n'implique pas nécessairement les mêmes parties que la procédure ayant donné lieu à la dé- cision ayant acquis l'autorité de la chose définitivement jugée. En effet, le requérant dans une action en responsabilité contre l'État obtient, en cas de succès, la condamnation

90 CJ CEDEAO, Affaire Mme Isabelle Ameganvi et al. c. l'Etat Togolais, Arrêt N° ECW/CCJ/ JUG/06/12, du 13 mars 2012.

de celui-ci à réparer le dommage subi, mais pas nécessairement la remise en cause de l'autorité de la chose définitivement jugée de la décision juridictionnelle ayant causé le dommage. En tout état de cause, le principe de la responsabilité de l'État inhérent à l'ordre juridique communautaire exige une telle réparation, mais non la révision de la décision juridictionnelle ayant causé le dommage ».[91]

The statement by the ECJ is completely correct regarding the formal legal force because the decision by the ECOWAS Court of Justice does not demand the reversal of the decision by the court giving rise to the damage.[92] The formal legal force of the national court therefore remains untouched.[93] Regarding the substantive reason, the applicable law at national level is the national constitutional law and at regional level (ECOWAS), the international law. The ECOWAS Court of Justice therefore monitors the adherence to the African Charta and the principles of international law (Art. 38 of the Amendment Agreement). The plaintiffs in fact desire the compliance to national constitutional law and the fundamental freedoms guaranteed in the constitution by the respective state organ before the Constitutional Court. The applicants or plaintiffs additionally desire the declaration of a violation by the signatory state at international level through the ECOWAS Court of Justice.

This preliminary remark means that both instances decide according to different standards and apply relatively different legal regulations. In this regard, it is not surprising if a regional Court of Justice, established by the Member States in order to monitor the Charta, reaches a wholly different conclusion than the national Constitutional Court of a Member State.

It is the task of the international court to close possible loopholes that may arise when national courts misinterpret and incorrectly apply the human rights found in the national constitutional order. In this respect, international law has a different function compared to national law of the signatory states.[94] The task of the ECOWAS Court of Justice to close such

---

91 CJUE, N°C-224/01, Arrêt (20/09/2003), Affaire Köbler v. Republik Österreich [Republic of Austria], par. 39.

92 Breuer, Staatshaftung für judikatives Unrecht [State liability in case of judicial injustice], 400.

93 Breuer, Staatshaftung für judikatives Unrecht [State liability in case of judicial injustice], 401.

94 Kamto, Charte africaine, instruments internationaux de protection des droits de l'homme, Constitutions nationales: Articulation respectives, in: Flauss/Lambert-Abdelgawad (Publ.), L'application nationale de la Charte africaine des droits de l'homme et des peuples, 11 (31).

loopholes can be justified by an interpretation of the African Charta according to international law (further explanations regarding this point in "Justification of the Derogation of the Legal Force" in chapter 4). The Court of Justice rightly decided in its decision of 22 November 2010 regarding the case of Togo that the Togolese Constitutional Court did not adhere to the standards of Art. 7 in the Charta and Art. 10 of the Universal Declaration of Human Rights.

This occurs based on the national and law-shaping effects of declaratory judgments by the Court of Justice. In conclusion, the ECOWAS Court of Justice is not a court of cassation. As a result, its declaratory judgment does not invalidate the formal legal force of national judgments. The decision of how the declaratory judgment should be implemented without derogating from the legal force remains with the sentenced Member State. However, its verdict has a cassatory effect on national level resulting from international responsibility of the sentenced state

V. Appeal proceedings (de lege ferenda)

Art. 25 paragr. 1 of the Protocol (A/P1/7/91) states:

> « La demande en révision d'une décision n'est ouverte devant la Cour que lorsqu'elle est fon- dée sur la découverte d'un fait de nature à exercer une influence décisive et qui, au moment du prononcé de la décision, était inconnu de la Cour et du demandeur, à condition toutefois qu'une telle ignorance ne soit pas le fait d'une négligence».
>
> "An application for revision for a decision may be made only when it is based upon the dis- covery of some fact of such a nature as to be a decision factor, which fact was, when the de- cision was given, unknown to the Court and also to the party claiming revision, provided always that such ignorance was not due to negligence".

Furthermore, the application to resume must contain prescribed reference points. For example, Art. 93 paragr. 2 of the rules of procedure of the Court of Justice stipulates that the application to resume must meet the following requirements:

> « *La demande* doit en outre:
> a) spécifier l'arrêt attaqué;
> b) indiquer les points sur lesquels la demande est basée;

c) indiquer les moyens de preuve tendant à démontrer qu'il existe des faits justifiant la révision et à établir que le délai prévu à l'article précédent a été respecté;
d) indiquer les moyens de preuve tendant à démontrer qu'il existe des faits justifiant la ré vision et à établir que le délai prévu à l'article précédent a été respecté».

"In addition such *application* shall:
a) specify the judgment consteded;
b) indicate the points on which the judgment is contested;
c) set out the fact on which the application is based;
d) indicate the nature of evidence to show that there are facts justifying revision of the judgment, and that the time limit laid down in Art. 92 has been observed".

The judgment actually develops legal force in a formal and substantive regard after official notification of the ruling. However, if a decisive fact is discovered in hindsight which was neither known to the Court of Justice nor to the parties to the dispute an application to resume may be submitted to the Court of Justice. The conditions for the resumption of the proceedings are provided in Art. 25 paragr. 1 of the Protocol (A/P1/7/91) and Art. 93 paragr. 2 of the rules of procedure of the Court of Justice . Thus, the application to resume is admissible if it is submitted within a period of three months after gaining knowledge of the facts that were not taken into account by the Court of Justice during its decision-making process.

Regarding the procedure, one must differentiate between the decision regarding the admissibility of the application and the substantive decision of appeal. In the admissibility phase, the Court of Justice must first determine whether the application to resume is, indeed, introducing new points that were not taken into account in the decision following the main proceedings (Art. 25 paragr. 2. of Protocol A/P1/7/91). If the application is admissible a special meeting of the Court of Justice ensues during which it decides on the points that are still open after hearing the parties to the dispute in a private session. The admissibility of the review application does not postpone the execution of the main decision according to Art. 27 Protocol (A/SP.1/01.05) (alter Art. 25 of Protocol A/P1/7/91) and Art. 94 of the rules of procedure of the Court of Law.

The resumption contemplated so far only refers to facts that were not taken into account in the decision by the Court of Law (Art. 25 paragr. 2. of Protocol A/P1/7/91). However, the regulation in Art. 25 paragr. 2. of the Protocol (A/P1/7/91) does not provide for a possibility to resume based on gross injustice by the ECOWAS Court of Justice. This legal situation may in future jeopardise the system for the protection of human rights because, unlike in the ECtHR system there are no legal remedies against the declaratory judgment by the ECOWAS Court of Justice available to the plaintiff. Moreover, there is no commission, according to the current provisions of the Court of Justice, which would be responsible for reviewing the decision in the first instance. It is recommended to provide a possibility *de lege ferenda* for the resumption of the proceedings due to gross procedural errors. This, however, should be limited to especially difficult and exceptional cases. The possibility should serve to remove gross procedural injustice in the declaratory decision. Furthermore, the possibility to resume the proceedings should be admissible if the legal matter concerns a serious question with respect to the interpretation or application of the Charta. The system of the ECtHR already offers some criteria according to Art. 43 in conjunction with Art. 44 ECHR.

The modification of a final decision is not unknown in the legal system of the Member States.§ 133 section 1 of the Constitution of Ghana allows for this possibility. Thus, Art. 54 of the Rules of Procedure of the Supreme Court in Ghana defines the reason for a resumption more precisely as follows:

> "The Court may review any decision made or given by it on the following grounds –
> (a) exceptional circumstances which have resulted in miscarriage of justice;
> (b) discovery of new and important matter or evidence which, after the exercise of due diligence, was not within the applicant's knowledge or could not be produced by him at the time when the decision was given."[95]

As impermeable as the final decision by the Court of Justice may be, it is quite imaginable to make provision for an appeal mechanism before the ECOWAS Court of Justice. This would be an instrument which the Court of Justice as well as the parties to the dispute can take advantage of in order to allow for a subsequent correction of gross procedural injustice. The ECOWAS Court of Justice is not only a human rights court.[96] Especially for this reason review procedures should be provided for. With the possi-

95 Ghana's Supreme Court Rules, 1996 (C. I 16), Art. 54.

96 Extensive presentation regarding the original jurisdictions of the Court of Law can be found in the introduction of the present paper.

bility of a resumption of the proceedings due to gross procedural errors the basic problem of judicial injustice[97] will also be removed at the level of international law. Like national legal systems, the regional legal order should also consider the possibility of resuming proceedings in case of judicial injustice. The proposition is based on the assumption that international courts also represent bearers of sovereign power. They therefore exercise a sovereign power of jurisdiction. Logically, the injustices caused by their actions should be removed by recourse to legal action.[98]

Moreover, it is advisable to establish a chamber, similar to the one at the ECtHR, which has the competence to adjudicate on a complaint against a judgment of the first formation of the Court of justice, if it is determined that legally significant questions which are of crucial importance for the entire legal system arise in a dispute. The establishment of such a chamber logically requires judges with sufficient knowledge in human rights litigation. Judgments made by this chamber should be seen as guiding judgments for the entire legal order. They should, therefore, be considered to be leading or pilot decisions (see also the section regarding leading decisions or pilot decisions). Therefore, the material prerequisites with respect to monitoring should be strictly regulated in the Grand Chamber. The renewed assessment is granted by the Grand Chamber if the legal matter causes a serious question of interpretation or application of the African Charta or the respective Protocols or a serious question of general significance.[99] It is also recommended that in legal matters including questions of general significance the ECOWAS Court of Justice should be composed differently with regard to the number of judges. Indeed, the number of judges at the ECtHR regarding the composition of the Grand Chamber is increased to 17 judges According to Art. 24 paragr. 1 of the Rules of Procedure of the ECtHR.

E. Legal Force According to Art. 15 of the Amendment Agreement

Upfront, one question must be asked: Why should the interpretation of Art. 15 paragr. 4 of the amendment agreement be presented in a separate

97 Breuer, Staatshaftung für judikatives Unrecht [State liability in case of judicial injustice], 1.

98 Breuer, Staatshaftung für judikatives Unrecht [State liability in case of judicial injustice], 3.

99 Schaffrin, in: Karpenstein/Mayer, ECHR-commentary, 2. edition, Art. 44, Rn. 6.

section? This can be justified on the grounds that interpretation belongs to the most difficult tasks of a judge at international law level. Especially because of the sovereignty of the signatory states the will of the state parties must always be determined.[100] Furthermore, the question of res judicata as the decisive element regarding the finality of a judgment. Consequently, research of the interpretation in terms of Art. 15 paragr. 4 of the Amendment Agreement is required because the aim of the interpretation is to establish the true intention of the signatory states with regard to every term that is used.[101]

Regarding the interpretation of Art. 15 of the Amendment Agreement, the Vienna Convention on the Law of Treaties (in the following referred to as VCLT) is quoted. One must note the rules of interpretation in Art. 31 and 32 of the VCLT in the interpretation of international treaties. Regarding the point in time, there is a prohibition of retroactivity according to Art. 4 VCLT. In this context, the VCLT applies in ECOWAS Community instruments because the ECOWAS Founding Treaty of 1975 represents a concluded agreement under international law, after the VCLT. Moreover, the ECOWAS Amendment Agreement of 1993 falls within the material scope of application of the VCLT since it represents an intergovernmental agreement (Art. 1 VCLT). It is questionable whether all ECOWAS Member States ratified the VCLT. This question remains unimportant for the prohibition of non-retroactivity in Art. 4, because the rules stipulated in Art. 31 and 32 embody the general rules under customary international law. Therefore, both regulations regarding the interpretation of the ECOWAS-judicial instruments are applicable under customary international law.

After this preliminary observation, we will now examine the meaning of Art. 15 paragr. 4 of the Amendment Agreement regarding the requirements as per Art. 31 and 32 VCLT. This is because in the legal matter Ameganvi vs the Republic of Togo[102] the question arose whether and to what extent the signatory states are bound by the declaratory judgment of the ECOWAS Court of Justice. The signatory states made no respective changes with regard to the binding effect of the decision by the Court of

100 McNair, The Law of Treaties, 364, 366.

101 De Visscher, Problèmes d'interprétation des judicaires en Droit International Public, 50; McNair, The Law of Treaties, 366.

102 CJ CEDEAO, Affaire Isabelle Ameganvi v. Republique Togo, N °ECW/CCJ/JUD/06/12 (13/03/2012), available at: www.courtecowas.org (last accessed on 20/04/2015).

justice in the reform of 2005 which enabled the access to the Court through direct individual complaints. Hence, the interpretation of Art. 15. paragr. 4 of the Amendment Agreement of 1993 must be referred to. In the following, the rule of interpretation in Art. 31 and 32 VCLT will be discussed.

I. Rule of Interpretation of Art. 31 VCLT

The rules of interpretation regarding an agreement under international law are laid out in Art. 31 VCLT. According to this, a convention should first be interpreted according to its usual wording (1). Should there still be uncertainties after this step, a systematic (2), historical (3) and teleological (4) interpretation of the agreement come alternatively into effect. Insofar as the international law is perceived as non-static law, an effective approach to interpreting the convention is needed. The agreement should thus be interpreted in an evolutionary and dynamic manner (5).

1. Literal Interpretation

The interpretation of Art. 15 of the Amendment Agreement should first be done according to the wording. The first general rule of interpretation of Art. 31 VCLT is the literal interpretation. In this respect, Art. 31 paragr. 1 stipulates:

> « Un traité doit être interprété de bonne foi suivant le sens ordinaire à attribuer aux termes du traité dans leur contexte ».
>
> "A treaty shall be interpreted in good fair in accordance with the ordinary meaning to be given to the terms of the treaty in their context and in the light of its object and purpose".

The fundamental rule of interpretation is mainly the adherence to the requirement of good faith (*pacta sunt servanda*) which concerns a moral obligation of the parties to the agreement.[103] Moreover, the literal interpretation of the wording of the agreement under international law has the function to maintain the rule of law by protecting the true will of the signatory

103 De Visscher, Problèmes d'interprétation des judicaires en Droit International Public, 50.

states. However, it must be pointed out that the VCLT has opted for the objective interpretation of agreements under international law.[104] Literal interpretation means: the interpretation of the original text of the agreement. In order to better understand the meaning of binding force, it is recommended to quote the original text of Art. 15 paragr. 4 of the Amendment Agreement. The original version in French of Art. 15 paragr. 4 of the Amendment Agreement read as follows:

> « Les arrêts de la Cour de Justice ont force obligatoire à l'égard des Etats Membres, des Institutions de la Communauté, et des personnes physiques et morales. »

In the original English version:

> "Judgments of the Court of Justice shall be binding on the Member States, the Institutions of the Community and on individual and corporate bodies".

The meaning of the text seems to immediately be comprehensible. It says that the decisions of the Court of Law are legally binding to the Member States, the institutions of the Member States and to natural and legal persons. However, legal regulations are often not as easy to comprehend as they seem at first. A peculiar example can be seen in the first judgment by the ECOWAS Court of Justice in 2004.[105]

Thereby, the Court of justice focused extensively on the word "peut" or "may", which is to be found in Art. 9 paragr. 3 of Protocol A/P1/7/91 (06/07/1991).[106] As McNair discussed, it can happen that the word "Mutter" for the purpose of a testator has a completely different meaning than the meaning a judge would attribute to it according to habitual linguistic usage.[107] Therefore, all possible interpretations regarding the binding forces provided in this provision, must be analysed, because after closer inspection of this regulation, only a paraphrase of the binding effect can be

---

104 Bleckmann, Völkerrecht [International Law], Rn. 367.

105 CCJ ECOWAS, Afolabi v. FEDERAL REPUBLIC OF NIGERIA, Judgment N° ECW/CCJ/ JUD/01/04/04 (27/04/2004), in: Community Court of Justice, ECOWAS, Law Report (2004–2009), 1 ff.

106 CCJ ECOWAS, Afolabi v. FEDERAL REPUBLIC OF NIGERIA, Judgment N° ECW/CCJ/ JUD/01/04/04 (27/04/2004), par. 18, in: Community Court of Justice, ECOWAS, Law Report (2004–2009), 1 ff.

107 McNair, The Law of Treaties, 367.

determined.[108] However, this regulation does not inform on which concrete consequences follow from a declaratory judgment for the sentenced Member State. What is to be understood needs to be interpreted and explained by those applying the law.

On closer inspection of the provision, one may assume that the signatory states wish to establish an abstract and general regulation regarding the legal effect for this provision. When stated in such general terms, it must then be further clarified by the judges of the Court of justice. The process of specifying such abstract-general norms in turn requires constant creativity by those applying the law.[109] The advantage in this case is that the judge receives further scope for interpretation.[110] When determining the meaning of this provision, one can assume that an obligation is created following a judgment by the Court of justice for the Member States and the Institutions of the Community as well as natural and legal persons to adhere to the final decision by the Court of justice. It is questionable, whether a positive obligation can be deduced from the provision because, as already mentioned, one can see at first glance that the addressees of the decision are subject to a negative obligation to comply.

Furthermore, many questions with respect to Art. 15 paragr. 4 of the Amendment Agreement remain unanswered. E.g. the question whether the signatory states not participating in the individual complaints' procedure should also be bound by the declaratory judgment. Unlike Art. 32 paragr. 3 of the SADC-Tribunal Protocol, the provision in Art. 15 paragr. 4 of the ECOWAS Amendment Agreement does not give any information regarding who exactly and to which extent is bound by the legal decision of the ECOWAS Court of Justice. There is a certain danger that the limitation to the wording could lead to completely different results than originally intended and that are undesirable for the parties (compared to Art. 31 paragr. 2 VCLT).[111] Since an interpretation of the wording cannot help us here any further, it must also be referred to the other rules of interpretation according to Art. 31 VCLT because, despite the top position of

---

108 Heckötter, Die Bedeutung der Europäischen Menschenrechtskonvention und der Rechtspre- chung des EGMR für die deutschen Gerichte [The importance of the European Convention for Human Rights and the jurisdiction of the ECtHR for the German courts], 45.

109 Cremer, Entscheidung und Entscheidungswirkung [Decision and the Effect of the Decision], in: Grote/Marauhn, ECHR/GG, consociational commentary, chapter 4, Rn. 118.

110 Bleckmann, Völkerrecht [International Law], Rn. 370.

111 McNair, The Law of Treaties, 367.

the literal interpretation in Art. 31 paragr. 1, it should not be deduced that this method of interpretation (literal) is superordinate compared to other rules of interpretation.[112] Quite the opposite: the equality of the rules stipulated in Art. 31 VCLT is expressed in the heading of this article. This point of view was confirmed by the International Law Commission when it did not provide a hierarchy between the rules of interpretation. The commission rather stated:

> « En mettant le titre de l'article (règle générale d'interprétation) au singulier, et en soulignant la relation, d'une part, entre les paragraphes 1 et 2 et, d'autre part, entre le paragraphe 3 et les deux paragraphes qui le précèdent, la Commission a voulu indiquer que l'application des moyens d'interprétation prévus dans l'article constituait une seule opération complexe. »[113]

Therefore, the other methods of interpretation will be discussed in the following sections.

2. Systematic Interpretation

In the term "systematic interpretation" the word "system" is of decisive importance. Therefore, the basis that every rule of law represents a system is addressed. According to the rule of interpretation stipulated in Art. 31 paragr. 2 VCLT, there is inter alia the reference to a systematic interpretation in the following words:

> « Aux fins de l'interprétation d'un traité, le contexte comprend, outre le texte, préambule et annexes inclus:
> a) Tout accord ayant rapport au traité et qui est intervenu entre toutes les parties à l'occa- sion de la conclusion du traité;
> b) Tout instrument établi par une ou plusieurs parties à l'occasion de la conclusion du trai- té et accepté par les autres parties en tant qu'instrument ayant rapport au traité ».

112 Ipsen, Völkerrecht [International law], 6. edition, § 12, Rn. 12.

113 Annuaire de la Commission du Droit international (1966), Volume II, 245; and also De Visscher, Problèmes d'interprétation des judicaires en Droit International Public, 51.

This fundamental rule of systematic interpretation has been confirmed by the International Court of Justice in its well-known opinion regarding the case of Namibia:

> « De plus, tout instrument international doit être interprété et appliqué dans le cadre de l'ensemble du système juridique en vigueur au moment où l'interprétation a lieu».[114]

The ECOWAS Amendment Agreement of 24 July 1993 and the associated Additional Protocol form a system.[115] When interpreting individual regulations, the interpreter should not lose sight of the entire system. The individual term must rather be interpreted in conjunction with the entire text of the evolved system. In graphical terms: The entire rule of law is like a chain. Every single norm represents a link in this closed chain. As soon as one of the links in this chain fails, the entire system collapses. It is therefore recommended to carefully interpret the meaning of each individual norm.

It follows from the aforementioned that the interpretation of an agreement under international law requires the adherence to the principle of unity and to avoid contradictions.[116] The regulations in the entire legal system are coordinated in such a way that the meaning of one of the regulations can only be recognised by taking the meaning of the others into consideration. More specifically, the judges of the ECOWAS Court of Justice must pay attention that contradictions between Art. 15 paragr. 4 of the Amendment Agreement and the legal consequences desired in Art. 9.4 (in conjunction with Art. 10 d) of Additional Protocol A/SP.1/01/05 (19/01/2005) are avoided when interpreting: This is the purpose of the systematic interpretation. One must differentiate in this respect between logical contradictions and discrepancies in the assessment.[117] Logical contradictions occur whenever certain behaviour is allowed by norm A in the jurisdiction and is prohibited by norm B in the same jurisdiction. Discrepancies in the assessment, however, concern the question of a different assessment of the legal consequences of norm A and those of norm B. Therefore,

114 Conséquences Juridiques pour les Etats de la présence continue de l'Afrique du Sud en Na- mibie nonobstant la Résolution 276 (1970) du Conseil de Sécurité, Avis Consultatif, CIJ, Recueil des Arrêts (1971), 16 (35), par. 53.

115 Ebobrah, A critical Analysis of the human rights mandate of the ECOWAS Community Court of Justice, 12, available at: http://docs.escr-net.org/usr_doc/S_Ebobrah.pdf (letzter Zu- griff am 16.05.2015).

116 Bleckmann, Völkerrecht, Rn. 354.

117 Bleckmann, Völkerrecht, Rn. 354.

those applying the law must always take care to assess the legal consequences of different norms in the same way.[118] All this requires the interpreter to sufficiently acknowledge the inner connection between the individual legal principles of the rule of law.

3. Historical Interpretation

It should be pointed out that there is no mention of human rights in the original founding agreement of 1975. The original goals of the Community were of a commercial nature. Especially for this reason, the Court of justice was in 1991 intended to settle disputes of a commercial nature. Only in the Amendment Agreement of 1993 did the signatory states decide that they had to employ the adherence to human rights as a fundamental prerequisite in order to reach their economic goals. This is taken into account in the preamble of the Amendment Agreement.[119] Despite this reference, there was no possibility to submit individual complaints before the ECOWAS Court of Justice. Only after the complaint of Afolabi vs Nigeria was declared admissible in 2004 [120] did the signatory states decide to amend the Protocol of 1991 of the Court of justice by introducing the Protocol of 2005. The Court of Law should include this development as a basis for the historical interpretation of the agreement.[121]

However, it must be stated that the interpretative task regarding the human rights disputes is not all that easy. The difficulties are such that the Court of justice had been originally established to settle disputes of an economic nature. Therefore, the personal as well as factual areas of responsibility of the Court of justice were only meant to settle disputes of an economic nature and only for the signatory states (Art. 9 of Protocol A/P.I/7/91). The rules of procedure were issued with this in mind in 2002. When the signatory states decided to confer a human rights competence to the

118 Bleckmann, Völkerrecht, Rn. 354.

119 Clause 4 of the preamble of the Amendment Agreement (of 24/07/1993 in Cotonou).

120 Afolabi v. Nigeria, Case N°ECW/CCJ/APP/01/03 (27/04/2004), in: Community Court of Jus- tice, ECOWAS, Law Report (2004–2009), 1 ff.

121 Ebobrah, A critical Analysis of the human rights mandate of the ECOWAS Community Court of Justice, 13, available at: http://docs.escr-net.org/usr_doc/S_Ebobrah.pdf (last accessed on 16/05/2015).

Court with the Additional Protocol A/SP.1/01/05[122], they did not sufficiently consider all legal consequences. There is in particular the question of obligations on the side of the signatory states after a declaratory judgment by the Court of justice with regards to a human rights violation. Neither the Additional Protocol A/SP.1/01/05 (2005) nor the rules of procedure of the Court of justice (2002) define the scope of the decision-making competence of the Court and subsequently the obligation of the signatory parties. Therefore, the historical interpretation is especially important. It must be referred to the historical events in the region – such as described in the introduction of the present study.

In 2001, with the Protocol on Good Governance, human rights and the adherence to the rule of law finally take centre stage in the legal order of the Community and were set as a benchmark for the assessment by the signatory states of their will to integrate. As a central actor regarding the enforcement of human rights as stipulated in the Charta, the role of the Court of justice is very much in demand. The historical background of this development must therefore be paid more attention when interpreting a norm. Step by step, the Court should steer the actions of the signatory states according to this interpretation technique because the West African states have given the Court of justice the responsibility to decide in human rights disputes, in order to accompany the process of democratisation in the region by a court.[123] The ECOWAS Court of Justice rightly referred to the historical context in the legal matter Afolabi vs Nigeria[124] as an interpretation aid by stating:

> "The court is to collect from the nature of subject, from the words and from the context of the protocol, the true intent of the contracting parties, when the provisions of a statute are apt and clear."[125]

With the reference to "context of the protocol" the historical aspect of the interpretation is referred to in this passage of the judgment. Granting the ECOWAS Court of Justice with the competence to adjudicate in human

---

122 Protocole Additionnel A/SP.1/01/05 (19/01/2005) Portant Amendement du Protocole (A/P.1/7/91) Relatif à la Cour de Justice de la Communauté.

123 Alter/Helfer/McAllister, A new international human right court for West Africa: the ECOWAS Community Court of Justice, in: The American Journal of International Law (2013), 737 (777).

124 Afolabi v. Nigeria, case N°ECW/CCJ/APP/01/03 (27/04/2004), in: Community Court of Jus- tice, ECOWAS, Law Report (2004–2009), 1 ff.

125 Afolabi v. Nigeria, case N°ECW/CCJ/APP/01/03 (27/04/2004), par. 52, in: Community Court of Justice, ECOWAS, Law Report (2004–2009), 1 ff.

rights disputes is in fact based on a deficit of legal protection at national and continental level. Indeed, it can be determined that, despite the establishment of constitutional courts since the third wave of democratisation, there has been no tangible development in the human rights situation in the signatory states. At continental level, the individual complaint before the African Court for Human Rights remains conditional.[126] It follows from these historical events that the regional courts of justice on the continent fulfill a particular task with regards to the protection of human rights.[127]

All this speaks for a constructive interpretation of the enabling provision of the ECOWAS Court of Justice, in order to reach the goal set out in Additional Protocol A/SP.1/01/05 (19/01/2005).

4. Teleological Interpretation

Every agreement represents an answer to a certain problem.[128] Teleological interpretation means that every term of the agreement must be interpreted with regards to its object and purpose. Regarding the teleological interpretation, the question arises of how Art. 15 paragr. 4 of the Amendment Agreement is to be interpreted in order to take account of the object and purpose of Protocol A/SP.1/01/05 (19/01/2005). According to Art. 31 paragr. 1 VCLT, object and purpose of the agreement has a special meaning besides the wording of the agreement:

> « Un traité doit être interprété de bonne foi suivant [...] et à la lumière de son objet et de son but ».

In order to determine object and purpose of the agreement the operative text of the agreement, the preamble as well possible addenda are available. Therefore, it must be stated that the teleological interpretation only refers to the written norm and follows the objective approach of interpreting a contract.[129] This view is correct because the purpose alone gives informa-

126 Viljoen, International Human Rights Law in Africa, 2nd éd, 487.
127 Ebobrah, Litigating Human Rights before Sub-Regional Court in Africa: Prospects and challenges, in: African Journal of International and Comparative Law (2009) 17, 79 (86).
128 Bleckmann, Völkerrecht [International Law], Rn. 362; Cross/Bell, Statutory Interpretation, 22.
129 Ipsen, Völkerrecht [International Law], 6. edition, § 12, Rn. 15.

tion regarding the more specific meaning which can be assigned to every term or article in the agreement.[130]

It is regrettable in this regard that the ECOWAS Court of Justice oriented itself according to the rules of interpretation of Sir Gerald Fitzmaurice in the key reasoning of the decision.[131] According to a study carried out by Sir Gerald Fitzmaurice regarding the decisions of the International Court of Justice, there are five rule of interpretation:

> "I. Actuality (or textual interpretation);
> II.Natural or Ordinary Meaning;
> III.Integration (or interpretation of the treaty as whole);
> IV.Effectiveness (ut res magis valeat quam pereat);
> a. Subsequent Practice; Contemporaneity (interpretation of texts and terms in the light of their normal meaning at the date of the conclusion)".[132]

However, there were problems with this rule of interpretation during the preparatory work at the Vienna Convention on the Law of Treaties. Indeed, the International Legal Commission highlighted the fact that, due to the divergence at the forum, these rules by Sir Fitzmaurice could not be codified.[133]133 Voices in literature as well as the practice of international courts show that the rules of interpretation as stipulated in Art. 31 VCLT have reached a character of customary international law. According to McNair, the parties to disputes may advocate different opinions regarding the rule of interpretation. One of the parties might demand a liberal interpretation while the other party might demand a more restrictive interpretation.[134] In order to avoid such disputes, it is necessary to orient oneself to the rules of interpretation in Art. 31 VCLT as these rules have an undisputed statute under international customary law.

It is therefore regrettable that the ECOWAS Court of Justice limits the question of legal force and its competence solely to Art. 15 paragr. 4 of the Amendment Agreement. The Amendment Agreement only contains general rules and principles. These rules were concretised by the subsequent protocols to the Amendment Agreement. The subsequent protocols de-

---

130 De Visscher, Problèmes d'interprétation des judicaires en Droit International Public, 62.

131 CCJ ECOWAS, Afolabi v. FEDERAL REPUBLIC OF NIGERIA, Judgment N° ECW/CCJ/ JUD/01/04/04 (27/04/2004), par. 35.

132 McNair, The Law of Treaties, 364; Sall, La Justice de l'intégration, 276.

133 Annuaire de la Commission du Droit international (1966), Volume II, 244.

134 McNair, The Law of Treaties, 365.

scribe the competence of the Court of justice clearer and more extensively than the Amendment Agreement.[135] The teleological interpretation aims to give the agreement an effective impact.

5. Principle of effectiveness and evolutive/dynamic interpretation

With regards to the interpretation of an agreement under international law, Art. 31 paragr. 3.c VCLT also refers to generally accepted principles in international law. Indeed, Art. 31 paragr. 3.c VCLT stipulates:

> « Il sera tenu compte, en même temps que du contexte: […] c) De toute règle pertinente de droit international applicable dans les relations entre les parties ».
>
> "There shall be taken into account, together with the context […] c) any relevant rules of international law applicable in the relations between the parties".

By interpreting according to object and purpose, other principles of interpretation have taken shape at an international law level and have become general rules of interpretation.[136] In this regard, the principles of effectivity and dynamic interpretation as in Art. 15 paragr. 4 of the Amendment Agreement (1993) must be taken into consideration. With reference to the Principle of Effectivity, the ECtHR insists that the rights guaranteed by the Convention are not illusory and theoretical, but that it is the object and purpose of the convention to protect rights that are practical and effective.[137]

The judgment by the ECOWAS Court of Justice develops a binding effect towards the Member States according to Art. 15 Abs. 4 of the Amendment Agreement. In the case of an individual complaint procedure, an *inter-parte* binding effect can be deduced from this. This means that the sen-

135 Sall, La Justice de l'intégration, 282.

136 Ipsen, Völkerrecht [International Law], 6. edition, § 12, Rn. 16.

137 Frowein, in: Frowein/Peukert, Europäische Menschenrechtskonvention [European Human Rights Convention]. EMRK commentary, 3. edition, introduction, Rn. 8; Meyer-Ladewig, Europäische Menschenrechtskonvention[European Human Rights Convention], hand commentary, 2. edition, Note, Rn. 36; Alter/Helfer/McAllister, A new international human right court for West Africa: the ECOWAS Community Court of Justice, in: The American Journal of International Law (2013), 737 (750).

tenced state and the plaintiff must acknowledge the final judgment. As already explained,[138] the participating parties to the procedure are bound by the formal legal force of the declaratory judgment. Here, the question must be asked what is included in the binding effect for the sentenced state as well as what should be understood regarding the scope of the binding effect provided for in Art. 15 of the Amendment Agreement. Thus, an interpretation of the legal force regulation, which takes the principle of effectivity into account, is needed. According to the effective interpretation requirement under international law, an agreement under international law is to be interpreted in such a way that the goal as well as the purpose of regulation is reached as best as possible. This includes that the intended efficiency is achieved[139]. The intention of the signatory states can be deduced from the special meaning they attribute to a term. To this effect, Art. 31 paragr. 4 VCLT states:

> « Un terme sera entendu dans un sens particulier s'il est établi que telle était l'intention des parties. »

> "special meaning shall be given to a term if it is established that the parties so intended"

Moreover, the principle of „necessary implication" should be considered during interpretation because with the adoption of an Additional Protocol and the concomitant admissibility of individual human rights complaints before the Court of justice, all Member States must reckon with the fact that the legal effect must go over and above what the signatory states had originally intended. Subsequently, one should also anticipate an extended authority of the Court of justice . With the adoption of Protocol A/SP.1/01/05 of 2005 the necessary implications for the interpretation of Art. 15 of the Amendment Agreement are to be included.[140] This means that in order to explore the meaning of thisregulation, it should not be referred only to this regulation but to all contractual agreements between the parties to the agreement, which are referred to at the time of the interpretation and which best serve the desired purpose of the regulation. Subsequent changes of the legal opinion regarding the legal system are to be considered by way of evolutionary interpretation.

---

138 See also the section regarding formal legal force (s. p. 38).
139 Ipsen, Völkerrecht [International Law], 6. edition, § 12, Rn. 16.
140 Ipsen, Völkerrecht [International Law], 6. edition, § 12, Rn. 16.

Moreover, it must be noted that the dispute between "dynamic interpretation" and "evolutionary interpretation" will not be discussed. The reason being that a Court of justice does not have the authority to modify the content of the norm. The interpreter, i.e. the judge, rather takes changes in societal opinions into account through evolutionary interpretation of the norm.[141] Therefore, the term "evolutionary interpretation" is preferable. The question concerning evolutionary interpretation is whether the original understanding of the term under international law is to be taken into account or whether one should rather orient oneself more closely to the changed legal opinion of the signatory states.[142] In Art. 31 paragr. 3 the time factor in the rule of interpretation has already been discussed:

« Il sera tenu compte, en même temps que du contexte:
a) De tout accord ultérieur intervenu entre les parties au sujet de l'interprétation du traitéou de l'application de ses dispositions;
b) De toute pratique ultérieurement suivie dans l'application du traité par laquelle est établi l'accord des parties à l'égard de l'interprétation du traité ».

"There shall be taken into account, together with the context:
(a) any subsequent agreement between the parties regarding the interpretation of the treaty or the application of its provisions;
(b) any subsequent practice in the application of the treaty which establishes the agreement of the parties regarding its interpretation

In order to fully understand the contemporary meaning of Art. 15 paragr. 4, the internal context of the Amendment Agreement together with Protocol A/SP.1/01.05 of 2005 must be consulted. The reference to this Protocol is significant for the interpretation of the binding effect because the regulation in Art. 15 paragr. 4 was provided for at a point in time when individual complaints were not admissible before the Court of justice . Furthermore, many regulations in Protocol A/P1/7/91 of 1991 were amended by the Protocol A/ SP.1/01.05 of 2005. However, the content of Art. 15

141 Matscher, Die Methoden der Auslegung der EMRK in der Rechtsprechung ihrer Organe, in: Schwind (Publ.), Aktuelle Fragen zum Europarecht aus der Sicht in- und ausländischer Gelehrter, 102 (108). [The methods of interpretation by the ECHR in the jurisdiction of its organs,..., Current questions regarding the European law from the viewpoint of domestic and foreign scholars.].

142 Wildhaber, De l'évolution des idées sur les missions de la Cour Européenne des Droits de l'Homme, in: Promoting Justice, Human Rights and Conflict Resolution through International Law (2007), 639 (645).

paragr. 4 of the Amendment Agreement has remained untouched. This status quo represents an inevitable source of conflict because the binding effect of a decision regarding an individual complaint is not necessarily the same as in a decision by the states regarding a complaint. It must be noted that the Member States have not ignored a limitation of the binding effect in a personal respect when working on Protocol (A/ P1/7/91) in 1991. A limitation of the legal effect on the parties and on the object of dispute was not entirely unknown to the Member States at this point in time. Quite the opposite, they made express provision for this regarding the review procedure according to Art. 27 paragr. 5 A/SP.1/01.05 (old Art. 25 paragr. 5 of Protocol A/P1/7/91). Even according to the current status of the development in international law regarding human rights disputes within the rule of law of the Community, many questions remain unanswered with regard to the interpretation of Art. 15 paragr. 4 of the Amendment Agreement. The question is therefore whether all Member States are concerned bound by the legal force of a declaratory judgment finding a violation of human rights between a signatory state and an individual plaintiff. This is a question of the subjective and objective limits of the legal effect (this aspect is extensively discussed in chapter 2). The subjective limit concerns the parties to the dispute and the objective limit concerns the scope of the legal effect over and above the case that was decided on. This is the question of the cross-case legal force. The legal question that the individual plaintiff raises in a human rights dispute is the question of his personal situation in regards to the respondent (the concerned Member State). Therefore, the legal effect concerns both parties to the procedure. However, the answer by the Court of justice regarding the raised legal question has an effect over and above the case, which must be taken into account in the entire legal order in the Community.[143]

Moreover, the rules of procedure of the ECOWAS Court of Justice were determined in 2002. Despite the fact that Protocol A/SP.1/01.05 of 2005 approved the admissibility of the individual complaint three years later, the rules of procedure (2002) of the Court of justice has not been amended. There is no answer to the question of why there is no respective regulation neither in Art. 15 paragr. 4 of the Amendment Agreement (1993) nor in the Additional Protocol A/SP.1/01.05 (2005). Therefore, the application of evolutionary interpretation is very helpful in this respect. As the International Court of justice said in its statement regarding the case of

143 Klein, Should the binding effect of the judgments of the European Court of Human Rights be extended?, in: Mahoney/Matscher/Petzold/Wildhaber, 705 (706).

Namibia, regulations in agreements under international law and the development of legal opinions play an important role in the interpretation of the terminology. The IGH stated in this regard:

> « [L]a Cour doit prendre en considération les transformations survenues dans le demi-siècle qui a suivi et son interprétation ne peut manquer de tenir compte de *l'évolution que le droit a ultérieurement* connue grâce à la Charte des Nations Unies et à la coutume ».[144]

The temporal element in interpretation has been acknowledged for a long time by the International Court of Justice (ICJ) as a rule of interpretation. Following the evolutionary interpretation invented by the ICJ, these regulations concerning agreements under international law are to be interpreted together with the international law in force at the time of the interpretation and their respective understanding.[145] Therefore, the time factor plays an important role regarding the scope of the binding effect of Art. 15 paragr. 4, regarding individual complaints. In the legal matter of Costa Rica vs Nicaragua, the ICJ has confirmed its case law regarding the interpretation with the following words:

> « Cela ne signifie pas qu'il ne faille jamais tenir compte du sens que possède un terme au moment où le traité doit être interprété en vue d'être appliqué, lorsque ce sens n'est plus le même que celui qu'il possédait à la date de la conclusion. D'une part, la prise en compte de la pratique ultérieure des parties, au sens de l'article 31 3-*b)* de la convention de Vienne, peut conduire à s'écarter de l'intention originaire sur la base d'un accord tacite entre les parties. D'autre part, il existe des cas où l'intention des parties au moment même de la conclusion du traité a été, ou peut être présumée avoir été, de conférer aux termes employés – ou à certains d'entre eux – un sens ou un contenu évolutif et non pas intangible, pour tenir compte notam- ment de l'évolution du droit international. En pareil cas, c'est précisément pour se conformer à la commune intention des parties lors de la conclusion du traité, et non pas pour s'en écarter, qu'il conviendra de tenir compte du sens que les

144 Conséquences Juridiques pour les Etats de la présence continue de l'Afrique du Sud en Namibie nonobstant la Résolution 276 (1970) du Conseil de Sécurité, Avis Consultatif, CIJ, Recu- eil des Arrêts (1971), 16 (35), par. 53 (emphasis by the Author).

145 Ipsen, Völkerrecht, 6. edition, § 12, Rn. 21.

termes en question ont pu acquérir à chacun des moments où l'application du traité doit avoir lieu ».[146]

The difficulty in interpreting Art. 15 paragr. 4 of the Amendment Agreement is that the ECOWAS Court of Justice itself combines the competences of the ECJ and ECtHR. Has the extent of an obligation arising from a judgment been extended through the admissibility of individual complaints before the Court of justice ? Through the adoption of both competences, the signatory states could have adjusted the limitation of the regulations regarding legal force. Unfortunately, this was not the case. Due to a lack of adjustment of contractual regulations regarding the weight of the legal force on the decision by municipal courts in general and constitutional courts of Member States in particular, one must rely on the specification by the judges. The interpretation of the regulations of the Amendment Agreement of 1993 in general and Art. 15 paragr. 4 Amendment Agreement in particular should be made according to the basic rules of evolutionaryinterpretation by the International Court of Justice .[147] Such a regulation should not be interpreted statically but must be interpreted in an evolutionary manner. Thus, the following practice between states plays an important role. As a result, the original intention of the signatory states is of secondary importance.[148] What the signatory states will express in future rather corresponds with their contemporary intent. Thus, the Amendment Agreement and its respective normative regulations should be understood as a "living instrument".[149]

Future behaviour of the signatory states serves as an interpretation aid within the framework of the rules of interpretation as per Art. 31 VCLT. It should be mentioned in this context that the requirement to respect human rights has, step by step, taken on new dimensions. The ECOWAS rule of law for example expresses their supremacy through the guidelines in the Protocol of Good Governance. This prohibits any reform of the constitutional order or reform of the electoral law six months before elections.

---

146 CIJ, differend relatif à des droits de navigations et des droits connexes, Costa Rica c. Nica ragua, Recueil des Arrêts (13.08.2009), par. 64.

147 Conséquences Juridiques pour les Etats de la présence continue de l'Afrique du Sud en Namibie nonobstant la Résolution 276 (1970) du Conseil de Sécurité, Avis Consultatif, CIJ, Recu- eil des Arrêts (1971), 16 (35), par. 53.

148 Payandeh, Internationales Gemeinschaftsrecht [International Community Law], 322.

149 Payandeh, Internationales Gemeinschaftsrecht [International Community Law], 322.

This temporal development of the requirement of the respect for the rule of law and human rights should be considered when interpreting any legal regulation regarding the individual complaint and its consequences.

II. Effects of Legal Force of other Regional Human Rights Courts

Other regional organisations, such as the East African Community, SADC and CEMAC, exist on the African continent. Regarding a legal comparison of the human rights jurisdiction, only those of the East African Court of justice and the SADC Tribunal are to be examined. Therefore, the legal force of the East African Court of justice will be discussed upfront (1). Subsequently, the SADC Tribunal will be introduced in this regard (2). Beyond the African continent, the ECtHR (3) and the Inter-American Court of Human Rights (4) represent interesting objects for comparison.

1. East African Court of Justice

The start of the effort regarding a regional organisation in East Africa can be dated to the period after the signatory states received independence. At first, three states participated in the project of a mutual regional market. In 1967, Kenya, Tanzania and Uganda founded an economic community by the name of EAC (East African Community).[150] This project crumbled in the year 1977 due to political differences and allegations of mutual interference between the concerned signatory states. Officially, the failure of the Community was due to a lack of political will by the signatory states.[151] In 1999 there was a revival of the efforts to establish an economic community. Subsequently, the agreement for the creation of the EAC was signed on 30 November 1999. At first only the states of Tanzania, Uganda and Kenya were again parties to the agreement. It came into force on 7 July 2000. Burundi and Ruanda are also among the members of the EAC

150 Also see § 3 of the preamble of the founding treaty (Treaty for the establishment of the East African Community, as amended on 14th December, 2006 and 20th August, 2007).

151 As in paragraph 4 of the preamble of the founding treaty (Treaty for the establishment of the East African Community, as amended on 14th December, 2006 and 20th August, 2007).

since 1 July 2007 and South Sudan recently (March 2016) became party to the agreement according to Art. 3 of the founding treaty.

The organs of the Community are listed in Article 9 of the founding treaty. Among these organs of the Community is the East African Court of Law (East African Court of Justice). It is responsible for the interpretation and application and for monitoring the implementation of the guidelines in the founding treaty (Art. 23 of the founding treaty). The organisation, competence of the Court of justice as well as the obligations of the signatory states regarding the decisions of the Court of justice will be briefly addressed in the following.

Regarding the organisation of the Court of justice , it consists of two chambers.

In this respect, Art. 23 paragr. 2 of the founding treaty stipulates:

> "The Court shall consist of a First Instance Division and an Appellate Division. 2. The First Instance Division shall have jurisdiction to hear and determine, at first instance, subject to a right of appeal to the Appellate Division under Art. 35 A, any matter before the Court in ac cordance with the Treaty".

This regulation is supplemented by Art. 24 paragr. 2 of the founding treaty. Thereby, the first chamber (First Instance Division) consists of ten judges. In contrast, the second chamber (Appellate Division) consists of no more than five judges. The heads of state elect the president and the vice-president of the Court of justice from the second chamber (Appellate Division).

It must be mentioned at this point that the appointment of the members of the Court of justice and the president and the vice-president of the Court of justice in particular could lead to an impairment of the independence of the Court of Law. As experience within the West African Community (ECOWAS) has already shown, the appointment of the judges by the heads of state may lead to an impairment of the independence of the ECOWAS Court of Justice. Therefore, an independent institution was established with the purpose of selecting judges of the ECOWAS Court of Justice (see above).

Regarding the authority of the Court of justice, the Court has a consultative as well as a contentious jurisdiction. In its contentious jurisdiction, the factual and the personal areas of competence of the Court of justice are regulated contractually. Regarding the factual and the personal competence of the Court of justice it has the competence to interpret the founding treaty. Moreover, the factual area of competence of the Court of Law also includes the monitoring of the application of the founding treaty (Art. 27 paragr. 1 of the founding treaty). Interestingly, it was established that the Court of Law would, in future, receive other competences including, among others, the human rights competence (Art. 27 paragr. 2 of the founding treaty). Concerning the personal competence, the signatory states may approach the Court of Law by way of an infringement procedure (Art. 28 paragr. 1 of the founding treaty). Similarly, Art. 29 of the founding treaty stipulates that the general secretary may approach the Court of Law on the grounds of a breach of contract by a Member State. Furthermore, complaints by natural and legal persons are admissible before the Court of Law. Moreover, Art. 30 paragr. 1 of the founding treaty stipulates:

> "1. Subject to the provisions of Article 27 of this Treaty, any person who is resident in a Part ner State may refer for determination by the Court, the legality of any Act, regulation, direc tive, decision or action of a Partner State or an institution of the Community on the grounds that such Act, regulation, directive, decision or action is unlawful or is an infringement of the provision of this Treaty".

On closer inspection of this regulation, it is clear that no particular prerequisite regarding citizenship of the authorized persons is required. Consequently, every natural person and not only citizens of the respondent signatory state, has the capacity to sue . Thus, expatriates or stateless persons are also authorised to bring a claim before the East African Court of Law. The only prerequisite is the lawful residence in one of the Member States of the Community.

Moreover, Art. 34 of the founding treaty provides that a preliminary procedure based on the model of Art. 267 TFEU. According to 34 of the founding treaty, national courts are authorised to submit to the Court of Law, in a concrete legal dispute, a legal question regarding the interpretation or application of the instruments of the Community if they deem this to be necessary. This possibility is to be welcomed as it prevents diverging interpretations and applications of the founding treaty depending on a particular signatory state.

A certain problem with interpretation can be seein in paragraph 3 of Art. 30 of the founding treaty. This regulation grants the Court of Law a negative competence. Art. 30 paragr. 3 of the founding treaty reads verbatim as follows:

> „The Court shall have no jurisdiction under this Article where an Act, regulation, directive, decision or action has been reserved under this Treaty to an institution of a Partner State".

The question of which concrete matter is referred to the national instance could arise. Disputes may occur due to the fact that a signatory state, according to its interpretation of the founding treaty, claims the competence regarding the matter that may at the same time fall in the area of competence of the Court of Law. Regarding its consultative competence, every contracting party can, according to Art. 28 paragr. 2 of the founding treaty, approach the Court of Law if there are doubts whether their actions infringed an act of the Community. Furthermore, the other organs of the Community, such as the Conference of the Heads of States, seek the advice of the Court of Law regarding legal questions with regard to the founding treaty (Art. 36 of the founding treaty).

Regarding the obligations of the signatory states with respect to the judgments of the Court of Law, two regulations should be pointed out. The founding treaty stipulates a general obligation to comply in Art. 38 paragr. 3:

> „A Partner State or the Council shall take, without delay, the measures required to implement a judgment of the Court".

This general obligation to comply refers to an obligation to omit as well as an obligation to act. However, a special regulation is provided for regarding the obligation to perform. Art. 44 of the founding treaty stipulates in this context that the implementation of an order to pay a sum of money should be executed according to the regulations of the respective Member State. Art. 44 of the founding treaty (EAC) can be compared to Art. 24 of Additional Protocol A/SP.1/01/05 (ECOWAS). However, in Art. 44 of the founding treaty (EAC)the reference of whether it is also to be applied regarding the signatory states' obligation to pay is missing. The regulation only mentions a "pecuniary obligation on a person". It may be deduced by means of interpretation that the general obligation to comply in Art. 38 paragr. 3 of the founding treaty (EAC) regarding the signatory states also applies to the obligation to pay. This is different from Art. 24 of Additional Protocol A/SP.1/01/05 (ECOWAS) in conjunction with Art. 15 of the Amendment Agreement (ECOWAS), where the signatory states are explicitly named with regard to the general obligation to comply as well as for the special obligation to pay in both regulations.

In the following, the human rights competence will be discussed in more detail. Indeed, the East African Court of Law clearly does not avail of a human rights competence. From a substantive legal point of view, however, the African Charta on Human and Peoples' Rights is to be applied.[152] According to Art. 27 paragr. 2 of the founding treaty (EAC):

> "The Court shall have such other original, appellate, human rights and other jurisdiction as will be determined by the Council at a suitable subsequent date. To this end, the Partner States shall conclude a protocol to operationalise the extended jurisdiction."

However, the preparatory work for the drafting of a Protocol has not yet been concluded. Regarding the question whether the East African Court of Law avails of a human rights competence, the following has been phrased in the legal matter Katabazi:

> "Does this Court have jurisdiction to deal with human rights issues? The quick answer is: No it does not have."[153]

Nonetheless, the Court of Law elaborated on its arguments:

> "[T]hen Article 6 sets out the fundamental principles of the Community which governs the achievement of the objectives of the Community, of course as provided in Article 5 (1)".[154]

In the end, the EACJ deduced its competence from the purpose of Art. 6, 5 and 27 of the founding treaty. This purposeful method of interpretation regarding the justification of the individual jurisdiction is welcomed by some authors.[155] The EACJ's assumption is based on the principle of *Pacta Sunt Servanda* because the interpretation by the Court of Law is part of the founding treaty of the East African Community.[156]

---

152 Ebobrah, Litigating Human Rights before Sub-Regional Court in Africa: Prospects and challenges, in: African Journal of International and Comparative Law (2009) 79 (88); Viljoen, In- ternational Human Rights Law in Africa, 2nd éd., 491 and 494.

153 Katabazi and other v. Secretary General of the East African Community and the Attorney General of the Republic of Uganda, Reference No.1 of 2007 (1st November 2007), 14, available at: www.eacj.org (last accessed on 08/04/2015).

154 Katabazi and other v. Secretary General of the East African Community and the Attorney General of the Republic of Uganda, Reference No.1 of 2007 (1st November 2007), 15, available at: www.eacj.org (last accessed on 08/04/2015).

155 Viljoen, International Human Rights Law in Africa, 2nd éd., 490.

156 Kamanga, 'Fast-Tracking' East African Integration and Treaty Law: *Pacta Sunt Servanda*,
Betrayed?, in: Journal of African and International Law (2010), 697 (697).

2. SADC Tribunal

SADC represents the development community in Southern Africa (Southern African Development Community). The first corner stones of a regional organisation in Southern Africa were established in July 1979 in Arusha (Tanzania). However, we can only speak about a regional community in its actual sense after the adoption of the founding treaty in 1992. This treaty has been amended several times. The last amendment of the founding treaty took place in 2009 in Kinshasa (Democratic Republic of Congo). With the joining of the Democratic Republic of Congo (28/02/2004) and the Republic of Madagascar (21/02/2006), there are currently fifteen signatory states in the region.

One of the permanent institutions of the community, according to Art. 9 of the founding treaty, is the Court of justice of the community (in the following referred to as the SADC Tribunal). The establishment of the SADC Tribunal took place in 2000 by the adoption of the Protocol on the Court of Law (07/08/2000) in Windhoek.[157] It also has its seat in Windhoek. However, the SADC Tribunal may hold external sessions according to Art. 13 of the Protocol, if special circumstances so require. According to the provisions in Art. 16 of the founding treaty, the SADC Tribunal is an independent court meant to settle all disputes submitted to it. To this effect, Art. 16 of the founding treaty states:

> "The Tribunal shall be constituted to ensure adherence to and the proper interpretation of the provisions of this Treaty and subsidiary instruments and to adjudicate upon such disputes as may be referred to it".

In the following, the organisation, competence, and the impact of rulings by the SADC Tribunal are briefly presented.

Regarding the organisation of the Court , it is composed of ten judges (Art. 3 of the Protocol). Five of these judges are permanently in office (Art. 3 paragr. 2 of the Protocol). The appointment of the judges is done by each Member State according to Art. 4 paragr. 1 of the Protocol, whereby the last decision of the final assumption of office is taken according to the proposal by the Conference of the Heads of State (Art. 4 Abs. 4 des Protocol). As a permanent court, the judges enjoy immunity also after retiring from office according to Art. 10 of the Protocol.

157 Protocol on Tribunal and Rules of Procedure thereof (Windhoek, 07/08/2000).

The authority of the political organs to appoint the judges presents a danger to the independence of the judges. As shown in the case of the ECOWAS Court of Justice, it is recommended that an independent organ is established, which is responsible for appointing the judges. This would guarantee the right to an impartial court, as can be learned from Art. 7 of the African Charta on Human and Peoples' Rights.

With regard to the rationae materiae and personal competences of the SADC Tribunal, the Court of Law represents an international court. Regarding the substantive competence, according to Art. 14 of the Protocol, it is competent to settle disputes regarding the interpretation and application of the founding treaty and the associated Additional Protocol. The applicable law before the SADC Tribunal is the international law, principles under international law and its own jurisdiction (Art. 21.b of the Protocol).

In the personal area of competence, the signatory states as well as natural and legal persons are eligible to apply (Art. 15 of the Protocol). With regards to natural and legal persons it must, however, be stated that the admissibility of the application requires the prior exhaustion of the national legal process. In this sense, Art. 15 paragr. 2 stipulates:

> "No natural or legal person shall bring an action against a Member State unless he or she has exhausted all available remedies or is unable to proceed under the domestic jurisdiction".

This regulation shows a significant difference between the SADC Tribunal and the ECOWAS Court of Justice because, as analysed above, the individual complaints are admissible before the ECOWAS Court of Justice without prior exhaustion of all possible legal remedies.

In this regard, the unifying function by way of the preliminary ruling procedure afther the modell of Art. 267 TFEU plays an important role for the SADC-Tribunal. The SADC Tribunal also exercises a consultative function. In this context, either the Conference of the Heads of State or the Council may ask the Court of Law for advice (Art. 20 of the Protocol in conjunction with Art. 16 of the founding treaty).

Regarding the obligations of the signatory states stemming from the decision of the SADC Tribunals, the brief formulation of Art. 16 paragr. 5 of the founding treaty must be referred to. It must be pointed out that all of the mentioned areas fall into the exclusive jurisdiction of the SADC Tribunal. This can be deduced from Art. 17, 18 and 19.

Regarding its human rights competence, it must be pointed out that the authorisation of the SADC-Tribunal regarding an individual human rights complaint has already caused a fierce debate within the commission during preparatory work on the Protocol regarding the court.[158] Eventually, the possibility was rejected in the adopted protocol.[159] Logically, there is no catalogue of human rights that needs to be observed by the signatory states. However, the African Charta is applied as the acknowledged and mutual human rights instrument on the continent.[160] Despite the lack of an explicit authorisation, the SADC Tribunal has deduced and affirmed its competence in three cases against Zimbabwe, just like the EACJ, out of the express authorisation by the founding treaty.[161] Art. 4 paragr. 3 of the founding treaty states:

> "SADC and its member States shall act in accordance with the following principles […] (c) human rights, democracy, and the rule of law".

Moreover, the SADC Tribunal may develop its case law on the basis of Art. 21 paragr. 2 of the SADC Tribunal's Protocol which reads:

> "The Tribunal shall develop its own Community jurisprudence having regard to applicable treaties, general principles and rules of public international law and any rules and principles of the law of States."

Further proceedings are regulated in Art. 6 paragr. 1 of the founding treaty:

> "Member States undertake to adopt adequate measure to promote the achievement of the objectives of SADC and shall refrain from taking any measure likely to jeopardise the sus- tenance of its principles, the achievement of its objectives and the implementation of the provision of this Treaty."

The binding force and the binding effect of the judgments of the SADC-Tribunal are formulated even more briefly. Art. 16 paragr. 5 of the founding treaty namely reads:

> "The decisions of the Tribunal shall be final and binding."[162]

---

158 Viljoen, International Human Rights Law in Africa, 2nd éd., 492; Ebobrah, Human rights developments in sub-regional court in Africa during 2008, in: African Human Rights Law Jour- nal (2009), 312 (334).

159 Viljoen, International Human Rights Law in Africa, 2nd éd., 492.

160 Viljoen, International Human Rights Law in Africa, 2nd éd., 494.

161 Viljoen, International Human Rights Law in Africa, 2nd éd., 492.

162 The binding effect of the legal decision by the Tribunal is complemented by Art. 24 paragr. 3 and Art. 32 paragr. 3 of the SADC Tribunal Protocol.

According to the wording, there is no possibility for the SADC Tribunal to order concrete corrective measures in case of the finding of a violation. However, in the case Campbell vs. the state of Zimbabwe it ordered to take all necessary measures that serve to make amends regarding the situation of the plaintiff and possibly pay compensation.[163] More specifically, the SADC Tribunal ordered the Republic of Zimbabwe, on the mutual application of Flick and Campbell, to implement the first judgment in the Campbell case by granting the plaintiff payment.[164] A difficult relationship between the regional Court of Law and the national courts developed in the jurisdiction of the SADC Tribunal.[165] This led to a situation where the activities of the SADC Tribunal were suspended in August 2010.

The Inter-American Court of Human Rights has more decision-making powers than courts of equal standing on the European and African continents.

3. ECtHR

The European Court of Human Rights became one of the most efficient protection systems for human rights after the Second World War. Before the organisation and the competence of the ECtHR are presented, it seems necessary to briefly summarise the historical background. The history of the ECtHR is logically tied to the adoption of the European Convention on Human Rights. The states of the European Council realised that the prevention of serious violations of human rights requires the establishment of an efficient human rights system within the European Council. The ECHR is an agreement under international law developed by the member states of the European Council. According to Art. 1 of the statute of the European Council it is the obligation of the European Council to ensure the protection of human rights and fundamental rights. The international protection of human rights was a basic concern of the United Na-

163 Viljoen, International Human Rights Law in Africa, 2nd éd., 493.

164 Judgment available at: http://www.sadc-tribunal.org/?cases=louis-karel-flick-othe rs-v-the- republic-of-zimbabwe (last accessed on 16/05/2015); see also Cowell, The Death of the Southern African Development Community Tribunal's Human Rights Jurisdiction, in: Human Rights Law Review (2013), 153 (161).

165 Nkhata/Ebobrah, Is the SADC Tribunal under judicial siege in Zimbabwe? Reflections on Etheredge v Minister of State for National Security Responsible for Lands, Land Reform and Re- settlement and Another, in: The Comparative and International Law Journal of Southern Africa (2010), 81 (90).

tions after the Second World War. Therefore, the fundamental idea behind the ECHR was to transform the Universal Declaration on Human Rights of 1948 into a document under international law at a European level.[166] In order to end the terrible human rights violations, thestates of the European Council developed a human rights instrument in a relatively short time.[167] As a result, the ECHR was adopted on 04/11/1950 in Rome and came into force on 03/09/1953 through ratification by the first 10 member states of the European Council. However, the first version of the convention designed the monitoring system in such a cautious manner that the human rights protection was not even efficient within the European Council. The original system can be compared entirely with the current American human rights protection system and the African Court on Human and People's Rights.[168] The European Commission for Human Rights even then received the competence to decide in individual complaints. This, however, required a respective declaration of submission by the member states of the European Council. Only after the inception of the 11th Additional Protocol[169] was the ECtHR established.

Regarding the organisation of the ECtHR: According to Art. 19 of the ECHR it is a permanent Court of Law. There are four different compositions of the ECtHR depending on the weight and the significance of each case to be decided. It can be constituted by a single judge, or sit in committees of three judges, in chambers of seven judges or in a Grand Chamber with seventeen judges (Art. 26 of the ECHR). Special rules regulate the sitting of the Grand Chamber and the sitting is of an exceptional nature because it can only deal with a case if a party requests the presentation of documents and a commission of five judges declares the referral to be admissible (Art. 43 paragr. 2 ECHR). The referral means that the legal matter refers to a serious question of interpretation or application of the convention. Regarding the election of judges, one has to refer to the highly democratic legitimation of the judges because the judges are elected according to the provisions in Art. 22 of the ECHR by the parliamentary as-

---

166 Meyer-Ladewig, Europäische Menschenrechtskonvention [European Convention on Human Rights], hand commentary, 3. edition, Einl.[introduction], Rn. 1 f.

167 Meyer-Ladewig, Europäische Menschenrechtskonvention [European Convention on Human Rights], hand commentary, 3. edition, introduction, Rn. 1 f.

168 Comparison: Art. 8 paragr. 3 (Protocol on the Statute of the African Court of Justice and Human Rights) with Art. 62 paragr. 1 (American Convention on Human Rights).

169 This Protocol came into force on 1 November 1998.

sembly of the European Council. This, in turn, guarantees a certain independence from the member states and from the executive organs of the European Council. This is a special feature of the ECtHR in comparison to other international courts of justice.[170]

Regarding the personal competence of the ECtHR: Here, every signatory party may approach the Court of justice with regards to an alleged human rights violation according to the convention or the associated Additional Protocols. This counterfactual scenario represents the inter-state complaint (Art. 33 of the ECHR).

This must be distinguished from the individual complaint. Art. 34 ECHR stipulates:

> « La Cour peut être saisie d'une requête par toute personne physique, toute organisation non gouvernementale ou tout groupe de particuliers qui se prétend victime d'une violation par l'une des Hautes Parties contractantes des droits reconnus dans la Convention ou ses protocoles. Les Hautes Parties contractantes s'engagent à n'entraver par aucune mesure l'exercice efficace de ce droit. »

> "The Court may receive applications from any person, nongovernmental or group of individ- uals claiming to be the victim of violation by one of the High Contracting Parties of the rights set forth in the Convention or Protocols thereto. The High Contracting Parties undertake not to hinder in any way the effective exercise of this right".

It can be ascertained from this regulation that the circle of those entitled to apply before the ECtHR is as broad as possible. Its objective is not only to include the citizens of the respondent signatory state, but also every natural or legal person. Therefore, expatriates and stateless persons also have the capacity to sue before the ECtHR. The decisive prerequisite for admission is laid out in Art. 35 paragr. 1 of the ECHR. According to this article, the ECtHR can declare an application admissible after all national legal remedies have been exhausted. Furthermore, a period of six months after the final national decision must have passed.

In a factual regard, the ECtHR has the authority to interpret and apply the ECHR and the associated Additional Protocols according to Art. 32 of the ECHR. A complaint can, in this sense, be rejected *rationae materiae* as inadmissible if the case does not fall within the scope of the Convention or

---

170 Meyer-Ladewig, Europäische Menschenrechtskonvention [European Convention on Human Rights], hand commentary, 3. edition, Art. 22, Rn. 2.

one of the Protocols. Should a dispute regarding the competence of the Court arise, it will itself decide on possible conflicts of competence (Art. 32 paragr. 2).

The obligations of signatory states arising from the judgments of the EC-tHR can be ascertained from Art. 46 paragr. 1. According to Art. 46 paragr. 1 of the ECHR:

> « Les Hautes Parties contractantes s'engagent à se conformer aux arrêts de la Cour dans les litiges auxquels elles sont parties. »

> "The High Contracting Parties undertake to abide by the final judgment of the Court in any case to which they are parties."

The reference to the phrase "in case to which they are parties" is important because it clearly expresses the personal limit or the subjective aspect [171] of res judicata regarding the declaratory judgement by the ECtHR. This reference is unfortunately, absent in the regulation of Art. 15 paragraph 4 ofthe ECOWAS Amendment Agreement of 1993. This absence results in the fact that a certain confusion must be noted regarding the interpretation of the binding effect res judicata in the human rights jurisdiction of the ECOWAS Court of Justice. However, Art. 46 paragraph 1 ECHR also causes a few problems with regard to the legal effect of the decision on merits by the ECtHR.[172] After more detailed examination of this regulation, it can be noted: Art. 46 paragraph 1 describes the duty of compliance or the obligation of implementation of the judgements by the ECtHR. This regulation does not clarify which concrete measures the signatory states must take regarding the implementation.[173] This complies with the peculiar nature of the judgements by the ECtHR because they only have a declaratory character. For this reason, there is no immediate obligation to act, tolerate or

171 Mückl, Kooperation oder Konfrontation? – Das Verhältnis zwischen Bundesverfassungsge-richt und europäischem Gerichtshof für Menschenrechte, in: Der Staat 44 (2005), 403 (420).
[Cooperation or Confrontation? – The Relationship between the Federal Constitutional Court and the Court of Law for Human Rights, in: The State 44.].

172 Cremer, Zur Bindungswirkung von EGMR-Urteilen [Regarding the Binding Effect of ECtHR judgements]. Comment regarding the Görgülü-ruling by the Federal Constitutional Court of 14/10/2004, in: EuGRZ (2004), 683 (690).

173 Rohleder, Grundrechtschutz im europäischen Mehrebenensystem, 44 [The protection of fundamental rights in the European multi-level system, 44].

omit in a certain way based on the declaratory judgement.[174] In no way does the declaratory judgement possess a design effect. The ECtHR clearly confirms this in its judgement in the legal matter Pakelli vs Germany:

> « [E]lle constate, à propos de la première demande, que la Convention ne lui attribue compé- tence ni pour annuler l'arrêt de la Cour fédérale ni pour ordonner au gouvernement de dé- savouer les extraits incriminés ».[175]

Despite this lack of specification of the content of the obligation set out in Art. 46 paragraph 1, there is at least an obligation to implement the declaratory judgement. Consequently, a signatory state may, after a declaratory judgement, no longer allege that its conduct had been in compliance with the convention.[176] An obligation to cease and desist follows, as a direct result that is. if the violation of the convention persists.[177]

Moreover, Art. 41 ECHR provides further references to the content of the obligations resulting from the declaratory judgement. In this respect, the right to order adequate compensation is conferred to the ECtHR in the case that the national law is directed against a comprehensive reparation of the violation of the convention. Acc. to Art. 41 ECHR:

> « Si la Cour déclare qu'il y eu violation de la Convention ou de ses protocoles, et si le droit interne de la Haute Partie contractante ne permet d'effectuer qu'imparfaitement les conséquences de cette violation, la Cour accorde à la Partie lésée, s'il y a lieu, une satisfaction équitable. »

> "If the court finds that there has been a violation of the Convention or the protocols thereto, and if the internal law of the High Contracting

174 Cremer, Zur Bindungswirkung von EGMR-Urteilen [Regarding the Binding Effect of ECtHR judgements]. Comment regarding the Görgülü-ruling by the Federal Constitutional Court of 14/10/2004, in: EuGRZ (2004), 683 (690).

175 CEDH, No. 8398/78, Arrêt (25/04/1983), Affaire Pakelli c. Allemagne, par. 45.

176 Klein, Should the binding effect of the judgements of the European Court of Human Rights be extended? in: Mahoney/Matscher/Petzold/Wildhaber, 705 (707).

177 Frowein, in: Frowein/Peukert, Europäische Menschenrechtskonvention. EMRK-Handkom- mentar, 3. edition, Art. 46, Rn. 6ff; Polakiewicz, Die Verpflichtungen der Staaten aus den Urteilen des Europäischen Gerichtshofs für Menschenrechte, 1993, 251. [European Human Rights Convention. ECHR hand commentary 3rd edition, Art. 46, Rn. 6ff; Polakiewicz, The obligations by countries resulting from the judgements by the European Court of Human Rights, 1993, 251.].

Party concerned allows only partial reparation to be made, the Court shall if necessary, afford just satisfaction to the injured party."

Due to the lack of a more detailed specification regarding the specific content of the obligation as per the declaratory judgement, the ECtHR has at least cautiously pointed out that it is left up to the signatory states to decide how they prefer to implement the obligations as per declaratory judgement on a national basis.[178] Polakiewicz rightly regrets that the ECtHR did not take the case Marckx as an opportunity to further specify the content of the obligations as per the judgement.[179] Depending on the nature or urgency of the individual case, the ECtHR has made a welcome step forward through the evolutive interpretation by the ECHR to order concrete measures in order to facilitate the implementation of the declaratory judgement. In light of the wording adopted by the ECtHR, the ordering of concrete corrective measures takes place either in the salient reasons for the decision[180] or in the binding tenor of the judgement.[181] According to the prevailing scholarly opinions, only the tenor of the judgement is, however, relevant and binding.[182] Judge Malinverni, especially for this reason, regrets, in his concurring opinion of the legal matter Kudac, that the

178 ECtHR (GK), Marckx v. Belgien (13.06.1979), Ziffer 58 = EuGRZ 1979, 454 [Marckx vs Belgium(13/06/1979), clause 58 = EuGRZ 1979, 454]; Polakiewicz, Die Verpflichtungen der Staaten aus den Urteilen des Europäischen Gerichtshofs für Menschenrechte, 1993, 251. [The obligations of countries resulting from judgements by the European Court of Human Rights, 1993, 251].

179 Polakiewicz, Die Verpflichtungen der Staaten aus den Urteilen des Europäischen Gerichts- hofs für Menschenrechte, 1993, 250. [The obligations of countries resulting from judgements by the European Court of Human Rights, 1993, 250].

180 CEDH, Nr. 56581/00, Arrêt (01/03/2006), Affaire Sejdovic c. Italie, par. 126; CEDH, Nr. 15869/02, Arrêt (23/03/2010), Affaire Cudac c. Lituanie, par. 79; CEDH, Nr. 2555/03, Arrêt (18/01/2011), Affaire Guadagnino c. Italie et France, par. 81; ECtHR, Nr. 74969/01, Urteil (26.02.2004), Rechtssache G. v. Deutschland, Ziff. 64.[Judgement (26/02/2004) legal matter G. vs Germany, clause 64.].

181 CEDH, Nr. 71503/01, Arrêt (08/04/2004), Affaire Assanidzé c. Géorgie, par. 14 (dispositif), par. 202 et 203 (motif); CEDH, Nr. 14556/89, Arrêt (31/10/1995), Affaire Papamichalopoulos et autres c. Grèce, par. 2 (dispositif); CEDH, Nr. 28342/95, Arrêt (23/01/2001), Affaire Brumàrescu c. Roumanie, par. 22 (motif), par. 1 (dispositif).

182 Cremer, Zur Bindungswirkung von EGMR-Urteilen [Regarding the Binding Effect of ECtHR judgements]. Anmerkung zum Görgülü-Beschluß des BVerfG vom 14/10/2004, in: EuGRZ (2004), 683 (690), [Comment regarding the Görgülü-ruling by the Federal Constitutional Court of 14/10/2004, in: EuGRZ (2004), 683 (690)] thus also the judge Malinverni regarding the case Kudak:

ECtHR does not express such specifically intended results in the tenor of the judgement.[183]

Ordering specific measures does not compare with the direct repeal of national court judgements which violate human rights. By ordering concrete measures, the Court of only shows which consequences under international law are to be drawn from the declaratory judgement.[184] A direct repeal does not matter at this point. Rem restitution is a mechanism of restitution of criminal conduct by a signatory state, recognised under international law. The consequences of a breach of international law are not just limited to the payment of a sum of money. Rather, this payment is in most cases an accessory to the obligation of restitution.[185] The ECtHR has rightly referred to the judgement of the permanent International Court of justice in order to apply rem restitution to its full extent.[186]

4. The Inter-American Court

The Inter-American Court of Human Rights (in the following: the Court of Law) nowadays represents the central control body in the American system of human rights protection. Before we touch on the effects of its rulings, it is advisable to take a quick glance at the history and the competence of the Court of Law.

The founding of the Inter-American organisation in its contemporary form has its origin in the Bogotá Pact of 1948. With this pact, the *Organization of American States* (OAS) was founded. The starting point of a re-

---

CEDH, Nr. 15869/02, Arrêt (23/03/2010), Affaire Cudac c. Lituanie, opi- nion concordante du juge Malinverni, à laquelle se rallient les juges Casadevall, Cabral Barreto, Zagreberlsky et Popovic, par. 4.

183 CEDH, Nr. 15869/02, Arrêt (23/03/2010), Affaire Cudac c. Lituanie, opinion concordante du juge Malinverni, à laquelle se rallient les juges Casadevall, Cabral Barreto, Zagreberlsky et Popo- vic, par. 2.

184 Breuer, Zur Anordnung konkreter Abhilfemaßnahmen durch den EGMR [Regarding the order of concrete corrective measures by the ECtHR], in: EuGRZ (2004), 257 (261); Heckötter, Die Bedeutung der Europäischen Menschenrechtskonvention und der Recht- sprechung des EGMR für die deutschen Gerichte [The meaning of the European Convention on Human Rights and the jurisdiction of the ECtHR regarding German courts], 64.

185 Arangio-Ruiz, Second Report on State Responsibility, UN Doc. A/CN.4/425 (09.06.1989), § 137.

186 CEDH, Nr. 14556/89, Arrêt (31.10.1995), Affaire Papamichalopoulos et autres c. Grèce, par. 36 et 38.

gional system of human rights protection within the OAS is the American Declaration of the Rights and Duties of Man that was issued on the 2nd of May 1948 within the framework of the founding of the OAS. This declaration, however, was not legally binding. It can therefore only be viewed as a political document (because the Court of Law only later in a legal opinion attributed the legal nature to this declaration). Subsequent to this declaration, the American Convention on Human Rights (American Convention on Human Rights, 22/05/1969) was adopted more than twenty years later in San José (Costa Rica). This Convention became effective with the eleventh ratification instrument on the 18th of July 1978. The Convention makes provision for the Court of Law and the Commission. This means that the basis of the Inter -American Court of Human Rights must be taken from theAmerican Convention on Human Rights.

The competence and the effect of rulings by the Court of Law can thus be presented. In order to better explain the competence of the Court of Law, most of the following references regard its competence. But based on the admissibility requirements of a complaint before the Court of Law, the Commission will also be discussed (see explanation below). In order to monitor the human rights granted in the Convention, the Convention created two important organs. According to the wording in Art. 33:

> "The following organs shall have competence with respect to matters relating to the fulfil- ment of the commitments made by the States Parties to this Convention: the Inter-American Commission on Human Rights [...]; and the Inter-American Court of Human Rights".

Both the Inter-American Court and the Commission are comprised of seven judges (Art. 34 and Art. 52 of the Convention). The judges are chosen from a list of candidates proposed by the signatory states of the OAS. This means that not only the parties to the pact may propose a candidate for the position as a judge, but also every member state of the OAS (Art. 53 paragraph 2 of the Convention). The general assembly of the OAS has the last word in the decision of who may hold the office of judge. Therefore, the election of the judges takes place with the majority of votes by the Member States in the general assembly of the OAS (Art. 53 paragraph 1 of the Convention). There is a peculiarity regarding the organisation of the Inter -American Court of Human Rights compared to the other regional courts of justice, such as the ECOWAS Court of Justice: the Inter-American Court sits at regular meeting periods which are necessary to fulfil its function (Art. 11 in the Rules of Procedure). The majority of the judges may decide, on the president judge's initiative, that an extraordinary meeting should be held (Art. 12 in the Rules of Procedure). Therefore, the Court of Law is not a permanent court[187] like the ECtHR. According to Art. 3 of the statute, its current seat is in San José, Costa Rica.[188]

However, the Court of Law is not automatically competent for all Member States of the OAS. This requires a separate declaration of competence. Acc. to Art. 62 paragraph 1 of the Convention:

> "A State Party may, upon depositing its instrument of ratification or adherence to this Convention, or at any subsequent time, declare that it recognises as binding, ipso facto, and not requiring special agreement, the jurisdiction of the Court on all matters relating to the interpretation or application of this Convention".

This regulation limits the scope of the Convention as a regional human rights instrument. It cannot be expected that all Member States of the OAS will readily submit the declaration of submission. This makes the American human rights system comparable to the system of the African Court of Justice because even within the framework of the African human rights system, a separate declaration of submission by the Member States regarding the competence of the African Court of Justice is required.[189] It must be noted that the declaration of competence can be viewed in two ways. It constitutes a negative as well as a positive authority of competence regarding the jurisdiction of the Court of Law toward the Member States of the OAS. However, the Commission acts on behalf of all the Member States of the OAS (Art. 35 of the Convention).

With regard to the personal competence, those persons who are entitled to apply before the Court of Law are, acc. to Art. 61 paragraph 1, rather restricted. Accordingly, only the Commission and the signatory states have the capacity to sue and be sued through the submission of a complaint before the Court of Law. Therefore, direct individual human rights complaints before the Court of Law are inadmissible. Here, a close collaboration between the Commission and the Court of Law must be noted. Re-

---

187 Figari Layus, Überblick über das interamerikanische Menschenrechtssystem [Overview of the Inter-American Human Rights System, in: MenschenRechtsMagazin (2008), 56 (60), [in: HumanRightsMagazine (2008), 56 (60)].

188 Art. 3 of the Statute of the Inter-American Court of Human Rights (Adopted by the General Assembly of the OAS at its Ninth Regular Session, held in La Paz Bolivia, October 1979 according to Resolution N°448).

189 Vergleich: Art. 8 Abs. 3 (Protocol on the Statute of the African Court on Human and Peoples' Rights) mit Art. 62 Abs. 1 (American Convention on Human Rights).

garding the admissibility of individual human rights complaints, the Commission has the competence to assess whether the admissibility requirements in Art. 46 of the Convention have been met. This competence of the Commission to rule with regard to individual human rights complaints was one of the successes of the second extraordinary Inter-American Conference in Rio de Janeiro in 1965. During this summit the Commission's mandate was extended by a corresponding amendment of its statute.[190] According to Art. 46 paragraph 1.a of the Convention, individual human rights complaints are only admissible when the national legal remedies have been exhausted. The Commission can declare individual human rights complaints inadmissible if the aforementioned admissibility prerequisites set out in Art. 46 of the Convention are not fulfilled. The prior control procedure of the Commission before the Court of Law in turn shows the limited effect of the Inter-American Commission onHuman Rights for the citizens in this region.

Regarding the substantive jurisdiction of the Court of Law, the Inter-American Court on Human Rights rules on the interpretation and application of the Inter-American Convention on Human Rights. Strictly speaking, the Court of Law rules on human rights violations. However, one must differentiate between advisory competence and contentious jurisdiction. The signatory states may request, according to the regulations in Art. 64, the opinion of the Court of Law regarding the interpretation of the Convention and of other human rights instruments (Art. 64 paragraph 1 of the Convention). In this case, the Court of Law issues a legal assessment of the national act of law and the regional human rights convention (Art. 64 paragraph 2 of the Convention). Within the framework of this consultative competence, the Court of Law has specified the significance of the *American Declaration of the Rights and Duties of Man* as the legal source of obligations under international law by the OAS Member States.[191] The contentious jurisdiction follows the procedure laid out in Art. 61 in conjunction with Art. 48 and 50 of the Convention.

---

190 Figari Layus, Überblick über das interamerikanische Menschenrechtssystem, in: MenschensRechtsMagazin (2008), 56 (59). [Overview of the Inter-American Human Rights System, in: MenschenRechtsMagazin [in: HumanRightsMagazine]. (2008), 56 (59).

191 Interpretation of the American Declaration of the Rights and Duties of Man within the Framework of Article 64 of the American Convention on Human Rights, Advisory Opinion OC- 10/89, July 14, 1989, Inter-Am.Ct.H.R. (Ser. A) N °. 10 (1989).

Regarding the obligations of the signatory states that ensue from the judgements of the Inter-American Court on Human Rights acc. to Art. 68 of the Convention and Art. 31 paragraph 1 of the Rules of Procedure, the judgements of the Court of Law are final and incontestable. Therefore, there are no legal remedies available against this legal process. The signatory states are subject to the following obligations acc. to Art. 68 of the American Convention on Human Rights:

> « 1. Les Etats parties à la présente Convention s'engagent à se conformer aux décisions ren- dues par la Cour dans tout litige où elles sont en cause.
> 2. Le dispositif de l'arrêt accordant une indemnité pourra être exécuté dans le pays intéressé conformément à la procédure interne tracée pour l'exécution des jugements rendus contre l'Etat. »[192]

> "1. The States Parties to the Convention undertake to comply with the judgement of the Court in any case to which they are parties.
> 2. The part of a judgement that stipulates compensatory damages may be executed in the coun- try concerned in accordance with domestic procedure governing the execution of judgements against the state."

Here, the same problem emerges as in Art. 46 paragraph 1 of the ECHR. Because of the manner in which Art. 68 paragraph 1 of the Inter-American Convention on Human Rights is worded, it does not provide any information regarding the reach of the declaratory judgement's binding effect. Thus, our opinions regarding the scope of the binding effect acc. to Art. 46 paragraph 1 of the ECHR are applicable *mutatis mutandis*. A special dispensation can be noted when looking at Art. 68 paragraph 2 of the Inter-American Convention on Human Rights.[193] Namely, that the enforcement of the claim for damagses as the part of the declaratory judgment which

192 Übersetzung der originalen Fassung durch [translation of the original version by] Bourgorgue-Larsen/Úbeda de Torres, in: Les Grandes Décisions de la Cour Interamericaine des Droits de l'Homme, 792.

193 Neuman, Import, Export, and Regional Consent in the Inter-American Court of Human Rights, in: European Journal of International Law (2008), 101 (102); Rota, Chronique de jurispru- dence de la Cour interaméricaine des Droits de l'Homme, in: Centre de Recherche pour les Droits Fondamentaux (CDRF) (2009), 189 (191 und 194); Gialdino, Le Nouveau Règlement de la Cour Interaméricaine des Droits de l'Homme, in: Revue Trimestrielle des Droits de l'Homme (2005), 981 (980); Mazzuoli, The Inter-American human rights protection system: Structure, functioning and effectiveness in Brazilian law, in: African Human Rights Law Journal (2011), 194 (203).

grants monetary damages, is left to the national enforcement procedure law of the signatory State concerned. Kokott rightly points out that the effectiveness of Art. 68 paragraph 2 depends on the manner in which the state liability law is implemented in the individual signatory states.[194] Insofar, paragraph 2 of Art. 68 of the Inter-American Convention is comparable to Art. 24 paragraph [sic] of the ECOWAS-Protocol A/P1/7/91 (06/07/1991)[195]. However, there is an important peculiarity within the system of the Inter-American Convention on Human Rights.[196] This peculiarity is found in Art. 63 paragraph 1 of this Convention. In fact, Art. 63 paragraph 1 expressly provides the Inter-American Court with the authority to order concrete corrective measures if it is determined that it is in the sense of the implementation of the judgement. It is helpful in this respect to understand the gist of the regulation. Art. 63 paragraph 1 of the Inter-American Convention on Human Rights[197] reads as follows:

> « Lorsqu'elle reconnait qu'un droit ou une liberté protégés par la présente Convention ont été violés, La Cour ordonnera que soit garantie à la partie lésée la jouissance du droit ou de la liberté enfreints. Elle ordonnera également, le cas échéant, la réparation des conséquences de la mesure ou de la situation à laquelle a donné lieu la violation de ces droits et le paiement d'une indemnité juste à la partie lésée. »[198]

> "If the Court finds that there has been a violation of a right or freedom protected by this Convention, the Court shall rule that the injured Party be ensured the enjoyment of his right or freedom that was violated. It shall also rule if appropriate, that the consequences of the measure or situation that constituted the breach of such right or freedom be remedied and that fair compensation be paid to the injured party".

---

194 Kokott, Der Interamerikanische Gerichtshof für Menschenrechte und seine bisherige Pra- xis, in: ZAöRV (1984), 806 (819). [The Inter-American Court for Human Rights and its present practice, in: ZAöRV (1984), 806 (819). This regulation can be compared to Art. 44 of the founding treaty of the East African Community Scheme.

195 See also: Art. 6 of Protocol A/SP.1/01/05 (19/01/2005).

196 Hilling, Le système interaméricain de protection des droits de l'homme: le modèle européen adapté aux réalités latino-américaines, in: Revue Québécoise de Droit International (1991–1992), 210 (214).

197 Signed in San José, Costa Rica, on 22/11/1969.

198 Translation of the original version by Burgorgue-Larsen/Úbeda de Torres, in: Les Grandes Décisions de la Cour Interaméricaine des Droits de l'Homme, 791.

In light of this regulation, the Inter-American Court has ordered concrete corrective measures to convicted Member States in many of its decided cases.[199] The comparative considerations can now be summarized:

The ECtHR and the Inter-American Court for Human Rights have interpreted the Human Rights Conventions in their respective areas of application in such an evolutive manner that they made a great contribution to the development of the protection of human rights.[200] Moreover, a mutual influence of the systems can be observed due to the reciprocal reference to jurisdiction in similar cases.[201] This reciprocal reference can be justified based on the commonality of human rights instruments.[202]

After a comparative observation on a continental level in Africa, the following results can be noted: The African Charter represents the general standard for review regarding the competence on human rights for all three regional courts on the continent.[203] Other than the East African Court of Law and the SADC-Tribunal who must find their own way with regard to its competence in human rights disputes,[204] the ECOWAS Court

199 Neuman, Import, Export, and Regional Consent in the Inter-American Court of Human Rights, in: European Journal of International Law (2008), 101 (104); Kokott, Der Interamerikani- sche Gerichtshof für Menschenrechte und seine bisherige Praxis, in: ZAöRV (1984), 806 (816) [The Inter-American Court for Human Rights and its present practice, in: ZAöRV (1984), 806 (816); Huneeus, Court resisting Court, in: Cornell International Law Journal (2011), 101 (114).

200 Neuman, Import, Export, and Regional Consent in the Inter-American Court of Human Rights, in: European Journal of International Law (2008), 101 (106).

201 Neuman, Import, Export, and Regional Consent in the Inter-American Court of Human Rights, in: European Journal of International Law (2008), 101 (104, 111, 114, 116); Olinga, Les Emprunts normatifs de la Commission Africaine Droits de l'Homme et des Peuples aux systèmes européen et Interaméricain de Garantie des Droits de l'Homme, in: Revue Trimestrielle des Droits de l'Homme (2005), 499 (500).

202 Padilla, An African Human Rights Court: Reflections from the perspective of the In- ter-American system, in: African Human Rights Law Journal (2002), 185 (186); Murray, A compa- rison between the African and European Court of Human Rights, in: African Human Rights Journal (2002), 195 (215, 216).

203 Enabulele, Reflections on the ECOWAS-Community Court Protocol and the Constitutions of Member States, in: International Community Law Review (2010), 111 (138).

204 Viljoen, International Human Rights Law in Africa, 2nd éd., 490; Alter/Helfer/McAllister, A new international human rights court for West Africa: the ECOWAS Community Court of Ju- stice, in: The American Journal of International Law (2013), 737 (739).

of Justice has an express legal competence in human rights issues.[205] Surprisingly, the ECOWAS Court ofJustice has a restrictive self-understanding. In contrast, the East African Court of justice and the SADC Tribunal tend to interpret their respective bases of authority in a broad sense.[206]

One of the important consequences of the interpretation of the African Charter by the new regional courts for the protection of human rights on the continent is that the interpretation of the Charter by the courts develops a binding effect for the convicted signatory states and its organs [sic].[207]

It must be pointed out that an excessively strong position of the regional courts could, due to the loss of sovereignty, lead to a lack of acceptance. In the worst case scenario, this could lead to a withdrawal of the authorisation by some of the signatory states. This was the case within the Southern African Development Community (SADC) in 2010, where the activities of the SADC Tribunal were suspended. Within the ECOWAS Community, such intentions were observed with regard to the Republic of Gambia after a conviction. This luckily did not lead to a withdrawal by the Republic of Gambia. It must be pointed out that the withdrawal of the authorisation or the suspension of the ECOWAS Court of Justice can hardly be imagined because, unlike the other regional organisations in Africa, the ECOWAS Member States are obliged to observe the guidelines of the Protocol of Good Governance. A withdrawal from the Additional Protocol A/SP.1/01/05 would in turn constitute a violation of the Protocol of Good Governance. Therefore, the events of August 2010 regarding the SADC-Tribunal are not applicable to the ECOWAS Community. It also depends on the historical development of the ECOWAS Community as described in the introduction of the analysis.

---

205 Alter/Helfer/McAllister, A new international human right court for West Africa: the ECOWAS Community Court of Justice, in: the American Journal of International Law (2013), 737 (739).

206 Ebobrah, Litigating Human Rights before sub-regional court in Africa: Prospects and challenges, in: African Journal of International and Comparative Law (2009), 79 (91).

207 Olinga, La première décision, au fond de la Cour africaine des droits de l'homme et des peuples, in: La Revue des droits de l'Homme (2014), 2 (2); Rousseau, Droit International Public, Tome I, p. 248.

F. Manifestations of Legal Force of the Judgements of the ECOWAS Court of Justice

The decision by the Court of justice is a purely declaratory judgement which, as such, has a declaratory effect.[208] However, the declaratory nature of the judgement does not diminish the legal force of the decision. The formal legal force thus takes effect once the decision by the Court of Law has been issued. Nevertheless, the declaratory judgement has a constitutive effect within the national legal system of the convicted Member State.[209] In the following, the formal and substantive legal force of the decision by the Court of justice will be discussed.

Here, the obligation of the convicted signatory state resulting from a judgement by the Court of Law needs to be considered. Acc. to Art. 15 paragraph 4 of the Amendment Agreement, the decisions of the Court of justice develop a binding effect on the Member States, the institutions of the Community as well as all natural and legal persons. It is clear from this provision that the signatory states must observe the judgements by theECOWAS Court of Justice . This in turn results in an obligation to also implement the judgements. For this reason, the legal force of the decision will be discussed before the question of the binding effect is addressed. The following questions are examined in this section: Does the declaratory judgement have an effect on the initial proceeding violating human rights? Does the declaratory judgement lead to an automatic break of the legal force?

With regard to the binding effect: the starting point in establishing the effect under international law of the declaratory judgement by the Court is described in Art. 15 paragraph 4 of the Amendment Agreement. Since the Court of Law has the final jurisdiction regarding the interpretation and application of the founding treaty and the corresponding Additional Protocol, formal legal force takes effect after the judgement has been pronounced (I). The content of a formal and final decision is decisive for the parties to the proceedings. Therefore, the object of the legally binding decision is no longer available to the parties to the proceedings. Hence, a substantive legal force takes effect (II). Consequently, the legal force brings

208 Schaffrin, Rechtskraft der Entscheidung[Legal Force of the Decision], in: Karpenstein/Mayer, EMRK, 2. edition, Art. 27 paragraph 2, Rn. 7.

209 Szymczak, La Convention européenne des droits de l'Homme et le juge constitutionnel national, 266.

about fundamental legal consequences for the convicted signatory state (III).

I. Formal Legal Force

The binding effect requires a court decision. This is a legally binding sentence by the Court of Law. Essentially, the binding effect represents a logical consequence of the legal force. After an admissible individual complaint, the Court of Law decides whether or not the complaint is justified. The complaint will be rejected if the application is unjustified in the Court of Law's opinion. This means that the national measure does not contravene the provisions of the African Charter. On the other hand, the Court of Law might declare the contested conduct by the Member State to be incompatible with the provisions of the Charter. The sentence by the Court of Law in the operative part of the judgement is final and enters into formal legal force with its pronouncement to the parties to the dispute. The commencement of the formal legal force represents the irrevocability of the judgement because there is no legal remedy regarding the judgement by the Court of justice . The formal legal force therefore has two significant consequences, namely: the non-appealability and the irreversibility of the judgement. For this purpose, Art. 19 paragraph 2 of the Protocol (A/P1/7/91) expressly stipulates that after their pronouncement, the decisions by the Court of Law immediately enter into legal force. Furthermore, there is no other legal action available against the judgements by the Court of Law acc. to Art. 19. Paragraph 3 of the Protocol (A/P1/7/91). Moreover, the Court of Law decides only once on each object of dispute. While the non-appealability expresses the effect of the formal legal force towards the parties to the dispute, the irreversibility concerns the effect towards the Court of Law. This means that neither the parties are allowed to seek another instance, nor may the Court of Law alter the judgement retrospectively. Consequently, this can be regarded as the irrevocability of the judgement.

II. Substantive res judicata

With regard to substantive res judicata, the question concerning the procedural binding effect must be asked. The following aspects of the binding effect of res judicata will be presented: the content of substantive res judicata, the extent of the legal force (1), the scope and approximate consequence of substantive res judicata and finally, the limit of the legal force. The limits of substantive res judicata are examined in the following regarding their objective (2), subjective (3) and temporal (4) aspects.

1. Extent of the Legal Force

Substantive res judicata refers to the pronounced opinion in the operative part of the judgement by the Court of Law. Regarding the procedural aspects, substantive res judicata hinders a renewed submission of a complaint regarding the same object of dispute. Therefore, substantive res judicata must be regarded as an obstacle to legal proceedings under international law. The content of the judgement is decisive and binding for the parties to the dispute.[210] However, the question must be asked, whether the principal reasons of the decision and the determination of facts are part of the legal force. Some voices in literature are in favour of a unity between the principal reasons of the decision and the operative part of the judgement. The principal reasons of the decision in the declaratory judgement are to be taken into account when implementing the judgement because here the Court of Law shows the required action in order to remove the violation. There is rarely a detailed "description of the criminal act"[211] to be found in the operative part of the judgement. Should the aforesaid be left in place, one can assume that the ECOWAS Court of Justice has already found the judgement by the Togolese Constitutional Court in the legal matter Ameganvi in the initial case to be expressly in violation of human rights in its principal reasons for the decision, when the Court of Law made the point that:

> « Il résulte des faits de la cause que les Requérants n'ont jamais exprimé leur volonté de dé- missionner ».[212]

---

210 Cremer, Zur Bindungswirkung von EGMR -Urteilen [Regarding the binding effect of judgements by the ECtHR]. Anmerkung zum Görgülü-Beschluß des BVerfG vom [Comment regarding the Görgülü judgement by the Federal Constitutional Court of] 14/10/2004, in: EuGRZ (2004), 683 (690).

211 Okresek, Die Umsetzung der EGMR-Urteile und ihre Überwachung [The implementation of judgements by the ECtHR and how they are monitored], in: EuGRZ (2003), 168 (171).

212 CJ CEDEAO, Affaire Isabelle Ameganvi v. Republique Togo, N °ECW/CCJ/JUD/09/11s (07.10.2011), par. 63.

Further, the Court of Law expressly confirms what the violation consists of by pointing out:

> « [L]a Cour constitutionnelle à statuer comme elle l'a fait, privant ainsi les Requérants de leur mandat, sans qu'ils aient été entendus, et ce en violation des dispositions pertinentes de la Déclaration Universelle des Droits de L'Homme et de la Charte Africaine des Droits de l'Homme et des Peuples ».[213]

By using these words in the principal reasons in the judgement, the Court of Law is expressly drawing attention to the fact that it decides in the last instance on the monitoring of the African Charter. At the same time, it expresses therelativisation of the legal force of national constitutional courts in human rights disputes.[214]

2. Objective limit of the legal force

The objective limit of the legal force refers to the legal issue raised in the object of the dispute. The determination of the violation of this primary duty is the basis for the validity of the object of the dispute. The answer to the raised legal issue represents the objective limit of the legal force. Accordingly, the content of the statements by the Court of Law, expressed in the operative part with regard to the specific object of the dispute, unfold. The reasons for the judgement serve the interpretation and the communication of the operative part. It is possible that the Court of Law may refer to one of its previous judgements. This reference only serves to give reasons for the concrete legal dispute and is therefore not legally binding.[215]

3. Subjective limit of the legal force

The subjective limit of the legal force primarily regards the personal limit of the declaratory judgement. First and foremost, a declaratory judgement

---

213 CJ CEDEAO, Affaire Isabelle Ameganvi v. Republique Togo, N °ECW/CCJ/JUD/09/11 (07.10.2011), par. 66.

214 Kane, La Cour de justice de la CEDEAO à l'épreuve de la protection des droits de l'homme, Mémoire de Maitrise, Université Gaston Berger (2012–2013), 46.

215 Tsikrikas, Die Wirkungen der Urteile des Europäischen Gerichtshofs im Vertragsverlet- zungsverfahren [The effects of judgements by the European Court of Justice in infringement proceedings, 57.

develops an *inter-partes* effect (a). This is not to say that the legal force is without consequence for Member States, who are not part of the proceedings (b).

a. Inter-partes-legal force

From a subjective legal perspective, the legal force refers to the parties to the dispute who are involved in the individual complaint proceedings, namely the plaintiff and the Member State, whose act of public authority is invalidated by the Court of Law due to an incompatibility with the Charter.[216]

Art. 15 of the Amendment Agreement, however, lacks the concept of the party although the same regulation concerns the effects of the legal force of an individual complaint, and thus concerns the party status[217]of the individual in proceedings under international law. The question must at least be asked, whether one should assume the regulation of an *erga-omnes* relationship based on the unchanged wording.

b. Erga-omnes impact of the legal force in practice

The binding effect res judicata of a decision under international law must always be differentiated from the impact of a judgement by a national constitutional court. The *res judicata* acc. to Art. 106 of the Togolese Constitution comprises of the entire national legal system *de jure.* On the contrary, the *res judicata* of the ECOWAS Court of Justice is limited to a particular object of dispute and parties to a dispute. In principle, the decisions of the Court of Law develop an *inter-partes*-effect. Since the given formal legal force solely concerns the parties to the proceedings, other Member States

216 Mückl, Kooperation oder Konfrontation? – Das Verhältnis zwischen Bundesverfassungsge- richt und europäischem Gerichtshof für Menschenrechte [Cooperation or confrontation? – the relationship between the Federal Constitutional Court and the European Court of Human Rights], in: Der Staat [The State], 44 (2005), 403 (411).

217 Mückl, Kooperation oder Konfrontation? – Das Verhältnis zwischen Bundesverfassungsge- richt und europäischem Gerichtshof für Menschenrechte [Cooperation or confrontation? – the relationship between the Federal Constitutional Court and the European Court of Human Rights], in: Der Staat [The State], 44 (2005), 403 (420).

are not affected by this. This means that every decision is binding for the convicted signatory state and the plaintiff. However, the development of regional law and the demand for respect of human rights at ECOWAS-level show that all signatory states should adjust their actions to comply with the provision of ECOWAS-standards. An "adjustment" of the national legal system is necessary in the light of the jurisdiction by the International Human Rights Court.[218]

Hence the distinction in the literature between the binding effect res judicata (convicted Member State and individual plaintiff) and the persuasion effect (other Member States).[219]

Consequently, the question must be asked whether the judgements by the ECOWAS Court of Justice can generate legal obligations for non-participating member States.[220] In the restrictive sense, and based on the subjective limits of the legal force, the non-participating Member States are not bound by the legal force. The legal force rather only extends to the plaintiff and the Member State convicted in the proceedings (i.e. the respondent). Furthermore, the Court of Law does not judge in the field of human rights in abstracto[221] but rather always on application by a plaintiff against a Member State in a specific case. However, the judgements by the Court of justice specify the standards and the claim of validity by the African Charter within the constitutional community, toward which all Member States should orientate their action. Due to the duty of realization of theCharter by the Court of justice, the judgements by the Court have a

---

218 Cremer, Zur Bindungswirkung von EGMR-Urteilen. [Regarding the binding effect of judgements by the ECtHR]. Anmerkung zum Görgülü-Beschluß des BVerfG vom 14.10.2004 [Comment regarding the Görgülü judgement by the Federal Constitutional Court of] 14/10/2004, in: EuGRZ (2004), 683 (693); dazu auch: Okresek, Die Umsetzung der EGMR-Urteile und ihre Überwachung, in: EuGRZ (2003), 168 (174) [see also: Okresek, the implementation of ECtHR judgements and their supervision, in: EuGRZ (2003), 168 (174)].

219 Ress, Wirkung und Beachtung der Urteile der Straßburger Konven- tionsorgane, in: EuGRZ (1996), 350 (351) [Effect of and Compliance with the judgements of the Straßburg Convention organs in: EuGRZ (1996), 350 (351)]; Okresek, Die Umsetzung der EGMR-Urteile und ihre Überwachung, in: EuGRZ (2003), 168 (168) [see also: Okresek, the implementation of ECtHR judgements and their supervision, in: EuGRZ (2003), 168 (168)].

220 Mellech, Die Rezeption der EMRK sowie der Urteile des EGMR in der französischen und deutschen Rechtsprechung, 75 [The reception of the ECHR and the judgements of the ECtHR in the French and German jurisdiction, 75].

221 Mellech, Die Rezeption der EMRK sowie der Urteile des EGMR in der französischen und deutschen Rechtsprechung, 76. [The reception of the ECHR and the judgements of the ECtHR in the French and German jurisdiction, 76].

normative orientation function within the Community. The most important advantage of the *erga-omnes*-effect is the avoidance of future complaints against other Member States who are, in principle, not affected by the legal force. The general effect of the judgements therefore disburden the Court of justice and, at the same time, serve to avoid the conviction of the other Member States.[222]

In the system of convergence of constitutional principles such as ECOWAS', one can assume that the jurisdiction by the Court of justice develops an *erga-omnes*-effect toward all national courts of Member States. The *erga-omnes*-binding effect has the advantage to avoid a divergent level of protection through the Charter within the same legal system of the Community.

This especially also applies to the Court of justice which represents a pedagogic legal instrument within the overall legal system of the Community. Thus, the decisions by the ECOWAS Court of Justice, in practice, act as precedent for the courts of Member States and, in particular, for the constitutional courts which play an exemplary role with regard to state law. Therefore, a uniform human rights standard is established within the constitutional order within the Community.[223] It is the task of the Court of Law to ensure a uniform West African standard for human rights. This goal can only be reached if a uniform human rights development can be achieved through its decisions. Just as at the European level (ECHR), the Protocol on Good Governance promotes a common West African development of human rights within the legal order of ECOWAS. At the European level, the German Federal Constitutional Court has rightly pointed out that:

> „[D]ie Heranziehung der Europäischen Menschenrechtskonvention und der Rechtsprechung des Europäischen Court of Law für Menschenrechte als Auslegungshilfe auf der Level des Verfassungsrechts über den Einzelfall hinaus dient dazu, den Garantien der Menschenrechts- konvention in der Bundesrepublik Deutschland möglichst um-

222 Schilling, Deutscher Grundrechtsschutz zwischen staatlicher Souveränität und menschen- rechtlicher Europäisierung [German constitutional protection between the sovereignty of the state and Europeanisation in terms of human rights], 109.

223 Pache, Die europäische Menschenrechtskonvention und die deutsche Rechtsordnung [The European Convention on Human Rights and the German legal system], in: EuR (2004), 393 (409).

fassend Geltung zu verschaf- fen, und kann darüber hinaus Verurteilung der Bundesrepublik Deutschland vermeiden ver- helfen".[224]

Furthermore, the orientation effect applies to the legislative, the judicial and the executive powers. There are already examples of Member States within theEuropean framework, who are not directly affected by a declaratory judgement by the ECtHR, but who have carried out precautionary legal changes, in order to comply with the standard of the Convention through jurisdiction by the ECtHR. Among these countries are the Netherlands and Austria. Austria had namely, in the case Zimmermann and Steiner vs Switzerland, taken action with the alleviation of the Constitutional Court and the Supreme Administrative Court [sic].[225] The Netherlands also reacted accordingly with the Act of 27/10/1982 to the effect of the Marckx judgement vs Belgium on the discriminating regulations of the Dutch legal system.[226]

The binding effect, however, goes beyond the individual case and generally takes effect on all national cases with the same criteria because, with the conviction, the responding Member State carries three responsibilities [sic], namely:

- The obligation of termination;
- The obligation of compensation and granting of just reparation;
- and the obligation to take measures to prevent further violations in the future.

The two first obligations principally concern the decided case. The last obligation refers to all further potential cases, which would lead to another conviction of the Member State, should they end up before the ECOWAS Court of Justice. It is precisely for this reason, that it is imperative that the Member State concerned take measures to remove or, if necessary, put an end to the offences which gave rise to the violation.[227] The declaratory judgements by the ECOWAS Court of Justice therefore serve as an inter-

224 BVerfGE [German Constitutional Court] 128, 326 (326).

225 Okresek, Die Umsetzung der EGMR-Urteile und ihre Überwachung [The implementation of judgements by the ECtHR and their supervision], in: EuGRZ (2003), 168 (170).

226 Zitiert nach: Okresek, Die Umsetzung der EGMR-Urteile und ihre Überwachung [The implementation of judgements by the ECtHR and their supervision], in: EuGRZ (2003), 168 (170).

227 Ress, Die Europäische Menschenrechtekonvention und die deutsche Rechtsordnung [The European Convention on Human Rights and the German legal system], in: EuGRZ (1996), 337 (350).

pretation aid for the affected Member State's own national affairs. Hence, the declaratory judgement develops a national multi-case legal effect.

Above all, the goal of the Amendment Agreement and the Protocol A/ SP.1/ 01/05 is to achieve a uniform adherence to the human rights as guaranteed by the Charter throughout the Community. After the case Koraou e. g., no Member State would now allege that e.g. slavery is lawful in its own legal system. This is because the ECOWAS Court of justice has already made a final decision that this conduct represents a serious violation of the African Charter. Should there be similar conduct within a member State that was not judicially reviewed, it should take national measures to ensure that this violation is terminated. Therefore, this Member State has the advantage of sparing itself of such a judicial review or to prevent it. Moreover, the jurisdiction of the ECOWAS Court of Justice creates the basis for a dialogue between the courts. The national legal practice of the Member States is based on the case law of the Court of justice in order to justify its own decisions. This dialogue can be implicit or explicit (discussed in more detailed in chapter 4).

4. Time-boundary of the legal force

The formal legal force takes effect at the time the judgement is announced. This point in time is significant because it can only be measured by this point in time whether any future complaint has already been covered by the res judicata that took place. In other words: Should there be a future plea relating to aspects of the object of the dispute, the Court of justice , in order to assess a new individual complaint and to decide whether it concerns the same case which it has already decided on, orientates itself on the date of the announcement of the declaratory judgement.[228] In this context, the point in time is an important "*repère*" regarding the assessment of the legal force. Moreover, the point in time plays an important role with regard to an application for review: in order to decide whether the points in question in the application for review were already known to the individual plaintiff at the point of the commencement of the res judicata. Should this question be answered in the affirmative, then the application for re-

228 Heckötter, Die Bedeutung der Europäischen Menschenrechtskonvention und der Recht- sprechung des EGMR für die deutschen Gerichte [The meaning of the European Convention on Human Rights and the jurisdiction of the ECtHR for German courts], 43.

view would be rejected as inadmissible (this has been dealt with in more detail in chapter 2).

III. Legal consequences of the legal force for the convicted signatory state

Three types of obligations arise from the declaratory judgement with regard to government liability principles under international law:
- The obligation to cease and desist;
- The obligation of reparation;

The obligation to accommodate reparation and the prevention of future violation through applicable preventive measures.[229]

This list means that the obligation to cease and desist (1) is to be differentiated from the compensation obligation (2).[230] The accommodation of reparation or compensation and the prevention of future violation conform with the consequence in future time of the declaratory judgement (3)

1. The obligation to cease and desist

The obligation to cease and desist, or of "termination" regarding the violation of obligations under international law can be defined as the obligation by the Convention state to terminate a violation determined by an instance under international law. This includes an obligation to remove or stop a continuing unlawful offence under international law. The obligation to terminate, in a restrictive sense, can be deduced from Art. 1 of the African Charter on Human Rights. Acc. to Art. 1 of the Charter:

> « Les Etats Membres de L'Organisation de l'Unité Africaine, parties à la présente Charte, reconnaissent les droits, devoirs et libertés énoncés dans cette Charte et s'engagent à adopter des mesures législatives ou autres pour les appliquer ».

---

229 Polakiewicz, Die Verpflichtungen der Staaten aus den Urteilen des Europäischen Gerichts hofs für Menschenrechte [The obligations by the states arising from the judgements by the European Court of Human Rights], 52 ff.

230 Polakiewicz, Die Verpflichtungen der Staaten aus den Urteilen des Europäischen Gerichts- hofs für Menschenrechte [The obligations by the states arising from the judgements by the European Court of Human Rights], 53.

> "The Member States of the Organisation of African Unity to the present Charter shall recog- nize the rights, duties and freedoms enshrined in this Charter and shall undertake to adopt legislative or other measure to give effect to them".

It can be deduced, by implication, that the Member States commit themselves to also refrain from all measures opposed to the rights within the Charter.[231] In case the ECOWAS Court of Justice determines a violation of the Charter and the violation continues at the time of the declaration, the Court of Law may order the convicted Member State to take measures at a national level in order to terminate the violation. Along with this, the order is to be seen as an *appeal* to the primary obligation of the Member States stipulated in Art. 1 of the Charter.[232] This is coherent: according to the provision in Art. 1, the Member States are obliged to guarantee the human rights embedded in the Charter to all persons subject to their respective sovereign territory. Withholding the guaranteed human rights is a typical case of an ongoing violation.[233] Should it be necessary for the decision to establish that this obligation has been denied, the Court of justice is entitled to order the removal of the cause of the violation of the Convention.[234] The obligation to terminate must hereby be regarded as the direct consequence of the primary obligation.[235]

It can be noted from the aforementioned that the obligation to terminate must be strictly differentiated from the obligation to compensate. This distinction is important because, in terms of the legal consequences in

---

231 Heckötter, Die Bedeutung der Europäischen Menschenrechtskonvention und der Rechtspre- chung des EGMR für die deutschen Gerichte [The meaning of the European Convention on Human Rights and the jurisdiction of the ECtHR for German courts], 49.

232 Vgl. Breuer, Zur Anordnung konkreter Abhilfemaßnahmen durch den EGMR [Regarding the order of concrete corrective measure by the ECHR], in: EuGRZ (2004), 257 (259); Verdross/Simma, Universelles Völkerrecht [Universal International law], 3rd edition, § 1294.

233 Polakiewicz, Die Verpflichtung der Staaten aus den Urteilen des Europäischen Court of Law für Menschenrechte [The obligations by the states arising from the judgements by the European Court of Human Rights], 64.

234 Heckötter, Die Bedeutung der Europäischen Menschenrechtskonvention und der Rechtsprechung des EGMR für die deutschen Gerichte [The meaning of the European Convention on Human Rights and the jurisdiction of the ECtHR for German courts], 49.

235 Vgl. Breuer, Zur Anordnung konkreter Abhilfemaßnahmen durch den EGMR [Regarding the order of concrete corrective measure by the ECHR], in: EuGRZ (2004), 257 (260).

the area of a state's responsibility, additional measures may be required from the responsible signatory state.[236] The obligation of non-recurrence as well as the obligation of termination may be considered.[237] Ultimately, the obligation of termination can be understood as the obligation to remove the cause of the violation. The best way to terminate a violation of international law is via legislative reforms of national law. In this regard, the ICJ explains in its interpretation of the Avena-case:

> « Un Etat qui a valablement contracté des obligations internationales est tenu d'apporter à sa législation les modifications nécessaires pour assurer l'exécution de des engagements pris ».[238]

Thus, the obligation of compensation is also included.

2. The obligation of compensation

In contrast to the obligation of termination, the obligation of compensation is the duty of the convicted Member State to reverse the activity of violation as much as possible. All measures should thus be taken in order to reach a situation as if the violation had not occurred. In this sense, the reparation could qualify as an obligation to eliminate the consequences of this act and restore the orderly condition.[239] The Permanent International Court of Justice summarises the obligation to eliminate the consequences as follows:

---

236 Verdross/Simma, Universelles Völkerrecht, 3. edition, § 1294; so auch: Heckötter, Die Bedeu- tung der Europäischen Menschenrechtskonvention und der Rechtsprechung des EGMR für die deutschen Gerichte [The meaning of the European Convention on Human Rights and the jurisdiction of the ECtHR for German courts], 50.

237 Breuer, Zur Anordnung konkreter Abhilfemaßnahmen durch den EGMR [Regarding the order of concrete corrective measure by the ECHR], in: EuGRZ (2004), 257 (260).

238 CIJ, Demande en interprétation de l'arrêt du 31 mars 2004 en l'Affaire Avena et autres res- sortissants mexicains (Mexique c. États-Unis d'Amérique), Arrêt du 19 janvier 2009, par 8.

239 Heckötter, Die Bedeutung der Europäischen Menschenrechtskonvention und der Rechtsprechung des EGMR für die deutschen Gerichte [The meaning of the European Convention on Human Rights and the jurisdiction of the ECtHR for German courts], 50 f.

> « [L]e principe essentiel qui découle de la notion même d'acte illicite et qui semble se dégager de la pratique internationale, notamment de la jurisprudence des tribunaux arbitraux, est que la réparation doit, autant que possible, effacer toutes les conséquences de l'acte illicite et rétablir l'état qui aurait vraisemblablement existé si ledit acte n'avait pas été commis».[240]

No easier *escape route*[241] may be provided under international law that would stand in the way of the obligation of compensation by the International Court of Justice. Should such misconduct be present, yet another violation of International Law would exist because, after a declaration of unconventionality, the Member State in question carries an obligation to reach results. Based on the declaratory judgement, all opposing national legal acts must be set aside.[242]

a. Order to reinstate the initial proceedings in the operative part of the judgement

As shown, the responsible signatory state carries a triple obligation of transposition under international law: the obligation to terminate, to compensate and to prevent comparable acts in the future. Thus, importance must further be attached to the legal nature of the act by the state that violates international law. When it comes to judgements regarding the violation of international law, the resumption of the initial proceedings represents an appropriate remedy to implement the declaratory judgement on a national level. This view can also be justified through the jurisdiction by the ECtHR. In more recent decisions which involved violations of procedural safeguards, the ECtHR always stresses the point that the appropriate form of compensation is in principle the provision of new proceedings or

240 Affaire relative à l'usine de CHORZÓW (demande en indemnité) (fond), CPJI, Série A N° 17 (13/09/1928), 47.

241 Cremer, Zur Bindungswirkung von EGMR-Urteilen. Anmerkung zum Görgülü-Beschluß des BVerfG vom 14.10.2004, in: EuGRZ (2004), 683 (692). [Regarding the binding effect of judgements by the ECtHR. [Comment regarding the Görgülü judgement by the Federal Constitutional Court of] 14/10/2004, in: EuGRZ (2004), 683 (692);].

242 Okresek, Die Umsetzung der EGMR-Urteile und ihre Überwachung, in: EuGRZ (2003),
168 (171) [see also: Okresek, the implementation of ECtHR judgements and their supervision, in: EuGRZ (2003), 168 (171)].

the resumption of the proceedings on application by the concerned party under national law.[243]Thus, a renewed assessment of the object of the dispute must take place with particular regard to the ECOWAS decision. This is the logical way to do justice to the national obligation to terminate the measure in violation of human rights. For the convicted state, the finding of the violation means the existence of an offence under international law. The existence of this offence under international law,[244] arising from the conviction, triggers the termination or the elimination obligation of the offence that led to the conviction.

The judgement by the ECOWAS Court of Justice constitutes a performance-triggering declaratory judgement. The decision by the ECOWAS Court is, in principle, a declaratory judgement. However, this declaratory judgement gives rise to an obligation of the responsible Member State. Arising from the declaratory judgement, a duty to act is laid on the responsible contracting state.

From this, the Court can or should indirectly make provision for the implementation of its judgement. This is done by way of ordering concrete measures in the tenor of the judgement. The Court of justice would make an important contribution to the effective implementation of the judgement by ordering the implementing measures in the tenor of the declaratory judgement in order to fully comply with the restoration obligation (Cudak, Seydovic und Görgülü).[245] Although the Court of Justice does not avail of any competence to directly intervene in the national legal system, there are numerous ways in which the ECOWAS Court of justice can explicitly point to a certain measure that may provide a remedy for the removal of the national human rights violation. The ECtHR has sometimes made use of this method of wording in its recent jurisdiction, in order to

---

243 Peukert, in: Frowein/Peukert, Europäische Menschenrechtskonvention. EMRK-Kommen tar, [European Human Rights Convention. ECHR commentary], 3rd edition, Art. 6, Rn. 140, 185; Breuer, Zur Anordnung konkreter Abhilfemaßnahmen durch den EGMR, in: EuGRZ (2004), 257 (263); Rohleder, Grundrechtsschutz im europäischen Mehrebenen- system [Protection of human rights in the European multi-level system], 76; CEDH, N. 71503/01, Arrêt (08.04.2004), Affaire Assanidzé c. Géorgie, par. 202; CEDH, Nr. 15869/02, Arrêt (23/03/2010), Affaire Cudac c. Lituanie, par. 79; CEDH, Nr. 1620/03, Arrêt (28.06.2012), Affaire Schütz c. Allemagne, par. 17.

244 Schilling, Deutscher Grundrechtsschutz zwischen staatlicher Souveränität und menschen- rechtlicher Europäisierung [Protection of the German constitutional law between state sovereignty and Europeanisation], 110.

245 Rohleder, Grundrechtsschutz im europäischen Mehrebenensystem [Protection of constitutional law in the European multi-level system], 141.

explain to the convicted Member State, which results the ECtHR expects from the declaratory judgement. In its Görgülü-decision of 26 February 2004, the ECtHR pointed out that from the obligation in Art. 46 ECHR "follows e.g. that a judgement in which the Court of justice observes a violation, obligates the responding state in legal terms not only to a just compensation of the concerned parties, but also to possibly take individual measures regarding its national legal system under the auspices of the ministerial committee, in order to stop the violation determined by the Court of justice and to remedy the consequences as much as possible."[246] After the establishment of an infringement, the convicted Member State must do or refrain from doing something. The continuation of the situation which existed before thedeclaratory judgement constitutes an ongoing offence by the convicted signatory state. In this respect, and with regard to the system of protection by the ECOWAS Court of Justice, these questions may also be asked: How is the enforcement by way of the individual complaint procedure before the ECOWAS Court of Justice useful if no reparation is carried out at a national level after the finding of a violation of the Charter? Thus, the question of the result-oriented binding legal effect of the declaratory judgement arises. It follows that the tenor of the judgement, as well as the salient reasons for the decision, should be regarded as a unit because the salient reasons for the decision are signposts regarding the implementation of the declaratory judgement: the main reasons for the decision in the declaratory judgement already provide information regarding the national conduct, in which the wrongdoing is rooted. The order, especially in the tenor of the judgement, has the advantage of being able to accelerate the implementation of the declaratory judgement.[247]

However, it should be clarified that the manner in which the state is expected to render compensation is left to the convicted state's discretion. However, the binding requirement and the efficiency of the declaratory judgement by the Court of justice is to be observed. The logical way to achieve an effective implementation of declaratory judgements, is to repeal the legally binding national decision in violation of human rights. The law

246 ECtHR, Urteil vom 26.02.2004, G.v. Deutschland, Beschwerde Nr. 74969/01, Ziff. 64.
[Judgement of 26/02/2004, G.v. Germany, complaint No. 74969/01, clause 64.

247 Schaffarzik, Europäische Menschenrechte unter der Ägide des Bundesverfassungsgericht, in: Die öffentliche Verwaltung. Zeitschrift für öffentliches Recht und Verwaltungswissenschaft (2005), 860 (864). [European human rights under the aegis of the Federal Constitutional Court, in: The Public Administration. Magazine for Public Law and Administrative Science (2005), 860 (864).].

of state responsibility represents the fundamental basis of this obligation under international law. The obligation deriving from the compensation means that the guarantee under procedural law as per Art. 7 paragraph 1 of the Charter must be included in formal and substantive terms. The safeguarding of the procedural guarantee (the admissibility of the individual complaint and the associated declaratory judgement by the ECOWAS Court of Justice) has the purpose of ensuring the exercise of the plaintiff's substantive human rights. This institution of legal force does not preclude the obligation to repeal. The legal force is ensured in such a manner if the underlying national judgement does not infringe on the obligation under international law of the prosecuted Member State. The legally binding decisions by national courts of law are not sacrosanct based on these obligations by the state under international law.

b. Justification of the order to reinstate

The resumption of the original national proceedings in violation of human rights is an effective means of reparation. There are many reasons in favourof such an approach. First of all, the declaration by the Court of justice does not possess direct national executive power. As a result of the fact that the decisions by the Court do not have a direct penetrative effect regarding the national judgements in violation of human rights, the Court of justice does not have the competence to repeal the national judgement. Secondly, the national courts have a greater degree of factual proximity and can therefore better judge the concrete circumstances of the case which should lead to the effective implementation of the declaratory judgement. Moreover, the ECOWAS Court of Justice may not speculate with regard to the result of the original national proceedings. In fact, it is unthinkable that the judges in Abuja ask themselves the question: How would the proceeding have ended if the national violation by the Constitutional Court had not taken place? In other words: How would the national constitutional complaint have proceeded if the Constitutional Court had complied with the right to a fair trial provided for in Art. 7 Abs. 1 of the Charter? The ECOWAS Court of Justice cannot consider such questions in the declaratory judgement. It cannot therefore predict the answer.

The resumption of the original proceedings after the conviction of the Member State also provides practical reasons for justification. The national Constitutional Court is closer to the facts and can therefore judge the case better, while considering the main arguments the ECOWAS Court of Justice made. The initiation of the possibility to resume also takes the sovereignty of the sued Member State into consideration. Furthermore, the ECOWAS Court of Justice is, as a general rule, not a trial judge. The initiation of trial resumption in favour of the convicted plaintiff represents the logical solution of the comparison between *res judicata* and *restitutio in integrum*. The answer to the question regarding the result of the original national proceedings in violation of human rights can only be comprehensively answered by the Constitutional Court considering the salient points made by the ECOWAS Court of Justice. The resumption of the national complaint proceedings therefore offers the only way to fulfil the obligation of the prosecuted Member State as per the convention in the case of concluded violations.

3. Obligation to take preventative measures

This requires the convicted Member State to take all measures necessary to prevent a repetition of the criminal misconduct in future cases. The preventive obligations of the convicted Member State are owed in certain cases. Should the declaratory judgement e.g. show a structural deficit in the national organisation of courts, the defendant signatory state is subject to an obligation to take preventive measures.[248] The *guarantees of non-repetition of the wrongful act*[249] are seen by Arangio-Ruiz even as an *obligation of result.*[250] This view is accurate because the obligations under international law, especially in the area of human rights, possess an objective character. Beyond the case that was decided, the convicted member State is expected to take measures to prevent a repetition. The causes that could give rise to future offences are to be removed as a precautionary measure. In this context, ECtHR correctly pointed out in the Deweer case [251]:

248 Polakiewicz, Die Verpflichtung der Staaten aus den Urteilen des Europäischen Court of Law für Menschenrechte [The obligations by the states arising from the judgements by the European Court of Human Rights], 155.

249 Arangio-Ruiz, Second Report on State Responsibility, UN Doc. A/CN.4/425 (09/06/1989), § 148 ff.

250 Arangio-Ruiz, Second Report on State Responsibility, UN Doc. A/CN.4/425 (09/06/1989), § 157.

251 ECtHR, Urteil vom 27.2.1980, Nr. 6903/75 [judgement of 27/2/1980, no. 6903/75] – Deweer v. Belgien [Belgium] = EuGRZ 1980, 667.

« [A]u surplus, les paragraphes 1 et 2 de l'article 11 de la loi de 1945–1971 restent en vigueur [...], de sorte que qu'ils peuvent à chaque instant donner lieu à une application combinée comme dans le cas de M. Deweer. *Le principal problème soulevé par l'affaire demeure par conséquent posé; il dépasse la personne et les intérêts du requérant et de ses héritiers.* »[252]

A further reason for the obligation to take preventive measures is that the individual legal situation of the plaintiff is paramount in the declaratory judgement. The Court of justice rather postulates the misconduct of the Member State in the declaratory judgement. Therefore, the convicted signatory state must restore the legal situation of the plaintiff under international law, but must also take measures to prevent similar cases in the future. The Court of justice doesn't have to stipulate such follow-up measures in the tenor of the judgement. Taking into account the finding in the individual case, the obligation to take preventive general measures in future is activated.[253] The objective obligation stemming from the declaratory judgement is thereby finally affirmed.[254] In general, three types of preventive measures can be differentiated..[255] They involve the publication of the declaratory judgement and the announcement of the same to the national authorities. Moreover, the convicted Member State should introduce reforms designed to prevent similar violations in the future. As a last consequence of the declaratory judgement, it must be considered that instructions should be given to the enforcement authorities to take the

252 ECtHR, Urteil vom 27.2.1980, Nr. 6903/75, Ziff. 38[judgement of 27/2/1980, no. 6903/75, clause 38], Deweer v. Belgien [Belgium] = EuGRZ 1980, 667 (Hervorhebung des Verfassers) [(emphasis by the author)].

253 Polakiewicz, Die Verpflichtung der Staaten aus den Urteilen des Europäischen Court of Law für Menschenrechte [The obligations by the states arising from the judgements by the European Court of Human Rights], 153.

254 Ress, „Die Einzelfallbezogenheit" in der Rechtsprechung des Europäischen Gerichtshofs für Menschenrechte, in: Völkerrecht als Rechtsordnung – Internationale Gerichtsbarkeit – Menschenrechte, FS für H. Mosler [The relatedness of "the individual case" in the jurisdiction by the European Court of Human Rights, in: International law as a legal system – international jurisprudence – human rights, FS for H. Mosler] (1983), 719 (744).

255 Polakiewicz, Die Verpflichtung der Staaten aus den Urteilen des Europäischen Court of Law für Menschenrechte [The obligations by the states arising from the judgements by the European Court of Human Rights], 150 f.

declaratory judgement into account with regards to their areas of competence.[256]

The Member States not participating in the individual proceedings are excluded from the formal res judicata. Although the declaratory judgement has no effect regarding the judgement towards the Member States that are not part of the proceedings, the declaratory judgements by the ECOWAS Court of Justice have a regulatory character of the African Charter within the Community. The declaratory judgements raising fundamental normative questions of general importance, such as the prohibition of slavery, should be implemented by all Member States within their respective sovereign territories.

In conclusion, other Member States are factually bound by declaratory judgements. The Member States should be bound to the decisions by the Court of justice in the same way that they are bound to the instruments of the Community. Particularly because the regulation regarding the binding effect (Art. 15 paragraph 4 of the Amendment Agreement) makes no difference between the binding effect on the parties to the agreement participating and not participating in the proceedings. Due to this silence of the text, the legal effect must be deduced from general rules of international law. Moreover, the objective meaning of the regulation in Art. 15 paragraph 4 of the Amendment Agreement should be taken into account in the legal effect of the declaratory judgement. From the aforesaid it can thus be established: the declaratory judgement by the Court of justice does not establish a cross-case effect for the entire legal order of the Community according to the analogous interpretation of Art. 15 paragraph 4 of the Amendment Agreement.[257] Therefore, in principle, no legal obligation to implement the judgement arises for the signatory states that are not part of the proceedings. However, a declaratory judgement represents the current meaning of the African Charter for the entire legal order of the Community. Therefore, a quasi *erga-omnes*-effect is ascribed to the declaratory judgements.

---

256 Polakiewicz, Die Verpflichtung der Staaten aus den Urteilen des Europäischen Court of Law für Menschenrechte [The obligations by the states arising from the judgements by the European Court of Human Rights], 150.

257 Rohleder, Grundrechtsschutz im europäischen Mehrebenensystem [Protection of constitutional law in the European multi-level system], 230.

G. Justification for Breaching the Legal Force: Function to Close Loopholes

At this stage, the question must be asked of how the human rights competence of the ECOWAS Court of Justice can be explained. There are two fundamental justifications, namely the structural problems within the national law of some of the Member States (I) as well as the bias of the national courts in some of the cases (II). However, the human rights competence of the Court of justice is accompanied with several problems (III).

I. Entry Barriers for individual complaints according to national law

It must be pointed out upfront that the constitutional acknowledgement of the rule of law and the civil and human rights have become a reality in the process of democratisation.[258] Nevertheless, the rights and principles have yet to be implemented by the Constitutional Court. The constitutional regulations are faced, in particular, with a certain resistance by the state authorities.[259] That is because there is a long tradition of authoritarian regimes on the African continent with a concentration of state authorities in favour of a single executive.[260] The complete overview of the legal system of the ECOWAS Member States paints a colourful picture of the possibility of access to the constitutional complaint. On the one hand, there are Member States which permit constitutional complaints. On the other hand, there are Member States that impose strict access requirements. This, in turn, constitutes a contravention of the right to an effective com-

---

258 Du Bois de Gaudusson, Défense et Illustration du constitutionnalisme en Afrique après quinze ans de pratique du pouvoir, in: Renouveau du droit constitutionnel. Mélanges en l'honneur de Louis Favoreu, 609 (611).

259 Du Bois de Gaudusson, Défense et Illustration du constitutionnalisme en Afrique après quinze ans de pratique du pouvoir, in: Renouveau du droit constitutionnel. Mélanges en l'honneur de Louis Favoreu, 609 (617); Diop, La Justice constitutionnelle au Sénégal. Éssai sur l'evolution, les enjeux et les réformes d'un contre-pouvoir juridictionnel, 263.

260 Gonidec, Constitutionnalismes Africains, in: African journal of international and compara- tive Law (1996), 23 (43); Benedek, Durchsetzung von Rechten des Menschen und der Völker in Afrika auf regionaler und nationaler Ebene [Enforcing the rights of the individual and the peoples in Africa on a regional and national level], in: ZaöRV (1994), 150 (151).

plaint.[261] Lastly, there are signatory states who make access to the Constitutional Court or an equally legal instance possible but obstruct the actual realisation of this possibility.

The principle of subsidiarity in international law is based on the fundamental idea that the obligation to adhere to agreements under international law is first and foremost the task of the signatory states. In order to enforce the rights in the African Charter, the signatory states represent the original addressees of such obligations.[262] International law entrusts, so to speak, the respective contracting party with the adherence to these obligations. Since the signatory states have a priority position regarding the adherence to the obligations under international law, they must provide for national measures and procedures that lead to the adherence of these obligations. Only once it has been determined that a signatory state cannot fulfil or has violated its obligation is the international instance called upon, as a subsidiary remedy, by which to enforce international law.

What does it mean when the signatory state cannot fulfil its obligation? This means that the state has not taken measures to fulfil its obligations under international law. Alternatively, the signatory state has taken such measures but they turn out to be insufficient.

Within the ECOWAS legal system, the task of monitoring the adherence to the African Charter falls directly on the ECOWAS Court of Justice without the need for national legal remedies having to have been exhausted.[263] How can the derogation of the general practice of international law be explained within the ECOWAS human rights protection? There are several reasons for this: on the one hand, human rights complaints are either not admissible before national courts or they are admissible, but the requirements for admissibility are strict.[264] On the other hand, the direct admissibility of the individual complaint is to be remedied by the principle of effective legal protection.

Among the signatory states that allow constitutional complaints without such strict admissibility requirements is, first of all, Benin (Art. 122 of the

---

261 Nicaise, Jurisprudence constitutionnelle, in: Afrilex N°4, 353 (359), available at http:// cerdradi.u-bordeaux4.fr/la-revue-afrilex.html (last accesses on 20/01/2015).

262 Breuer, Staatshaftung für judikatives Unrecht, 3.

263 Onoria, The African Commission on Human and Peoples' Rights and the exhaustion of local remedies under the African Charter, in: African Human Rights Law (2003), 1 (3).

264 Österdahl, Implementing Human Rights in Africa. The African Commission on Human and Peoples' Rights and Individual Communications, 173.

Constitution of Benin). With regard to such Member States, it can be presumed that they have theoretically fulfilled their procedural legal obligation to protect under Art. 7 paragraph 1 of the Charter. However, in many other Member States, such as Togo for example, individual constitutional complaints are strictly inadmissible. It will be discussed in the following how the inadmissibility of the constitutional complaint (1) and the strict requirements for the individual constitutional complaint (2) justify the direct constitutional role of the ECOWAS Court of Justice. This legal situation forms the basis ofthe role of the ECOWAS Court of Justice as a guarantor of effective legal protection in West African States (3).

1. Inadmissibility of a national human rights complaint

First of all, we will look at the Member States that do not allow an individual constitutional complaint. The primary obligation to adhere to human rights and fundamental freedoms is provided for by the Member States of the ECOWAS Community. It is therefore necessary that the Member States open up constitutional guarantees to their citizens in order to fulfil this obligation. It is regrettable that many Member States do not allow individual constitutional complaints access to the Constitutional Court. Art. 99 of the Togolese Constitution stipulates:

> « La Cour constitutionnelle est la plus haute juridiction en matière constitutionnelle. Elle est juge de la constitutionnalité de la loi et elle garantit les droits fondamentaux de la personne humaine et les libertés publiques. Elle est l'organe régulateur du fonctionnement des institutions et de l'activité des pouvoirs publics ».

From a substantive point of view, this regulation sufficiently guarantees individual rights and fundamental freedoms. With this constitutional regulation, it is certain that the Togolese Constitution guarantees human rights and that the Constitutional Court monitors the fundamental rights and freedoms of the people. However, neither in the constitution nor in the supplementary constitutional act[265] is there any reference to how citizens can legally exercise the rights guaranteed under the constitution. In terms of competence, the question must be asked as to whether constitutional law allows constitutional complaints by natural and legal persons directly before the constitutional court as the Constitutional Court represents the

265 See Art. 27 to 32 of the *Loi Organique* (Togo) N°2004–004 of 01/03/2004.

natural guardian of fundamental freedoms.[266] However, a direct constitutional complaint by natural and legal persons to the Constitutional Court is, on closer inspection of the constitutional regulations and the rules of procedure of the Constitutional Court, not admissible. This means that whilst human rights are sufficiently guaranteed in the constitution, there are no procedural guarantees to realise these rights. Therefore, the Togolese Constitutional Court has declared a complaint by members of parliament in the initial proceedings to be inadmissible. Furthermore, the court confirms that there are no legal remedies against its judgements:

> « Qu'aucune autorité civile ou militaire, qu'aucune institution, fut-elle internationale, ne peut s'opposer à une décision de la Cour».[267]

These findings already represent an infringement against the procedural guarantee as per Art. 7 paragraph 1 of the African Charter on Human and Peoples' Rights.[268] The only possibility to find a judicial guarantee of individual human rights in the Togolese constitutional system is the co-called procedure of *Exception d'inconstitutionnalité.*[269] This procedure only affects the complaint with regard to the unconstitutionality of a law. Even in this case, natural persons are not directly admissible before the Constitutional Court with regard to a complaint. On the contrary, they must prove the objection of unconstitutionality of the act before the national courts. The national courts alone are directly entitled to make submissions for the procedure *Exception d'inconstitutionnalité* before the Constitutional Court. Moreover, another question arises concerning which constitutional guarantee applies if the act has entered into force in a constitutional manner but is used by legal practitioners and authorities in an unconstitutional manner. The constitution is quiet on this point. Therefore, citizens are powerless against much injustice by the judiciary and against the unconsti-

266 Nicaise, Jurisprudence constitutionnelle, in: Afrilex N°4, 353 (359), Available at http:// cerdradi.u-bordeaux4.fr/la-revue-afrilex.html (last accessed on 20/01/2015).

267 Cour constitutionnelle du Togo, Décision N°E-002/2011 vom 22. June 2011, available at: http://www.courconstitutionnelle.tg/ (last accessed on 22/06/2015).

268 Germelmann, Das rechtliche Gehör vor Gericht im europäischen Recht, 29.

269 Art. 104 paragr. 6 Constitution of Togo of 14 October 1992; Art. 96 paragr. 4 Constitution of Guinea of 07 May 2010; Art. 96 Constitution of Ivory Coast of 23 July 2000. Vgl. Abebe, Towards more liberal standing rules to enforce constitutional rights in Ethiopia, in: African Human Rights Law (2010), 407 (418).

tutional behaviour of the executive.[270] Thus, just to take the case of Togo, in February 2005, once Faure Gnassingbé[271] came to power, many human rights violations and constitutional infractions were determined, but as a constitutional judge wrote: the Constitutional Court could not take action in this case, as there was no possibility in the constitutional system for the Constitutional Court to make an official decision.[272]

2. Strict prerequisites for admissibility for the human rights complaint

There are also constitutional systems which provide for the possibility of a constitutional complaint. The prerequisites are, however, so selective that theyrarely lead to an effective constitutional guarantee.[273] It is, however, well-known that the Constitutional Court represents a „rampart“ of fundamental rights in a democratic system.[274] Especially for this reason, a restriction of the prerequisite of admissibility before Constitutional Courts is, at the same time, an impairment of individual human rights and fundamental freedoms. Indeed, e.g. the constitutional system of Togo allows the constitutional complaint but also requires the meeting of conditions, making its realisation more difficult [sic].[275] The legal situation constitutes a serious and ongoing violation of the constitutional guarantee with regard to the rights in the African Charter because the constitutional complaint counts as one of the procedural guarantees. Unfortunately, this is not the case in some Member States within the ECOWAS legal system. Acc. to Art. 152 of the Constitution of Burkina Faso, e.g., those who are entitled

270 Onoria, The African Commission on Human and Peoples' Rights and the exhaustion of local remedies under the African Charter, in: African Human Rights Law (2003), 1 (21).

271 The current State President of Togo.

272 Maman-Sani, Vacance de la présidence de la République: la constitution togolaise à l'épreuve des faits, in: Revue nigérienne de droit (2006), 11 (28).

273 Koussetogue Koude, Peut-on à bon droit parler d'une conception africaine des droits de l'homme?, in: Revue Trimestrielle des Droits de l'Homme (2005), 539 (541).

274 Diop, La justice constitutionnelle au Sénégal. Éssai sur l'evolution, les enjeux et les réfor- mes d'un contre-pouvoir juridictionnel, 254.

275 Benedek, Durchsetzung von Rechten des Menschen und der Völker in Afrika auf regionaler und nationaler Level [Enforcing the rights of the individual and the peoples in Africa on a regional and national level], in: ZaöRV (1994), 150 (151).

to submit a complaint to the Constitutional Court are stipulated rather restrictively:

> « Le Conseil constitutionnel est saisi par le Président du Faso, le Premier Ministre, le Présent de l'Assemblée Nationale, et un cinquième (1/5) au moins des membres de l'Assemblée Na- tionale ».[276]

These prerequisites for admission represent a limitation of the right to an effective complaint.[277] This should be corrected at ECOWAS-level particularly because it does not represent a "*self-executing*" instrument under international law.[278] In order to allow implementation at a national level, the constitutional systems of the Member States recognise the African Charter as a firm component of the *bloc de constitutionnalité.*[279] Nevertheless, one must wait and see how those seeking justice will be able to exercise the provisions of the African Charta in court.[280]

---

276 The requirements have been relatively more favourable under the new constitution after the completion of the first edition of this book. See Art. 157 of the Loi Constitutionnelle N°072-2015/CNT amending the Constitution of Burkina Faso.

277 Onoria, The African Commission on Human and Peoples' Rights and the exhaustion of local remedies under the African Charter, in: African Human Rights Law (2003), 1 (21).

278 Flauss, L'effectivité de la Charte Africaine des Droits de l'Homme et des Peuples dans l'or- dre juridiques des Etats Parties contractantes: Bilan et Perspectives, in: Flauss/Lambert-Abdelgawad (Publ.), L'application nationale de la Charte africaine des droits de l'homme et des peuples, 247 (249).

279 Flauss, L'effectivité de la Charte Africaine des Droits de l'Homme et des Peuples dans l'or- dre juridiques des Etats Parties contractantes: Bilan et Perspectives, in: Flauss/Lambert-Abdelgawad (Publ.), L'application nationale de la Charte africaine des droits de l'homme et des peuples, 247 (248).

280 Flauss, L'effectivité de la Charte Africaine des Droits de l'Homme et des Peuples dans l'ordre juridiques des Etats Parties contractantes: Bilan et Perspectives, in: Flauss/Lambert-Abdelgawad (Publ.), L'application nationale de la Charte africaine des droits de l'homme et des peuples, 247 (249).

3. The ECOWAS Court of Justice as guarantor of the effective protection of human rights

As shown in the introduction of the present paper, the ECOWAS Court of Justice did not originally constitute a human rights court.[281] The settling of human rights disputes at continental level was reserved for other institutions. The signatory states of the Charter became aware that the actual improvements of the human rights situation at continental level require procedural mechanisms.[282] In order to specify this finding, two institutions were installed. The African Charter on Human Rights and Peoples' Rights was adopted in 1981. Art. 1 prescribes the signatory states with the primary obligation to observe human rights as stipulated in the Charter. The organs of the convention put in place to monitor the contractual obligations are the African Commission as well as the African Court on Human and People´sRights.[283] In principle, the African Court on Human Rights and Peoples' Rights embodies the natural monitoring organ in regards to the guaranteed human rights in the African Charter. This Court , in particular, has the authority to determine a human rights violation on application by individual complainants and to order corrective measures. The judgement of the African Court develops a binding effect for the signatory states.

The African Commission for Human Rights and Peoples' Rights was established acc. to the instructions in Art. 30 of the Charter. Therefore, the doctrine describes the Commission as the primary judiciary body on the African continent.[284] Regarding its mandate, the Commission avails of an extensive authority. According to the regulation in Art. 45 paragraph 2 of the Charter, the following subjects of reference are bestowed on the Commission: the promotion of human rights and peoples' rights; protection of

---

281 Ebobrah, A rights-protection goldmine or a waiting volcanic eruption? Competence of, and access to, the human rights jurisdiction of the ECOWAS Community Court of Justice, in: African Human Rights Law Journal (2007), 307 (312); Ndiaye, La protection des droits de l'homme par la Cour de justice de la CEDEAO, Mémoire de Master II, Université Montesquieux Bordeaux IV, 14.

282 Gumedze, Bringing communication before the African Commission on Human Rights and Peoples' Rights, in: African Human Rights Law Journal (2003), 118 (128).

283 Österdahl, Implementing Human Rights in Africa. The African Commission on Human and Peoples' Rights and Individual Communications, 177.

284 Ebobrah, Legitimacy and feasibility of human rights realisation through regional economic communities in Africa: the case of ECOWAS, 85; Elsheikh, The future relationship between the African Court and the African Commission, in: African Human Rights Law Journal (2002), 252 (253).

human rights and peoples' rights; interpretation of the regulations in the Charter on request by a state party, an organ of the then OAU (Organisation of African Unity) or of an organisation recognised by the OAU. This list and sequence clarify which weight is laid on human rights regarding the Commission's function. In addition, the Commission represents an investigative Commission (Art. 45 paragraph 1 of the Charter). Regarding the procedure before the Commission, it must be stated that the complaint by a state was preferred to the individual complaint. Generally, the signatory states may submit complaints directly to the Commission (Art. 49 of the Charter). Regarding the individual complaint before the Commission, one must use the interpretation of Art. 55 paragraph 1 as there is no clear definition for the individual complaint according to the wording of the regulation. Rather, they are recorded in Art. 55 paragraph 1 of the Charter as other "notifications". On the other hand, individual complaints are not directly admissible before the Commission. The possibility of access for individual complaints has been restricted by the fact that the chairperson of the Commission must, with regard to submitted notifications, obtain the votes of the members of the Commission before each session. The members of the Commission then decide with an absolute majority of votes (Art. 55 of the Charter). The fundamental prerequisite for this is the exhaustion of the national legal procedures (Art. 56 paragraph 5 of the Charter). With regard to the binding effect, it must be pointed out that the decisions are not binding (Art. 59 of the Charter). However, the Commission has slowly developed recommendations.[285]

The human rights mission by the Commission was apparently not sufficient.[286] Not only were the possibilities of submission limited to the persons entitled to complain, but the decisions by the Commission were also not binding. Therefore, the signatory states of the organisation of the African Union adopted an Additional Protocol to the Charter with regard to the African Court on Human and Peoples' Rights in the year 1998. This took effect in January 2004. This allowed the first judges of the African Court on Human and Peoples' Rights to take office.[287] In July 2004, it had

285 Ebobrah, Legitimacy and feasibility of human rights realisation through regional economic communities in Africa: the case of ECOWAS, 85.

286 Ebobrah, Legitimacy and feasibility of human rights realisation through regional economic communities in Africa: the case of ECOWAS, 87; Wachira, African Court on Human Rights and Peoples' Rights: Ten years on and still no justice, 8.

287 Ebobrah, Legitimacy and feasibility of human rights realisation through regional economic communities in Africa: the case of ECOWAS, 87.

been decided that the African Court on Human and Peoples' Rights should become part of the African Court of Justice.[288] This proposal was adopted by the signatory states with the passing of an Additional Protocol regarding theAfrican Court of Justice in 2009.[289] However, the Protocol regarding the African Court of Justice has developed the control system at a continental level very carefully, so that the rights embedded in the Charter in favour of the individual can hardly be realised. Indeed, a separate declaration of submission by the signatory states is required for the admissibility of the individual complaint. In this context, Art. 8 paragraph 3 of Additional Protocol (2009) stipulates:

> « Tout Etat partie, au moment de la signature ou du dépôt de son instrument de ratification ou d'adhésion, ou à tout autre période après l'entrée en vigueur du Protocole peut faire une dé- claration acceptant la compétence de la Cour pour recevoir les requêtes énoncées à l'article 30 (f) et concernant un Etat partie qui n'a pas fait cette déclaration».
>
> "Any Member State may, at the time of signature or when depositing its instrument of ratifi- cation or accession, or at any time thereafter, make a declaration accepting the competence of the Court to receive cases under Article 30 (f) involving a State which has not made such a declaration."

It is hereby confirmed that individual complaints are not automatically admissible before the African Court of Justice (human rights section). Therefore, the new African Court of Justice does not automatically have jurisdiction over individual complaints.[290] The individual complain arguing an infringement of the Charter is only admissible if the Member State con-

---

288 Kindiki, The Proposed Integration of the African Court of Justice and the African Court on Human and Peoples' Rights: Legal difficulties and merits, in: African Journal of International and Comparative Law (2007–2009), 138 (138); Ipsen, Völkerrecht [International Law], 6. edition, § 7, Rn. 13; Dujardin, La Cour Africaine de Justice et des Droits de l'Homme: Un Projet de fusion opportune et progressiste des juridictions panafricaines par l'Union Africaine, in: Revue Juridique et Politique (2007), 511 (513).

289 The original designation in both official languages is: « Protocole portant Statut de la Cour Africaine de Justice et des Droits de L'Homme » or "Protocole in the Statute of the African Court of Justice and Human Right".

290 Mubiala, L'accès de l'Individu à la Cour Africaine des Droits de l'Homme et des Peuples, in: Promoting Justice, Human Rights and Conflicts Resolution through international Law (2007), 369 (371).

cerned has made a particular declaration.[291] According to this declaration, the signatory state must acknowledge the competence of the African Court of Justice in this regard. Without this declaration of competence, individual complaints are rejected as inadmissible by the Court of Justice. Article 30 (f) of this Protocol confirms the conditional requirements for the authority on individual complaints as follows:

> « Les entités suivantes ont également qualité pour saisir la Cour de toute violation d'un droit garanti par la Charte africaine des droits de l'Homme et des peuples, par la Charte africaine des droits et du bien-être de l'enfant, le Protocole à la Charte africaine des droits de l'homme et des peuples relatif aux droits de a femme en Afrique ou par tout autre instrument juridique pertinent relatif aux droits de l'homme, auxquels sont parties les Etats concernés [...] (f) les personnes physiques et les organisations non-gouvernementales accréditées auprès de l'Union ou de ses organes ou institution, sous réserve des dispositions de l'article 8 du protocole »

> "The following entities shall also be entitled to submit cases to the Court on any violation of a right guaranteed by the African Charter, by the Charter on the Rights and Welfare of the Child, the Protocol to the African Charter on Human and Peoples Rights on Rights of Women in Africa, or any other legal instrument relevant to human rights ratified by States Parties concerned [...] (f) Individual or relevant Non-Governmental Organisations accredited to the African Union or to its organs, subject to the provisions of Article 8 of the Protocol".

A condition of this sort does not create an easy situation for the individual complainant because it cannot be expected that all Member States readily submit this necessary declaration of submission in due time.[292] Indeed, the signatory states had agreed on the idea of a Court on Human Rights at a continental level. They are, however, not prepared to submit the necessary

291 Olinga, Regard sur le Premier Arrêt de la Cour Africaine des Droits de l'Homme et des Peuples, Cour africaine des droits de l'homme et des peuples, Michelot Yogogombaye c. Sénégal, 15 décembre 2009, in: Revue Trimestrielle des Droits de l'Homme (2010), 749 (752).

292 Nach derzeitigem Ratifizierungsstand haben nur 16 Vertragsstaaten das Protokoll über den Gerichtshof ratifiziert, Ratifizierungsstand [According to the current ratification status, only 16 signatory states have ratified the Protocol regarding the Court of Law], ratification status available at: http://www.african-court.org/fr/ (last accessed on 26/08/2015).

declaration.[293] Subsequently, the African Court of Justice has little opportunity to examine the legal matter submitted to it in detail.[294] As a result, the individual complaints by persons living in the territory are systematically declared inadmissible by the African Court of Justice if the provisions as per Art. 8 i. c. w. Art. 30 of the Additional Protocol (2009) are not met.[295] The regional legal process within the ECOWAS Community therefore represents the guarantor of effective legal protection. Based on the futility on a continental as well as national level, the task of monitoring the Charter falls to the ECOWAS Court of Justice. The admissibility of the individual complaint before the ECOWAS Court of Justice should fulfil the requirements of the reason of fairness in Art. 7 paragraph 1 of the African Charter.

It can, from the aforementioned, be established that only the ECOWAS Court of Justice can guarantee an effective protection of human rights for the persons living in the territory of the Community. After reviewing the constitutional systems of the Member States it can be deduced that the possibility for theindividual complaint to be submitted to the ECOWAS Court of Justice can be justified by a deficient legal protection in most member States.[296] It can be deduced from this that the ECOWAS Court of Justice has a supranational role as a Constitutional Court. The ECOWAS acts as a guarantor due to the failure of the national legal protection system. For, as shown in the introduction (Chapter 1), the goal of the Community is, the safeguarding of the human rights guaranteed in the Charter within the legal system of the Community. Hence, the principle of effective legal protection is being applied. This principle is based on the idea that the complainant is given the opportunity to raise attention to his rights. However, if it is established that the national procedure does not provide him with sufficient legal remedies, as in the case of the Togolese constitutional code of procedure, through which the constitutional guarantees cannot be safeguarded by way of a constitutional complaint, the direct admissibility of the individual complaint at Community level is justified.

293 O'Shea, A critical reflection on the proposed African Court on Human and Peoples' Rights, in: African Human Rights Law Journal (2001), 285 (287).
294 Bhoke, Judgement in the First Case before the African Court on Human and Peoples' Rights a Missed Opportunity or a Mockery of International Law in Africa?, in: Journal of African and International Law (2010), 187 (228).
295 Barsac, La Cour africaine de Justice et des droits de l'homme, 42.
296 Österdahl, Implementing Human Rights in Africa. The African Commission on Human and Peoples' Rights and Individual Communications, 173.

The same applies if the national legal system formally provides constitutional guarantees but if these are not carried out on a fair basis (case Koraou vs Niger). However, the Court of justice is not authorised to act *ex-officio*. According to the previous basis of authority, an *ex-officio*-action would be seen as a transgression of competence. It can only be employed on application. This prerequisite adheres to the principle *nullo actore, nullus iudex* (i.e. if there is no plaintiff, there is no judge).

In conclusion, it appears that the transfer of the human rights competence to the ECOWAS Court of Justice is based on the fact that, on the one hand, there are obstacles at a continental level[297] and, on the other hand, the guarantee of the human rights enshrined in the Charter is in jeopardy.[298]

The disregard of the constitutional state and the contempt for human rights and fundamental rights within national legal systems of the Member States was the reason for an extension of the competence of the ECOWAS Court of Justice in 2005. In the preamble of the Protocol A/SP.1/01/05 it is expressly pointed out that the extension of the responsibility of the Court of Law is meant to serve the removal of the obstacle to realise the goals of the Community. These goals mainly include the effective guarantee of the rights in the African Charter and the democratic principles within the entire system of the Community. The Court of justice embodies the assurance of this guarantee and the safeguarding of the human rights recognised in the Charter. The Court of justice is, so to speak, the guardian of the African Charter on Human Rights and peoples' Rights within the ECOWAS legal system. The only problem is that, in terms of competence, the relationship between the ECOWAS Court of Justice and the African Court of Justice is not clearly defined.[299]

297 Wachira, African Court on Human Rights and People's Rights: Ten years on and still no justice, 15.

298 Onoria, *The Locus Standi* of Individual and Non-State Entities before Regional Economic Integration Judicial Bodies in Africa, in: Journal of African and International Law (2010), 91 (95).

299 Barsac, La Cour africaine de justice et des droits de l'homme, 46.

II. Possible Conflict of Interest of the Constitutional Court of a Member State

The procedural guarantees represent a positive obligation by the signatory states (2). It is thereby left up to the signatory states on how they would like to meet their obligations with regard to the procedural guarantees. However, it can be gathered from the African Charter that the national courts must be organised in such a way that structural as well as organisational problems should not arise. However, it can be gleaned from an examination of the legal systems of the ECOWAS Member States that there is a certain prejudice of the judges. Therefore, the legal criteria of a judges' bias must be focused on more closely (1).

1. Elements of the complaint of a conflicted court

The constitutional regulations guarantee the independence of the constitutional judges with regard to other organs of the state for exemple acc. to Art. 102 of the Togolese Constitution:

> « Les membres de la Cour Constitutionnelle, pendant la durée de leur mandat, ne peuvent être poursuivis ou arrêtés sans autorisation de la Cour Constitutionnelle sauf les cas de fragrant délit. Dans ce cas, le Président de la Cour Constitutionnelle doit être saisi immédiatement et au plus tard dans les quarante-huit heures. »

Although the constitutional regulations guarantee the independence of the constitutional judges, it cannot be excluded that the constitutional judges may issue biased judgements based on personal interests. This can be explained: the independence of the judges is the objective aspect regarding the performance of official duties. There is, however, a subjective aspect, namely the impartiality of the judges. The impartiality of the judges must be strictly differentiated from the independence. There are many cases regarding the jurisprudence of Member States which leave no doubt as to the diffidence of the judges in general and that of constitutional judges in particular.[300] Within the francophone African judicial area, the Constitu-

300 Tambedou, De l'indépendance du Pouvoir Judiciaire au Sénégal, in: Revue Juridique et Politique (2008), 271 (276).

tional Court is regarded as the "chien de garde"[301] of the constitution and the fundamental freedoms as enshrined in it. However, with regard to the performance of official duties, a certain proximity of the constitutional judges to politics can be noted.[302] This fact can be established by the interference of the executive in the functioning and jurisdiction of the constitutional courts.[303] The suspicion becomes blatant when the Constitutional Court contributes to a challenge of the guarantee of the constitution. An example of a definitive failure of its office was delivered by the Togolese Constitutional Court in 2005 during the transfer of power after the death of the State President .[304] Bias represents a justified objection to the official performance of the judges in the constitutional process. This is always the case when objective facts are established that could lead a rationally thinking individual to doubt the impartiality and objectivity of the judges.[305] Furthermore, it should be demonstrated that the judicature in general, and the jurisdiction of national constitutional courts in particular, is under political pressure at a national level. Due to the special task of the courts, especially the constitutional courts, compliance with the law is a fundamental prerequisite for an impartial court when enforcing human rights.

---

301 Koupokpa, La perte du mandat par un parlementaire pour cause de démission ou de l'exclu- sion de son parti en cours de législature en Afrique noire francophone, in: Revue Togolaise des Sciences Juridiques (2013), 65 (78).

302 Ahadzi-Nonou, Les nouvelles tendances du constitutionalisme africain, in: Afrique Juri- dique et Politique (2002), 35 (43); Diop, La justice constitutionnelle au Sénégal. Éssai sur l'evolu- tion, les enjeux et les réformes d'un contre-pouvoir juridictionnel, 263.

303 Tambedou, De l'indépendance du Pouvoir Judiciaire au Sénégal, in: Revue Juridique et Politique (2008), 271 (276).

304 Maman-Sani, Vacance de la présidence de la République: la constitution togolaise à l'épreuve des faits, in: Revue nigérienne de droit, N°09 décembre 2006, 11 (28); Kokoroko, L'ap- port de la Jurisprudence constitutionnelle africaine à la consolidation des acquis démocratiques, in: Revue Béninoise des sciences juridiques et administratives (2007), 85 (95); Kessougbo, La Cour constitutionnelle togolaise et la régulation de la démocratie au Togo, in: Revue Béninoise des sciences juridiques et administratives (2005), 59 (96).

305 Koupokpa, L'indépendance de la Cour de justice de la CEDEAO, Communication donnée au colloque international de Lomé, organisé par le Centre de Droit Public de Lomé et le départe- ment de Droit administratif de la Faculté de Droit de L'Université de Gand (02.03.2012), Lomé, 4; Decaux/Imbert/Pettiti, La convention Européenne des Droits de l'Homme, Commentaire article par article, Art. 6, 261; Grabenwarter, Europäische Menschenrechtskonvention [European Human Rights Convention], 4. edition, § 24, Rn. 45; Matscher, Der Gerichtsbegriff der EMRK [The concept of a court by the ECHR], in: FS Baumgärtel, 363 (376).

Even though it is recognised that the filing of a suit before international courts is subject to the exhaustion of all national legal remedies, this can be justified by the principle of subsidiarity to the international complaint procedure. However, adherence to the principle of subsidiarity in the West African context is currently problematic when it comes to the the guarantee of the constitutional courts as a civil right as national judges in many countries tend to render judgements in favour of the most powerful political player, be it an individual or a state body, such as the executive in some cases (The case Korau vs Niger or the case Fall Ameganvi vs Togo).

This could hinder the neutrality or impartial jurisdiction, as shown by the decision of the Togolese Constitutional Court. Voices in literature quite rightly point out that the decisions rendered by the constitutional courts in the African legal system are in some cases "orientated", biased or erring in law.[306] This bias by the national judges, which, without fail, leads to a threat to the protection of human rights, must be removed by the guardian of the regional protection of human rights. The ECOWAS Court of justice has determined the right to a fair trial regarding initial proceedings. It must be pointed out that the ECOWAS signatory states have undertaken the process of democratisation since the 1990s. This means that the principle of the rule of law and the adherence to fundamental freedoms by governmental authorities is in need of a legal culture. This can only be achieved if a functioning judicial system exists. Currently, the executive is struggling to enforce the principles of the rule of law. This is clearly because the principle of the separation of powers is hardly ever adhered to. The executive tries to impose a certain dominance in the constitutional system of the state.[307] The violation of the principle of separation of powers leads to a situation whereby the judicial power is exposed to pressure by the executive. The fragility of new democracies can be noted, in particular, in this factual dependency of the jurisdiction.

In conclusion, it can be noted that there are, on the one hand, structural problems in the procedural orders of Member States as a sign of a deficit of legal protection within the signatory states. At the same time, these structural problems represent an obstacle to an effective protection of human rights within national law. This situation justifies the admissibility of a di-

306 Adeloui, L'autorité de la chose jugée par les juridictions constitutionnelles en Afrique, in: Revue Togolaise des Sciences Juridiques (2012), 54 (73, 75).

307 Kessougbo, La Cour constitutionnelle togolaise et la régulation de la démocratie au Togo, in: Revue Béninoise des sciences juridiques et administratives (2005), 59 (96).

rect human rights complaint before the ECOWAS Court of Justice. On the other hand, the declaration of competence of the African Court on Human Rights as an admissibility requirement constitutes a serious obstacle at continental level.

2. Conflicted judges as a violation of the positive obligation of the Member State

Up til now, the State has been regarded as the violating party of the guaranteed human rights in the Charter. With the positive obligation of the Member State, the question is addressed in which respect the Member State is to be viewed as the guarantor of human rights. The violation of this obligation by the State can only be measured with this in mind. It is self-evident that the positive obligation is to be understood as the obligation by the signatory states to take measures to realise the recognised human rights. According to Art. 1 of the Charter:

> « Les Etats membres de l'Organisation de l'Unité Africaine, partie á la présente Charte, re- connaissent les droits, devoirs et libertés énoncés dans cette Charte et s´engagent á adopter des mesures législatives ou autres pour les appliquer ».
>
> "The Member States of the Organisation of African Unity parties to the present Charter shall recognize the rights, duties and freedom enshrined in this Charter and shall undertake to adopt legislative or other measures to give effect to them."

The obligation laid out in the provisions is a primary obligation under international law. The signatory states have a positive duty to realise these rights because the adherence to the contractual rights is to be regarded primarily as the task of the individual contracting states. Every signatory state shall take national measures to achieve this contractual goal. The national judicial guarantee of the aforementioned human rights comes into consideration. Only if this guarantee fails at a state level can the international guarantee be considered as an alternative. The international protective organ materialises the collective measure mutually provided for by the contracting states in order to close the deficit at a national level. The procedural guarantee is seen as the minimum in respect of the material legal guarantee. In other words: The infringement of material human rights is eliminated by the procedural guarantee.[308] Thus, procedural warranties help in implementing substantive rights. Through the procedural guarantee, it is up to the human rights entities to have the violation of their rights examined by an impartial court.

The state must take positive and recognisable measures which must serve the independence of the control authorities. In this sense, the procedural guarantees are taken into account in addition to the substantive rights. In total, the contractual state carries two positive protective obligations: substantive protective duties and procedural protective duties. Only in the procedural guarantee can the right to an impartial trial be realised.

However, it must be pointed out that the judicial power exercised by theECOWAS Court of Justice entails several problems.

III. Foreseeable problems of the ECOWAS jurisdiction

Here, the question must be asked whether problems with the jurisprudence in convicted member State may arise that are caused by the human rights jurisdiction of the Communal Court. In the following, a comparison of the national legal certainty and the equity under international law is demonstrated (1). Nonetheless, the judicial power exercised by the ECOWAS Court of Justice could entail some problems (2). These can only be resolved if a dialogue between the two legal systems can be established (3).

1. Challenge to legal certainty

The suggested resumption of the national initial proceedings based on a superseding legal effect causes tension between the legal certainty and the correct decision. As discussed, judgements by a constitutional court develop an effect with regard to the facts and the design. The design effect causes a legal situation for the parties to the proceedings or in favour of third parties that should be ensured by principles of a constitutional state: This is the principle of legal certainty. This results in the right of protection of the confidence of third parties. The prohibition of repealing constitutional judgements has the advantage of securing this legal protection. The role of

308 Dröge, Positive Verpflichtungen der Staaten in der Europäischen Menschenrechtskonven tion [Positive obligations of the states within the European Human Rights Convention], 61.

the international instance consists, however, in ensuring the accuracy and correctness of the occurrence of national legal acts such as judicial decisions. A decision that is taken after taking the human rights standards into account should be given preference compared to the decision in violation of human rights because fairness and justice have more weight than legal certainty. The legal certainty which follows from a misjudgement in constitutional proceedings is in turn a threat to legal peace and thus legal certainty because, if citizens no longer have confidence in the justice system, they will go another route, namely political unrest.

This situation would in turn be an obstacle in ensuring peace.

As a result, the correction by the ECOWAS Court of Justice of a constitutional court decision which violates human rights is preferable in order to ensure legal peace within the entire constitutional system of the Community. Whoever benefitted under national law from the contravention of the convention should not be better off than the individual complainant at an international law level. The rights of the successful individual complainant are more deserving of protection than those of the third party in the initial proceedings. From a justice point of view, the immutability of the legal force leads to non-acceptable situations, in the face of gross procedural injustice. Moreover, the exceptional overcoming of the legal effect due to gross procedural injustice serves both justice as well as legal certainty. The resumption, especially of such decisions which produce obvious injustice within the national legal system, constitute definitive legal certainty.

2. Overburdening of the Court of Justice and proposed solutions

In view of a population density of approx. 300 million inhabitants[309], the seven judges (in Abuja, Nigeria) are hardly able to guarantee the right to a fair trial within a reasonable period (Art. 7 paragraph 1 of the African Charter) if the lodging of regional individual complaints before the ECOWAS Court of Justice would not be subject to the prior national exhaustion of legal remedies. There is, however, the possibility to anticipate such problems. The possible alternative solutions may be realised from the perspective of the Court of justice (a) as well as from the perspective of the Member States (b).

309 In addition, see http://news.abidjan.net/h/426775.html (last accessed on 25/02/2015).

a. Landmark and pilot judgments as a possible solution

There are various possibilities of how a quasi-constitutional function could be assigned to the Court .

The function of the ECOWAS Court of Justice regarding the setting of principles: It can be determined from the preamble of Protocol A/PS. 1/01/05 that the admissibility of the individual human rights complaint has a main objective and a secondary objective. It is the main objective that the Court of justice should guard the adherence to human rights in its jurisdiction. The performance of this task is in the general interest of the Community because the realisationof the integration process and the unified adherence to international obligations of the Member States can only be achieved if the regional Court of justice is able to ensure a unified interpretation and application of the African Charter. There are many sections in the Community Agreement where in the least the commitment of the Community to the Charter and the democratic principles are expressed (Preamble of the Amendment Agreement).

The secondary objective is to grant the possibility of effective legal protection to every citizen through a direct human rights complaint at a regional level. The realisation of the secondary objective serves the main objective (in the general interest of the Community). For these reasons, the National Constitutional Courts consult the principles emerging from the ECOWAS Court of Justice in addition to their own jurisdiction. This consultation of the human rights principles from the ECOWAS Court of Justice in the constitutional jurisdiction should serve the objective to strengthen the ECOWAS-standards in all signatory states. In this context, two possibilities from the operative practice of the ECtHR could contribute to the relief of the Court of justice . Namely, the passing of landmark judgments and of pilot judgments.

The Court of justice can make landmark judgments. These must be adhered to by the National courts because the decisions of the Court are always based on the most current status of the Charter's development. The signatory states are bound by the Charter in the same way as they are bound to the decisions by the Court of justice in this respect. Now the question must be asked: How do legal practitioners in Member States know that a certain decision by the Court of justice is a landmark judgment? There are criteria with regards to this that may usually be of help when it comes to their identification. This concerns namely the legal question, and the Court 's answer to this question – this answer must be a counter-position regarding the same question in previous case law with regard to the same question –, the time and the main reasons for the decision. Or behaviour that the Court of justice would have declared compatible with the African Charter, might be declared by it incompatible at a later point in time. The opposite is also possible. This modus operandi at least takes the further development of the understanding of human rights on state and international level into account.[310] With regard to such changes in case law, the time limit of the legal force is expressed.[311]

The legal opinion of the Court of justice may change due to various factors. The change might be based on a need to coordinate the law. In this case, the Court confirms a human-rights-friendly tendency of the majority of the signatory states. The tendency justifies a change in case law. This approach does not represent a transgression of competences because in order to interpret the agreements under international law, the subseaquent practice by the signatory states is to be taken into consideration acc. to Art. 31 VCLT. The Court of justice should use the evolutive approach of this regulation to develop the law.[312]Judicial power after all counts to the most important functions of the Community. Therefore, the development of the law by way of landmark judgments is in conformity with international law. Especially for this reason the national legal systems of the Member States should continue to orientate themselves according to the current status of the human rights jurisdiction by the Court of justice . The content of the Charter is mirrored, so to speak, in the judgments of the ECOWAS Court of Justice.

The ECOWAS Court of Justice should primarily play its part as a Constitutional Court through its pilot judgments and landmark judgments. A pilot judgment represents a particular decision by the ECtHR (a kindred regional Court), which is passed to adress a structural problem of a respondent state. A pilot judgment is passed if several subsequent complaints of the respondent member State involve the same problem. According to the

310 Polakiewics, Die Verpflichtung der Staaten aus den Urteilen des Europäischen Court of Law für Menschenrechte, 49. [The obligations by countries resulting from the judgments by the European Court of Human Rights, 49.].

311 Polakiewics, Die Verpflichtung der Staaten aus den Urteilen des Europäischen Court of Law für Menschenrechte, 50. [The obligations by countries resulting from the judgments by the European Court of Human Rights, 50.].

312 Cremer, Zur Bindungswirkung von EGMR-Urteilen. Anmerkung zum Görgülü-Beschluß des BVerfG vom 14.10.2004, in: EuGRZ (2004), 683 (694). [Regarding the binding effect of judgments by the ECtHR. [Comment regarding the Görgülü judgment by the Federal Constitutional Court of] 14/10/2004, in: EuGRZ (2004), 683 (694);].

decision-making practice of the ECtHR, such problems can be of an organisational as well as a structural nature.[313] The ECtHR defined the practice of pilot judgments as follows:

> « La Cour a estimé que lorsqu'elle constate une violation découlant d'une situation à caractère structurel concernant un grand nombre de personnes, des mesures générales au niveau natio- nal peuvent s'imposer dans le cadre de l'exécution de ses arrêts. Cette approche juridiction- nelle adoptée par la Cour pour traiter les problèmes systémiques ou structurels apparaissant dans l'ordre juridique National est désignée par l'expression ‹ procédure d'arrêt pilote ›. Celle- ci a avant tout pour vocation d'aider les Etats contractants à remplir le rôle qui est le leur dans le système de la Convention en résolvant ce genre de problèmes au niveau National, en sorte qu'ils reconnaissent par là même aux personnes concernées les droits et libertés définis dans la Convention, comme le veut l'article 1, en leur offrant un redressement plus rapide tout en allégeant la charge de la Cour qui, sinon, aurait à connaître de quantités de requêtes sem- blables en substance ».[314]

In case of such a failure of the legal system within the respondent Member State, a pilot judgment is issued. The ECOWAS Court of Justice may pass pilot judgments in order to confirm its role as a Constitutional Court. In such judgments, the general interest, rather than the individual interest of the individual plaintiff is expressed. The practice of pilot judgments can only be effective at a national level if an expansion of the legal force regarding the national parallel proceedings takes place. Only in this way can a renewed sentencing of the Member State in subsequent proceedings, the object of the complaint being based on the same behaviour of the Member State, be avoided. This corresponds to the thought behind the obligation to comply: resulting from the declaratory judgment, the respondent Member State has the obligation, not only to change its behaviour toward the individual complainant so as to conform to the convention, but also, in a preventive fashion regarding all other National parallel cases suffering from the same type of infringement, to remedy the situation according to the declaratory judgment. This has the advantage of preventing a repeat conviction of the Member State. This is consistent because, if the other na-

313 Die Definition des Piloturteils lässt sich dem Urteil Sejdovic gegen Italien entnehmen: CEDH, Nr. 56581/00, Arrêt (01.03.2006), Affaire Sejdovic c. Italie, par. 120.

314 CEDH, Nr. 56581/00, Arrêt (1.3.2006), Affaire Sejdovic c. Italie, par. 120.

tional cases of the same Member State reach the ECOWAS Court of Justice, this Court would, without a doubt, arrive at the same result.[315] This also does not represent a contravention of the factual and personal limit of the legal force. Indeed, the legal force limits itself to the parties to the proceedings. This means that the relevance of the declaratory judgment refers at least to a certain object of dispute.[316] The broader effect already supported in the literature[317] is based on the basic idea of the obligation to provide a general effective national legal protection as a consequence of the declaratory judgment.

b. The solution from the perspective of the national legal system

From the perspective of the national constitutional systems of the Member States, it must be ensured that the human rights guaranteed in the constitutions are also protected from a procedural point of view, in order to prevent violations under international law.

The principle of subsidiarity: This international law principle takes state sovereignty into account, as it is designed to effect primarily to the Member States' own responsibility to adhere to their obligations under international law. The primary obligation to monitor the adherence to human rights is the equal responsibility of both national Constitutional Courts and national courts. Therefore, it is recommended to introduce the subsidiary principle in theprotective system of the Community whenever all Member States allow for the direct constitutional complaint by natural and legal persons in their respective legal systems. Art. 7 par. 1 of the Charter namely implies the obligation of the Member States to provide a legal process against the violation of individual fundamental rights and hu-

---

315 Rohleder, Grundrechtschutz im europäischen Mehrlevelssystem, 273 [Protection of constitutional law in the European multi-level system], 273.

316 Cremer, Zur Bindungswirkung von EGMR-Urteilen. Anmerkung zum Görgülü-Beschluß des BVerfG vom 14.10.2004, in: EuGRZ (2004), 683 (690). [Regarding the binding effect of judgments by the ECtHR. Comment regarding the Görgülü judgment by the Federal Constitutional Court of] 14/10/2004, in: EuGRZ (2004), 683 (690);].

317 Mückl, Kooperation oder Konfrontation? – Das Verhältnis zwischen Bundesverfassungsge richt und Europäischem Court of Law für Menschenrechte, Der Staat 44 (2005), 403 (420).
[Cooperation or confrontation? – the relationship between the Federal Constitutional Court and the European Court of Human Rights], in: Der Staat [The State], 44 (2005), 403 (420).

man rights. This would meet the obligation to the right and access to a court. This includes the obligation to allow national constitutional complaints against all measures of state powers. These substantive guarantees are ineffective if, in order to enforce them, the constitutional principle of fairness is not adhered to.[318] Effective legal protection is primarily the task of the signatory states. These will safeguard such if good procedural legal conditions are created on a national level. But even in this case, the guarantee as per Art. 7 par. 1 of the Charter must be ensured so that the Member States do not create theoretical opportunities at a national level without contributing to an effective legal protection system. The judicial systems of the Member States must have identifiable objective characteristics which comply with the principle of fairness. The constitutional guarantees include the right to a hearing in an equitable manner before an independent and impartial court of law[319] as well as the right to a decision and execution in an appropriate time period. In short, the procedural guarantee assumes that the trial takes place on a fair basis before a court of law (see Art. 6 ECHR). The compliance with this obligation will reduce an overload of the ECOWAS Court of Justice. Moreover, no parallel complaint pending before National courts and the ECOWAS Court of Justice need to be feared. However, the Court of justice should always have the last word, with regard to judicial decisions by Member States.

From the above, a dialogue between the regional Human Rights Court and National Constitutional Courts seems necessary, which would, in turn, serve to improve and ensure an effective human rights protection.

3. Dialogue between both levels

ECOWAS Court of Justice case law will not be static but dynamic. It is possible that the Court of justice issues a change in case law with regard to certain questions in order to continuously take into account the improved development status of human rights within the Community and taking into account the practice of other comparable international courts. Such

318 Okresek, Die Umsetzung der EGMR-Urteile und ihre Überwachung, in: EuGRZ (2003), 168 (168). [the implementation of ECtHR judgments and their supervision, in: EuGRZ (2003), 168 (168)].

319 Peukert, in: Frowein/Peukert, Europäische Menschenrechtskonvention. EMRK-Kommentar [European Human Rights Convention. ECHR-commentary], 3. edition, Art. 6, Rn. 112.

changes in the jurisdiction towards an improved direction should be seen by other Constitutional Courts of Member States as precedent judgment within the framework of the dialogue process between the regional courts and the Constitutional Courts of Member States. This dialogue which is already taking place between judicial bodies at a national level can be transferred to the relationship between the ECOWAS Court of Justice and the National courts of the Member States.[320] The aim of the dialogue between the two levels is to avoid a clash between the two legal systems, i.e. to prevent a conflict of jurisdiction between national courts and the international ECOWAS Court of Justice. It is therefore recommended that there is an exchange of and reference to case law between both legal systems.[321] This dialogue should be carried out in both directions. Furthermore, a collaboration between both (ECOWAS-level and National level) should be promoted. In order to resolve alleged or actual conflicts between the national Constitutional Courts, or courts with comparable competences, and the ECOWAS Court of Justice, the idea of complementarity of the guarantee is useful.

This discussion within the multi-level systems can be implicit or explicit. The dialogue is referred to as explicit if the courts of both legal systems quote each other. This is the case in the decision N° DCC 15–027 of the Constitutional Court of Benin.[322] When it quoted the judgment by the ECOWAS Court of Justice in the legal matter of Mamadou Tandja vs the Republic of Senegal when explaining its own legal interpretation. The exchange should not only be used with regards to its organisational and structural aspects. There also needs to be an improved interlocking of international law and state law with a strong mutual consideration regarding the interpretation of both international and national law.[323]

320 Diop, La justice constitutionnelle au Sénégal. Éssai sur l'evolution, les enjeux et les ré- formes d'un contre-pouvoir juridictionnel, 191.

321 Cremer, Zur Bindungswirkung von EGMR-Urteilen. Anmerkung zum Görgülü-Beschluß des BVerfG vom 14.10.2004, in: EuGRZ (2004), 683 (694). [Regarding the binding effect of judgments by the ECtHR. Comment regarding the Görgülü judgment by the Federal Constitutional Court of] 14/10/2004, in: EuGRZ (2004), 683 (694)].

322 Décision DCC 15–027 (12.02.2015), available at: www.cour-constitutionnelle-benin.org (last accessed on 25/04/2015).

323 Peters, Legal systems and constitutionalisation: Regarding the redefinition of the relationships, in: DÖV (2010), 3 (55); Häberle, Europäische Verfassungslehre, 6. edition, 92. [European Constitutional Theory, 6th edition, 92].

Chapter 4 The Reception of the Legal Force in theNational Legal System

The exercise of its jurisdiction by the ECOWAS Court of Justice creates a legal force. How does the national constitutional order perceive this binding force of the legal effect? At the same time, this also poses the question of the national status of international law within the national legal systems of the Member States. It will at this stage be shown how the binding effect issued at the level of international law is implemented into the national legal order. The declaratory judgment does not automatically breach the national legal force. However, this declaratory judgment has significant legal consequences for the domestic legal system of the concerned state. The question whether the legal effect is welcome or not welcome within the national legal order must be primarily answered on the basis of national law. This question is of decisive importance because the implementation of judgments by international courts depends on how they are treated at a domestic level. The removal of any obstacles to implementation depends on the national law of signatory states.[1] Therefore, the question of interaction[2] between international law and national law of Member States must be asked. In the same manner, the questions must be asked of, firstly, what provisions are made by the ECOWAS legal regulations regarding the legal effect of its decisions and, secondly, how the domestic legal systems of the Member States regard the guidelines under international law regarding the legal effect from a legal point of view. In order to determine whether the legal effect possesses a national enforcement character, reference must be made to both Community and national legislation. The effectiveness of the binding effect of the declaratory judgment in this specific case depends on the Togolese code of procedure (for example) and the ECOWAS regu-

1 Enabulele, Reflections on the ECOWAS-Community Court Protocol and the Constitutions of Member States, in: International Community Law Review 12 (2010), 111 (113).

2 Cremer, Zur Bindungswirkung von EGMR-Urteilen. Anmerkung zum Görgülü-Beschluß des BVerfG vom 14.10.2004 (2004), in: EuGRZ (2004), 683 (692). [Regarding the binding effect of judgments by the ECtHR. Comment regarding the Görgülü judgment by the Federal Constitutional Court of] 14/10/2004, in: EuGRZ (2004), 683 (692)].

lation.[3] The interaction of the National legal system and theECOWAS Community's legal system creates good conditions for an effective implementation of declaratory judgments by the Community's Court . All this demands, on the one hand, is the interpretation of the pertinent guidelines of the Court of justice and the determination of the binding effect of the decision and on the other hand, the examination of national regulations of constitutional orders by the Member States regarding the reception of the binding effect. This preliminary question is also important because many problems regarding the implementation of international law do not regard the ratification of international law but the national effectiveness of international law. In this respect, African countries do show a presentable history of ratification of international law but, unfortunately, show behaviour that is open to criticism regarding its domestic implementation.[4]

For a better understanding of the reception of the legal force into the national legal system in the signatory states, the importance of the African Charter in the domestic legal system must first of all be demonstrated A) because the national concretisation of the declaratory judgment (B) depends on which rank is assigned to the Member States' constitutional regulations. Nevertheless, the failure to comply with the implementation obligation has consequences under international law to the detriment of the convicted signatory state (C).

A. Preliminary Question: Binding Force of International Law and the ECOWAS Judgments

A preliminary question is defined as a legal question raised before the main question (question préjudicielle) can be discussed. In this case, the preliminary question does not entirely deviate from the sense of law provisions.The special characteristic of the preliminary question raised corresponding with this thought process is differently defined. It concerns the clarification of the question of the status of international law within the

3 Cremer, Zur Bindungswirkung von EGMR-Urteilen. Anmerkung zum Görgülü-Beschluß des BVerfG vom 14.10.2004 (2004), in: EuGRZ (2004), 683 (695).[Regarding the binding effect of judgments by the ECtHR. Comment regarding the Görgülü judgment by the Federal Constitutional Court of] 14/10/2004, in: EuGRZ (2004), 683 (695)].

4 Enabulele, Reflections on the ECOWAS-Community Court Protocol and the Constitutions of Member States, in: International Community Law Review 12 (2010), 111 (126).

domestic legal systems of the Member States in a normative respect. Contrary to the meaning of the legal provisions, this preliminary question does not require a concrete case before a national court.In order to answer all these questions, the ranking of international law is discussed in francophone (I) as well as Anglophone countries (II). It should not be overlooked that since the Protocol of Good Governance came into force there has been a degree of convergence of constitutional principles within the ECOWAS signatory states (III).

I. Binding Force of the International Law in francophone Member States

Which rank is given to international law in the domestic legal system of Member States (1), is a preliminary question to be resolved before the question regarding the national concretisation of the legal force of the ECOWAS judgment will be discussed. What is more is the consideration of whether the reciprocity principle under International law can be applied in this case (2).

1. Question of rank

It may come as a surprise why, in the context of the investigation into the validity of a constitutional court decision and the institution of an in rem restitution according to International guidelines, a consideration of the domestic status should be necessary. This question, however, should be clarified for two reasons: if International law is ranked below the constitution, the consequence for the implementation of an unconstitutional International rule becomes legally relevant.[5] International law may only be applied when the constitution is changed accordingly. This means that if the decision by the Court of justice , i.e. a judgment in accordance with International law, violates the constitution, it can only be observed if the regulation which is in violation has been changed in advance.

In the initial case, this question of rank was central to the debate regarding the domestic implementation of the declaratory judgment. The government, as well as the Togolese Constitutional Court, refused to implement the judgment of the Court of justice in the initial case. The reasons

5 Adeloui, L'autorité de la chose jugée par les juridictions constitutionnelles en Afrique, in: Revue Togolaise des Sciences Juridiques (2012), 54 (74).

they gave for this were, amongst others, that the decisions by the Constitutional Court were final. There was no further instance above the Constitutional Court.[6]

Such reasoning is understandable from a certain perspective. Fundamentally speaking it is not wrong if the signatory states prevent the implementation of declaratory judgments by the Court of justice . The declaratory judgment basically means that the decision by the Constitutional Court was made in violation of the Convention. The implementation of such a judgment means that the concerned state would accept the violation of the constitutional principle of finality of the decision. This, in turn, would indicate that the International law is ranked above the constitution. At any rate, this constellation equals a displacement of the constitutional principles by the International law. Thus, the judgment under International law that was issued would rank above the constitutional law. This is precisely what the state did not want to accept in the initial case. From the viewpoint of the hierarchy of norms this refusal is justified because, at the level of the domestic legal system, the constitution receives a higher rank. International law is ranked below the constitution. Since the declaratory judgment has International legal content, it would be second in rank in the hierarchy of norms. The legal consequences of the constellation of norms are interesting: A norm under International law that infringes on a constitutional principle (e.g. the finality of legal force) cannot be implemented[7] unless a change to the constitution was made beforehand.

It must, however, be taken into consideration that constitutional norms and International law belong to different legal systems. They take different principles into account. Even in case of a certain relationship between International law and constitutional law, every legal system is independent of the other – as soon as the signatory states have signed and ratified an International treaty. The consequences of this mean that International law demands a domestic implementation, regardless of the constitutional norms that are inconsistent with it. Therefore, the signing parties must, during the conclusion of the agreement, give attention to their constitutional principles before the treaty is signed. Once signed, International law must be easily enforceable and implementable. Therefore, from the point

---

6 Adeloui, L'autorité de la chose jugée par les juridictions constitutionnelles en Afrique, in: Revue Togolaise des Sciences Juridiques (2012), 54 (74).

7 See criticism of the government in the initial case: Adeloui, L'autorité de la chose jugée par les juridictions constitutionnelles en Afrique, in: Revue Togolaise des Sciences Juridiques (2012), 54 (74).

of view of International law, a conflicting constitutional principle does not play a role. This is precisely the meaning of the regulation in Art. 26 of the Vienna Convention on the Law of Treaties. The International Court of Justice also confirms this interpretation in its Avena-judgment.[8]

The *question of rank*[9] is therefore important because the National enforceability of human rights instruments depends on the respective National legal system giving these instruments meaning[10] and which rank the International instrument has within the legal system of the Member State. In order to clarify this preliminary question, the constitutional provisions regarding the ranking of International law will be discussed in the following. First of all, Art. 142 of the Togolese constitution must be explained. It states that:

> « Les traités ou accords régulièrement ratifiés ou approuvés ont, dès leur publication, une autorité supérieure à celle des lois, sous réserve, pour chaque accord ou traité, de son appli- cation par l'autre partie ».

After detailed examination of this provision, three basic requirements must be met in order for International law to be valid on a National level: the rule-consistent ratification, the publication in the official state gazette and the application of the reciprocity principle. The domestic question of the rank of International law will be analysed through a systematic examination of all constitutional regulations regarding International law and the constitution. International treaties in general, and the Charter in particular, are directly applicable at a National level as long as they have been properly ratified and published in the government gazette (Art. 142 of the Togolese Constitution)[11]. Ever since the publication of the ECOWAS Amendment Agreement and the associated Additional Protocol, the instruments of International law have a direct National legal force. Therefore, no additional implementation measures are necessary. However, this provision contains a number of uncertainties. Its vague and broad wording

8 CIJ, Demande en interprétation de l'arrêt du 31 mars 2004 en l'Affaire Avena et autres res- sortissants mexicains (Mexique c. Ètats-Unis d'Amérique), Arrêt du 19 janvier 2009, par. 8.

9 Mellech, Die Rezeption der EMRK sowie der Urteile des EGMR in der französischen und deutschen Rechtsprechung, 19 ff. [The reception of the ECHR and the judgments of the ECtHR in the French and German jurisdiction, 19 ff].

10 Tama, Droit International et africain des droits de l'homme, 131.

11 See: Oumarou, La Cour constitutionnelle du Niger et le contrôle de conformité des traités et accords internationaux à la Constitution: Remarques sur la Jurisprudence CIMA, in: Revue Juridiques et Politiques (2008), 503 (505).

allows for two hypotheses with regards to the interpretation of Art. 142 of the Togolese Constitution, because the regulation does not clarify whether a differentiation based on the content-related rank of the norm is to be done with regards to the question of rank. Fundamentally, the following questions must be asked: what does « *autorité supérieure* à celle des lois » in the regulations of Art. 142 in the Togolese Consituttion mean? Which « loi » is meant in this regulation? The constitutional legislator leaves this question unanswered. Scholarly opinions point to « loi » in the broadest sense. The term « loi » means, according to the understanding of the civil tradition any general and abstract provision inevitably containing a legal command.[12]

> « [Une] autorité supérieure à toute loi, peu importe sa place dans la hiérarchie des normes»[13].

What this means is that after proper ratification and publication of the International law it is directly given a status below that of constitutional law, on national level. Based on the order of validity in Art. 142 of the Togolese Constitution, all International treaties ratified by Togo receive a status above ordinary law.

These agreements are ranked below the constitution. Regarding the African Charter on Human Rights and Peoples' Rights, however, it must be pointed out that the Charter is incorporated into the constitution and is an integral part of the constitution. The principle of reciprocity prevailing in International law, and embedded in Art. 142 of the Togolese Constitution, does not apply here. Due to the special character of the Charter in the Community's Constitution of ECOWAS and in the constitutional system of the Member States, a "constitutional instrument of West African Countries"[14] must be surmised. In any case the Charter enjoys in that regard the status of customary international law. These two conditions were adhered

---

12 Eissen, Le statut juridique interne de la Convention devant les juridictions répressives, in: Cohen-Jonathan, Droits de l'homme en France, 1 (6); Grewe, The reception of the ECHR in Germany, in: dies./Gusy, Human Rights, 106 (115); Sauve/Pauti, in: Thierry/Decaus, Droit International, 237 (240).

13 Amselek, Une fausse idée claire: la hiérarchie des normes juridiques, in: Renouveau du Droit constitutionnel. Mélanges en l'honneur de Louis Favoreu, 983 (1013).

14 Fall/Sall, Une constitution régionale pour l'espace CEDEAO: le protocole sur la démocratie et la bonne gouvernance, available at: http://la-constitution-en-afrique.org/article-34239380. html (last accessed on 16/05/2015); Adjolohoun, Droits de l'homme et justice constitutionnelle en Afrique: le modèle béninois, 95.

to in the African Charter on Human Rights. Now, the question remains whether the other conditions have been met with regards to the unconditional entry into force of the Charter. Regarding liability, it does not make a difference which domestic rank the Charter receives. Ranking by National constitutional law has no consequence for the obligation to comply. The Member State concerned cannot argue that the Charter and the legal regulations of ECOWAS only receive their rank above the ordinary law within the state-internal hierarchy of norms.[15]This transnational constitutional content of the Charter – based on the proclaimed constitutional convergence of West-African states in the Protocol on Good Governance and Democracy from 2001 – confirms a special status of the Charter for all constitutional systems in Member States. Therefore, the principle of reciprocity can also not be applied here.[16]

2. Principle of reciprocity

The principle of reciprocity has its origins in customary International law and establishes a legitimate objection to non-compliance with the obligation under International law.[17] The International treaty is to be applied unconditionally, insofar as the basic principle of reciprocity according to the monistic legal tradition is met. However, this principle cannot be applied to the African Charter on Human Rights for the following reasons:

- objective obligations in the Charter;
- Validity of the principle of reciprocity only for bilateral International treaties;
- Existence of a control organ within the system of the Charter.

The exclusion of the applicability of the principle of reciprocity is based on the objective obligations in the Charter. The obligations ensuing from the

15 Schaffarzik, Europäische Menschenrechte unter der Ägide des Bundesverfassungsgerichts, in: DÖV (2005), 860 (861). [European human rights under the aegis of the Federal Constitutional Court, in: DOV (2005), 860 (861).].

16 Rohleder, Grundrechtsschutz im europäischen Mehrlevelssystem, 169. [Protection of constitutional law in the European multi-level system, 169].

17 Simma, Das Reziprozitätselement in der Entstehung des Völkergewohnheitsrechts, 45.[The element of reciprocity in the inception of customary International law, 45.].

Charter are of an objective nature.[18] This excludes the so-called principle exceptio *non adimpleti contractus*. In concrete terms, it cannot solely depend on the compliance to the human rights laid out in the Charter by the other signatory states. The Togolese state must also meet its obligations. Every signatory state is obligated to unilaterally adhere to recognised human rights and account to International institutions. The goals of the Charter are therefore superordinate in such a way that the signatory states to the Charter must not provide for their own but for a mutual interest in the adherence to the human rights stipulated in the Charter (the guarantees according to the Charter) for all persons in the territory of the signatory states.[19] According to the wording in Art. 142 of the Togolese Constitution it can already be noted that the principle of reciprocity can only be applied to bilateral treaties. This is due to « l'autre partie contractante ». The limitation to the other signatory party and not the other signatory parties confirms the exclusion of the principle of reciprocity regarding multilateral treaties.[20] Therefore, the conduct of the other signatory states is insignificant regarding the adherence to the obligations stipulated in the Charter. After comparing the constitutional system of the ECOWAS Member States, the African Charter on Human Rights and Peoples' Rights receives a special status. This gives the Charter the legal nature of a special International treaty. In confirmation of this special status of the Charter, the adherence to the obligations is transferred from the Charter to the ECOWAS Court of Justice.

Moreover, it must be pointed out that the African Charter belongs to the *bloc de constitutionnalité* of the constitutional system of the Member States. The term *bloc de constitutionnalité* means that all constitutional regulations which the constitutional court refers to in its decision-making process.[21]A number of voices in literature see the *bloc de constitutionnalité* as

---

18 Cohen-Jonathan, La fonction quasi constitutionnelle de la Cour Européenne des Droits de l'Homme, in: Renouveau du Droit constitutionnel. Mélanges en l'honneur de Louis Favoreu, 1127 (1128).

19 See also Mellech, Die Rezeption der EMRK sowie der Urteile des EGMR in der französi- schen und deutschen Rechtsordnung, 16. [The reception of the ECHR and the judgments of the ECtHR in the French and German jurisdiction, 16].

20 Mellech, Die Rezeption der EMRK sowie der Urteile des EGMR in der französischen und deutschen Rechtsordnung, 16. [The reception of the ECHR and the judgments of the ECtHR in the French and German jurisdiction, 16].

21 Adeloui, L'insertion des engagements internationaux en droit interne des États africains, in: Revue Béninoise des Sciences Juridiques et Administratives (2011), 51 (85).

the standard of review for International treaties and the constitutionality of the laws.[22] This means that the International treaties do not belong to the standard of review of the constitutional conduct of the state organs. However, the Charter and the Universal Declaration of Human Rights of 1948, as well as the two International pacts of 1966, receive a special status in the constitutions of the member states of ECOWAS . Indeed, the mentioned human rights treaties are referred to in the preambles of the constitutions. The Togolese constitutional legislator expressly points out that the Charter is an integral part of the constitution. This particular statute of the Charter needs to be explained further:

- The human rights enshrined in the Charter have constitutional status. The constitutional legislator, as well as all other state powers, must align their actions according to the Charter. In this context, the Charter constitutes a standard of review regarding the actions of state organs.
- The Constitutional Court guarantees the adherence to the human rights enshrined in the Charter in the same manner as those in the constitutional regulations.

These annotations speak for the complementarity of the roles between the Constitutional Courts and the ECOWAS Court of Justice. Remarkably, the Constitutional Court of Benin referred to the Judgment DCC 10–049[23] as well as the Protocol on Good Governance and Democracy from 2001 in the ECOWAS Protocol and the African Charter on Human and Peoples' Rights in its reasoning in justifying the control of the constitutionality of an electoral act. The Constitutional Court of Benin explained in this judgment:

> « Ne pas censurer la loi abrogative, c'est autoriser les députés à violer le protocole A/SP1/12/01 de la CEDEAO et par conséquent l'article 147 de la Constitution qui confirme la suprématie de la norme supranationale sur la norme juridique Nationale».[24]

Furthermore, the Constitutional Court reaffirmed the reference to the Charter in another consideration in this judgment:

---

22 Chantebout, Droit constitutionnel, 27 éd., 2010, 596; Bernhardt, The Convention and Dome- stic Law, in: Macdonald/Matscher/Petzold (Publ.), The European System for the Protection of Human Rights, 25 (27).

23 Cour constitutionnelle du Bénin, Décision DCC 10–049 (05.04.2010), available at: www. cour-constitutionnelle-benin.org (last accessed on 25/04/2015).

24 Cour constitutionnelle du Bénin, Décision DCC 10–049 (05/04/2010), available at: www. cour-constitutionnelle-benin.org (last accessed on 25/04/2015).

> « [I]l s'ensuit que l'ensemble des dispositions de ces textes internationaux font partie inté-grante de la Constitution béninoise et ont une valeur supérieure à la loi ».[25]

Based on the aforementioned it should be noted, that the ECOWAS signatory states ascribe a special role to the Charter in their respective National constitutional systems. At Community level, this special status is attached to the transfer of the jurisidiction to the ECOWAS Court of Justice to monitor the adherence to the human rights as stipulated in the Charter. Organs have been set up to ensure adherence to the human rights guaranteed in the Charter. These include the African Commission on Human Rights, the African Court on Human and Peoples' Rights and – within the ECOWAS legal system – the newly established ECOWAS Court of Justice. The roles assigned to all mentioned International organs are complementary.

II. Binding Force in Anglophone Member States

It is necessary for the validity of a treaty under International law that the signatory states have signed and ratified the agreement. Furthermore, the effectivity of a treaty depends on how it is integrated into the National legal system and how it is applied.[26] What is important is that the Anglophone Member States, stemming from the legal tradition of Common Law, are not familiar with the concept of a hierarchy of norms.[27] However, with regards to the comprehensive effectivity of International law, this re-

---

25 Cour constitutionnelle du Bénin, Décision DCC 10–049 (05.04.2010), available at: www. cour-constitutionnelle-benin.org (last accessed on 25/04/2015).

26 Oppong, Legal Aspects of Economic Integration in Africa, 191.

27 Mückl, Kooperation oder Konfrontation? – Das Verhältnis zwischen Bundesverfassungsge- richt und Europäischem Court of Law für Menschenrechte, in: Der Staat 44 (2005), 403 (405) [Cooperation or confrontation? – the relationship between the Federal Constitutional Court and the European Court of Human Rights], in: Der Staat [The State], 44 (2005), 403 (405)]; Tou- fayan, When British Justice (in African Colonies) Point Two Ways: On Dualism, Hybridity and the Genealogy of Juridical Negritude in Taslim Olawale Elias, in: Leiden Journal of International Law (2008), 377 (396); Landauer, Things Fall Together: The Past and Future Africas of T.O. Elias's Africa and Development of International Law, in: Leiden Journal of International Law (2008), 351 (352).

quires a further legal step at the domestic level of these Member States.[28] The implementation of international law by the national assembly of the respective Member State is indeed necessary for the enforcement of an instrument of International law in all English-speaking ECOWAS Member States. In this regard, the respective provision of Art. 12 par. 1 of the Constitution of Nigeria of 1999 reads as follows:

> "No treaty between the federation and any other country shall have the force of law except to the extent to which any such treaty has been enacted into law by the National Assembly."[29]

Such a constitutional requirement is also contained in the constitutions of other Member States that are not Anglophone countries.[30] Art. 11 of the Constitution of the lusophone Republic of Cape Verde is an exception in that regard .[31] Art. 11 (3) of the Constitution of the Republic of Cape Verde reads:

> "The legal acts emanating from the relevant organs of the supranational organisations of which Cape Verde is member, shall enter directly into force in the domestic legal order".[32]

---

28 Okene/Eddie-Amadi, Bringing Rights Home: The Status of International Legal Instruments in Nigeria, in: Journal of African and International Law (2010), 409 (410).

29 Ekhator, Improving access to environmental justice under the African Charter on Human and Peoples' Rights: The role of NGOS in Nigeria, in: African Journal of International and com- parative Law (2014), 63 (69).

30 Art. 75 Abs. 2 Verfassung Ghana vom 8. May 1992, geändert durch Verfassungsänderungs- gesetz vom 16. December 1996; Art. 10 d Verfassung Sierra Leone vom 3. September 1991; Art. 79 (c) the Constitution of The Gambia of 16 January 1997; Art. 57 i. conn. with Art. 34 iii. b Constitution of Liberia of 19 October 1983; Art. 56 par. 8 the Constitution of Guinea-Bissau of 16 May 1984, Amendment of 11 May 1991 are considered herein. Available at: http://www.constitutionnet.org/files/Guinea- Bissau%20Constitution.pdf *(last accessed on 14/05/2015).*

31 Ouguergouz, L'application Nationale de la charte africaine des droits de l'homme par les autorités Nationales en Afrique occidentale, in: Flauss/Lambert-Abdelgawad (Publ.), L'application Nationale de la charte africaine des droits de l'homme et des peuples, 163 (166); Enabulele, Reflections on the ECOWAS Community Court Protocol and the Constitutions of Member States, in: International Community Law Review 12 (2010), 111 (124).

32 The Constitution of Cap Verde of 05/09/1992, available at: http://www.constitutionnet.org/vl/ item/constitution-republic-cape-verde-1992 (last accessed on 15/05/2015).

According to these constitutional provisions, Parliament has transformed the African Charter e.g. through a so-called „African Charter Act“ in Nigeria into National law.[33] This dualism is regrettable in the sense that a ratified but not nationally implemented International law instrument will be declared inapplicable by National courts.[34] More specifically, the legal regulations within ECOWAS as well as the judgments by the Court of justice in this regard, are invalid due to a lack of implementation.[35] The practical legal consequences of comparable regulations are also well-known within the legal system of SADC. This concerned the dispute regarding Art. 231 of the South African Constitution and the effect of the SADC-Treaty on the National legal system.[36] For these reasons, voices in Anglophone literature disputethe direct binding effect of the instruments of the Community within the ECOWAS legal system and therefore the judgments by the ECOWAS Court of Justice with regards to the anglophone Member States. To justify their rejection of the binding effect, they refer to the dualistic legal tradition.[37] Through the ratification of the Amendment Agreement and the Additional Protocols of francophone West African countries, all International law-instruments receive their rank above the law. Therefore, the final decisions by the ECOWAS Court of justice develop the same legal effect as the instruments of the Community that the judgments by the Court of justice refer to.

Voices in literature speak of a direct legal effect of the African Charter based on its special nature.[38] It has already been mentioned above that the judgments by the ECOWAS Court of Justice are final and incontestable

33 Egede, Bringing Human Rights Home: An Examination of the Domestication of Human Rights Treaties in Nigeria, in: Journal of African Law (2007), 249 (250).

34 Enabulele, Reflections on the ECOWAS Community Court Protocol and the Constitutions of Member States, in: International Community Law Review 12 (2010), 111 (125).

35 Ouguergouz, L'application Nationale de la charte africaine des droits de l'homme par les autorités Nationales en Afrique occidentale, in: Flauss/Lambert-Abdelgawad (Publ.), L'application Nationale de la charte africaine des droits de l'homme et des peuples, 163 (166).

36 Oppong/Niro, Enforcing Judgments of International Court in National Court, in: Journal of International Dispute Settlement (2014), 1 (7).

37 ECOWAS Vanguard, „Issues for an ECOWAS of People“, Volume 2, Issues 4, Feb. 2013, 7.

38 Ouguergouz, L'application Nationale de la charte africaine des droits de l'homme par les autorités Nationales en Afrique occidentale, in: Flauss/Lambert-Abdelgawad (Publ.), L'application Nationale de la charte africaine des droits de l'homme et des peuples, 163 (167).

and may not be reviewed or changed by any other court. The nature of the respective national legal order of the Member States is, therefore "*self-executing*".[39] According to this, no national implementation measures are required to render the judgments of this Court of Law effective.

Opinion: It makes no difference whether the legal system of the Member State belongs to the dualistic or the monistic system. Moreover, the International law and the decision by the ECOWAS Court of Justice are legally binding. The status assigned to International law within the National law of the signatory states does not play a role.[40] The special character of the Charter within the constitutional order of the Community clarifies that it is a *self-executing* norm and as such does not need a particular implementation measure within the respective constitutional system in order to receive validity at a National level. The Charter even belongs to the *bloc de constitutionnalité* in francophone West African countries, i.e. one of the standards of constitutional interpretation. In Anglophone countries, the Charter is mentioned in the respective preambles. Furthermore, the Member States have waived their sovereignty in this regard by transferring the jurisdiction to the ECOWAS Court of Justice concerning the final authority of the Constitutional Courts or the Supreme Court.[41]

With regards to liability, it does not matter which domestic rank the Charter is given. The determination of the rank by the National Constitutional Court is of no consequence to the obligation of compliance. The concerned Member State cannot submit that the Charter and the ECOWAS legal regulations are only given the rank above basic law within the domestic hierarchy of norms.[42] Therefore, the ECOWAS Court of Justice alone has the right to speak the last word on whether a Member State's

39 Rohleder, Grundrechtsschutz im europäischen Mehrlevelssystem, 163. [Protection of constitutional law in the European multi-level system, 163].

40 Kilian, Die Bindungswirkung der Entscheidungen des Europäischen Gerichtshofs für Men- schenrechte auf die Nationalen Gerichte der Mitgliedstaaten der Konvention zum Schutze der Men- schenrechte und Grundfreiheiten vom 4. November 1950, 114. [The Binding Effect of Decisions taken by the European Court of Law for Human Rights with regards to the National Court of the Member States regarding the Convention on the Protection of Human Rights and Constitutional Freedoms of 4 November 1950, 114].

41 Pache, Die Europäische Menschenrechtskonvention und die deutsche Rechtsordnung [The European Convention on Human Rights and the German legal system], in: EuR (2004), 393 (400).

42 Schaffarzik, Europäische Menschenrechte unter der Ägide des Bundesverfassungsgerichts, in: DÖV (2005), 860 (861). [European human rights under the aegis of the Federal Constitutional Court, in: DOV (2005), 860 (861).].

conduct infringes on human rights or not. The declaratory judgments by the ECOWAS Court of Justice, therefore, do not need a special measure of recognition in order to be executed. Whether monism or dualism, the result remains the same: The Member States are subject to an obligation to comply.[43] In light of the development of human rights case law, the dualistic principle is nowadays to be regarded as antiquated.[44]

III. Principle of the convergence of constitutions

It must be stated in advance that the constitutions of ECOWAS Member States are predominantly influenced by International law.[45] The Protocol on Good Governance from 2001 is denoted as the Constitution of the ECOWAS Community.[46] It expressly orders the Member States to assign the jurisdiction on human rights matters to the ECOWAS Court of Justice.[47] The fact that all signatory states have recognised the Charter and the associated human rights in the preambles of the Constitutions of the Member States, the Charter receives the validity of International customary law

43 Kilian, Die Bindungswirkung der Entscheidungen des Europäischen Gerichtshofs für Men- schenrechte auf die Nationalen Gerichte der Mitgliedstaaten der Konvention zum Schutze der Men- schenrechte und Grundfreiheiten vom 4. November 1950, 114. [The Binding Effect of Decisions taken by the European Court of Law for Human Rights with regards to the National Court of the Member States regarding the Convention on the Protection of Human Rights and Constitutional Freedoms of 4 November 1950, 114].

44 Bernhardt, The Convention and Domestic Law, in: Macdonald/Matscher/Petzold (Publ.), The European System for the Protection of Human Rights, 25 (30).

45 Sall, Le Droit International dans les nouvelles constitutions africaines, in: Revue Juridique et Politique (1997), 339 (340).

46 Fall/Sall, Une constitution régionale pour l'espace CEDEAO: le protocole sur la démocratie et la bonne gouvernance, available at: http://la-constitution-en-afrique .org/article-34239380. html (last accessed on 16.05.2015); Alter/Helfer/McAllister, A new International human rights court for West Africa: the ECOWAS Community Court of Justice, in: The American Journal of International Law (2013) Vol. 107, 737 (775); Kane, La Cour de justice de la CEDEAO à l'épreuve de la protection des droits de l'homme, Mémoire de Maitrise, Université Gaston Berger (2012- 2013), 14; Cowell, The impact of the protocol on good governance and democracy, in: African Journal of International and Comparative Law (2011), 331 (333).

47 Alter/Helfer/McAllister, A new International human rights court for West Africa: the ECOWAS Community Court of Justice, in: The American Journal of International Law (2013), 737 (757).

within the order of the Community. The obligations in the Protocol of Good Governance are not only directed at the governments of the signatory states. There is more involved: it is not just about actions of the government but also of those of the legislature and the judiciary. Addressees of the responsible governance are, so to speak, all government officials.[48]

Moreover, the Charter belongs to the *bloc de constitutionnalité* of the respective constitutional order of each Member State. Member States have establishhed in their constitutional tradition that it is possible that the human rights guaranteed in the Charter can be violated by organs of the state despite their affiliation to the respective Constitution. In this sense, e.g. the Constitutional Court of Benin expressly refers its jurisdiction to the Protocol:

> « Ces fraudes massives étaient du reste contraire aux principes de la transparence et de la fiabilité garantis les articles 4 et 5 des protocoles de la CEDEAO sur la démocratie et la bonne gouvernance ».[49]

In order to reduce this risk, the Member States have created another way at ECOWAS level to ensure that sufficient attention is paid to the Charter. This task was transferred to the ECOWAS Court of Justice. This means that the Member States are aware that even the Constitutional Courts, who are primarily supposed to guard the rights in the Charter, can fail. Therefore, a possible correction measure at International level was created in the Community. Thus, the Constitutional Courts and the ECOWAS Court of Justice have a common complementary task: to give the African Charter an effective binding force for all persons under the sovereignty of the Community.[50] Notwithstanding the state-internal hierarchy of norms, the norms of International law develop unreserved assertiveness, especially in the area of human rights.[51] It would jeopardise the purpose of the Protocol

48 Dolzer, "Good governance": neues transNationales Leitbild der Staatlichkeit? [a new transNational role model in statehood?], in: ZaöRV (2004), 535 (535).

49 Cour constitutionnelle du Bénin, Décision DCC 10–049 (05.04.2010), available at: www. cour-constitutionnelle-benin.org (last accessed on 25/04/2015).

50 Mückl, Kooperation oder Konfrontation? – Das Verhältnis zwischen Bundesverfassungsge- richt und Europäischem Gerichtshof für Menschenrechte, in: Der Staat 44 (2005), 403 (431). [Cooperation or confrontation? – the relationship between the Federal Constitutional Court and the European Court of Human Rights], in: Der Staat [The State], 44 (2005), 403 (431)].

51 Schaffarzik, Europäische Menschenrechte unter der Ägide des Bundesverfassungsgerichts, in: DÖV (2005), 860 (863). [European human rights under the aegis of the Federal Constitutional Court, in: DOV (2005), 860 (863).].

if the obligation under International law, would receive a different meaning depending on the involved Member State.

In the legal matter of Togo vs the Parliamentarians, the government stated that the ECOWAS Court of Justice did not have any competence to order a removal of the consequences of the violation of human rights because such an order would constitute an infringement of Art. 106 of the Togolese Constitution. The ECOWAS Court of Justice did not share this view of the government and therefore rejected the order of a retrial.

Following the entry into force of the Amendment Agreement of 1993 and the associated Additional Protocol, the Member States are prohibited from preventing the application of the obligations under International law which they have adopted from the agreement with reference to their National law. This is because, acc. to Art. 26 of the Vienna Convention (VCLT), International treaties must be adhered to due to the requirement of good faith. Furthermore, the view of both the Togolese government and the concurring opinion of the ECOWAS Court of Justice in the above case , are acc. to Art. 27 VCLT not cogent and therefore dissatisfactory. Art. 27 VCLT reads:

> “A party may not invoke the provisions of its internal law as justification for its failure to perform a treaty. This rule is without prejudice to article 46“

In connection with the competence of the ECOWAS Court of Justice and the obligation of implementation by the Member States, the Togolese government could e.g. refer to Art. 106 of the Togolese Constitution in order to reject the competence to review decisions by the Constitutional Court. This objection is not valid because such a restriction of competence should have been foreseen by the signatory states during the drafting of the agreement. As long as such regulations do not find expression in provisions in the agreement, the recourse to conflicting domestic law must be rejected. They must logically adjust their entire legal system, including the Constitution, to adhere to the guidelines of the obligations of the Community under International law.[52] At this point, a comparison with the competence of the ECtHR is of interest. The Member States indeed have made provision for a certain limitation of the judicial power of the ECtHR in

52 Giegerich, Wirkung und Rang der EMRK in den Rechtsordnungen der Mitgliedstaaten [Effect and rank of the ECHR in the legal systems of Member States], in: Dörr/Grote/Marauhn (Publ.), EMRK/GG, 2. edition, Kap. 2, Rn. 19.

Art. 41 ECHR. In light of dynamic interpretation, the ECtHR even deems this limitation partially incompatible with the purpose of the Convention.

In summary, it can be said that: when it comes to the interpretation of the legal regulations within ECOWAS, it does not matter whether these regulations are indeed valid within the domestic legal systems and which National legal status they have been assigned. It is not up to the Court of justice to worry about the question of National validity and state-internal hierarchies of norms when it comes to the legal regulations within ECOWAS.[53]

B. National Articulation of Legal Force

It is irrelevant whether the concerned signatory state has already paid compensation or not. It is the purpose of the declaratory judgment to effect a concrete measure at domestic level. In implementing the decision of the Court of justice, the defendant has a duty to reach a result. The convicted Member State is namely subject to an obligation to succeed or obligation to achieve results. Due to this obligation to achieve results, the convicted signatory state must do everything possible that will lead to a termination or restoration of the original status quo in accordance with the Convention. Even if the judgment by the Court of justice is of a purely declaratory character, the plaintiff must not endure an ongoing violation after the declaratory judgment. Rather, it is the duty of the State to design National procedural regulations in such a manner that the continuation of the violation is terminated or, if necessary, a compensation is paid. The aim of the obligation to achieve results is to enable the declaratory judgment to be enforced or implemented in practice. Based on this obligation to achieve results, the declaratory judgment has a conceptualising effect on domestic law. The design effect is then expressed in the annulment an adaptation of judgment the domestic Constitutional Court ruling. A concrete example can be clearly noted in the aforementioned case. The parliamentarians

53 Egede, Bringing Human Rights Home: An Examination of the Domestication of Human Rights Treaties in Nigeria, in: Journal of African Law (2007), 249 (278); Enabulele, Reflections on the ECOWAS-Community Court Protocol and the Constitutions of Member States, in: Internatio nal Community Law Review 12 (2010), 111 (127). Also: Schaffarzik, Europäische Menschen- rechte unter der Ägide des Bundes Constitutional Court, in: DÖV (2005), 860 (861) [European human rights under the aegis of the Federal Constitutional Court, in: DOV (2005), 860 (861)].

who occupy seats in parliament after the judgment in violation of human rights by the Constitutional Court, must, indeed, give up their seats. After a successful human rights complaint, the plaintiffs are entitled to demand their seats back. How this will be taken forward in detail is to be clarified by means of the binding effect of national procedural law (I) and the indirect binding effect of the state organs (II).

I. National procedural binding force

The declaratory judgment has procedural consequences for the domestic legal system of the convicted Member State. The resumption is available to the Member State as an adequate means of reparation of the violation regarding the convention. The domestic concretisation of the compensation takes place by reopening the original proceedings (1). The resumption of the original proceedings is meant to sufficiently effect the change in the the National court's legal opinion (2) in order to reflect the substantive legal effect of the ECOWAS judgment. Moreover, the legal decision by the Court of justice sets the precedent for domestic parallel cases (3). *De lege ferenda,* the declaratory judgment by the Court of justice should be the basis for a *Question Prioritaire de Conformité* (4).

1. Resumption of the initial proceedings

The cause of the declaratory judgment issued against the respondent was the judgment of a violation of human rights by the Constitutional Court. In order to restore the status quo according to the Charter, this cause must be terminated.[54] Several conditions are necessary in order for the resumption of original proceedings. The resumption of the proceedings is not opposed to the institution of legal force.

54 Mückl, Kooperation oder Konfrontation? – Das Verhältnis zwischen Bundesverfassungsgericht und Europäischem Gerichtshof für Menschenrechte, in: Der Staat 44 (2005), 403 (404).
[Cooperation or confrontation? – the relationship between the Federal Constitutional Court and the European Court of Human Rights], in: Der Staat [The State], 44 (2005), 403 (404)].

a. Prerequisites for a resumption

At this point, it must be differentiated between a completed violation (*violation consommée*) and violations that could be eliminated through future changes. Because, due to the conviction, the Court of justice orders the convicted Member State to terminate the persisting violations, the omission of repeated offences and to take measures to prevent future violations. Therefore, the question arises of what happens should the violation be complete. This means that the legal situation of the plaintiff cannot be restored in hindsight. This addresses the question of the impossibility of performance at International law level. In case of impossibility, the criteria of the obligation of restitution have been stipulated by the Permanent International Court of Justice with the following words:

> « Restitution en nature, ou, si elle n'est pas possible, paiement d'une somme correspondant à la valeur qu'aurait la restitution en nature. »[55]

The restitution has become impossible due to the fact that the violation concerns a completed event.[56]

However, National court decisions contrary to International law are vulnerable due to the obligation of restitution.[57] This addresses the question of the infringing act as the restitution depends on the manner in which the violation came about. There are many such cases in which the possibility

55 Affaire relative à l'usine de CHORZÓW (demande en indemnité) (fond), CPJI, Série A N° 17 (13.09.1928), 47.

56 Cremer, Zur Bindungswirkung von EGMR-Urteilen. Anmerkung zum Görgülü-Beschluß des BVerfG vom 14.10.2004, in: EuGRZ (2004), 683 (691) [Regarding the binding effect of judgments by the ECtHR. Comment regarding the Görgülü judgment by the Federal Constitutional Court of] 14/10/2004, in: EuGRZ (2004), 683 (691)].; Kilian, Die Bindungswirkung der Entscheidungen des Europäischen Gerichtshofs für Men- schenrechte auf die Nationalen Gerichte der Mitgliedstaaten der Konvention zum Schutze der Men- schenrechte und Grundfreiheiten vom 4. November 1950, 200. [The Binding Effect of Decisions taken by the European Court of Law for Human Rights with regards to the National Court of the Member States regarding the Convention on the Protection of Human Rights and Constitutional Freedoms of 4 November 1950, 200].

57 Cremer, Zur Bindungswirkung von EGMR-Urteilen. Anmerkung zum Görgülü-Beschluß des BVerfG vom 14.10.2004, in: EuGRZ (2004), 683 (691). [Regarding the binding effect of judgments by the ECtHR. Comment regarding the Görgülü judgment by the Federal Constitutional Court of] 14/10/2004, in: EuGRZ (2004), 683 (691)].

of resumption is excluded due to the nature of the matter[58]. E.g. a responding state is convicted based on the overly long duration of the trial,[59] or the plaintiff was arrested and released without any criminal proceedings. In such cases, the granting of appropriate damages offers a reasonable compensation in order to do justice to the interests of the individual plaintiff. Except from such cases in which the restitution is impossible due to the nature of the infringing act, a resumption of the proceedings in most cases represents the only possibility for *restitutio in integrum*. This is typically the violation of the Right to a fair trial acc. to Art. 7 par. 1 of the Charter.

The legal force of National courts is in no way an insurmountable obstacle to the effectiveness of the judgment under International law. However, the resumption of the trial cannot be carried out ex officio. This results from the fact that the declaratory judgment is not directly binding to the National instance (This is discussed in detail). It is, therefore, recommended to reopen the proceedings of restitution on application by the plaintiff.[60] The concerned signatory state has a duty to act due to the declaratory judgment: the obligation of implementation. The implementation can be made more concrete through the resumption. The content of the obligation is to restore the original status quo. The restoration is made in the form of a reinstatement into the previous state of affairs. Depending on the nature of the violation, the retraction of the violating National legal act or the violating measure must primarily be considered. The legal force cannot be preferred to the duty to implement.[61] In the case of a decision by the Constitutional Court, a resumption of the proceedings in favour of the convicted plaintiff (after his successful complaint by taking action under

---

58 Polakiewicz, Die Verpflichtung der Staaten aus den Urteilen des Europäischen Gerichtshofs für Menschenrechte, 98.[The obligation of countries resulting from the judgments by the European Court of Human Rights, 98.].

59 Ress, Die Europäische Menschenrechtskonvention und die deutsche Rechtsordnung [The European Convention on Human Rights and the German legal system], in: EuGRZ 1996, 337, 351.

60 Kilian, Die Bindungswirkung der Entscheidungen des Europäischen Gerichtshofs für Men- schenrechte auf die Nationalen Gerichte der Mitgliedstaaten der Konvention zum Schutze der Men- schenrechte und Grundfreiheiten vom 4. November 1950, 108. [The Binding Effect of Decisions taken by the European Court of Law for Human Rights with regards to the National Court of the Member States regarding the Convention on the Protection of Human Rights and Constitutional Freedoms of 4 November 1950, 108].

61 Schaffarzik, Europäische Menschenrechte unter der Ägide des Bundesverfassungsgerichts, in: DÖV (2005), 860 (867). [European human rights under the aegis of the Federal Constitutional Court, in: DOV (2005), 860 (867)].

International law) must be considered. This is coherent because, according to the principle of *restitutio in integrum*, the convicted signatory state must restore the state of affairs for the plaintiff in such a way as if the Charter had not been violated. Only if a complete reparation turns out to be impossible due to the nature[62] of the matter, is compensation the only other alternative. It must be pointed out that the restoration to the previous status quo does not preclude a just compensation. On the contrary, the restoration in the form of a reinstatement of the previous state of affairs can be done together with an appropriate compensation. It is already accepted in the literature on International law that both obligations, i.e. the natural restitution and the payment of compensation, may go hand in hand.[63]

Furthermore, the legal force is not breached, but rather overcome, by the resumption of the original proceedings on application by the plaintiff, The exceptional overcoming of the legal force based on the jurisdiction by the ECtHR has already been accepted in German constitutional case law. The Federal Constitutional Court has outlined:

> „Entscheidungen des Europäischen Court of Law für Menschenrechte, die neue Aspekte für die Auslegung des Grundgesetzes enthalten, stehen rechtserheblichen Änderungen gleich,die zur Überwindung der Rechtskraft einer Entscheidung des Bundesverfassungsgerichts führen können".[64]

Many legal systems within the European judicial area provide for a resumption of proceedings after a conviction by the ECtHR. E.g. § 359 par. 6 of the German Crimimal Procedure Code. The Swiss Constitutional Process Law makes even more explicit provision for a resumption of the original constitutional complaint, should the ECtHR have determined a violation bySwitzerland. At this point it is advisable to quote the regulation:

> « Art. 122: Violation de la Convention européenne des droits de l'hommeLa révision d'un arrêt du Tribunal fédéral pour violation de la

---

62 Peukert, in: Frowein/Peukert, Europäische Menschnrechtskonvention. EMRK-Kommentar[European Human Rights Convention. ECHR-commentary], 3. edition, Art. 41, Rn. 3

63 Schilling, Deutscher Grundrechtsschutz zwischen staatlicher Souveränität und menschen- rechtlicher Europäisierung, S. 113; Ipsen, Völkerrecht, § 41, Rn. 66. [Protection of the German constitutional law between state sovereignty and Europeanisation of human rights, p. 113; Ipsen, International law§ 41, Rn. 66].

64 BVerfGE 128, 326 (326).

Convention de sauvegarde des droits de l'homme et des libertés fondamentales du 4 novembre 1950 (CEDH) peut être demandée aux conditions suivantes : a. la Cour européenne des droits de l'homme a constaté, dans un arrêt définitif, une violation de la CEDH ou de ses protocoles; b. une indemnité n'est pas de nature à remédier aux effets de la violation; c. la révision est nécessaire pour remédier aux effets de la violation ».[65]

The constitutional sovereignty of the signatory state is not opposed to the obligation to restitution.[66] This is coherent as the individual human and fundamental rights recognised in the Charter are not at the disposition of the National constitutional legislator. The conditions of a resumption of the proceedings do not play a significant role in the procedure to implement the judgment.[67] In Austria, for example, in addition to fair compensation, domestic measures are provided for in order to meet the obligation of restitution (§ 33 StPO, renewal of the criminal proceedings acc. to §§ 363a to 363c StPO).[68]

Moreover, the question must be asked which arguments for action the winning individual plaintiff should put forward before the National courts. Following this, one should ask which reasons the judgment of the National court should contain when going over the new facts of the case. For the main proceedings are, as shown, concluded and have therefore entered into legal force. The decision by the ECOWAS Court of Justice serves as a guideline for the constitutional assessment of the case when the National Constitutional Court reconsiders judgment of the case.[69] The fact that a Constitutional Court has to reconsider an individual complaint fol-

65 La loi fédérale sur le Tribunal fédéral du 17 juin 2005, entrée en vigueur le 1er janvier 2007; siehe dazu: CEDH, Nr. 10577/04, Arrêt (26.07.2007), Affaire Kressler c. Suisse, par. 18.

66 Cremer, Zur Bindungswirkung von EGMR-Urteilen. Anmerkung zum Görgülü-Beschluß des BVerfG vom 14.10.2004, in: EuGRZ (2004), 683 (696). [Regarding the binding effect of judgments by the ECtHR. Comment regarding the Görgülü judgment by the Federal Constitutional Court of] 14/10/2004, in: EuGRZ (2004), 683 (696)].

67 Pettiti, Le réexamen d'une décision pénale française après un arrêt de la Cour Européenne des Droits de L'Homme: La loi française du 15 juin 2000, in: Revue Trimestrielle des Droits de l'Homme (2001), 3 (12).

68 See: Okresek, Die Umsetzung der EGMR-Urteile und ihre Überwachung, in: EuGRZ 2003, 168 (171). [The implementation of ECtHR judgments and their supervision, in: EuGRZ (2003), 168 (171)].

69 Mückl, Kooperation oder Konfrontation? – Das Verhältnis zwischen Bundesverfassungsge- richt und Europäischem Gerichtshof für Menschenrechte, in: Der

lowing a declaratory judgment of the ECtHR in favour of the successful human rights complainant despite having previously declared it judgment inadmissable is now well-known in the jurisdiction of the German Constitutional Court ever since the Görgülü case.[70] Therefore, there is no loss of sovereignty should the Constitutional Court render the declaratory judgments by the ECOWAS Court of Justice effective. Based on the exemplary role of the Constitutional Court, the effective implementation of International judgments by the Constitutional Court would be seen as a sign of respect for the rule of law. This is also primarily the demand of the Protocol on Good Governance of 2001. By consulting this Protocol in the judgments of the Constitutional Court of Togo in 2009, the opinion is confirmed that this Protocol represents a supra-National Constitution for the West African Community.[71] The Constitutional Court expressly quotes the Protocol on Good Governance of 2001 in the salient reasons for the decision. However, the Constitutional Court cannot act *ex nihilo*.[72] It requires regulations with regard to the constitutional process to simplify the execution of the resumed proceedings. The court judgments and especially those by the Constitutional Courts must have a legal basis. The Constitution, the acts supplementing the Constitution (the *lois organiques*) and the rules of procedure of the Constitutional Court are the legal bases for the Constitutional Courts. Here, a reason for a resumption should be recorded.

The determination of the violation of human rights by the ECOWAS Court of justice should be recorded in the acts supplementing the Constitution either as "*erreur de droit*"[73] or as a new fact, which represents a rea-

---

Staat 44 (2005), 403 (414) [Cooperation or confrontation? – the relationship between the Federal Constitutional Court and the European Court of Human Rights], in: Der Staat [The State], 44 (2005), 403 (414)].

70 The Federal Constitutional Court had at first declared the complaint inadmissible: BVerfG (Chamber), a decision of 31/07/2001. After a successful human rights complaint before the ECtHR, the proceedings is again presented to the Federal Constitutional Court. As a reaction to the declaratory judgment by the ECtHR, the Federal Constitutional Court has accepted the renewed constitutional complaint submitted to it for decision-making and sustained the complaint, comp. BVerfGE 111, 307 – Görgülü.

71 See the judgment by the Constitutional Court of Togo: Décision N°C-003/09 du 09 Juillet 2009.

72 Cremer, Entscheidung und Entscheidungswirkung [Decision and Effect of the Decision], in: Dörr/Grote/Marauhn, EMRK/GG, 2. edition, chapter 32, Rn. 91.

73 Adeloui, L'autorité de la chose jugée par les juridictions constitutionnelles en Afrique, in: Revue Togolaise des Sciences Juridiques (2012), 54 (68, 69); DCC 98–098 du 11 décembre 1998; DCC 02–134 du 18 décembre 2002 de la Cour constitutionnelle du Bénin.

son for resumption. This is because the Constitutional Court did not take sufficient account of the aspects relevant to human rights decisions when dealing with the first final decision that violated human rights. In particular, there are already factors in some West African constitutional systems that lead to a relativisation of the legal force of judgments by Constitutional Courts.[74] Under the european jurisdiction the Federal Constitutional Court of the Federal Republic of Germany has rightly pointed out that the regional human right Court has better knowledge regarding the current status and the development of human rights with respect to the current conditions („*à la lumière des conditions d'aujourd'hui*"). Therefore, the jurisdiction of the ECOWAS Court of Justice lends itself as an aid for the interpretation when it comes to the resumption of a trial.

It is recommended that the National Constitutional Court and the courts quote the supporting reasons of the ECOWAS Court of Justice in the declaratory judgment in the resumed trial because the act of violation by the concerned state is to be found in the salient reasons of the judgment. For this reason, the International judgment is also decisive for the domestic Constitutional Court in justifying its own opinion.

As far as the successful individual plaintiff is concerned, he refers directly to the declaratory judgment of the ECOWAS Court of Justice.[75] These are the substantive consequences of the legal force, as the substantive legal force of the ECOWAS judgment should be decisive in the renewed consideration of the facts by the domestic Constitutional Court.[76] In other words: the cause of the action in the retrial represents the declaratory judgment by the ECOWAS Court of Justice. This opinion also confirms the most recent jurisdiction by the European Court of Human Rights.[77] It

74 Adeloui, L'autorité de la chose jugée par les juridictions constitutionnelles en Afrique, in: Revue Togolaise des Sciences Juridiques (2012), 54 (68, 69).

75 Kilian, Die Bindungswirkung der Entscheidungen des Europäischen Gerichtshofs für Men- schenrechte auf die Nationalen Gerichte der Mitgliedstaaten der Konvention zum Schutze der Men- schenrechte und Grundfreiheiten vom 4. November 1950, 107. [The Binding Effect of Decisions taken by the European Court of Law for Human Rights with regards to the National Court of the Member States regarding the Convention on the Protection of Human Rights and Constitutional Freedoms of 4 November 1950, 107].

76 Cremer, Zur Bindungswirkung von EGMR-Urteilen. Anmerkung zum Görgülü-Beschluß des BVerfG vom 14.10.2004 [Regarding the binding effect of judgments by the ECtHR. Comment regarding the Görgülü judgment by the Federal Constitutional Court of 14/10/2004], in: EuGRZ 2004, 683 (698).

77 Maestriv. Italian, Urteil der Großen Kammer vom 17.02.2004, Ziffer 47[Judgment by the Great Chamber of 17/02/2004, Clause 47].

states that the resumption of the violating action or sovereign measure represents an appropriate measure of restitution.[78] Because of this, the reference to the resumption of the trial should be mentioned in the declaratory judgment so that is can be implemented effectively. Without this exceptional overturning of the final decision of the National Constitutional Court, Art. 15 par. 4 of the Amendment Agreement would be null and void which would not correspond with the will of the signatory states.[79]

b. Justification of the obligation to resume

The individual possibility to complain from within the ECOWAS legal circle is to be seen as formal justice. The guarantee in Art. 7 par. 1 of the Charter, together with Art. 9 and 10 of Protocol A/SP./01/05 is a procedural guarantee of effective legal protection because, with the opening up of this possibility to complain, an individual plaintiff is entitled to a procedural guarantee at the international level. This procedural guarantee primarily derives from Art. 1a of the Charter:

> « Toute personne a le droit à ce que sa cause soit entendue. Ce droit comprend : le droit de saisir les juridictions Nationales compétentes de tout acte violant les droits fondamentaux qui lui sont reconnus et garantis par les conventions, les lois, règlements et coutumes en vigueur ».

This guarantee would not be of great importance for the plaintiff if no substantive legal consequences would arise in his individual case. The procedural law is rather meant to concretise the substantive right. What good is a declaratory judgment without revising the National judgment in favour of the plaintiff? The disguise of legal force should not be a justification to uphold Constitutional Court judgments opposed to the Charter.[80] Thus, every signatory state carries the responsibility when a violation is declared

78 Bernhardt, The Convention and Domestic Law, in: Macdonald/Matscher/Petzold (Publ.), The European System for the Protection of Human Rights, 25 (37).

79 Schaffarzik, Europäische Menschenrechte unter der Ägide des Bundesverfassungsgerichts [European human rights under the aegis of the Federal Constitutional Court], in: DÖV (2005), 860 (867).

80 Breuer, Von Lyons zu Sejdovic: Auf dem Weg zu einer Wiederaufnahme konventionswidrig zustande gekommener Nationaler Urteile? [On the way to a resumption of National judgments that have come about in a manner contrary to the Convention], in: EuGRZ 2004, 782 (786).

to undertake everything to remove any kind of obstacle to the implementation. These measures could be a reopening of a trial despite final judgments or a legislative act.[81]

Thus, the possibility of individual complaints after the granting of a declaratory judgment triggers a substantive change in the legal situation at National level in favour of the plaintiff. The formal justice, i.e. the procedural guarantee at ECOWAS legal level serves substantive justice. The resumption is a realisation of this substantive justice. After the declaratory judgment has been issued, the plaintiff has not yet felt the benefit of the specific change of his rights. This rather happens once a favourable resumption of the original proceedings take place. Only then does the plaintiff experience the effect of the procedural guarantee, as prescribed by Art. 7 par. 1 of the Charter.

The change in legal opinion of a Constitutional Court or Supreme Court is not foreign to constitutional legal systems. For example, § 129 par. 3 of the Constitution of Ghana stipulates:

> "The supreme Court may, while treating its own previous decision as normally binding, de part from a previous decision when it appears to it right to do so, and all other courts shall be bound to follow the decisions of the Supreme Court on questions of law."

Such constitutional regulations should be welcomed as the interpretation of the Constitution is a dynamic process. The case law of a Constitutional Jurisdictions namely follows societal change and meets its needs. Regarding the judgments of the ECOWAS Court of Justice, the same thought can be applied with regards to the legal consequences of a declaratory judgment. The case of the the Federal Constitutional Court of Germany can repeatedly be recalled when it has revised its legal opinion following a divergence between itself and the ECtHR.[82]

---

81 Kilian, Die Bindungswirkung der Entscheidungen des Europäischen Gerichtshofs für Men- schenrechte auf die Nationalen Gerichte der Mitgliedstaaten der Konvention zum Schutze der Men- schenrechte und Grundfreiheiten vom 4. November 1950, 201. [The Binding Effect of Decisions taken by the European Court of Law for Human Rights with regards to the National Court of the Member States regarding the Convention on the Protection of Human Rights and Constitutional Freedoms of 4 November 1950, 201].

82 Mückl, Kooperation oder Konfrontation? – Das Verhältnis zwischen Bundesverfassungsge- richt und Europäischem Court of Law für Menschenrechte [Cooperation or confrontation? – the relationship between the Federal Constitutional Court and the European Court of Human Rights], in: Der Staat 44 (2005), 403 (410).

From the above, the regulations demand from the constitutional procedural law of Member States that the jurisdiction must be adjusted to the legal development within the ECOWAS Community. It is in fact conceivable that the declaratory judgment of the ECOWAS Court of Justice should be one of the reasons for a change in legal opinion of Constitutional case law. Consequently, § 129 par. 3 of the Constitution of Ghana needs to be supplemented with respect to the guidelines of ECOWAS instruments.

2. Declaratory judgment by the ECOWAS Court of Justice as a prohibition of enforcement

It is questionable whether the application for the resumption of the original proceedings hinders the execution of the final constitutional judgment. It is important to remember at this point that the judgment by the Constitutional Court that has entered into legal force develops certain effects (this was already addressed to in Chapter 1,). In its core, this application cannot be assigned any restrictive effect as far as the execution is concerned. However, as a result of the renewed consideration of the case after a second final constitutional judgment, the enforcement of the first judgment in violation of human rights is suspended.[83] These legal consequences should be provided for in National procedural law or respectively in court procedure regulations. The domestic measure in violation of the Charter and which has been declared as such by the ECOWAS Court of Justice is no longer enforceable. The convicted Member State must cease the execution of such measures in order to avoid a renewed violation of the Charter. Therefore, the declaratory judgment serves at National level as an interdiction against an execution.[84]

However, the Constitutional Court cannot remove the legal consequences that were set in motion in the past. Rather, the legal force is valid based on the first judgment issued in violation of human rights. The only solution in this constellation is the cessation of the execution in future.

83 Vgl. Hoffman-Holland, Resumption of a closed trial made final bya judgment], in: Graf (Publ.), Strafprozessordnung [Criminal Procedure Code], § 360, Rn. 1.

84 Heckötter, Die Bedeutung der Europäischen Menschenrechtskonvention und der Recht- sprechung des EGMR für die deutschen Gerichte [The meaning of the European Convention on Human Rights and the jurisdiction of the ECtHR for German courts], 256.

The declaratory judgment by the ECOWAS Court of Justice hence develops an *ex-nunc*-effect at a National level. Even though third parties may have possibly benefitted from the constitutional judgment in violation of human rights, the known principles of unjust enrichment in civil law cannot be applied to their full extent.[85]

3. Effects Transcending the Individual Case

It has been demonstrated above that the declaratory judgment can be extended to the legal systems of other Member States. Now the question must be asked whether the same cross-case effect is imaginable for parallel cases at domestic level. Above all, the ECOWAS legal system does not expressely limit the effect of its decision on the decided legal matter for. However, the system of the ECHR specifies that the signatory states are only obligated in legal matters to which they are a party (Art. 46 par. 1 der ECHR).[86]

Another argument for the legally binding parallel cases on national level is that the declaratory judgment represents a significant legal consequence on national level for the winning individual plaintiff by way of the resumption of the original proceedings. However, the declaratory judgment only develops a direct effect for the parties to the trial before the ECOWAS Court of Justice, and thus only for the individual plaintiff and the responsible Member State. However, the concerned Member State is required to transfer the consequences of the final declaratory judgment by the ECOWAS Court of Justice to comparable domestic cases.[87] The transfer of legal consequences has the advantage for the Member State of avoiding another future conviction.

---

85 Pestalozza, Verfassungsprozeßrecht [Constitutional Process Law], 3. edition, § 20, Rn. 74 f.

86 Rohleder, Grundrechtsschutz im europäischen Mehrlevelssystem [Protection of constitutional law in the European multi-level system], 273.

87 Rohleder, Grundrechtsschutz im europäischen Mehrlevelssystem [Protection of constitutional law in the European multi-level system], 273.

4. ECOWAS Court of Justice Decisions as the basis for QPC

From a comparable point of view, the jurisdiction of the ECOWAS Court of Justice can represent the legal basis of a *Question Prioritaire de Conformité* before the courts of the Member States. The mechanism in constitutional law of the *Question Prioritaire de Constitutionnalité* (QPC) is actually a common institution of procedural law before the French Conseil constitutionnel. The analysis of the QPC requires an account of the relevant French constitutional regulation. Art. 61–1 of the French Constitution reads as follows :

> « Lorsque, à l'occasion d'une instance en cours devant une juridiction, il est soutenu qu'une disposition législative porte atteinte aux droits et libertés que la Constitution garantit, le Conseil constitutionnel peut être saisi de cette question sur renvoi du Conseil d'État ou de la Cour de cassation qui se prononce dans un délai déterminé».[88]

The basic functioning of the system of the QPC is atypical.[89] It is a hybrid system for this mechanism represents a combination of an abstract and concrete judicial review.[90] In principle, the QPC is triggered by the question of a normal party to the process, i.e. a citizen, who disputes the constitutionality of a legal norm applicable to a concrete case.[91] However, the proceedings which ensue do not function like the preliminary ruling procedure within the framework of Art. 267 TFEU before the ECJ. Contrary to the preliminary ruling procedure, here a significant idiosyncrasy arises: Only the highest courts in the various stages of the proceedings are entitled to appeal before the Constitutional Council because the highest domestic courts function as a filter during the assessment of the QPC. This means that the court which is presented with the question, may not decide on the constitutionality of the disputed legal norm. On the contrary, the question is directed to the respective highest court (Cour de Cassation or Conseil d'État). Thus, the pending proceedings must be suspended until the highest court or, where appropriate, the Constitutional Council has reached a decision on the constitutionality of the law. The filtering process

88 Art. 61–1 de la Constitution du 04 octobre 1958 suivant la modification du 23 juillet 2008.
89 Preußler, Question prioritaire de constitutionnalité, 31.
90 Preußler, Question prioritaire de constitutionnalité, 31.
91 Cartier, Le positionnement tactique et stratégique des acteurs du procès face à la QPC, in: ders. (Publ.): La QPC, le procès et ses juges, 53 (53).

takes place at the level of the highest court. Should the question be considered to require presentation, it will be transferred to the Constitutional Council for a decision. This means that only the Constitutional Council is authorised to decide on constitutionality. This shows that the QPC is a legal remedy in the event of a concrete legal dispute. For this reason, the QPC has both the legal nature of a concrete and an abstract judicial review. Nevertheless, this is not a complete abstract control measure.[92] It must be pointed out that when it comes to the admissibility of the trial, it is not necessary that the disputed legal norm is decisive for the outcome of the pending procedures. Rather, it is sufficient that the respective legal norm represents a violation of the human and civil rights guaranteed in the Constitution.

Regarding the signatory states to ECOWAS, it must be pointed out that a comparable mechanism is not entirely unknown to the constitutional systems of the signatory states. Literally all francophone West African states have a comparable procedure referred to as "*Procédure de l'exception d'inconstitutionnalité*". Therefore, Art. 104 par. 6 of the Togolese Constitution stipulates:

> « Au cours d'une instance judiciaire, toute personne physique, ou morale peut, ‹ *in limine li- tis* ›, devant les cours et tribunaux, soulever l'exception d'inconstitutionnalité d'une loi. Dans ce cas, la juridiction sursoit à statuer et saisit la Cour constitutionnelle».[93]

Due to the fact that the object of the dispute is not the legal dispute as such, but rather the constitutionality of the law, this trial is called a *procédure de l'exception d'inconstitutionnalité.* Indeed, every citizen can dispute the constitutionality of a law that has already entered into legal force during the legal dispute. The court before which the proceedings are pending is obliged to submit them. In this case, the legal dispute is suspended and the question of constitutionality of the disputed law is referred to the

92 Preußler, Question prioritaire de constitutionnalité, 37.

93 Art. 104 par. 6 Verfassung von Togo vom 14. Oktober 1992 [Constitution of Togo of 14 October 1992]; Art. 122 Verfassung Benin vom 11. Dezember 1991[Constitution of Benin of 11 December 1991]; Art. 132 par. 1 Verfassung Niger vom 25. November 2010[Constitution of Niger of 25 November 2010]; Art. 96 par. 4 Verfas- sung Guinea vom 07. May 2010 [Constitution of Guinea of 07 May 2010]; Art. 96 Verfassung Elfenbeinküste vom 23. July 2000[Constitution of Ivory Coast of 23 July 2000]; Kanté, Models of Constitutional Jurisdiction in Francophone West Africa, in: The Journal of Comparative Law (2008) Vol. 3, 158 (160).

Constitutional Court.[94] However, there is no possibility in the current legal situation to assess the incompatibility of a legal norm with the African Charter and the respective constitutional case law by the ECOWAS Court of Justice. Therefore, the mechanism of the QPC should contribute to closing loopholes with certain adjustments in this regard.

This mechanism of the QPC can be applied to the domestic orientation effect of the ECOWAS judgment because the jurisprudence of the ECOWAS Court of Justice is part of the meaning and capacity of the African Charter within the constitutional order of the Community. Whenever the conformity to International law of a norm, in light of the African Charter, and with it the jurisprudence of the ECOWAS Court of Justice, is doubted by the disputing parties, there must be domestic mechanisms in place, which enable such questions to be indicatively answered. This would produce a cross-case effect of the decision by the ECOWAS Court of Justice. However, the corresponding adjustment must be pointed out. The description and importance of the QPC should be adjusted because the *Question Prioritaire de Constitutionnalité* is based on the question of compatibility with the French Constitution. At this point, the question should be described as a *Question Prioritaire de Conformité* (in the following referred to as *QPC*) as those seeking justice should ask the question of the compatibility (Conformité) with the African Charter and the case law of the ECOWAS Court of Justice. This reference is important because the African Charter, together with the jurisdiction by the Court of justice , represents an instrument of autonomy. The task of the national Constitutional Courts would therefore, be to assess whether the allegation, primarily made against a legal norm with regards to the African Charter or against the case law of the Court of Law, has any foundation. In this respect, the national

94 Art. 24 LO und Art. 122 Verf B; *Mipamb*, L'exception d'inconstitutionnalité en droit togolais, available at: www.courconstitutionnel.tg (last accessed on 22/06/2015); Bado, Verfassungs- gerichtsbarkeit und Demokratisierung im frankophonen Westafrika, Länderstudie/Togo[Constitutional Jurisdiction and democratisation in Francophone West Africa, country study Togo], 11, ab- rufbar unter [available at]: http://intlaw-sgiessen.de/fileadmin/user_upload/bilder_und_dokumente/forschung/ westafrikaprojekt/workingpapers/Draft_WP_2014_benin.pdf (last accessed on 02/07/2015); Cour constitutionnelle du Bénin, Décision DCC 10–117 (08.09.2010) available at: www. cour-constitutionnelle-benin.org (last accessed on 25/04/2015); Cour constitutionnelle du Bénin, Décision DCC 10–149 (28.12.2010), available at: www.cour-constitutionnelle-benin.org (last accessed on 25/04/2015).

Constitutional Courts would contribute to consolidate the meaning of the African Charter and the case law of the Court of justice at a National level.

The mechanism of the QPC should entail many advantages. First of all, the domestic *erga-omnes*-effect of the jurisdiction by the ECOWAS Court of Justice is established by the domestic Constitutional Courts.[95] Indeed, the decision by the domestic Constitutional Courts has an automatic *erga-omnes*-effect. In this sense, regarding the capacity of the *QPC*-judgment in the domestic legal system, the French Constitutional Council emphasises in established case law judgment:

> « Considérant que cette déclaration d'inconstitutionnalité prend effet à compter de la date de publication de la présente décision ; que, d'une part, elle est applicable à toutes les procédures dans lesquelles les réquisitions du procureur de la République ont été adressées postérieurement à la publication de la présente décision ; que, d'autre part, dans les procédures qui n'ont pas été jugées définitivement à cette date, elle ne peut être invoquée que par les parties non représentées par un avocat lors du règlement de l'information dès lors que l'ordonnance de règlement leur a fait grief » [96]

The same tenor can be recommended for the proposed *QPC* in the domestic constitutional order of ECOWAS. By declaring the *QPC*-decision of the Constitutional Court compatible with ECOWAS case law, it also has an *erga-omnes*-effect on the Court of Justice's decision. When accepting the compatibility of a legal norm with the Charter or with the decision by the ECOWAS Court of Justice, it must then be expressly referred to the respective decision by the Court of Law. Accordingly, the domestic acknowledgement of the decision by the ECOWAS Court of Justice by the Constitutional Court of Benin must be welcomed. In fact, regarding the definition of an arbitrary arrest, the Constitutional Court of Benin expressly referred to the relevant judgment by the ECOWAS Court of Justice:

> « Notons que pour déterminer à partir de quand une arrestation et une détention sont jugées arbitraires, la Cour de Justice de la CEDEAO, dans son arrêt N°ECW/CCJ/JUD/05/10 du 08 novembre 2010 prononcé dans l'espèce Mamadou TANDJA contre État du Niger a rappelé

95 Bernabé/Cartier, L'introduction d'un nouveau gène dans le procès, in: Cartier (Publ.): La QPC, le procès et ses juges, 1 (21).

96 Conseil Constitutionnel, N°2011–160 QPC (09.09.2011), M. Hovanes A.; Conseil Constitu- tionnel, N°2010–15/23 QPC (23.07.2010), Région Languedoc-Roussillon et autres.

> que les conclusions de la « Commission des Droits de l'Homme de l'Organisation des Nations Unies, en déterminant le mandat du groupe de travail sur la détention arbitraire a considéré comme arbitraires les privations de liberté qui, pour une raison ou une autre sont contraires aux normes Internationales pertinentes énoncées dans la Déclaration universelle des droits de l'Homme ou par les instruments internationaux pertinents ratifiés par les États ».[97]

This modus operandi should be applied to the mechanism of the QPC. Even if the French Constitutional Council does not always expressly refer to the jurisdiction by the ECtHR when it comes to the *QPC*, a convergence of legal practices between the two legal systems can be seen in renowned statemtents by the Constitutional Council.[98] Moreover, with the introduction of the *QPC*, the contribution of the litigants to the communitarisation and consolidation of constitutional jurisprudence will be decisively recognisable in the constitutional system of ECOWAS. Furthermore, by introducing the *QP*C the Member States would avoid further convictions because the proposal is based on the assumption that the litigants should have the opportunity within the framework of the *QP*C, by way of a constitutional process, to remove a potential violation of their rights which is embedded in the African Charter. This is consistent: The application of a legal norm contrary to the Convention leads directly to a violation of the Convention and therefore the rights of the citizens. Therefore, the procedure of the *QP*C will contribute to the anticipation of the conviction of Member States. Finally, a unified application of the African Charter and judgments of the Court of justice will be established in Member States by the *QPC*. This consideration takes the idea of precautionary compliance with the obligations resulting from a declaratory judgment into account. Indeed, every Member State has three kinds of obligations in case of a conviction: the obligation to terminate, the obligation of reparation and the

---

97 Cour constitutionnelle du Bénin, Décision DCC 15–025 (12.02.2015), available at: www. cour-constitutionnelle-benin.org (letzter Zugriff am 27.04.2015).

98 Conseil Constitutionnel, N°2011–113/115 QPC (01.04.2011), M. Xavier P. et autres; Conseil Constitutionnel, N°2010–38 QPC (29.09.2010), M. Jean-Yves G.; Conseil Constitutionnel, N°2011- 147 QPC (08.08.2011), M Tarek J.; Conseil Constitutionnel, N°2011–185 QPC (21.10.2011),
M. Jean-Louis C.; Conseil Constitutionnel N°2011–223 QPC (12.02.2012), Ordre des Avocats au barreau de Bastia; Conseil Constitutionnel, N°2012–243/244/245/246 QPC (14.05.2012), Société Yvonne Républicaine et autre; Conseil Constitutionnel, N°2011–214 QPC (27.01.2012), Société COVED SA.

obligation of prevention. With the introduction of the *QPC*, the obligation of prevention will be met to a large extent.

However, the *QPC* as proposed here could entail a certain risk on both sides: If the highest domestic courts should avail of a monopoly without any control during the filtering process of the question to be referred to the Constitutional Courts, this, on one hand, entails the potential danger of an arbitrary refusal. This risk is already known in the French constitutional process.[99] Therefore, it is recommended that the highest court dealing with the question must be obliged to give reasons for a possible refusal of a submission to the Constitutional Court.[100] This would serve to enable a clean filtering process of the *QPC* at the highest courts. Furthermore, the litigants should have a legal remedy against the refusal of a reference of the *QPC*. On the other hand, the litigants may also misuse the *QPC* by possibly abusing it to delay the pending trial (as a *manoeuvre dilatoire*). It is therefore recommended that the objection of incompatibility with the relevant basis of the Charter or decision by the ECOWAS Court of Justice be clearly stated before the respective court for the admissibility of the *QPC*. The legal basis of the *QPC*-objection should also be clearly distinguished.

Moreover, it must be stated that the national Constitutional Courts could, in certain cases, issue more guarantees than the ECOWAS Court of Justice. This would be admissible since the regional system before the ECOWAS Court of Justice is, after all, a subsidiary protection system according to International practice.[101] Therefore, the domestic Constitutional Court has the primary task to protect the human rights as guaranteed in the African Charter from state interference. In this respect, the ECOWAS protection system represents a lower threshold (*plancher*).[102] The domestic constitutional systems may reach an upper limit with regard to guarantee-

99 Bernabé/Cartier, L'introduction d'un nouveau gène dans le procès, in: Cartier (Publ.): La QPC, le procès et ses juges, 1 (21).

100 Delanlssays, La motivation des décisions juridictionnelles relatives à la QPC au prisme de l'efficience, in: Cartier (Publ.): La QPC, le procès et ses juges, 133 (137).

101 Villiger, The principle of subsidiarity in the European Convention on Human Rights, in: Promoting Justice, Human Rights and Conflict Resolution through International law (2007), 623 (625).

102 In comparison, the ECHR represents the minimum standard in the European Council. Also: Lock, Das Verhältnis zwischen dem ECJ und Internationalen Gerichten [the relationship between the ECJ and International courts], 280; Villiger, The principle of subsidiarity in the European Convention on Human Rights, in: Promoting Justice, Human Rights and Conflict Resolution through International Law (2007), 623 (634).

ing the Charter. Such approaches are known e.g. between the ECtHR and the French Constitutional Council. Indeed, a certain divergence between the Constitutional Council and the ECtHR in favour of more legal protection in the French constitutional system can be noted. This constellation is shown in the decisions Nr. 2011–160 and Nr. 2010–15/23.[103] These two decisions clarify that the regional system represents a minimum standard and the National constitutional system can do even more. All things considered, this approach is to be welcomed, because the understanding of the principle of subsidiarity and the primary obligation of the signatory states are clear.

In the end, the introduction of the *QPC* would enable the litigant to challenge every legal norm, should there be legitimate doubts that it does not comply with the guarantees of the Charter and the established case law of the ECOWAS Court of Justice. Furthermore, the possibility of a *QPC* in the legal system of the Member State would contribute to a certain autonomisation of the African Charter regarding the constitutional jurisprudence of the Member States. This would be guaranteed if the Constitutional Courts would expressly refer to the African Charter and the relevant judgment by the ECOWAS Court of Justice regarding the assessment of the conformity of the *QPC* with National legal norms. The African Charter, within the framework of the *QPC,* would also be seen as a domestic tool of interpretation of the guarantee in the Convention. Furthermore, the relationship of the constitutional guarantee and the guarantee of the Charter would become clearer with the QPC. Regarding the question before domestic courts, the *QPC* would contribute to a differentiation between *Exception d'Inconstitutionnalité* and *Question Prioritaire de Conformité*, because both procedures are similar yet have a different legal basis. The *Exception d'Inconstitutionnalité* refers to the constitutional regulations whilst the *QPC refers* to the guarantees of the African Charter and the corresponding decision by the ECOWAS Court of Justice. After all, with the introduction of the *QPC,* the litigants would become rather familiar with the African Charter and the ECOWAS-case law because such would form the legal basis of their question. All in all, the *QPC* would help in the proposed way the Charter and the case law of the ECOWAS Court of Justice to become a vibrant legal source in the constitutional legal systems the

103 Conseil Constitutionnel, N°2011–160 QPC (09.09.2011), M. Hovanes A.; Conseil Constitu- tionnel, N°2010–15/23 QPC (23.07.2010), Région Languedoc-Roussillon et autres.

Member States (*droit vivant*). Thus, the mechanism contributes to making the guarantee of the Charter also justiciable within domestic law.

II. Effect on all state powers

Although the state is directly convicted, the violating act was not caused by the state itself. Addressee of the declaratory judgment is the concerned state organ, which committed the wrongdoing of the Member State. However, state organs are not party to individual complaint proceedings before the ECOWAS Court of Justice. Precisely because of this, only the involved signatory state is expressly named in the tenor of the declaratory judgment.[104] Nevertheless, the state organs of the sued Member State are indirectly affected by the judgment.[105] This raises the question of the effectiveness and the mode of action of the declaratory judgment on the National legal system of the responsible Member State. On which legal grounds are the state organs obliged to observe International law in general and the decisions by the ECOWAS Court of Justice in particular? This question begs further clarification because Art. 15 par. 4 of the Amendment Agreement does not provide indications of whether the legal decision by the ECOWAS Court of Justice also represents a legal obligation for the National state organs (1). It is, however, certain that the national Constitutional Courts have a special binding commitment (2).

104 Kilian, Die Bindungswirkung der Entscheidungen des Europäischen Gerichtshofs für Men- schenrechte auf die Nationalen Gerichte der Mitgliedstaaten der Konvention zum Schutze der Men- schenrechte und Grundfreiheiten vom 4. November 1950[The Binding Effect of Decisions taken by the European Court of Law for Human Rights with regards to the National Court of the Member States regarding the Convention on the Protection of Human Rights and Constitutional Freedoms of 4 November 1950], 113.

105 CIJ, Demande en interprétation de l'arrêt du 31. mars 2004 en l'Affaire Avena et autres ressortissants mexicains (Mexique c. États-Unis d'Amérique), Arrêt du 19. janvier 2009, par. 64; Kilian, Die Bindungswirkung der Entscheidungen des Europäischen Gerichtshofs für Menschen- rechte auf die Nationalen Gerichte der Mitgliedstaaten der Konvention zum Schutze der Menschen- rechte und Grundfreiheiten vom 4. November 1950[The Binding Effect of Decisions taken by the European Court of Law for Human Rights with regards to the National Court of the Member States regarding the Convention on the Protection of Human Rights and Constitutional Freedoms of 4 November 1950], 114.

1. Indirect legal force for all state organs

The silence by the signatory states during the adoption of this Amendment Agreement could be justified by assuming that the question of the binding effect for the organs of the convicted Member State was left up to the National law of the concerned signatory state.[106] Which domestic organ is affected depends on the content of the violating act.[107] Although the declaratory judgment only has a declarative character, it directly intervenes in the domestic legal system of the concerned convicted Member State. Thus, all public authorities are bound by the legal binding force.[108] The indirect power of the case law of the ECOWAS Court of Justice to affect all state organs can be derived from the principles of *restitutio in integrum* and effective legal protection.[109] The ICJ thus decided in the legal matter of Avena vs the United States as follows:

> « Le comportement de tout organe de l'État est considéré comme un fait de l'État d'après le droit International, que cet organe exerce des fonctions législatives, exécutives, judiciaires ou autres, quelle que soit la position qu'il occupe dans l'organisation de l'État, et quelle que soit sa nature en tant qu'organe du gouvernement central ou d'une collectivité territoriale de l'État ».[110]

In case of a constitutional judgment which led to a violation, the decision regarding reparations has an indirect effect on the case law of the Constitutional Court. Should it be a law that has been declared to be in violation of human rights by the Court of justice , it must be assumed that the parliament will take this decision into account in the legislative amendment procedure of the sentenced member state. A legal act of the executive

106 Enabulele, Reflections on the ECOWAS-Community Court Protocol and the Constitutions of Member States, in: International Community Law Review 12 (2010), 111 (113).

107 BVerfGE 111, 307 (323 in C I 2 d) – Görgülü.

108 Cremer, Zur Bindungswirkung von EGMR-Urteilen. Anmerkung zum Görgülü-Beschluß des BVerfG vom 14.10.2004, in: EuGRZ 2004, 683 (692). [Regarding the binding effect of judgments by the ECtHR. Comment regarding the Görgülü judgment by the Federal Constitutional Court of] 14/10/2004, in: EuGRZ (2004), 683 (692)].

109 Rohleder, Grundrechtsschutz im europäischen Mehrlevelssystem [Protection of constitutional law in the European multi-level system], 160.

110 CIJ, Demande en interprétation de l'arrêt du 31 mars 2004 en l'Affaire Avena et autres res- sortissants mexicains (Mexique c. Ètats-Unis d'Amerique), Arrêt du 19 janvier 2009, par. 63.

which leads to the violation of the Charter should be rectified by an appropriate measure.Everything, therefore, depends on the organ which was party to the violation.

It follows that the ECOWAS Court of Justice does not have to expressly name the concerned state organ responsible for the misconduct in the tenor of the judgment. The reason is clear: The specification of competence has already been regulated in domestic law. So to speak: The declaratory judgment is directed together with the to whom it may concern.[111]

The declaratory judgment is addressed to the state organs in their respective area of competence. With regard to the domestic courts, the successful plaintiff receives an enforceable claim to restitution executable under International law through the declaratory judgment. By qualifying the conduct of the state as a violation of human rights and consequently convicting the state, the Court of Justice has indirectly convicted the domestic court concerned. At this stage, it should be pointed out that the Court of justice does not have the power to directly intervene in the domestic legal proceedings. Therefore, its judgments do not have a direct effect.[112] However, on the part of the courts, there is the obligation to give effect to International judgments at a National level. However, the judiciary cannot decide *ex nihilo*.[113] To avoid an *ultra vires,* act the courts need a legal basis. It is therefore recommended to provide for reasons for a resumption through legislation on a National level in order to take the judgments by the ECOWAS Court of Justice into account. This principle of reparation, deduced from common International law, is confirmed for example by § 359 No. 6 of the German Criminal Procedure Code. As a result, provisions should be made for domestic compensation proceedings within the National legal systems in the ECOWAS Community. Failure to comply is a violation of Art. 7 par. 1 of the African Charter.

The task of the legislature concerning compliance with the judgment can be justified on many grounds . As long as there are no new legal or constitutional regulations with regards to the legal effect of the declaratory judgment by the ECOWAS Court of Justice, the National courts in gener-

111 Schaffarzik, Europäische Menschenrechte unter der Ägide des Bundesverfassungsgerichts [European human rights under the aegis of the Federal Constitutional Court], in: DÖV (2005), 860 (864).

112 Rohleder, Grundrechtsschutz im europäischen Mehrlevelssystem [Protection of constitutional law in the European multi-level system], 159.

113 Bernhardt, The Convention and Domestic Law, in: Macdonald/Matscher/Petzold (Publ.), The European System for the Protection of Human Rights, 25 (38).

al, and the Constitutional Courts in particular, are in a dilemma. Compliance with the ECOWAS judgment means an infringement of theconstitutional requirement of the finality of Art. 106 of the Constitution (of Togo). Should the Constitutional Court however remain unimpressed by the declaratory judgment, there would also be an infringement of International law because of the violation of the obligation of compliance of an International judgment.[114] An easing of the legal effect in Art. 106 of the Togolese Constitution is the only way to resolve this dilemma. Thus, it is necessary that the National constitution-amending legislator or the simple legislator take action.[115] A law in violation of human rights per se already creates a normative basis for a permanent violation of the declaratory judgment because those enforcing the law are bound by the legislation. Specialised courts are bound by the legal authorisations of the legislator and the Constitutional Courts to the decision-making authority of the constitutional legislator (or the constitution-amending legislator). They align their actions to the guidelines given by the legislator. This was recently confirmed by the French State Council when it rejected the resumption of a decision by the administrative court in violation of human rights from 1999.[116] By the executive and the judiciary acting according to the guideline of the law, a law in violation of human rights would be per se the strongest form of a breach of a declaratory judgment by the ECOWAS Court of Justice. This makes the task of the legislature of implementing the declaratory judgment even more urgent.

Many Member States of the European Council have recognised the danger of a violation of the Convention based on non-action of the legislature. In order to prevent recurring violations, Germany and France, e.g. have

---

114 Mückl, Kooperation oder Konfrontation? – Das Verhältnis zwischen Bundesverfassungsge- richt und Europäischem Court of Law für Menschenrechte [Cooperation or confrontation? – the relationship between the Federal Constitutional Court and the European Court of Human Rights], in: Der Staat, 44 (2005), 403 (422).

115 Kilian, Die Bindungswirkung der Entscheidungen des Europäischen Gerichtshofs für Men- schenrechte auf die Nationalen Gerichte der Mitgliedstaaten der Konvention zum Schutze der Men- schenrechte und Grundfreiheiten vom 4. November 1950[The Binding Effect of Decisions taken by the European Court of Law for Human Rights with regards to the National Court of the Member States regarding the Convention on the Protection of Human Rights and Constitutional Freedoms of 4 November 1950], 201.

116 Mellech, Die Rezeption der EMRK sowie der Urteile des ECtHR in der französischen und deutschen Rechtsprechung, 84. [The reception of the ECHR and the judgments of the ECtHR in the French and German jurisdiction, 84].

made statutory provisions for the resumption of proceedings. In Germany, it can be found in § 580 No. 8 of the Civil Procedure Act and in § 359 No. 6 of the German Criminal Procedure Act. In France, a retrial was introduced into the French Criminal Procedure Act with the announcement of the Act No. 2000–516 of 15 June 2000.[117] Such measures are to be welcomed in the states of the European Council because the continued validity of a law in violation of human rights and declared as such by the ECOWAS Court of Justice is a continuous criminal offence by the convicted Member State.[118] Therefore, the theoretical continued validity of the law is, after the conviction and its practical application, a permanent criminal offence of the Member State under International law. It is therefore necessary that the constitution-amending legislator creates conditions for a resumption of a trial after sentencing the state on the basis of Constitutional Court judgments in violation of human rights. Here, it must also be pointed out, taking into account the perspective of comparative law, that an amendment to the Constitution following an International judgment is nothing new. This is e.g. the case in some European countries which amended their constitutions as a consequence of and in accordance with judgments by the ECtHR.[119] In this context, Ress rightfully considers the

117 See also Art. 626–1 to 626–7 of Act No. 2000–516 of 15/06/2000. Acc. to Art. 626–1 CPP: « [Le réexamen d'une décision pénale définitive peut être demandé au bénéfice de toute personne reconnue coupable d'une infraction lorsqu'il résulte d'un arrêt rendu par la Cour européenne des droits de l'homme que la condamnation a été prononcé en violation des disposi- tions de la convention européenne de sauvegarde des droits de l'homme et des libertés fondamentales ou de ses protocoles additionnels, dès lors que, par sa nature et sa gravité, la violation cons- tatée entraîne pour le condamné des conséquences dommageables auxquelles ‹ la satisfaction équi- table › allouée sur le fondement de l'article 41 de la convention ne pourrait mettre un terme.»

118 Bernhardt, The Convention and Domestic Law, in: Macdonald/Matscher/Petzold (Publ.), The European System for the Protection of Human Rights, 25 (39); Ress, Die Europäische Men- schenrechtskonvention und die deutsche Rechtsordnung [The European Human Rights Convention and the German Legal System], in: EuGRZ 1996, 337 (252).

119 Rohleder, Grundrechtsschutz im europäischen Mehrlevelssystem [Protection of constitutional law in the European multi-level system], 175; such, Turkey has changed its Constitution on 03/10/2001 and on 31/12/2002 with reg. to Art. 13, 26 and 76 (see: Conseil de L'Europe, Comité des Ministres, Résolution intérimaire ResDH 2004, 38 du 02.06.2004.); also as a consequence of the judgment Incal vs. Turkey, judgment of 09/06/1998 Turkey has made changes to its Constitution, see Ress, Aspekte der Entfaltung des europäischen Menschenrechtss-

resumption as the only possibility to remedy a violation of the Convention.[120]

In some cases, the executive represents the state before International courts. Indeed, the Member State is represented by the respective government as the respondent in individual complaints proceedings before the ECOWAS Court of Justice. However, this does not mean that the government is to be regarded as a party before the regional human rights protection instance. It only acts as a representative of foreign affairs before the Court of justice .[121] Every Member State namely regulates the question of who is authorised to represent the state before International instances. As a result, it may occur that the reprimanded conduct of the state is an action by a state authority or the administration. The action of the signatory state that led to the conviction concerns all decisions in violation of human rights. In this sense, decision means all sovereignactions by the concerned Member States. Thus, it is clear that acts by the executive which are attributed to the signatory state should be repealed.[122] When determining a violation of the Charter, the executive's leeway for consideration to retract is reduced to nil because of the principle *restitutio in integrum*. The administration must comply with the declaratory judgment.[123] Due to the obligation to comply with the judgment, the declaratory judgment indirectly

chutzes, in: Jahrbuch der Juristischen Gesellschaft Bremen [Aspects of the development of the European protection of human rights] (2003), 17 (20); Sweden has also changed its Constitution after the case Sporrong a. Lönnroth vs Schweden of 23/09/1982 in accordance with the jurisdiction by the ECtHR, see also Rinsche, Die Welt nach Caroline – Rechtliche und faktische Umsetzung des EGMR-Urteils im Fall Hannover [The World after Caroline – legal and factual implementation of the ECtHR judgment in the case of Hanover], in: Mann/ Smid (Publ.), FS Damm (2005), 156 (159).

120 Ress, Die Europäische Menschenrechtskonvention und die deutsche Rechtsordnung [The European Human Rights Convention and the German Legal System], in: Eu- GRZ 1996, 337 (251).

121 Rohleder, Grundrechtsschutz im europäischen Mehrlevelssystem [Protection of constitutional law in the European multi-level system], 168.

122 Kilian, Die Bindungswirkung der Entscheidungen des Europäischen Gerichtshofs für Men- schenrechte auf die Nationalen Gerichte der Mitgliedstaaten der Konvention zum Schutze der Men- schenrechte und Grundfreiheiten vom 4. November 1950 [The Binding Effect of decisions taken by the European Court of Law for Human Rights with regards to the National Court of the Member States regarding the Convention on the Protection of Human Rights and Constitutional Freedoms of 4 November 1950], 203.

123 Mückl, Kooperation oder Konfrontation? – Das Verhältnis zwischen Bundesverfassungsge- richt und Europäischem Court of Law für Menschenrechte [Cooper-

binds the executive, in a broad sense. The conduct that led to the violation must be removed or terminated. Precautions must be put in place in order to prevent future violations. Thereby, the obligation to compensate can be enforced. The domestic Constitutional Courts are subject to a separate binding effect based on their position in the respective constitutional system of the Member States.

2. Special binding effect of the Constitutional Court

At this stage, the question must be asked: on which grounds may the ECOWAS Court of Justice assess constitutional courts judgments? For the status of a constitutional court expresses the sovereignty of the signatory state.[124] In order to guarantee the last decision-making competence of the Constitutional Court or Supreme Court, constitutional regulations are expressly provided for.[125] However, the degree of the binding effect of the ECOWAS Court of Justice is unrestricted. It does not depend on the position of the responsible state organ. Rather, as a state organ, the Constitutional Court (a) is just as liable toward the Member State as all other state organs. Moreover, Constitutional Courts or Supreme Courts play such an important role at a National level that they function as a role model (b).

---

ation or confrontation? – the relationship between the Federal Constitutional Court and the European Court of Human Rights], in: Der Staat, 44 (2005), 403 (414).

124 Kilian, Die Bindungswirkung der Entscheidungen des Europäischen Gerichtshofs für Men- schenrechte auf die Nationalen Gerichte der Mitgliedstaaten der Konvention zum Schutze der Men- schenrechte und Grundfreiheiten vom 4. November 1950 [The Binding Effect of Decisions taken by the European Court of Law for Human Rights with regards to the National Court of the Member States regarding the Convention on the Protection of Human Rights and Constitutional Freedoms of 4 November 1950], 114.

125 See also: § 129 par. 2 Constitution of Ghana of 16 December 1996; Art. 106 Constitution of Togo of 14 October 1992; Art. 124 Constitution of Benin of 11 December 1991; Art. 94 Constitution of Mali of 25 February 1992; Art. 134 Constitution of Niger of 25 November 2010; Art. 99 Constitution of Guinea of 07 May 2010; Art. 98 Constitution of Ivory Coast of 23 July 2000; Art. 159 Constitution of Burkina Faso of 02 June 1991; Art. 92 par. 2 Constitution of Senegal of 22 January 2001; Sect. 230, 232, 233, 235 Constitution of Nigeria of 29 May 1999; Art. 65 Constitution of Liberia of 06 January 1984; Art. 92 Constitution of Guinea Bissau of 16 January 1984; Sect. 126, 127 Constitution of The Gambia of 16 January 1997; Art. 229 par. 1 Constitution of Cape Verde of 23 November 1999; Art. 122 par. 1 Constitution of Sierra Leone of 03 September 1991.

Furthermore, even Constitutional Courts can infringe on the human rights guidelines through the execution of judicial powers (c).

a. The Constitutional Court as a state organ

The Constitutional Court is part of the National judiciary and as such carries the responsibility for and against the state. Every state is sovereign. The Constitution contains regulations that correspond with the attribution of sovereignty. However, unlike natural persons, the state itself cannot act. It needs organs that carry out certain National tasks on its behalf through natural persons referred to as organ administrators.[126] For this reason, the "actions of the organ administrators are attributed to the respective organ and via this to the state. The action of the organ administrator is, therefore, a direct action of the state".[127] In this sense, the attribution of the actions of the constitutional bodies to the state is therefore especially applicable at the International law level. Functionally, the Constitutional Court is to be regarded as both a court and also as the highest constitutional body of the state.[128] At the level of International law, the term state organ has an even broader meaning. Every official is included. The ICJ has defined the term with regards to the liability of the state based on actions in violation of International law as follows:

> « L'expression ‹ organe de l'État › utilisée [...] doit s'entendre dans son acception la plus large. Elle ne se limite pas aux organes du gouvernement central, aux hauts responsables ou aux personnes chargées des relations extérieures de l'État. Elle recouvre les organes publics de quelque nature et de quelque catégorie que ce soit, remplissant

126 Maurer, Staatsrecht I. Grundlagen, Verfassungsorgane, Staatsfunktionen [State Law I. Basics, Organs of the Constitution, Functions of the State], 4. edition, 391, Rn. 22.

127 Maurer, Staatsrecht I. Grundlagen, Verfassungsorgane, Staatsfunktionen [State Law I. Basics, Organs of the Constitution, Functions of the State], 4. edition, 391, Rn. 22.

128 See also Art. 114 Constitution of Benin of 11 December 1991; Art. 99 Constitution of Togo of 14 October 1992; Art. 152 Constitution of Burkina Faso of 02 June 1991; Art. 88 Constitution of Ivory Coast of 23 July 2000; Art. 94 Constitution of Guinea of 07 May 2010; Art. 120 Constitution of Niger of 25 November 2010; Art. 85 Constitution of Mali of 25. February 1992.

quelque fonction que ce soit et à quelque niveau que ce soit, y compris au niveau régional au local».[129]

As a court, the Constitutional Court carries out judicial power and is therefore part of the judiciary in the separation of powers.[130] As a general rule, it may only act as public authority of the Third Power[131] on application. In a numbe of ways, the Constitutional Court is a court and therefore a state organ. As a Court of Law, the decisions by the Constitutional Court develop final legal force in a substantive and formal regard. It is the very top of the judiciary in guarding the fundamental freedoms and human rights entrenched in the Constitution.As the highest constitutional organ, the Constitutional Court is subordinate to no other constitutional organ. Rather, it controls the actions of all other constitutional organs, in particular of the parliament and the president of the state according to the Constitution. If they exceed their competences, the Constitutional Court shall refer the other Constitutional organs to their respective areas of competence. At state level, its decisions develop the strongest effects on all state organs, including the legislature and everyone.[132]

b. Role Model Function of the National Constitutional Court

The special position of a Constitutional Court finds expression in the legal systems of the francophone West African states. That is to say, that they are not connected to the regular instance procedure.[133] In fact, the regulations

---

129 CIJ, Demande en interprétation de l'arrêt du 31. mars 2004 en l'Affaire Avena et autres ressortissants mexicains (Mexique c. États-Unis d'Amérique), Arrêt du 19. janvier 2009, par. 64.

130 Art. 88 Constitution of Senegal of 22. January 2001; see also Sodan/Ziekow, Grundkurs Öffentliches Recht [Basic Course Public Law], 5. edition, 130, Rn. 1; Benda/Klein, Verfassungsprozeßrecht [constitutional process law], 2. edition, § 4, Rn. 99.

131 Stern, Das Staatsrecht der Bundesrepublik Deutschland, Band [State Law of the Federal Republic of Germany, Volume] II, § 32 I 2, 335.

132 Maurer, Staatsrecht I. Grundlagen. Verfassungsorgane, Staatsfunktionen[State Law I. Basics, Organs of the Constitution, Functions of the State], 4. edition, 667, Rn. 9.

133 Art. 124 Constitution of Burkina Faso of 02 June 1991; Art. 113 Constitution of Togo of 14 October 1992; Art. 125 Constitution of Benin of 11 December 1991; Art. 102 Constitution of Ivory Coast of 23 July 2000; Art. 108 Constitution of Guinea of 07 May 2010; Art. 136 Constitution of Niger of 25 November 2010; Art. 81 Constitution of Mali of 25 February 1992.

of the Constitutional Court are stipulated in their own chapter.[134] As a result, it exercises its competence as the highest guardian of the Constitution independently and autonomously. Because the existence, the statute and the regulations regarding the competence of the Constitutional Court are provided for in the Constitution itself, the Constitutional Court has an important position within the constitutional framework.[135]The safeguarding of the human rights guaranteed by the Constitutional Court is first and foremost the task of the National Constitutional Court. In order to remove a certain discrepancy between the International jurisdiction on human rights and the decisions by National state organs of Member States, the Constitutional Court plays a model role. The Constitutional Court has, in this regard, a levelling task.[136] In otherwords, the Constitutional Court is a guide within the structure of a state. The domestic Constitutional Court is, so to say, *the highest* guardian[137] of the Charter within the National legal system. Moreover, the Constitutional Court plays a key role within the structure of the state.[138] It has the responsibility to make landmark judgments to consolidate the rule of law. The case law of the Constitutional Court has consequences for the entire domestic constitutional order. The Constitutional Court gives other state authorities the incentive to comply with International law at National level because the other state organs, such as the highest specialised courts and the legislature, base their actions on the control standards of the Constitutional Court.

Subsequently, it is clear that the respective Constitutional Court of the ECOWAS signatory states has the highest responsibility within the state structure, in particular with regards to the adherence to the judicial guarantee acc. to Art. 7 par. 1 of the Charter. Their role as "Co-Con-

134 Art. 152 Constitution of Burkina Faso of 02 June 1991; Art. 99 Constitution of Togo of 14 October 1992; Art. 114 Constitution of Benin of 11 December 1991; Art. 88 Constitution of Ivory Coast of 23 July 2000; Art. 93 Constitution of Guinea of 07 May 2010; Art. 120 Constitution of Niger of 25 November 2010; Art. 85 Constitution of Mali of 25 February 1992.

135 Stern, Das Staatsrecht der Bundesrepublik Deutschland, Band [State Law of the Federal Republic of Germany, Volume] II, § 32 II 2, 344.

136 Schaffarzik, Europäische Menschenrechte unter der Ägide des Bundesverfassungsgerichts [European human rights under the aegis of the Federal Constitutional Court], in: DÖV (2005), 860 (860).

137 Schaffarzik, Europäische Menschenrechte unter der Ägide des Bundesverfassungsgerichts, in: DÖV (2005), 860 (866). [European human rights under the aegis of the Federal Constitutional Court].

138 Sodan/Ziekow, Grundkurs Öffentliches Recht [Basic Course Public Law], 5. edition, § 16, Rn. 6.

troller" next to the ECOWAS Court of Justice, entails significant consequences regarding the implementation of the human rights entrenched in the Charter. However, it is clear that these conditions for appealing to the national Constitutional Courts do not make it easier to consolidate the legal principles. Especially the Constitutional Courts have the responsibility of entrenching the rule of law.[139] Should this primary responsibility fail, the violation must be removed at National level in hindsight. Consequently, this violation is the responsibility of the state under International law. The National Constitutional Court must then remedy this error retrospectively by reopening the original proceedings.[140]

In the following, the adherence to the legal decision by the ECOWAS Court of Justice will be briefly discussed. The declaratory judgment of the ECOWAS Court of Justice only has declarative character. In its role as the highest guardian of the Charter, the Constitutional Court should establish an *erga-omnes* binding effect for the Charter and the associated judgments by the ECOWAS Court of Justice at National level. Art. 106 of the Togolese Constitution and Art. 23 of the LO[141] read as follows:

> « Les décisions de la Cour Constitutionnelle ne sont susceptibles d'aucun recours. Elles s'im- posent aux pouvoirs publics et à toutes les autorités civiles, militaires et juridictionnelles. »

Especially because these two regulations ascribe the strongest effect to the decisions of the Constitutional Court, all other state powers should follow the understanding of the International law and the associated judgments by the ECOWAS Court of Justice before that of the Constitutional Court. Should the Constitutional Court reject the binding effect of the declaratory judgment by the ECOWAS Court of Justice, the other state powers would not have any reason to pay attention to the declaratory judgment by the Court of Law. They follow the opinion of the Constitutional Court and are closer and more open to the Constitutional Court than they are to

---

139 Diop, La justice constitutionnelle au Sénégal. Éssai sur l'évolution, les enjeux et les réfor- mes d'un contre-pouvoir juridictionnel, 268.

140 Also Cremer, Zur Bindungswirkung von EGMR-Urteilen. Anmerkung zum Görgülü- Beschluß des BVerfG vom 14.10.2004, in: EuGRZ 2004, 683 (698). [Regarding the binding effect of judgments by the ECtHR. Comment regarding the Görgülü judgment by the Federal Constitutional Court of] 14/10/2004, in: EuGRZ (2004), 683 (698)].

141 Loi Organique N°2004–004 (01.03.2004).

the ECOWAS Court of Justice.[142] The reason is obvious: The Constitutional Court is perceived as the highest court within the state structure and also as the "*pouvoir neutre*".[143]

c. The possibility of a judgment in violation of human rights

We will discuss the question, why the Constitutional Court of a Member State should be bound by the decision by the ECOWAS Court of Justice. At first glance, this binding effect is opposed to regulations, e.g. § 129 par. 2 of the Ghanaian Constitution. Nevertheless, the obligation of the Constitutional Court of the Member State can be justified. The constitutional regulations have a certain *kinship* with the human rights that are guaranteed in the Charter.[144]

However, assessment benchmarks by the Constitutional Court at their core are not to be confused with those of the ECOWAS Court of justice . The control measures of the Constitutional Court are different compared to those of the ECOWAS Court of Justice. Although the relevant human rights instruments and the Charter are applicable in the ECOWAS signatory states, the respective Constitutional Court assesses the constitutional complaint against the benchmark of the domestic constitutional law. For the suitability of these International obligations as a direct standard of examination in a Constitutional Court procedure is, according to the opinion of the majority in literature, rather limited.[145] Consequently, the Constitutional Court is in the service of the respective National Constitution. In contrast, the terms of the Human Rights Convention are to be interpreted autonomously by the ECOWAS Court of Justice.[146] Therefore, at

---

142 Heckötter, Die Bedeutung der Europäischen Menschenrechtskonvention und der Recht- sprechung des EGMR für die deutschen Gerichte [The meaning of the European Convention on Human Rights and the jurisdiction of the ECtHR for German courts], 139.

143 Herdegen, Constitutional Court als pouvoir neutre, in: ZaöRV (2009), 257 (258).

144 Benda/Klein, Verfassungsprozeßrecht[Constitutional Process Law], 2. edition, § 3, Rn. 71.

145 Benda/Klein, Verfassungsprozeßrecht [Constitutional Process Law], 2. edition, § 3, Rn. 64.

146 Bernhardt, The Convention and Domestic Law, in: Macdonald/Matscher/Petzold (Publ.), The European System for the Protection of Human Rights, 25 (34); Benda/Klein, Verfassungspro- zeßrecht [Constitutional Process Law], 2. edition, § 3, Rn. 66.

the level of International law, the African Charter, i.e. International law, represents the subject of assessment of the individual complaint against actions of the state. In this sense, the ECOWAS Court of Justice is directly at the service of the Charter. Actions by the state are directly assessed according to the guidelines of the Charter. There are, in fact, precedence cases in which some of the principles in the Constitutions do not comply with the human rights guidelines.[147] At European level, some Member States have changed their Constitutions because of the ECHR in order to reconcile them with the guidelines of the ECHR and ECtHR case law. All this confirms the autonomy of human rights despite the theoretical acknowledgement of their principles in the legal systems of Member States.[148] As far as the case law of the Constitutional Court is concerned, there are concrete examples in the West African judicial area, where sovereign acts of National Constitutional Courts have caused justified fears regarding the rule of law and the consolidation of democracy. The Togolese Constitutional Court must be quoted in this respect. In 2005, the Constitutional Court confirmed the unconstitutional transfer of power after the death of the former state president. This measure taken by the Togolese Constitutional Court has attracted particular attention within the International Community in general and the ECOWAS Community in particular.[149] Moreover, it is recognised within the West African Community that there is a convergence of constitutional principles. This convergence is reflected in the incorporation of the African Charter on Human and Peoples' Rights into the constitutional systems of the Member States. The ECOWAS Court of Justice is to be regarded as the authentic interpreter for the unification of the interpretation of these constitutional principles formed by the African Charter.[150] The ECOWAS Court of Justice alone has more knowledge regarding the current state of development of the Charter. It is therefore log-

147 CJ CEDEAO, Affaire Hissen Habré v. République du Sénégal, N °ECW/CCJ/JUD/06/10 (18/11/2010), available at: www.courtecowas.org (last accessed on 20/04/2015).

148 Bernhardt, The Convention and Domestic Law, in: Macdonald/Matscher/Petzold (Publ.), The European System for the Protection of Human Rights, 25 (34).

149 Regarding the failure of the Togolese Constitutional Court, see Kessougbo, La Cour constituti- onnelle togolaise et la régulation de la démocratie au Togo, in: Revue Béninoise des Sciences Juri- diques et Administrative (2005), 61 (97); Cowell, The impact of the protocol on good governance and democracy, in: African Journal of International and Comparative Law (2011), 331 (339).

150 Kilian, Die Bindungswirkung der Entscheidungen des Europäischen Gerichtshofs für Men- schenrechte auf die Nationalen Gerichte der Mitgliedstaaten der

ical that the Constitutional Courts of Member States are subordinate to the jurisdiction of this ECOWAS Court of justice .[151]

In summary: An overview of the constitutional regulations of Member States clearly shows that obstacles still remain on national level of the ECOWAS Member States which could block the implementation of the judgments by the Court of justice . The majority of the opinions in literature argue for the precedence of the ECOWAS-instrument and therefore in favour of the precedence of the judgments by the Court of justice above National constitutional regulations.[152] Member States cannot refer to the inaction of their organs in order to justify the lack of effectiveness of their obligations towards the ECOWAS Community.[153]

The ECOWAS Court of Justice has expressly deduced from Art. 15 par. 4 of the Amendment Agreement that it has no authority to order a direct revocation of measures in violation of human rights, as a command to state organs, in the tenor of a declaratory judgment. For this reason, the declaratory judgment does not develop a direct legal binding effect with regards to the state bodies of the responding Member State. Therefore, they are only indirectly affected by the obligation to comply with the judgment. Nevertheless, the declaratory judgment possesses a factual legal force towards the state organs because of the right to effective legal protection

---

Konvention zum Schutze der Men- schenrechte und Grundfreiheiten vom 4. November 1950[The Binding Effect of Decisions taken by the European Court of Law for Human Rights with regards to the National Court of the Member States regarding the Convention on the Protection of Human Rights and Constitutional Freedoms of 4 November 1950], 195.

151 BVerfGE, 74, 358 (370).

152 Enabulele, Reflections on the ECOWAS-Community Court Protocol and the Constitutions of Member States, in: International Community Law Review 12 (2010), 111 (135 und 136); Egede, Bringing Human Rights Home: An Examination of the Domestication of Human Rights Treaties in Nigeria, in: Journal of African Law (2007), 249 (253 und 284); Oppong/Niro, Enforcing Judg- ments of International Court in National Court, in: Journal of International Dispute Settlement (2014), 1 (21).

153 Egede, Bringing Human Rights Home: An Examination of the Domestication of Human Rights Treaties in Nigeria, in: Journal of African Law (2007), 249 (253 und 253); the SADAC-Tribunal has accurately rejected the opinion of the Zimbabwean government: Oppong/Niro, Enforcing Judgments of International Court in National Court, in: Journal of International Dispute Settle- ment (2014), 1 (7).

(Art. 7 of the Charter). Thus, the duty to remedy applies to all state.[154] The actual, indirect commitment of the state organs is based on an International legal obligation of the convicted Member State. The state organs are not a party before the ECOWAS Court of Justice, therefore this Court of justice cannot directly convict them. On the basis of the right to effective legal protection the Court should be able to give directives in the tenor of a declaratory judgment, on how this goal could be achieved at a domestic level. Such references have no direct effect on the domestic legal system of the convicted state. The signatory state alone is bound by them. It is helpful for the convicted state to understand which route the Court of justice expects. The guidelines in the tenor of the declaratory judgment create a sound basis for the immediate national implementation of the judgment. Moreover, the ECOWAS Court of Justice saves itself a renewed assessment of the same case by way of an interpretative judgment because with the clear statement in the tenor of the Court of justice s decision regarding the resumption of the domestic proceedings it can hardly be presumed that the parties will submit another application for the interpretation of the declaratory judgment. This is because an interpretation procedure is based on the ambiguity of the tenor which entails the expectation of the Court of justice towards the result of the reparations. With respect to the effective legal protection and an acceleration of the compliance with the judgment, it is necessary to point out to the affected state organs in the main reasons of the decision that they are to act in accordance with the Convention. The Court of Law can make use of the method to aid the effectiveness of the declaratory judgment. No exception can be deducted from the legal basis for the transfer of human rights competences to the ECOWAS Court of Justice as to which state action may be objected to before the Court of justice . Therefore, judgments by the Constitutional Court in violation of human rights are to be assessed by the ECOWAS Court of justice . With the declaration of a violation of human rights by these judgments, the resumption of the trial offers an appropriate solution to effectively grant the plaintiff their legal right. Based on the principle of non-appealability of final constitutional decisions, the National Constitutional Courts should be authorised to take sufficient account of the legal consequences of the declara-

154 Mückl, Kooperation oder Konfrontation? – Das Verhältnis zwischen Bundesverfassungsgericht und Europäischem Gerichtshof für Menschenrechte [Cooperation or confrontation? – the relationship between the Federal Constitutional Court and the European Court of Human Rights], in: Der Staat 44 (2005), 403 (417).

tory judgment by reopening the initial trial. In order to reach a compromise between justice in the individual case and legal certainty, National Constitutional Courts should order the cession of the enforcement for the future (*ex-nunc*-Wirkung) in the resumed trial. In this way the resumption of the proceedings serves the removal of the consequences of the legal force on a National level.

C. Consequences of Contempt of Judgments of the ECOWAS Court of Justice

The implementation of decisions by the ECOWAS Court of Justice represents an obvious, decisive step toward a better functionality of the mechanism instituted by Additional Protocol A/SP.1/01/05 for the direct individual complaint before the Court of justice . This goal can only be achieved if the Member States feel bound by the decision of the Court of Law and actually implement the latter in their domestic legal order. In this way, a functional legal system on Community level can slowly develop.[155] It is not a valid argument that the domestic law of the signatory states opposes the implementation of obligations under International law. This view is reiterated by the ICJ in its consistent case law, in particular in its latest judgmentinterpretation judgment in the case Avenas vs the United States. The ICJ namely states that:

> « La Cour n'a cessé de réaffirmer dans sa jurisprudence qu'un État ne saurait invoquer son droit interne pour justifier de ne pas avoir exécuté une obligation Internationale. Ainsi, en prenant les mesures qui leur incombent en vertu de l'arrêt Avena, les États-Unis ne sauraient invoquer vis-à-vis d'un autre État leur propre Constitution pour se soustraire aux obligations que leur imposent le droit International ou les traités en vigueur».[156]

Consequently, the question of sanction mechanisms in case of a violation of the obligation to implement arises (II). Is there a legal basis for an alternative solution in case of a violation of the obligation to implement (I)?

155 Gans, Die ECOWAS. Wirtschaftsintegration in Westafrika [ECOWAS. Economic Integration in West Africa], 71.

156 CIJ, Demande en interprétation de l'arrêt du 31 mars 2004 en l'Affaire Avena et autres res- sortissants mexicains (Mexique c. États-Unis d'Amérique), Arrêt du 19. janvier 2009, par. 8.

I. State liability due to a breach of the obligation to implement

Acc. to Art. 15 par. 4 of the Amendment Agreement, the signatory states are obliged to acknowledge the declaratory judgment by the Court of justice as legally binding. In case of a conviction to pay compensation, the content of the obligation to implement is obvious. In some cases, however, the obligation to implement is based on the withdrawal of the disputed legal act by the state in violation of the Convention – regardless of whether it was an act of the administration, a court judgment, a legal norm that directly affects the individual or any other conduct by the state.[157] It has been shown, that the obligations derived from the African Charter represent objective obligations for the signatory states. For this reason, the violation of the obligation is established under International law by the convicted Member State towards the individual plaintiff. Furthermore, the other signatory states also have a legitimate interest in the implementation of the declaratory judgment. This can be specified through the enforcement of the General State Liability Act under International law.[158] From the aforementioned, it can be said: With regards to the object of the dispute, i.e. the substantive legal force, the legal proceedings of State liability inevitably neither have the same parties nor the same object of the dispute as the final national decision establishing liability.[159] Thus, the difference of the object of the dispute with regard to the substantive legal force represents a significant advantage in avoiding pendency when a new possibility of appeal is opened (1).[160] Regarding the accountability of the signatory states because of a violation of the obligation to implement, it should be referred to the general rule of state responsibility as well as the sanction mechanisms within the ECOWAS Community (2).

157 Frowein, in: ders./Peukert, Europäische Menschenrechtskonvention. EMRK-Kommentar [European Human Rights Convention. ECHR-commentary], 3. edition, Art. 46, Rn. 2.

158 Combacau/Sur, Droit International Public, 7. éd., 520.

159 CJUE, N°C-224/01, Arrêt (20.09.2003), Affaire Köbler v. Republik Österreich, par. 39.

160 Breuer, Staatshaftung für judikatives Unrecht [State liability in case of judicial injustice], 402.

1. Introduction of a new complaint procedure due to a breach of the obligation to implement

Commonly, the injustice under International law only arises against the violated subjects under International law[161], which represent states or International organisations. Through the declaratory judgment, the convicted signatory state carries an obligation to implement. This implementation preferably takes the shape of compensation in case of an established violation or the termination obligation in case of of still continuing infringements. If this obligation to implement is violated, this results in new rights in favour of the individual plaintiff. Therefore, the individual plaintiff can first claim the obligation to implement at a state level. Should a violation of the obligation to implement be established, a second individual complaint is set in motion before the ECOWAS Court of Justice based on the violation of the obligation to implement.

The failure to comply with the judgment opens the opportunity to submit a new complaint to the Court of justice . The plea of non-compliance has a different legal basis than the plea for the violation of human rights. The possibility to submit a further individual complaint if a breach of the obligation to comply is determined would contribute to the effective legal protection. Indeed, such a possibility can be dogmatically justified: on one hand, there is no need to fear the breach of legal force by a renewed complaint against the convicted Member State because the fundamental elements of this complaint are different to those in the initial proceedings before this Court of justice . Here, the plaintiff submits the application based on a violation of a general objective violation of an obligation, namely, the obligation to observe the International commitment of the Member State (Art. 15 par. 4 of the Amendment Agreement). In contrast to the initial trial where the plaintiff asserts the violation of the individual and civil rights acknowledged in the Charter, the application in a resumption of the domestic proceedings refers to the declaratory judgment. In this respect, it is recommended to create an appellate court at Community level, which should not only be able to decide on a remedy against judgments in the first instance but also on the complaint of a violation of the obligation to implement.[162] In this sense, the declaratory judgment gives the claimant a

161 Schröder, in: Vitzthum/Proelß (Publ.), Völkerrecht [International Law], 6. edition, 7. section, Rn. 8.

162 Thus was the recommendation of the experts during the meeting in Guinea-Bissau, "Legal and Human Rights Experts Propose Measures for Improving the Ef-

subjective legal claim to the implementation of the judgment. For, the declaratory judgment, with all due caution, gives rise to a subjective obligation to perform in favour of the applicant.

From the above, the status of the individual as a subject of under International law can be perceived. In principle, International law establishes rights and duties between subjects under International law.[163] Therefore, the right of state responsibility forms a second corrective level[164] in case of unlawful conduct. Subsequently, the rules of state liability come into effect if and only when, should a subject under International law has infringed on its primary obligation through attributable action.[165] The fact that the individual may claim the imputability of an infringement of International law means that he is awarded the status of a subject under International law. While the individual was purely perceived as an object under International law, this opinion has increasingly been criticised in the second half of the twentieth century.[166] The situation has definitely changed with the regulation in Art. 34 ECHR and Art. 10 d in the Additional Protocol A/SP.1/01/05 (19/01/2005). Both regulations grant the individual a right to judicial legal protection under International law. Thereby, access to an International court and the introduction of court proceedings have been made possible. The question with regard to the legal order of ECOWAS remains, whether the individual has the same claim regarding the violation of the implementation of the judgment because the regulation in Art. 10 d A/SP.1/01/05 (19/01/2005) only allows for the complaint against the violation of the primary obligation by the signatory state, but not on the second corrective level.

2. Enforcement of general state liability law

Here, the function and purpose of state liability law at the International law level can be perceived. With regard to the violation of the obligation

---

ficiency of the ECOWAS Court in Imple- menting Human Rights Mandate", available at: www.courtecowas.org (last accessed on 18/04/2015).

163 Doehring, Völkerrecht [International Law], § 1, Rn. 17; Kau, Der Staat und der Einzelne als Völkerrechtssub- jekte [The State and the individual as subjects under International law], in: Vitzthum/Proelß (Publ.), Völkerrecht [International Law], 6. edition, 131 (140).

164 Ipsen, Völkerrecht International Law], 6. edition, § 28, Rn. 6.

165 Ipsen, Völkerrecht [International Law], 6. edition, § 28, Rn. 6.

166 Ipsen, Völkerrecht [International Law], 6. edition, § 7, Rn. 1.

to implement a declaratory judgment by the Court of justice , the general rule of customary International law is applicable (a). In addition, there are regional mechanisms of sanctions at ECOWAS-level (b).

a. Applicability of the general rules of customary International law

The states are responsible for attributable violations of International legal obligations according to International law. In the customary practice between states, the case law of International courts and the jurisprudence of International law, there is a consensus that the violation of International law by a state establishes its responsibility.[167]

The International law perceives the state as a unit. It does therefore not matter which state organ is responsible for the actual offence. What is important is the determination of the infringement of International law. The state cannot escape its obligation by attributing the action in violation of International law to another domestic organ.[168] In this respect, the legal actions of the legislature, the executive as well as the judiciary are attributable to the state. The independence of National courts cannot be an argument against the attribution of a violation of International law. Subsequently, the International Justice Commission stipulates in Art. 4 of the draft for state responsibility:

> "The conduct of any State organ shall be considered an act of that State under International law, whether the organ exercises legislative, executive, judicial or any other functions, what- ever position it holds in the organisation of the State, and whatever its character as an organ of the central Government or of a territorial unit of the State".[169]

167 Ipsen, Völkerrecht [International Law], 6. edition, § 28, Rn. 1; Schröder, in: Vitzthum/Proelß (Publ.), Völkerrecht [International Law], 6. edition, 7. section, Rn. 6.

168 Breuer, Staatshaftung für judikatives Unrecht [State liability in case of judicial injustice], 592; Van Genugten, Avena ou le system ju- ridique fédéral américain à l'épreuve, in: Hague Justice Journal (2008), 53 (58).

169 UN Doc. A/56/10, Chapter 2 (attribution of conduct to a state), Art. 4, 44; CIJ, Demande en interprétation de l'arrêt du 31 mars 2004 en l'Affaire Avena et autres ressortissants mexicains (Mexique c. États-Unis d'Amérique), Arrêt du 19 janvier 2009, par. 65; Koupokpa, L'indépendance de la Cour de Justice de la CEDEAO, Communication donnée au colloque International de Lomé, organisé par le Centre de Droit Public de Lomé et le département de Droit administratif de la Fa- culté de Droit de L'Université de Gand (02.03.2012), Lomé, 18.

From this, we should remember that the states are accountable for the injustice under International law that was caused by their courts. According to common International law, states are responsible for disregarding their obligations under International treaty law. As far as the system of protection within the ECOWAS Community is concerned, in the absence of a provision such as Art. 41 and 46 ECHR, the common principles of state responsibility under international law applies to the obligations of Member States arising from judgments by the Court of Law.[170] Should a sued Member State refuse to implement the binding final decision by the ECOWAS Court of justice , the general rules under International law regarding state liability are set in motion. The refusal of the obligation to comply represents a violation of the execution of the declaratory judgment.

Furthermore, the disregard or non-compliance with a declaratory judgment is a violation of the principle of supremacy of the rule of law. This basic principle in the Protocol on Good Governance from 2001 is a milestone in the framework of fundamental rights in the ECOWAS Community. This disregard is even classified in the system of the ECtHR as a serious infringement of the Convention and triggers a multitude of sanctions: the right of representation of the concerned Member State is withdrawn. In the case of Loisidou, the Ministerial Committee expressly referred to the serious nature of the violation in disregarding the declaratory judgment.[171] In the event of acquiescence, the sued Member State will be forced to declare its withdrawal.[172] Only once – in the years 1969 and 1970 – has this procedure been employed against Greece.[173]

b. Sanction mechanisms in the ECOWAS legal order

Apart from the general State Liability law described, ECOWAS makes provision for further sanctions based on the violation of an International obli-

170 Doehring, Völkerrecht [International Law], 2. edition, Rn. 838; Schilling, Deutscher Grundrechtsschutz zwischen staatlicher Souveränität und menschenrechtlicher Europäisierung [Protection of the German constitutional law between state sovereignty and Europeanisation of human rights], 113.

171 Interim Resolution of 24 July 2000 DH (2000) 105, HRLJ 000, 272.

172 See: Okresek, Die Umsetzung der EGMR-Urteile und ihre Überwachung []. [The implementation of ECtHR judgments and their supervision], in: EuGRZ (2003), 168 (172).

173 Compare the Resolution fo the Ministerial Committee Res. DH (70)1 (15/04/1970).

gation by the member States. Regarding the sanctions in case of a violation of the obligation to implement, the Community provides for many step by step possibilities. The sanctions are stipulated in Art. 77 of the Amendment Agreement. According to Art. 77:

> « 1. Sans préjudice des dispositions du présent Traité et des protocoles y afférents, lorsqu'un État membre n'honore pas ses obligations vis-à-vis de la Communauté, la Conférence peut adopter des sanctions à l'encontre de cet Etat. 2. Ses sanctions peuvent comprendre: (i) lasuspension de l'octroi de nouveau prêt ou de toute nouvelle assistance par la Communauté;
> (ii) la suspension de décaissement pour les prêts, pour tous les projets ou des programmes d'assistance communautaires en cours; (iii) le rejet de la présentation de candidature aux postes statutaires professionnels; (iv) la suspension du droit de vote; et (v) la suspension de la participation aux activités de la Communauté ».

> "Where a Member State fails to fulfil its obligations to the Community, the Authority may decide to impose sanctions on that Member State. These sanctions may include: (i) suspen- sion of new Community loans or assistance; (ii) suspension of disbursement on on-going Community projects or assistance programmes; (iii) exclusion from presenting candidates for statutory and professional posts; (iv) suspension of voting rights; and (v) suspension from participating in the activity of the Community."

With this regulation, it is clear: The other signatory states also have a direct interest in implementation. It is questionable, however, who should be responsible for employing the procedure against the failing Member State? The legal quality of the public International legal system and in particular based on the character of the African Charter as an instrument of human rights means that its violation is of greater importance for the other Member States. This thought is expressed in Art. 15 of the Supplementary Act A/SA.13/02/12 of 17 February 2012. To this end, acc. to Art. 15 par. 1 of the Supplementary Act A/SA.13/02/12 of 17 February 2012 gives the other Member States the primary right to submit an application for the declaration of non-compliance with the judgments by the Court of justice . Apart from the signatory states, also natural or legal persons may report a violation of the obligations under International law by the signatory states (Art. 15 par. 1 of the Supplementary Act). Finally, the institutions of the Community, as well as the Ministerial Committee and the Conference of the Heads of State, have the right to report (Art. 15 par. 1 of the Supplementary l Act A/SA.13/02/12).

However, the procedure of reporting the violation of an obligation differs depending on the plaintiff. Notfication of a violation of the obligation by natural as well as by legal persons, must be lodged with the ECOWAS Community representative in the concerned Member State acc. to Art. 15 par. 2 of Supplementary Act A/SA.13/02/12 . This means that an individual complaint before the ECOWAS Court of Justice in this regard is not provided for within the framework of Art. 15 par. 2 of the Supplementary Act A/SA.13/02/12 . Thus, the Court of justice has declared an individual complaint in this regard to be inadmissible with the argument that this legal recourse is only open to Member States.[174]

II. Monitoring and Implementation of the Decisions by the ECOWAS Court of Justice

The organs of the Community should ensure the execution of the declaratory judgment. The President of the European Court of Justice has quite rightly reprimanded the Federal Republic of Germany based on the delay of the implementation of judgments by the European Court of Human Rights.[175] The question must be asked, whether the ECOWAS legal system makes provision for an implementation mechanism (1). Due to a lack of implementation mechanisms, it is not surprising that some of the Member States do not implement the judgments into the domestic legal system (2).

1. Monitoring of the implementation

The execution of the implementation measures of the declaratory judgment is left to the sued Member State. According to the implementation practice of the ECOWAS judgments, it is regrettable that there is no institution within the Community that can directly monitor the implementa-

---

174 CJ CEDEAO, Affaire Hissein Habré v. République du Senegal, arrêt N° ECW/ CCJ/ RUL/05/13 (05.11.2013), available at: www.courtecowas.org (last accessed on 18/04/2015).

175 See Der Tagesspiegel of 08/12/2006, Meldung im Internet [Report on the Internet] available at: http://www. tagesspiegel.de/politik/International/europaeische r-menschenrechtshof-praesident-ermahnt- deutschland/784798.html (last accessed on 05/02/2015).

tion of the judgments by the Court of justice .[176] Moreover, there is no official procedure to inform the public on how the decisions by the Court of justice are implemented. It is therefore recommended to establish a body, which must follow up on the implementation as well as of implementation measures of the judgments by the Community's Court of justice . This was a demand by experts during a meeting in Guinea-Bissau. They demanded, among other things, the creation of an executive organ which must monitor the implementation of the judgments by the Court of justice .[177] Furthermore, this organ could compile an annual list which shows the status of implementation of the Court of justice judgments and which must be made public. In this context, it is currently difficult to monitor which member States have and have not implemented the judgments by the ECOWAS Court of Justice. The practice at the point in time of my conversation at the Court of justice in Abuja (Nigeria) was as follows: If there is no complaint regarding the non-implementation of a judgment, the Court assumes that the judgment has been implemented. Such a legal situation is not favourable for the plaintiff who is ultimately powerless towards the convicted Member State.

2. Status of the implementation according to previous practice by the ECOWAS Court of Justice

The consequences of the lack of a Community organ for the monitoring of the implementation measures are clearly noticeable. After an exchange with the Court Registrar, it can be concluded that the decisions by the Court of justice are not implemented equally by all Member States. To be even more concrete, the status of implementation (stand until July, 10th 2015) is as follows: Niger, Senegal, Liberia and the ECOWAS Commission have all implemented the decision of the Court of justice . Member States such as Gambia, Nigeria, Togo, Burkina Faso and Ghana have unfortunately *not* implemented the decision by the Court of justice . Moreover, it must be pointed out that, after several decisions against the Nigerian State, only

176 Lambert-Abdelgawad, L'exécution des arrêts de la Cour européenne des Droits de l'Homme, in: Revue Trimestrielle des Droits de l'Homme (2011), 939 (941).

177 "Legal and human rights experts propose measures for improving the efficiency of the ECOWAS court in implementing human rights mandate", available at: www.courtecowas.org (last accessed on 18/04/2015).

one decision has been implemented. Even the ECOWAS Commission has not yet implemented several decisions by the Court of Law.

In conclusion, it can be recommended that the ECOWAS-System provides provision for the possibility of monitoring the implementation of the declaratory judgments for the future and that the Court of justice itself will enforce the demand for implementation in the tenor of the judgment.[178]

178 Hamuli-Kabumba, La répression Internationale de l'esclavage. Les leçons de l'arrêt de la cour de justice de la Communauté économique des États de l'Afrique de l'ouest dans l'Affaire Hadijatou Mani Koraou c. Niger (27 octobre 2008), in: Revue québécoise de droit International (2008), 25 (56).

Chapter 5 Result and Concluding Comment

A. *Criticism of the Self-Restraint of the ECOWAS Court of Justice in the Ameganvi et al vs. Togo Case*

The criticism, directed at the self-limitation of the ECOWAS Court of Justice, can be viewed from three different perspectives: from a procedural perspective (II.), from a legal-substantive perspective (III.) and from the perspective of the basis of authorisation (I.).

I. Criticism of the Self-Restraint

1. Legal basis of the self-restraint

In clause 18 of the legal matter of Ameganvi et al vs Togo, the ECOWAS Court of Justice elaborated:

> « La Cour n'avait donc pas à aller au-delà de sa compétence pour se prononcer sur la demande de réintégration, qui, si elle était ordonnée, équivaudrait à l'annulation de la décision de la Cour Constitutionnelle pour laquelle la Cour de Justice de la Communauté n'a pas de compétence.»[1]

Such an elaboration can be noted several times in the rulings of the Court of justice .[2] The question now arises as to whether the rejection of the reinstatement order and the reasoning of the Court can be justified under International law.

In this clause, the Court of justice makes it expressly known that the authorisation of International courts, such as the ECOWAS Court of Justice,is dependent on the will of the signatory states. International organisa-

1 CJ CEDEAO, Affaire Isabelle Ameganvi v. Republique Togo, Arrêt N° ECW/CCJ/ JUG/06/12, (13.03.2012), par. 18.

2 CCJ ECOWAS, JERRY UGOKWE v. FEDERAL REPUBLIC OF NIGERIA, Judgment N° ECW/CCJ/JUD/03/05 (07/10/2005), par. 32, in: Community Court of Justice, ECOWAS, Law Report (2004–2009), 5; CJ CEDEAO, Affaire Moussa Léo Kéita v. Mali, Arrêt N°ECW/CCJ/ APP/05/06 (22.03.2007), par. 35; Sall, La Justice de l'intégration, 321.

tions, courts in particular, are established by subjects under International law. Their existence and tasks are thus dependent on the will of the subjects under International law. Therefore, they do not enjoy the same freedom as the states as per the principle of sovereignty.[3] Depending on the needs, they have more or fewer tasks. They may not extend their scope and power of action by themselves.[4] Therefore their competence is limited. Acting *ultra vires*[5] is therefore prohibited. In the fulfilment of its task, the ECOWAS Court of Justice may not exceed its competence. This is accurate in this respect, since the principle of limited authorisation is one of the fundamental principles of law of International organisations.[6] Particularly for this reason, the ECOWAS Court of Justice ensures that there is no transgression of its competence in its decision-making process. Because, in principle, it may only exercise its competence within the framework of its founding act.[7]

Furthermore, the signatory states have some discretion when it comes to the National realisation of obligations under International law.

What is disturbing in the legal practice of the Court of justice regarding the rejection of a possible cassation power is that the Court of does not state a reason why it does not consider itself to be authorised to control legally binding judgments of the National courts of the Member States. However, its legal position could derive from two important fundamental principles under International law: the limited authorisation and the margin of discretion by the state. As a result, however, the power of control can be derived from other principles under International law.

2. Implied authority

Indeed, the ECOWAS Court of Justice can refer to other principles of International law regarding the perception of its constitutional function. The International court organs have found possibilities, within the scope of

3 Ebobrah, Legitimacy and feasibility of human rights realisation through regional economic communities in Africa: The case of ECOWAS, 29.
4 Vitzthum, Völkerrecht, 4. edition, 4. Abschnitt, Rn. 189.
5 Vitzthum, Völkerrecht, 4. edition, 4. Abschnitt, Rn. 192.
6 Breuer, Zur Anordnung konkreter Abhilfemaßnahmen durch den EGMR [Regarding the order of concrete corrective measures by the ECtHR], in: EuGRZ (2004), 257 (259).
7 Ebobrah, Legitimacy and feasibility of human rights realisation through regional economic communities in Africa: The case of ECOWAS, 30.

their competence, which primarily serve the realisation of their task and the realisation of the purpose of their organisation.

There is no conditioning in the jurisdiction of the the ECOWAS Court of Justice's legal basis. It concerns the competence given to the Court . The limitation of the competence does not change the fact that the competence of the ECOWAS Court of Justice can be explained otherwise.[8] The theory under International law of limited authorisation does not change the fact that International courts such as the ECOWAS Court of Justice apply the instruments and techniques at their disposal in order to reach the objective and purpose they were established to fulfil. One of these techniques is interpretation. The purpose for the establishment of the Court of justice was to ensure effective legal protection within the entire legal system of the Community. The application of the principle of interpretation, i.e. the *effet utile*[9], serves the teleological interpretation of the Founding Protocol and the African Charter on Human and Peoples' Rights. To realise the goal of the Charter, an *implied power* of the ECOWAS Court of justice is created.[10] The signatory states must accept such an implied legal basis.[11] The safeguarding of the Charter requires a responsible realisation of this authorisation. Especially in the area of human rights, the implied authorisation proves to be logical.[12]

---

8 Heckötter, Die Bedeutung der Europäischen Menschenrechtskonvention und der Recht- sprechung des EGMR für die deutschen Gerichtev[The meaning of the European Convention on Human Rights and the jurisdiction of the ECtHR for German courts], 64.

9 Vitzthum, Völkerrecht, 4. edition, 4. Abschnitt, Rn. 190.

10 Katabazi and Others v. Secretary General of the East African Community and the Attorney General of the Republic of Uganda, Reference No. 1 of 2007 (01. November 2007), Ziff. 18, available at: www.eacj.org (last accessed on 08/04/2015); Ebobrah, Legitimacy and feasibility of human rights realisation through regional economic communities in Africa: The case of ECOWAS, 30.

11 Heckötter, Die Bedeutung der Europäischen Menschenrechtskonvention und der Rechtspre chung des EGMR für die deutschen Gerichte [The meaning of the European Convention on Human Rights and the jurisdiction of the ECtHR for German courts], 63.

12 Ebobrah, Litigating Human Rights before Sub-Regional Court in Africa: Prospects and challenges, in: African Journal of International and Comparative Law (2009), 79 (82); Ebobrah, Legitimacy and feasibility of human rights realisation through regional economic communities in Africa: The case of ECOWAS, 30; Ruffert/Walter, Institutionalisiertes Völkerrecht [institutionlised International law], 2. edition, 78; Klabbers, An Introduction to International Organisations Law, 3rd ed., 56.

There are many examples in the jurisprudence of the International Court of Justice in which the ICJ had not been explicitly authorised to order measures, did, however, draw conclusions from the implied power and e.g. ordered the release of US-American diplomats in Teheran.

This application of the implied authorisation may, however, not lead to rendering an explicit limitation provided for by the signatory states to be ineffective[13].But at no point have the ECOWAS Member States expressly excluded a restriction of the Court's review of judgments by a Constitutional Court. It is therefore clear: The restraint expressed by the ECOWAS Court of Justice is, in this context, rather questionable. The Court of justice 's self-conception may lead to a restriction of the authorisation, which is, in turn, incompatible with the will of the signatory states. Because reaching this goal is also one of the primary responsibilities of the Member States. The Member States therefore also carry responsibility, which is why the competence of the Court has been extended. A particular interest of a signatory state must not suppress the general interest of the entire Community. On the contrary, the Court of justice has, within the framework of its authorisation, a duty to interpret the Charter in accordance with international law in the interest of all persons within the sovereign territory of the Community. Especially the wording of the competence to act is formulated so broadly that the Court itself is responsible to derive its implied power from it.[14] It is authorised within the framework of this implied power to do everything possible that complies with the inherent rights in the Founding Treaty and Additional Protocols.[15] Moreover, it would lead to a weakening of the Court if its task was only to issue fixed judgments without there being any hope for the plaintiff.

It is plaintiff's personal interest, that his individual rights be duly respected following the declaration of a violation. The competence to declare a violation of the Charter can go as far as to order concrete measures which are meant to rectify the situation in contravention of the Convention. In the legal matter of Campbell vs Zimbabwe, the same broad inter-

13 Verdross/Simma, Universelles Völkerrecht, 3. edition, § 780, Punkt 2.

14 Vitzthum, Völkerrecht, 4. edition, 4. Abschnitt, Rn. 191.

15 Das ist ein in amerikanischer Gerichtshoheit bekanntes Prinzip der *implied power.* Dazu: Zuleeg, Internationale Organisation, Implied Powers, in: Bernhard (Publ.), EPIL II (1995), 1312 (1313). Vgl. ferner Köck, Die „implied powers“ der Europäischen Gemeinschaften als Anwen- dungsfall der „implied powers“ Internationaler Organisationen überhaupt, in: FS Seidl-Hohenvel- dern, 1988, 279 ff.

pretation of the Protocol can be noted.[16]The basis of this understanding of competence can be deduced from the ancillary competence developed by the ICJ in the Teheran case.[17] Even if the ECOWAS Court of justice does not have an express competence to order the termination of an act in violation of the Charter, an ancillary competence of the Court of justice can be deduced from the primary obligation of the Member States to order corrective measures. Prior to that, the Court must declare a violation of the primary obligation. Should there be such a violation, the Court of justice should be granted the ancillary competence. The ancillary competence of the Court of justice can be implicitly derived from Art. 1 of the Charter. Otherwise, there would be a prohibition norm derived from the authorisation. It follows that the ECOWAS Court of Justice is authorised to determine a breach of the primary obligation under International law and order its termination in the form of an obligation to terminate.[18] The reference to the ancillary competence giving the Court of justice the power to demand such corrective measures simplifies the implementation of the judgment.[19] The Court of Law should always be given an ancillary competence in case a violation has not yet been completed as in this case, the Member State still has the opportunity to guarantee the adherence to the primary obligation by terminating the violating act in hindsight. Only in the case of a completed event that is entirely in the past does the Court have the authorisation to order reparations on a different legal basis under International law (in detail see chapter 3).[20]

---

16 Ebobrah, Litigating Human Rights before Sub-Regional Court in Africa: Prospects and challenges, in: African Journal of International and Comparative Law (2009), 79 (84).

17 CIJ, Affaire relative au personnel diplomatique et consulaire des États-Unis à Téhéran, (États-Unis D'Amérique c. Iran), Arrêt du 29 Novembre 1979, par. 27; dazu EuGRZ 1980, 394 (403).

18 Breuer, Zur Anordnung konkreter Abhilfemaßnahmen durch den EGMR [Regarding the order of concrete corrective measures by the ECtHR], in: EuGRZ (2004), 257 (261); Heckötter, Die Bedeutung der Europäischen Menschenrechtskonvention und der Recht- sprechung des EGMR für die deutschen Gerichte [The meaning of the European Convention on Human Rights and the jurisdiction of the ECtHR for German courts], 64.

19 Heckötter, Die Bedeutung der Europäischen Menschenrechtskonvention und der Rechtspre- chung des EGMR für die deutschen Gerichte [The meaning of the European Convention on Human Rights and the jurisdiction of the ECtHR for German courts], 64.

20 Heckötter, Die Bedeutung der Europäischen Menschenrechtskonvention und der Rechtspre- chung des EGMR für die deutschen Gerichte[The meaning of the European Convention on Human Rights and the jurisdiction of the ECtHR for

In the absence of a prohibition norm,[21] the International court may do whatever it takes to concretise the goal of the agreement. In the legal matter of Katabazi vs the East African Community and Uganda[22], the East African Court of justice recognised its competence to review decisions by the highest courts of Member States. This took place despite a lack of regulations stemming from the basis of authorisation. The East African Court of justice has, namely, approved the access for National persons by interpreting the Founding Agreement, in particular Art. 27. In this case, although the East African Court of justice found that there was no express regulation in the Agreement to declare the complaint admissible, it took the the logical consequenceof the rule of law to affirm its competence:

> "While the Court will not assume jurisdiction to adjudicate on human rights disputes, it will abdicate from exercising its jurisdiction of interpretation under Article 27 (1) merely because the reference includes allegation of human rights violation."[23]

This statement by the East African Court of justice can be justified with the help of two principles, namely, the ancillary competence and the non-existence of a prohibition norm.[24]

3. Development of the law by International Courts

The international court organs have their jurisdiction through the will of states. From this, they are able to create the law through the developing case law. It must only be assumed, through the decision-making practice by the Court of Law, that the developed legal practice can be identified as

---

German courts], 50; Breuer, Zur Anordnung konkreter Abhilfemaß- nahmen durch den EGMR[Regarding the order of concrete corrective measures by the ECtHR], in: EuGRZ (2004), 257 (262).

21 Verdross/Simma, Universelles Völkerrecht [Universal International Law], 3. edition, § 1295.

22 Katabazi and Others v. Secretary General of the East African Community and the Attorney General of the Republic of Uganda, Reference No. 1 of 2007 (01 November 2007), available at: www.eacj.org (last accessed on 08/04/2015).

23 Katabazi and Others v. Secretary General of the East African Community and the Attorney General of the Republic of Uganda, Reference No. 1 of 2007 (01 November 2007), 16, available at: www.eacj.org (last accessed on 08/04/2015).

24 Verdross/Simma, Universelles Völkerrecht [unicersal International law], 3. edition, § 1295.

sufficiently meaningful to the signatory states.[25] The law-generating authority[26] is a logical consequence of the authorisation. Applicable law before international courts includes not only the Convention on international law, but also other legal sources which are listed in Art. 38 of the statute of the ICJ. One of these sources is mainly the jurisprudence of International courts. The development of the law is clearly expressed in the Protocol by the SADC Tribunal. Acc. to Art. 21 par. 2 of the SADC Tribunal-Protocol, the Court of Law should not only consider the Founding Agreement and the associated Protocols in its decision-making but also its own jurisdiction. The East African Court of justice is authorised with the following words in Art. 21 par. 2 of the SADAC Tribunal-Protocol:

> "The Tribunal shall develop its own Community jurisprudence having regard to applicable treaties, general principles and rules of public International law and any rules and principles of the law of States."

The National Constitution of the convicted Member States does not represent an "*écran National*", which should be opposed to the principle of effective legal protection of the Charter. Instead, the signatory states took themselves the task to guarantee the rights in the Charter for the subjects of their respective domestic legal system.[27] In this regard, the East African Court of justice states further:

> "It is to my mind unthinkable that in such circumstances the court should declare itself to be powerless and stand idly by".[28]

---

25 Grosche, Rechtsfortbildung im Unionsrecht [Law development in Union Legislation], 68.

26 Kelsen, Die Einheit von Völkerrecht und staatlichem Recht [The unity of International law and state legislation], in: ZaöRV 19 (1958), 234 (238).

27 Ouguergouz, L'application Nationale de la charte africaine des droits de l'homme par les autorités Nationales en Afrique occidentale, in: Flauss/Lambert-Abdelgawad (Publ.), L'application Nationale de la Charte africaine des droits de l'homme et des peuples, 163 (167); Somali, L'indépen- dance de la Cour Africaine des droits de l'homme et des peuples, théories et réalités, in: Revue Togolaise des Sciences Juridiques (2013), 51 (58); Badet, Commentaire de l'arrêt dame Hadidjatou Mani Koraou contre la République du Niger, CJ CEDEAO, in: Revue Béninoise des Sciences Juri- diques et Administratives (2010), 153 (178).

28 Katabazi and Others v. Secretary General of the East African Community and the Attorney General of the Republic of Uganda, Reference No. 1 of 2007 (01. November 2007), 20, available at: www.eacj.org (last accessed on 08/04/2015); Adeloui, L'autorité de la chose jugée par les juridictions constitutionnelles en Afrique, in: Revue Togolaise des Sciences Juridiques (2012), 54 (73).

From this and further statements by the East African Court of justice it can be concluded that the complainant is dependent on the action of the ECOWAS Court of Justice to obtain effective legal protection against interventions by the convicted signatory state. When interpreting and applying Art. 9 par. 4 (together with Art. 10 d) of the Additional Protocol A/SP.1/01/05 (19/01/2005), the ECOWAS Court of justice should take into account the principle that the signatory states, by means of the reform sought by this Additional Protocol, wish to guarantee practical and effective legal protection for the subjects within the territory of the Community.[29] It is therefore clear: A declaration without legal consequence for the convicted Member State is contrary to the goal of the reform carried out in 2005 and constitutes a violation of effective legal protection.

II. Criticism from a Constitutional Perspective

From a procedural perspective, a certain confusion of the cassation authority of a Court of justice and the role of the ECOWAS Court of Justice as a Constitutional Court is regrettable. In order to clarify this, the differentiation between object of dispute and party before National courts and the ECOWAS Court of Justice must, on the one hand, be addressed (1.), and on the other hand, the difference between the cassation authority of a Court of justice and the role as a Constitutional Court of the ECOWAS Court of Justice (2.) must be demonstrated.

1. Object of dispute and party to the dispute before National and the ECOWAS Courts of Justice

The object of dispute refers to the constitutional guarantee before the National Constitutional Court. Regarding the constitutional complaint, an act of state power is facing an individual plaintiff. From a constitutional point of view, the ECOWAS Court of Justice misjudges one of the most important principles of substantive legal force: The legal force is always

29 Meyer-Ladewig, Europäische Menschenrechtskonvention [European Convention on Human Rights]. Hand commentary, 2. edition, Art. 34, Rn. 3a.

tightly bound to the object of the proceedings or the dispute.[30] The ECJ has confirmed this with the following words:

> « Il y a lieu de considérer cependant que la reconnaissance du principe de la responsabilité de l'État du fait de la décision d'une juridiction statuant en dernier ressort n'a pas en soi pour conséquence de remettre en cause l'autorité de la chose définitivement jugée d'une telle décision. Une procédure visant à engager la responsabilité de l'État n'a pas le même objet et n'implique pas nécessairement les mêmes parties que la procédure ayant donné lieu à la dé- cision ayant acquis l'autorité de la chose définitivement jugée. En effet, le requérant dans une action en responsabilité contre l'État obtient, en cas de succès, la condamnation de celui-ci à réparer le dommage subi, mais pas nécessairement la remise en cause de l'autorité de la chose définitivement jugée de la décision juridictionnelle ayant causé le dommage. En tout état de cause, le principe de la responsabilité de l'État inhérent à l'ordre juridique communautaire exige une telle réparation, mais non la révision de la décision juridictionnelle ayant causé le dommage ».[31]

The objections therefore concern interventions by state organs. Thus, the legal force of the decision by the Constitutional Court does not oppose the control competence of the ECOWAS Court of Justice to review as the reasons for litigation before this Court of justice are different compared to those submitted to the National Constitutional Court. Also, the parties to the proceedings before the ECOWAS Court of Justice (signatory state and individual plaintiff) are not the same as those before the National Constitutional Court. Consequently, the legal force of the Constitutional Court and the legal force of the ECOWAS Court of Justice differ considerably from a personal and objective point of view. The East African Court of justice has quite rightly referred to the difference between the reasons for the suit brought before the Constitutional Court of Uganda and the basis of the claim brought before it in the legal matter of Katabazi[32], when reject-

30 Detterbeck, Streitgegenstand und Entscheidungswirkungen im öffentlichen Recht [The object of Dispute and the Effect of Legal Decisions in Public Law], 33.

31 CJUE, N°C-224/01, Arrêt (20.09.2003), Affaire Köbler c. Republik Österreich [The Republic of Austria], par. 39.

32 Katabazi and Others v. Secretary General of the East African Community and the Attorney General of the Republic of Uganda, Reference No. 1 of 2007 (01. November 2007), available at: www.eacj.org (last accessed on 08/04/2015).

ing the opinion of the Ugandan government. Thus, it dismissed the sanctity of *res judicata* on the part of the Ugandan government.[33]

2. Confusion in the Excercise of Jurisdiction

In the decision-making practice of the ECOWAS Court of Justice, a certain confusion between the possible cassatory authority and its role as a Constitutional Court on human rights disputes can be noted. In order to contain this confusion, an illumination of both authorities is necessary.

Upfront, the term cassation must be addressed. As a matter of fact, cassation means:

> « Annulation par la cour suprême d'une décision passée en force de chose jugée et rendue en violation de la loi ».[34]

From this definition, three attributes of a cassation court can be deduced:
- the cassation court is part of the same instance as the courts below;
- the cassation court has a cancellation competence;
- It is the task of the cassation court to safeguard the unified interpretation and application of state law.

In this definition it can be observed: The procedure before the National courts are part of a completely different sequence of instances in comparison to the proceedings at the level of International law (ECOWAS Court of Justice). However, the procedure for individual complaints before the ECOWAS Court of Justice meets none of the above-mentioned criteria and should therefore not be confused with a cassation court or equated with such. Consequently, this Court of justice does not have a cancellation competence such as the cassation court. Rather, the procedure established in Protocol A/SP.1/01/05 (19/01/2005) is an extraordinary legal measure. This

33 Katabazi and Others v. Secretary General of the East African Community and the Attorney General of the Republic of Uganda, Reference No. 1 of 2007 (01. November 2007), 14, available at: www.eacj.org (last accessed on 08.04.2015); Ebobrah, Litigating Human Rights before Sub-Regional Court in Africa: Prospects and challenges, in: African Journal of International and Comparative Law (2009), 79 (95).

34 Guinchard/Debard (Publ.), Lexiques des Termes Juridiques, 18ème Édition (2011), 121; Crei- felds, Rechtswörterbuch [legal Dictionalry], 19. edition, 650.

is a procedure of an extraordinary nature and therefore fulfils another task[35]. It serves the realisation of the primary obligation of the signatory states.[36]

It is comparable to the National procedure for Constitutional Courts. This procedure arises from the violation of the primary obligation of the signatory states.[37] The individual complaints procedure is an expression of the lack of legal protection in the National legal systems of the Member States. Within the framework of its competence, the Court of justice can only order concrete corrective measures as a consequence of its declaratory judgment. A repeal of the state's objected intervention is irrelevant.

The ECOWAS Court of justice itself has already performed its role as a Constitutional Court in the legal system of the Community by giving two fundamental judgments with constitutional characteristics in 2010. It had namaly convicted the Republic of Senegal in May 2010.[38] It concerned the violation of the non-retroactivity in the constitution-amending Act of 7 August 2008. In the tenor, the Court of Justice of the Republic of Senegal ordered that the principle of non-retroactivity needed to be observed in the amendment of the Constitution.The second decision in this regard concerns the arrest in breach of human rights of the former state president of the Republic of Niger, Mamadou Tandja. In its declaratory judgment, the Court of justice emphasised the need to respect the fundamental freedoms of the state president who had been deposed by a coup. Thus, the Court ordered the release of the former state president Mamadou Tandja.[39]

---

35 Katabazi and Others v. Secretary General of the East African Community and the Attorney General of the Republic of Uganda, Reference No. 1 of 2007 (01 November 2007), available at: www.eacj.org (last accessed on 08/04/2015); Ebobrah, Litigating Human Rights before Sub-Re gional Court in Africa: Prospects and challenges, in: African Journal of International and Com- parative Law (2009), 79 (95); Sall, La Justice d'intégration, 294; Peukert, in: Frowein/Peukert, Europäische Menschenrechtskonvention. EMRK-Kommentar [European Human Rights Convention. ECHR-commentary], 3. edition, 2009, Art. 34, Rn. 6.

36 Sall, La Justice d'intégration, 296; Meyer-Ladewig, Europäische Menschenrechtskonven- tion. Handkommentar, 2. edition, Art. 35 ECHR, Rn. 5 f.

37 Peukert, in: Frowein/Peukert, Europäische Menschenrechtskonvention. EMRK-Kommentar [European Human Rights Convention. ECHR-commentary], 3. edition, Art. 34, Rn. 6.

38 CCJ ECOWAS, Hissein Habre v. Republic of Senegal, Judgment N° ECW/CCJ/JUD/06/10 (18.11.2010), in: Community Court of Justice, ECOWAS, Law Report (2010), 71.

39 CCJ ECOWAS, Mamadou Tandjav. Republic of Niger, Judgment N° ECW/CCJ/JUD/05/10 (08.11.2010), in: Community Court of Justice, ECOWAS, Law Report (2010), 109.

The ECOWAS Court of Justice contributes to the protection of the human rights stipulated in the Charter against infringements by the state. Thereby, it was rightly qualified as a supra-National Constitutional Court.[40]

Prior to these two decisions, the Court of justice had in 2007 already expressly mentioned this aspect of its competence and thus its function as a Constitutional Court in the legal matter of Keita vs the Republic of Mali.[41] Should the order of reparations in case of Constitutional Court judgments inviolation of human rights be removed from the factual area of competence [42], the Additional Protocol would fail to fulfil its purpose. It is even more so astonishing and regrettable that in its first declaratory judgment on the case of dispute the Court of justice judgment extensively described the violating act in the main reasons of its decision.[43] The Court could have drawn this conclusion within the framework of a methodical, acceptable interpretation. This procedural aspect of the constitutional role of the ECOWAS Court of Justice is closely linked to the substantive content of the Charter.

3. Confusion regarding the applicable law

Criticism from a substantive perspective concerns, on the one hand, the applicable law and, on the other hand, the objective nature of the obligations resulting from the judgment.

---

40 Bolle, La Cour de Justice de la CEDEAO: une cour (supra)constitutionnelle?, in: La Constitution en Afrique (08.11.2010), available at www.la-constitution-en-afrique.org (last accessed on 08.03.2015); Kpodar, La communauté Internationale et le Togo: éléments de réflexion sur l'ex- tranéité de l'ordre constitutionnel, in: Revue Togolaise des Sciences Juridiques (2011), 38 (39).

41 CJ CEDEAO, Affaire Moussa Léo Kéita c. Mali, Arrêt N°ECW/CCJ/APP/05/06 (22.03.2007), par. 35; Ebobrah, A critical Analysis of the human rights mandate of the ECOWAS-Community Court of Justice, 26, available at: http://docs.escr-net.org/usr_doc/S_Ebobrah.pdf (last accessed on 01/03/2015).

42 Should the untouchability of the decisions in violation of human rights by the Constitutional Court be part of the *domestic juridiction domaine reservé* of the signatory states, the Member States would have made provision for such during the adoption fo the Founding Protocol and the Additional Protocol. See also: Vitzthum, Völkerrecht [International Law], 4. edition, 4. section, Rn. 195.

43 CJ CEDEAO, Affaire Isabelle Ameganvi v. Republique Togo, Arrêt N° ECW/ CCJ/ JUG/06/12, (13.03.2012), par. 18.

In the case of the National courts, the National law is applied. This means that the final judgments of National courts can be repealed by the National cassation court, should they be contrary to National law. In contrast, in the individual complaints procedure before the ECOWAS Court of Justice, International law is applied. Art. 19 par. 1 of Protocol A/P1/7/91 (19/01/2005) expressly points out that the International regulations are to be applied, i.e. the applicable principles under International law as per Art. 38 of the statute by the ICJ. This means that the declaratory judgment by the ECOWAS Court of Justice has a different function compared to the judgments of National courts of the Member States.

The obligations arising from declaratory judgments are of an objective nature. They have a cross-case effect in the convicted signatory state and a factual *erga-onmes*-effect for the Member States not party to the proceedings (see in more detail chapter 3).

It is the task of the ECOWAS Court of Justice, just as it is with a National Constitutional Court, to guarantee the safeguarding of certain fundamental freedoms and rights stipulated in the African Charter.[44]Especially for this reason, the individual complaint fulfils an objective function of legal protection that exceeds the mere declaratory judgment in a specific case. In the Marckx case, the ECtHR already expressly clarified the aspect of the cross-case effects of its declaratory judgment.[45] Therefore, the case law to be developed by the ECOWAS Court of Justice is in the general interest of the legal order of the Community.[46]

Comment: This case law by the Court of justice is dangerous in many aspects:

The constant rejection of the review of court judgments creates an obstacle for the signatory states with regards to the human rights competence of the ECOWAS Court of Justice. Indeed, it is in the hands of the Member States to create an obstacle by prematurely rendering judgments in violation of human rights by domestic courts, in order to seemingly fulfil the

44 Vgl. Peukert, in: Frowein/Peukert, Europäische Menschenrechtskonvention. EMRK-Hand- kommentar[European Human Rights Convention. ECHR-commentary], 3. edition, 2009, Art. 34, Rn. 6.

45 ECtHR (GK), case No. 6833/74, Marckx v. Belgium (13/06/1979), clause 58 = EuGRZ 1979, 454 (460).

46 Peukert, in: Frowein/Peukert, Europäische Menschenrechtskonvention. EMRK-Kommen- tar [European Human Rights Convention. ECHR-commentary], 3. edition, 2009, Art. 34, Rn. 9; Meyer-Ladewig, Europäische Menschenrechtskonvention, Hand- kommentar [European Human Rights Convention. ECHR-commentary], 2. edition, Art. 34, Rn. 3b.

legal bases against the review competence of the ECOWAS Court of Justice.[47] Bolle correctly viewed this narrow interpretation in an interpretative judgment as questionable self-limitation.[48]

From the above, it can be recommended that the Court of justice should amend its case law in this regard by differentiating between a possible cassation-competence and its function as a Constitutional Court within the legal system of the Community. The African Charter on Human and Peoples' Rights is an International treaty with objective obligations. It is necessary, particularly for this reason, to choose the interpretation that comes closest to the purpose of the treaty. In this context, the ECtHR clarified in the case Wemhoff vs Germany:

> « [S']agissant d'un traité normatif, il y a lieu d'autre part de rechercher l'interprétation la plus propre à atteindre le but et à réaliser l'objet de ce traité et non celle qui donnerait l'étendue la plus limitée aux engagements des Parties ».[49]

It is particularly regrettable that the ECOWAS Court of Justice includes the purpose of the later Additional Protocols in its interpretation only to a minimal extent. It thereby overlooks the fact that "the individual norms and parts of a system are to be seen rather as purposely linked to each other. A treaty with all its annexes, Additional Protocols, explanations etc. now represents – in its area a self-contained system as well as a National law".[50]

Through the previous case law, the Court of justice has given itself a self-limitation, thereby endangering the Charter. The Court may and should review final judgments by the Constitutional Courts if human rights are at stake. It is not a cassation if the Court of justice finds a violation in a domestic Constitutional Court´s judgment and demands that the signatory state draw the possible consequences from it. For these reasons and in light

47 Ebobrah, Litigating Human Rights before Sub-Regional Court in Africa: Prospects and challenges, in: African Journal of International and Comparative Law (2009), 79 (100).

48 Bolle, Quand la Cour de Justice de la CEDEAO s'autolimite, in: La Constitution en Afrique (08.04.2012), available at: www.la-constitution-en-afrique.org (last accessed on 08/03/2015).

49 Case Wemhoff v. Deutschland, ECtHR No. 2122/64, (27/06/1968), 20.

50 Matscher, Die Methoden der Auslegung der EMRK in der Rechtsprechung ihrer Organe [Methods of interpretation by the ECHR in the jurisdiction of its organs], in: Schwind (Publ.), Aktuelle Fragen zum Europarecht aus der Sicht in- und ausländischer Gelehrter [Current questions regarding the European Law from the viewpoint of domestic and foreign scholars], 103 (114).

of its previous case law, the ECOWAS Court of Justice has ridden itself of its task in this respect. It is not a cassation court according to domestic hierarchical understanding but the interpretation of its human rights competence should be undertaken in the future with particular care.

In conclusion: Should the International court have no competence to demand the application of the Charter under International law, the following dangers are to be feared:

- The signatory states are encouraged to continue to commit the same violations because they do not have to fear major repercussions apart from paying compensation to the victims of an established violation;
- The plaintiffs must endure a legal relationship contrary to human rights determined by the ECOWAS Court of Justice, despite the fact that their legal situation is in need of improvement;by refusing to review final National judgments, the signatory states enjoy an easy way out of avoiding the control competence by the ECOWAS Court of Justice.

III. *Marge Nationale d'appréciation* as a possible Limit to the Empowerment Authority?

The big problem international human rights organs are confronted with is the boundary between the guarantee under International law and the competence of the respective signatory state.[51]

1. The term *marge Nationale d'appréciation*

The National margin of discretion is to be seen as a source of tension between the requirement of effective protection of human rights and the granted autonomy of the signatory states.[52] The term *marge Nationale d'appreciation* invented by the European Commission on Human Rights ad-

51 Bernhardt, Internationaler Menschenrechtsschutz und Nationaler Gestaltungsspielraum, in: Völkerrecht als Rechtsordnung [International protection of human rights and National margin of discretion, in International Law as the rule of law], FS Mosler, 75 (75).

52 Bernhardt, Internationaler Menschenrechtsschutz und Nationaler Gestaltungsspielraum, in: Völkerrecht als Rechtsordnung[International protection of human rights and National margin of discretion, in International Law as the rule of law], FS Mosler, 75 (78).

dresses the question of how much leeway the Convention bodies of a signatory state share should be granted in the realisation of human rights. For the first time in the case Greece vs the United Kingdom[53], the term has been applied in more than 700 cases in the case law of the ECtHR.[54]

The characteristics of the term were demonstrated in the case Ireland vs the United Kingdom as follows:

> « Les limites du pouvoir de contrôle de la Cour [...] se manifestent avec clarté particulière dans le domaine de l'article 15. Il incombe d'abord à chaque État contractant, responsable de la vie de sa nation, de déterminer si un danger public la menace et, dans l'affirmative, jusqu'où il faut aller pour essayer de le dissiper. En contact direct et constant avec les réalités pres- santes du moment, les autorités Nationales se trouvent en principe mieux placées que le juge International pour se prononcer sur la présence de pareil danger comme sur la nature et l'étendue de dérogations nécessaires pour le conjurer. L'article 15 § 1 laisse en la matière une marge d'appréciation ».[55]

In the case Marckx[56], ECtHR already introduced the term *marge d'appreciation* when rejecting the order of concrete corrective measures. But this can be justified by the fact that, by the nature of the violation, the sued Member State had many possibilities to remove the violation.[57]

In this case, the discretion of the convicted member State is reduced to "zero". This should often be the case if the contravention against the guarantee of the Convention lies in a legislative act.[58] In this regard, Maurice Kamto, adds that the realisation of the African Charter is dependent on the margin of discretion in the decision-making by the signatory states.[59]

---

53 Affaire Hellénique contre Royaume-Uni, Annuaire de la Convention Européenne des Droits de l'Homme (1958–59) 2, 172 (177).

54 Greer, The margin of appreciation: interpretation and discretion under the European Con- vention on Human Rights, in: Human rights files No. 17, Council of Europe, 2000, 5.

55 CEDH (plénière), Affaire Irlande v. Royaume-Uni N°5310/71, (18.01.1978); par. 207.

56 ECtHR (GK), Marckx v. Belgium (13/06/1979), Ziff. 58 = EuGRZ 1979, 454.

57 ECtHR (GK), Marckx v. Belgien (13.06.1979), clause 58 = EuGRZ 1979, 454 (460).

58 Breuer, Zur Anordnung konkreter Abhilfemaßnahmen durch den EGMR [Regarding the order of concrete corrective measures by the ECtHR], in: EuGRZ (2004),268 (268).

59 Kamto, Charte africaine, instruments internationaux de protection des droits de l'homme, Constitutions Nationales: Articulation respectives, in: Flauss/Lambert-

2. Appreciation of reverting to the discretion of the state

The state's margin of discretion, however, is not unlimited.[60] It should be emphasised that the principle of effective legal protection is superior to the National margin of discretion.[61] Generally, the term of the state's margin of discretion is limited where the ECtHR has determined that the conduct of a Member State is not tolerable in a democratic society.[62] In the case of Ireland vs the United Kingdom, the ECtHR gave the concerned signatory state a certain prerogative with respect to its factual assessments but clearly stated its boundary:

> « Les États ne jouissent pas pour autant d'un pouvoir illimité en ce domaine. Chargée, avec la Commission, d'assurer le respect de leurs engagements (Art. 19), la Cour à compétence pour en décider s'ils ont excédé la stricte mesure des exigences de la crise [...]. La marge Nationale d'appréciation s'accompagne donc d'un contrôle européen ».[63]

In case of a violation of Art. 7 of the Charter, the ECOWAS Court of Justice should set clear boundaries where the discretion of the concerned Member State must be reduced to "zero". Consequently, the signatory state must draw the necessary consequences if the ECOWAS Court of Justice declared a judgment by the National Constitutional Court to be in violation of human rights.[64] The ECtHR already declared in many cases that the resumption of such judgments in violation of human rights is the suitable and appropriate way to remedy the violation.[65]

Abdelgawad (Publ.), L'ap- plication Nationale de la Charte africaine des droits de l'homme et des peuples, 11 (31).

60 Bernhardt, Internationaler Menschenrechtsschutz und Nationaler Gestaltungsspielraum, in: Völkerrecht als Rechtsordnung [International protection of human rights and National margin of discretion, in International Law as the rule of law], FS Mosler, 75 (82).

61 Greer, The margin of appreciation: interpretation and discretion under the European Con- vention on Human Rights, in: Human rights files No. 17, Council of Europe, 2000, 26.

62 Bernhardt, Internationaler Menschenrechtsschutz und Nationaler Gestaltungsspielraum, in: Völkerrecht als Rechtsordnung [International protection of human rights and National margin of discretion, in International Law as the rule of law], FS Mosler, 75 (84).

63 CEDH (plénière), Affaire Irlande v. Royaume-Uni N°5310/71, (18.01.1978); par. 207 (in fine).

64 CJ CEDEAO, Affaire Isabelle Ameganvi v. Republique Togo, N°ECW/CCJ/APP/12/10 (07.10.2011), par. 66.

65 CEDH, Affaire Somogyi v. Italie, N°67972/01, (10.11.2004), par. 86.

Even if it is regrettable that the ECtHR orders such measures only in the main reasons for its decision[66] and not in the tenor of a judgment, in the case Assanidze vs Georgia the plaintiff was immediately released, one day after issuing the judgment.[67] In particular, the discretion of the signatory states does not intervene in the procedural guarantee because this, in particular, is one of the core areas, in which state and subjective interests collide. The demand for impartial justice however has more weight than the margin of discretion (a)[68] as there is no conflict when it comes to the guarantees of justice between state interests and International law (b). Subsequently, the procedural guarantees represent an obligation to show result at the expense of the convicted signatory state.

a. Procedural guarantees as a basis for other human rights

In its judgment Assanidze vs Georgia, the ECtHR stipulates:

> « La Cour rappelle que ses arrêts ont u caractère déclaratoire pour l'essentiel et qu'en général il appartient au premier chef à l'État en cause de choisir les moyens à utiliser dans son ordre juridique interne pour s'acquitter de son obligation au regard de l'article 46 de la Convention, pour autant que ces moyens soient compatibles avec les conclusions contenues dans l'arrêt de la Cour [...] Toutefois, en l'espèce, la nature même de la violation constatée n'offre pas réel- lement de choix parmi différentes sortes de mesures susceptibles d'y remédier».[69]

---

66 Breuer, Zur Anordnung konkreter Abhilfemaßnahmen durch den EGMR [Regarding the order of concrete corrective measures by the ECtHR], in: EuGRZ (2004),257 (263).

67 Breuer, Zur Anordnung konkreter Abhilfemaßnahmen durch den EGMR [Regarding the order of concrete corrective measures by the ECtHR], in: EuGRZ (2004),257 (262).

68 Greer, The margin of appreciation: interpretation and discretion under the European Con- vention on Human Rights, in: Human rights files No. 17, Council of Europe, 2000, 28 f.

69 CEDH, N°71503/01, Arrêt (08.04.2004), Affaire Assanidzé c. Géorgie, par. 202; Peukert, in: Frowein/Peukert, Europäische Menschenrechtskonvention. EMRK-Handkommentar [European Human Rights Convention. ECHR-commentary], 3. edition, Art. 6, Rn. 140, 185; Breuer, Zur Anordnung konkreter Abhilfemaßnahmen durch den EGMR[Regarding the order of concrete corrective measures by the ECtHR], in: EuGRZ (2004), 257 (263); CEDH, N°15869/02, Arrêt (23.03.2010), Affaire Cudac c. Lituanie, par. 79; CEDH, N°1620/03, Arrêt (28.06.2012), Affaire Schütz c. Allemagne, par. 17.

Fundamental principles can be derived from this statement by the ECtHR. Regarding the procedural guarantees, the discretion of the signatory states has been reduced to "zero".[70] The reason is clear: The procedural guarantees are the basis for the realisation of other human rights. Therefore, the meaning of procedural guarantees should be clarified in relation to the paper at hand.How can the procedural guarantee be defined in terms of the present study? In order to answer this question, it is recommended to reflect on the (French and English) wording in Art. 7 par. 1 of the African Charter:

> « Toute personne a droit à ce que sa cause soit entendue. Ce droit comprend: a). le droit de saisir les juridictions Nationales compétentes de tout acte violant les droits fondamentaux qui lui sont reconnus et garantis par les conventions, les lois, règlements et coutumes en vigueur; b). le droit à la présomption d'innocence, jusqu'à ce que sa culpabilité soit établie par une juridiction compétente; c). le droit à la défense, y compris celui de se faire assister par un défenseur de son choix; d). le droit d'être jugé dans un délai raisonnable par une juridiction impartiale ».
>
> "Every individual shall have the right to have his cause heard. This comprises: (a) the right to an appeal to competent National organs against acts violating his fundamental rights as recognised and guaranteed by conventions, laws, regulations and customs in force; (b) the right to be presumed innocent until proven guilty by a competent court or tribunal; (c) the right to defence, including the right to be defended by counsel of choice; (d) the right to be tried within a reasonable time by an impartial court or tribunal".

The regulation in Art. 7 par. 1 of the Charter is to be divided into an organisational and a functional guarantee. Furthermore, the content of the regulation in Art. 7 par. 1 of the Charter encompasses the procedural guarantee regarding the principle of fairness.[71] The right to a fair procedure comprises, amongst others, the claim to impartiality and independence of

70 Rohleder, Grundrechtsschutz im europäischen Mehrlevelssystem [Protection of constitutional law in the European multi-level system], 76; Breuer, Zur Anordnung konkreter Abhilfemaßnahmen durch den EGMR [Regarding the order of concrete corrective measures by the ECtHR], in: EuGRZ (2004), 257 (263).

71 Grabenwarter, Europäische Menschenrechtskonvention [European Human Rights Convention], 4. edition, § 24, Rn. 26.

the presiding court.[72] A certain equity consideration can be noted behind Art. 7 of the Charter.[73] Thus, the principle of the requirement of fairness with respect to the structural and organisational elements of the procedural guarantee can be applied.[74] The independence and impartiality with regard to the organisational guarantee concern the decision-making body because, unlike the guarantee of independence, impartiality and the requirement of fairness, the claim to access to the court is not guaranteed absolutely.[75] Rather, the right to access to the court may be subject to limitations.[76] Even here, the principle of proportionality takes effect.[77]

Consequently, limitations are permissible as long as they serve a legitimate goal and there is a reasonable relationship between the applied means and the goals pursued.[78]

It is questionable, what the two organisational guarantees should be benchmarked against. For a lack of firm criteria to measure independence and impartiality of the court, the case law of International courts, as well as the doctrine, must be referred to.[79] According to ECtHR case law e.g. the independence of a court can be determined by the following features: the manner of the nomination of members of the court, the judges' term of offices, the existence of guarantees against external influences (protection against external influence) and finally the external appearance of the

72 Peukert, in: Frowein/Peukert, Europäische Menschenrechtskonvention. EMRK-Kommentar [European Human Rights Convention. ECHR-commentary], 3. edition, Art. 6, Rn. 1.

73 Djogbènou, Procès équitable, in: Annuaire Béninoise de Justice constitutionnelle (2013), 587 (613); Velu, Considérations sur les arrêts de la Cour européenne des droits de l'homme relatifs au droit à un procès équitable dans les affaires mettant en cause la Belgique, 17.

74 Matscher, Der Gerichtsbegriff der EMRK [The concept of court by the ECHR], in: Prütting (Publ.), FS Baumgärtel, 363 (366).

75 Szymczak, La Convention européenne des droits de l'homme et le juge constitutionnel national, 414.

76 Szymczak, La Convention européenne des droits de l'homme et le juge constitutionnel nati- onal, 415.

77 Delmas-Marty/Izorche, Marge Nationale d'appréciation et Internationalisation du droit: réflexions sur la validité formelle d'un droit commun pluraliste, in: McGill Law Journal (2000- 2001), 923 (954).

78 Grabenwarter, Europäische Menschenrechtskonvention[European Human Rights Convention], 4. edition, § 24, Rn. 49.

79 Tonnang/Fandjip, La Cour de Justice de la CEMAC et les règles du Procès équitable, in: Recueil Penant (2010) N°872, 329 (332); Dupuy, Les juridictions Internationales face au procès équitable. Le point de vue de la Cour Internationale, in: Delmas-Marty u. a. (Publ.), Variations autour d'un droit commun, 239 (244).

court. The ECtHR has expressed these criteria even more clearly in the legal matter of Bryan vs the United Kingdom:

> "In order to establish whether a body can be considered *independent* regard must be had, inter alia, to the manner of appointment of its members and to their term of office, to the existence of guarantees against outside pressures and to the question whether the body presents an ap- pearance of independence".[80]

With regards to the outer appearance, the maxim "justice must not only be done it must also be seen to be done" must be adhered to.[81] The criteria of independence mainly include the relationship of a court to the parties to the proceedings as well as to the executive. Here, it must be assessed whether the court as a whole and the individual judges entertain any relationship with the party and the executive.[82] What is more are the tenure of the judges and the freedom from instructions from other state powers. The freedom from instructions for the judges means that they may not be subject to any form of justification obligation.[83]

In total, independence means a formal freedom from instructions. Furthermore, the independence of the court and its members means the freedom from exterior coercion, pressure or influence; it is, so to speak, a state which puts the judge in a position that allows him to make his decisions solely on the basis of law and conscience.[84] Regarding tenure, the irremov-

80 ECtHR, No. 19178/91, Judgment (22.11.1995), Case of Bryan v. The United Kingdom, par. 37 (emphasis by the author); CEDH, N°22107/93, Arrêt (25.02.1995), Affaire Findlay c. Royaume-Uni, par. 73; CEDH, N°4/1998/907/1119, Arrêt (02.09.1998), Affaire Lauko c. Slovaquie, par. 63; CEDH, N°6878/75, 7238/75 Arrêt (23.06.1981), Affaire Le Compte c. Belgique, par. 57; Peukert, in: Frowein/ Peukert, EMRK-Kommentar [European Human Rights Convention. ECHR-commentary], 3. edition, Art. 6, Rn. 205.

81 Peukert, in: Frowein/Peukert, Europäische Menschenrechtskonvention. EMRK-Kommentar [European Human Rights Convention. ECHR-commentary], 3. edition, Art. 6, Rn. 205; CEDH, N°22107/93, Arrêt (25.02.1995), Affaire Findlay c. Royaume- Uni, par. 73.

82 Grabenwarter, Europäische Menschenrechtskonvention [European Human Rights Convention], 4. edition, § 24, Rn. 32; Matscher, Der Gerichtsbegriff der EMRK [The concept of court by the ECHR], in: Prütting (Publ.), FS Baumgärtel, 363 (370).

83 Grabenwarter, Europäische Menschenrechtskonvention [European Human Rights Convention], 4. edition, § 24, Rn. 35.

84 Matscher, Der Gerichtsbegriff der EMRK [The concept of court by the ECHR], in: Prütting (Publ.), FS Baumgärtel, 363 (369).

ability of the judges plays an important role.[85] Should there be a removal, its criteria must be objectively defined in detail. This may only be possible under special circumstances.[86] The ECtHR rightly decided in a particular case that a court had not been independent due to the fact that the respective decision-makers were too controlled by the government. The dependence of the court was, in particular, confirmed by the ECtHR because the nomination of the judges was subject to the assessment of the executive. Through the broad control authority by the executive, the judges received, from a legal point of view, the status of employees and it was therefore affirmed that they had been exposed to undue exterior coercion.[87]

One of the organisational guarantees, named in Art. 7 par. 1 of the Charter, describes impartiality.[88] It must be pointed out that impartiality and independence are closely connected. The reason is clear: The objectivity of a trial and the judicial decision depends on the impartiality and the independence of the decision-making body.[89] Nevertheless, these two procedural guarantees are not interchangeable because independence is a fundamental prerequisite for impartiality.[90] This basically refers to the subjective attitude of the judges. They should be above the parties and make their decisions properly and to their best knowledge and conscience, regardless of the person involved.[91] Thus, the impartiality is an independent criterion to be judged on by the ECOWAS Court of Justice.[92] In order to assess the impartiality, the actual and procedural circumstances of the indi-

85 Grabenwarter, Europäische Menschenrechtskonvention [European Human Rights Convention], 4. edition, § 24, Rn. 34.
86 Grabenwarter, Europäische Menschenrechtskonvention [European Human Rights Convention], 4. edition, § 24, Rn. 34.
87 CEDH, N°4/1998/907/1119, Arrêt (02.09.1998), Affaire Lauko c. Slovaquie, par. 64.
88 CC CEDEAO, Manneh c. République de la Gambie, Arrêt, N°ECW/CCJ/JUD/3/08 (05.06. 2008), par. 21, available at: www.courtecowas.org (last accessed on 16.07.2015).
89 Grabenwarter, Europäische Menschenrechtskonvention [European Human Rights Convention], 4. edition, § 24, Rn. 39.
90 Peukert, in: Frowein/Peukert, Europäische Menschenrechtskonvention. EMRK-Kommentar [European Human Rights Convention. ECHR-commentary], 3. edition, Art. 6, Rn. 213.
91 Peukert, in: Frowein/Peukert, Europäische Menschenrechtskonvention. EMRK-Kommentar [European Human Rights Convention. ECHR-commentary], 3. edition, Art. 6, Rn. 213.
92 Grabenwarter, Europäische Menschenrechtskonvention [European Human Rights Convention], 4. edition, § 24, Rn. 40.

vidual case must be taken into account. In this sense, one must differentiate between subjective and objective impartiality.[93]

Subjective impartiality is to be understood as the relationship between the members of a decision-making body and the parties to the proceedings. The close relationship between independence and impartiality is expressed through objective impartiality.[94] Because objective impartiality poses the question of whether the position held by a judge within the internal organisation of the court can cast doubts on his independence. If this question is answered in the affirmative, the judge would be biased.[95] Furthermore, a judges' objective partiality is given, if a judge holds different positions as *"juge d'instruction"* and as *"juge d'assise"* in the same proceedings.[96] A criminal judge who was actually involved in the early stages of the trial as a member of the prosecuting authorities is affected by the appearance of objective impartiality. Thus, it does not suffice that the concerned judge showed himself to be impartial during the public trial.[97] Furthermore, the danger of objective impartiality is given, if one and the same judge is involved in the civil or criminal jurisdiction with the same matter at different instances.[98]

Moreover, the core of the procedural guarantee is the requirement of fairness.[99] This includes many partial guarantees,[100] namely the require-

93 Decaux/Imbert/Pettiti, La convention Européenne des Droits de l'Homme, Commentaire article par article, Art. 6, 260; CEDH, N°22107/93, Arrêt (25.02.1995), Affaire Findlay c. Royaume-Uni, par. 73.; Gundel, Verfahrensrechte [procedural rights], in: Bernhardt/Merten (Publ.), Handbuch der Grundrechte in Deutschland und Europa, Band [Handbook on fundamental rights in Germany and Europe, volume] VI, § 146, Rn. 90.

94 Koupokpa, L'indépendance de la Cour de Justice de la CEDEAO, Communication donnée au colloque International de Lomé, organisé par le Centre de Droit Public de Lomé et le département de Droit administratif de la Faculté de Droit de L'Université de Gand (02.03.2012), Lomé, 4.

95 Grabenwarter, Europäische Menschenrechtskonvention [European Human Rights Convention], 4. edition, § 24, Rn. 45.

96 Decaux/Imbert/Pettiti, La convention Européenne des Droits de l'Homme, Commentaire article par article, Art. 6, 261.

97 Matscher, Der Gerichtsbegriff der EMRK [The concept of court by the ECHR], in: Prütting (Publ.), FS Baumgärtel, 363 (376).

98 Matscher, Der Gerichtsbegriff der EMRK [The concept of court by the ECHR], in: Prütting (Publ.), FS Baumgärtel, 363 (376).

99 Bertele, Souveränität und Verfahrensrecht [Sovereignty and procedural law], 180.

100 Mole/Harby, Le droit à un procès équitable, un guide sur la mise de l'article 6 de la Conven- tion européenne des droits de l'homme, 11.

ment of equality of arms, the right to view the case files, the right to a fair hearing (the right to a fair hearing as per Art. 7 par. 1 of the African Charter) and lastly the right to know the reasons for the decision.[101] For the parties to the dispute, the right to a fair hearing includes the right to receive the opportunity to make a statement regarding the facts of the case and the legal aspects during the entirety of the proceedings.[102]

Accordingly, the court must acknowledge the statements of the parties as well as the submitted evidence according to the requirement of fairness.[103] Furthermore, Art. 7 par. 1 of the African Charter includes the requirement of an even playing field. An even playing field as a procedural guarantee should be understood as the adherence to a certain equality of the parties during court proceedings. The requirement of an even playing field represents a core element of the right to a fair trial. It requires that each party to the proceedings, regardless of which court proceedings, receives an appropriate opportunity to present the facts during the proceedings.[104] Moreover, the principle of even playing field stipulates that the court proceedings must be conducted under conditions which exclude any disadvantage of one party to the proceedings in relation to the other parties to the proceedings. With regards to this, the ECtHR stated:

> « La Cour rappelle que le principe de l'égalité des armes – l'un des éléments de la notion plus large de procès équitable – requiert que chaque partie se voie offrir une possibilité raison- nable de présenter sa cause dans des conditions qui ne la placent pas dans une situation de désavantage par rapport à son adversaire ».[105]

---

101 Grabenwarter, Europäische Menschenrechtskonvention [European Human Rights Convention], 4. edition, § 24, Rn. 60.

102 Peukert, in: Frowein/Peukert, Europäische Menschenrechtskonvention. EMRK-Kommen- tar [European Human Rights Convention. ECHR-commentary], 3. edition, Art. 6, Rn. 142; Renoux, Le Conseil Constitutionnel et l'autorité judiciaire, l'élabora- tion d'un droit constitutionnel juridictionnel, 364.

103 Renoux, Le Conseil Constitutionnel et l'autorité judiciaire, l'élaboration d'un droit constitutionnel juridictionnel, 382.

104 Peukert, in: Frowein/Peukert, Europäische Menschenrechtskonvention. EMRK-Kommen tar[European Human Rights Convention. ECHR-commentary], 3. edition, Art. 6, Rn. 147; Grabenwarter, Europäische Menschenrechtskonvention [European Human Rights Convention], 4. edition, § 24, Rn. 60.

105 CEDH, Nr. 39594/98, Arrêt (07.06.2001), Affaire Kress c. France, par. 72; CEDH, N°32367/96, Arrêt (05.10.2000), Affaire Apeh Üldözöteinek c. Hongrie, par. 39; Szymczak, La Convention européenne des droits de l'homme et le juge constitutionnel National, 122.

The procedural guarantee demands further, regarding the right to view case files, that each participant of the trial will be notified of all evidence and statements submitted to the court.[106] Here, the goal is them give him the opportunity to comment on such. It, therefore, does not matter whether the material is relevant to the issue or not. In this context, the EC-tHR said in the legal matter of Kressler vs Switzerland:

> « Dans sa jurisprudence constante, la Cour a notamment affirmé que l'effet réel des observa- tions d'une autorité importe peu, mais que les parties à un litige doivent avoir la possibilité d'indiquer si elles es-timent qu'un document appelle des commentaires de leur part». [107]

This opinion by the ECtHR is justified because it does not matter whether the opposing party to the proceedings has actually made use of the advantage of having viewed the case files or not. Rather, it is important to assess whether such an advantage is an abstract existence and whether the opposing party to the proceedings could use this advantage should the need arise.[108]If one party has a knowledge advantage over the other participants to the proceedings and is able to draw procedural advantages from such, this would constitute a violation of the principle of fairness corresponding with Art. 7 par. 1 of the Charter (Art. 6 ECHR).[109] Moreover, it is irrelevant whether the determination of a violation has any substantial effect on the decision-making process.[110]

The procedural guarantees are the basis and prerequisite for the implementation of substantive human rights at domestic level. This view can be justified by the fact that most of the complaints concern the reprimand of procedural guarantees before domestic courts as well as before International courts.[111]

---

106 Germelmann, Das rechtliche Gehör vor Gericht im europäischen Recht [The legal hearing before a court in the European Law], 144; Bimpong- Buta, The role of the Supreme Court in the development of constitutional Law in Ghana, 377.

107 CEDH, N°10577/04, Arrêt (26.07.2007), Affaire Kressler c. Suisse, par. 30.

108 Grabenwarter, Europäische Menschenrechtskonvention [European Human Rights Convention], 4. edition, § 24, Rn. 61.

109 Grabenwarter, Europäische Menschenrechtskonvention [European Human Rights Convention], 4. edition, § 24, Rn. 64.

110 CEDH, N°32367/96, Arrêt (05.10.2000), Affaire Apeh Üldözöteinek c. Hongrie, par. 42.

111 Cohen-Jonathan, Quelques considérations sur la réparation accordée aux victimes d'une violation de la Convention Européenne des Droits de l'Homme, in: Les Droits de l'Homme au seuil du troisième millénaire. Mélanges en hommage à Pierre Lambert, 109 (109).

Thus, the differentiation between the *"obligations actives procédurales"* and *„droits substantiels"*[112] are of greatest importance for understanding of the following statement.

First of all, the question must be clarified to which area of expertise the regulation in Art. 7 par. 1 of the African Charter can be applied. The question can be asked because, contrary to Art. 6 ECHR, there is no differentiation in the type of procedure. Therefore, it can be presumed that Art. 7 par. 1 of the Charter finds application for all court procedures. Thus, the quality of the decision-making body does not play an important role. Furthermore, the applicable procedural law is irrelevant for the material scope of the regulation in Art. 7 par. 1 of the Charter. Subsequently, Art. 7 par. 1 of the Charter can be applied to civil, criminal as well as administrative court procedures.[113] However, the question must be asked of whether the adherence to the procedural guarantee, in particular, the principle of fairness in the Constitutional Court proceedings, is necessary. This question is justified because the constitutional procedural law is a special procedure. Thus, in the Kraska case the Swiss government was of the opinion that the adherence to the constitutional guarantee in Art. 6 ECHR should not be applied to the constitutional complaint.[114]

The ECtHR did not follow this interpretation in its judgment in the Kraska case.[115] Now, after the development of the jurisdiction of the ECtHR, it is confirmed that the procedural guarantees should also apply to proceedings before the Constitutional Court.[116] In this regard, the ECtHR expressly pointed out that it is irrelevant whether the proceedings before the Constitutional Court is a referral for a preliminary ruling or a constitu-

112 Cohen-Jonathan, Quelques considérations sur la réparation accordée aux victimes d'une violation de la Convention Européenne des Droits de l'Homme, in: Les Droits de l'Homme au seuil du troisième millénaire. Mélanges en hommage à Pierre Lambert, 109 (110).

113 Grabenwarter, Europäische Menschenrechtskonvention [European Human Rights Convention], 4. edition, § 24, Rn. 15.

114 CEDH, N°13942/88, Arrêt (19.04.1993), Affaire Kraska c. Suisse, par. 23.

115 CEDH, N°13942/88, Arrêt (19.04.1993), Affaire Kraska c. Suisse, par. 23.

116 EGMR, Nr. 47169/99, Urteil [judgment] (08/01/2004), legal matter of Voggenreiter vs Germany, clause 32; CEDH, N°20024/92, Arrêt (16.09.1996), Affaire Süssman c. Allemagne, par. 40; Graben warter, Europäische Menschenrechtskonvention [European Human Rights Convention], 4. edition, § 24, Rn. 15; Ndiaye, La protection des droits de l'homme par la Cour de justice de la CEDEAO, Mémoire de Master II, Université Mon- tesquieux Bordeaux IV, 72.

tional complaint against a court decision.[117] In the case Süssman vs Germany, the ECtHR emphasised that the plaintiffs wanted to enforce their substantive claim by questioning constitutional law. Thus, the ECtHR explained:

> « [E]lle estima que, si elle n'avait pas à se prononcer dans l'abstrait sur l'applicabilité de l'ar- ticle 6 par. 1 aux Cours constitutionnelles en général, il lui fallait néanmoins rechercher si des droits garantis aux requérants par ce texte avaient été touchés en l'espèce. Elle rappela aussi qu'en suscitant des questions de constitutionnalité, les intéressés utilisaient l'unique moyen-indirect- dont ils disposaient pour se plaindre d'une atteinte à leur droit de propriété ».[118]

The ECOWAS Court of Justice later confirmed this opinion in its jurisdiction.[119] The procedural guarantees are the prerequisite and basis for the realisation of the substantive human rights in Charter, such as the freedom of speech, the right to life.[120] There are two reasons which justify the view held in here. On one hand, the task of the adherence to human rights is first and foremost that of the signatory state. On the other hand, there is generally a principle of subsidiarity before International courts. Both reasons can be substantiated by the primary obligation and the exhaustion of the National legal remedies as a prerequisite for individual complaints before International instances.

The term 'primary obligation' and the principle of subsidiarity go hand in hand. The principle of subsidiarity is based on the assumption that it is primarily the task of the domestic bodies, the courts in particular, to en-

117 EGMR, Nr. 47169/99, Urteil (08.01.2004), legal matter of Voggenreiter vs Germany, clause 32.

118 CEDH, N°20024/92, Arrêt (16.09.1996), Affaire Süssman c. Allemagne, par. 39; Velu/Er- gec, La Convention Européenne des Droits de l'Homme, Art. 6, par. 425.

119 CJ CEDEAO, Affaire Ameganvi et al. c. État du Togo, N°ECW/CCJ/JUD/09/11 (07.10.2011), par. 66, available at: www.courtecowas.org (last accessed on 16.07.2015); Koupokpa, L'indépendance de la Cour de Justice de la CEDEAO, Communication donnée au colloque interna- tional de Lomé, organisé par le Centre de Droit Public de Lomé et le département de Droit administratif de la Faculté de Droit de L'Université de Gand (02.03.2012), Lomé, 20.

120 Dröge, Positive Verpflichtungen der Staaten in der Europäischen Menschenrechtskonven- tion [Positive obligations of the states within the European Human Rights Convention], 61.

sure the effective protection of human rights.[121] For the guarantee of substantive human rights, the respective domestic rules of law of the signatory states of the African Charter must, therefore, ensure such effective procedural guarantees. It follows that the effectiveness of the substantive rights depends on the adherence to procedural guarantees by the parties to the treaty. The closest connection between the substantive complaint and the procedural guarantee is clearly demonstrated in the Selmouni vs France case:

> « Cette règle se fonde sur l'hypothèse, objet de l'article 13 de la Convention – et avec lequel elle présente d'étroites affinités – que l'ordre interne offre un recours effectif quant à la vio- lation alléguée. De la sorte, elle constitue un aspect important du principe voulant que le mécanisme de sauvegarde instauré par la Convention revête un caractère subsidiaire par rap- port aux systèmes nationaux de garantie des droits de l'homme. Ainsi, le grief dont on entend saisir la Cour doit d'abord être soulevé, au moins en substance, dans les formes et délais prescrits par le droit interne, devant les juridictions Nationales appropriées ».[122]

Furthermore, from the violation of the procedural guarantee, the ECtHR drew the conclusion that Ireland had violated the substantive guarantee under Art. 3 ECHR in the O'Keeffe case.[123] This ECtHR's argument is logical because the procedural guarantees are the fundamental prerequisite for the realisation of the substantive rights entrenched in the Convention. The domestic courts have the primary task to protect these rights from unlawful interference. Therefore, the signatory states are required to establish effective legal remedies.[124] The ECOWAS Court of Justice proceeded in the same manner in the case of Koraou vs the Republic of Niger. Indeed, the Court of Law deduced a violation of the prohibition of slavery from the violation of the procedural guarantee. It can be seen from this that the ECOWAS Court of Justice demands from the Member States to establish procedural regulations which enable everybody who feels that his rights

---

121 Twinomugisha, The role of the judiciary in the promotion of democracy in Uganda, in: Af- rican Human Rights Law Journal (2009), 1 (8); Meyer-Ladewig, Europäische Menschenrechtskon- vention. Handkommentar [European Human Rights Convention. Commentary], 2. edition, Art. 35, Rn. 5.

122 CEDH, N°25803/94, Arrêt (28.07.1999), Affaire Selmouni c. France, par. 74.

123 CEDH, N°35810/09, Arrêt (28.01.2014), Affaire O'Keeffe c. Irlande, par. 187.

124 Villiger, Handbuch der Europäischen Menschenrechtskonvention [Handbook on the European Human Rights Convention], 2. edition, § 7, Rn. 112.

under the Charter have been violated to assert his rights before an independent and impartial court.[125]

In this context, the decision by the ECOWAS Court of Justice in the Ugokwe vs the Republic of Nigeria case is questionable in many respects. On the one hand, the election disputes fall within the area of factual competence of the Court of Law. In that respect, the opinion by the Court is unacceptable.[126] On the other hand, however, the Court had to assess whether the signatory state had ensured the procedural guarantees before the National courts of Nigeria with regards to the electoral disputes. This would have justified the connection of the procedural guarantees to the competence of the Court of Law. However, the ECOWAS Court of Justice, unfortunately, did not take this approach.[127] Thus, the violation of the plaintiff's right to a fair trial by Nigeria's Court of Appeal remained without legal protection at ECOWAS level.[128]

The particularity of the procedural guarantee can be determined, strictly speaking, with the comparison to the right to an effective complaint.[129] While the right to an effective complaint (Art. 13 ECHR, Art. 7 Abs. 1a of the Charter) leaves a certain margin of discretion for the signatory states,[130] there are particularities with respect to the procedural guarantee (Art. 7

125 CJ CEDEAO, Koraou c. Republique du Niger, N°ECW/CCJ/JUD/06/08 (27.10.2010), par. 85, available at: www.courtecowas.org (last accessed on 24/07/2015); Badet, Commentaire de l'arrêt dame Hadidjatou Mani Koraou contre la République du Niger, in: Revue Béninoise des Sciences Juridiques et Administrative (2010), 153 (170).

126 CCJ ECOWAS, Ugokwe v. The Federal Federal Republic of Nigeria, Judgment, N°ECW/ CCJ/JUD/02/05 (07.10.2005), par. 26, 33, available at: www.courtecowas.org (last accessed on 16/07/2015).

127 CCJ ECOWAS, Ugokwe v. The Federal Federal Republic of Nigeria, Judgment, N°ECW/ CCJ/JUD/02/05 (07.10.2005), par. 33, available at: www.courtecowas.org (last accessed on 16/07/2015).

128 CCJ ECOWAS, Ugokwe v. The Federal Federal Republic of Nigeria, Judgment, N°ECW/ CCJ/JUD/02/05 (07.10.2005), par. 19, 27, available at: www.courtecowas.org (last accessed on 16/07/2015); see also criticism Koupokpa, L'indépendance de la Cour de Justice de la CEDEAO, Communication donnée au colloque International de Lomé, organisé par le Centre de Droit Public de Lomé et le département de Droit administratif de la Faculté de Droit de L'Université de Gand (02.03.2012), Lomé, 17.

129 It must be pointed out that within the system of the African Charter, the regulations in Art. 6 and Art. 13 ECHR are integrated in Art. 7 of the African Charter *mutatis mutandis*.

130 CEDH, N°22414/93, Arrêt (15.11.1996), Affaire Chahal c. Royaume-Uni, par. 145.

par. 7 par. 1d. and Art. 6 ECHR). This can be justified by the fact that the right to an effective complaint must continue to be linked to other regulations of the respective Convention. Thus, the right to an effective complaint is an accessory right to other substantive pleas. However, the prerequisites in of the guarantees are, strictly speaking, stricter than the right to an effective domestic complaint.[131] The ECtHR even recognised the fact that procedural guarantees absorb the right to an effective domestic complaint. In this regard, the ECtHR explained:

> « Bref, il n'y a eu violation ni de l'article 13 (art. 13) ni, à cet égard, de l'article 6 par. 1 (art. 6–1), les exigences du premier (art. 13) étant d'ailleurs moins strictes que celles du second (art. 6–1) et entièrement absorbées par elles en l'espèce».[132]

Moreover, the procedural guarantees play an important role in a democratic state and are an external sign of the adherence to the principles of the rule of law.[133] Based on the role of the procedural guarantees for the enforcement of the principles of the rule of law, the International courts leave hardly any margin of discretion for the signatory states.[134] Furthermore, the ECOWAS Court of Justice demands, based on its importance for the enforcement of the principles of the rule of law, that the principle of fairness must also be adhered to in the constitutional procedural law because the rule of law requires the adherence to the procedural guarantees.[135] By referring to the Protocol on Good Governance from 2001 in connection with the procedural guarantees, the ECOWAS Court of Justice

---

131 Villiger, Handbuch der Europäischen Menschenrechtskonvention [Handbook on the European Human Rights Convention], 2. edition, § 19, Rn. 648; De Bruyn, Le Droit à un recours effectif, in: Les Droits de l'Homme au seuil du troisième millénaire, Mélanges en hommage à Pierre Lambert, 185 (191).

132 CEDH, N°15777/89, Arrêt (16.09.1996), Affaire Matos E Silva et al. c. Portugal, par. 64.

133 CEDH, N°4/1998/907/1119, Arrêt (02.09.1998), Affaire Lauko c. Slovaquie, par. 63; CEDH, Nr. 34869/05, Arrêt (29.06.2011), Affaire Sabeh El Leil c. France, par. 46; Bertele, Souveränität und Verfahrensrecht [Sovereignty and procedural law], 195.

134 CEDH, N°9024/80, Arrêt (12.02.1985), Affaire Colozza c. Italie, par. 32; CJ CEDEAO, Af- faire Ameganvi et al. c. État du Togo, N°ECW/CCJ/JUD/09/11 (07.10.2011), par. 67, available at: www.courtecowas.org (last accessed on 16/07/2015).

135 CJ CEDEAO, Affaire Ameganvi et al. c. État du Togo, N°ECW/CCJ/JUD/09/11 (07.10.2011), par. 66, available at: www.courtecowas.org (last accessed on 16/07/2015).

made it clear that the judicial protection prescribed by Art. y referring to the Protocol on Good Governance from 2001 in connection with the procedural guarantees, the ECOWAS Court of Justice made it clear that the judicial protection prescribed by Art. constitutional procedural law because [136]

b. Non-existence of a collision with National interests

For the assessment of the adherence to the rights in the Convention that contain procedural guarantees, several particularities apply. The assessment of the procedural guarantees, namely, follows a different pattern from the other rights of defense.[137] The usual assessment scheme is not applied. Rather, the monitoring body assesses whether the conduct of the state organsis reconcilable with the procedural guarantee in question. The reason is clear: The procedural guarantees are defined more concretely than the comparable rights of defense.[138] Furthermore, it is hardly imaginable that a conflict exists between the fairness principle and a National interest. Thus, discretion by the signatory states is, strictly speaking, excluded with respect to the procedural guarantees.[139] Public interests, such as National security or the protection of third parties, cannot justify a restriction of the right to an independent, impartial court and a fair trial. There are also no special circumstances in the interest of national security that could justify the limitation of the principle of fairness. The procedural guarantees are therefore to be viewed as universally implementable human rights.

---

136 CJ CEDEAO, Affaire Ameganvi et al. c. État du Togo, N°ECW/CCJ/JUD/09/11 (07.10.2011), par. 67, available at: www.courtecowas.org (last accessed on 16/07/2015).

137 Grabenwarter, Europäische Menschenrechtskonvention [European Human Rights Convention], 4. edition, § 18, Rn. 29.

138 Grabenwarter, Europäische Menschenrechtskonvention [European Human Rights Convention], 4. edition, § 18, Rn. 29.

139 Greer, The margin of appreciation: interpretation and discretion under the European Convention on Human Rights, in: Human rights files No. 17, Council of Europe, 2000, 28.

c. Procedural Guarantees as the resulting obligation

As discussed above, the right to access to courts is not an absolute right.[140] The substance of this right depends on the domestic reality in signatory states. Therefore, when it comes to the right to access to courts, a certain "*marge Nationale d'appreciation*" by the High Contracting Parties[141] applies and there is, therefore, no absolute obligation to create domestic courts.[142] However, the legal situation presents itself in a different light than the procedural guarantee of the principle of fairness. On the one hand, there is an obligation to achieve results and, on the other hand, a positive obligation.[143] The positive obligation is to be understood in the sense that the respective signatory state must provide for regulations through legislation that ensure the independence, impartiality and the principle of fairness.

Because as long as the courts exist, the signatory states must adhere to the procedural guarantees of Art. 7 par. 1 of the Charter.[144] Thus, the High Contracting States carry an "*obligation de résultat*" *when* it comes to procedural guarantees.[145] In this sense, the procedural guarantee receives more attention than the substantive human rights.[146] National discretion cannot interfere with the procedural guarantee. In principle, the right to a fair trial can only be adhered to if the signatory state can guarantee the impartiality and independence of the judiciary. In this context, the ECtHR expressly emphasises the absolute character of the impartiality and independence of the judiciary in the case Micallef vs Malta.[147] Absolute rights are first and

140 Decaux/Imbert/Pettiti, La convention Européenne des Droits de l'Homme, Commentaire article par article, Art. 6, 259.
141 CEDH, N°38695/97, Arrêt (15.02.2000), Affaire Garcìa Manibardo c. Espagne, par. 36; CEDH, N°9024/80, Arrêt (12.02.1985), Affaire Colozza c. Italie, par. 30; CEDH, N°24488/04, Arrêt (15.04.2009), Affaire Guillard c. France, par. 33; CEDH, N°34869/05, Arrêt (29.06.2011), Affaire Sabeh El Leil c. France, par. 47.
142 CEDH, N°38695/97, Arrêt (15.02.2000), Affaire Garcìa Manibardo c. Espagne, par. 39.
143 Decaux/Imbert/Pettiti, La convention Européenne des Droits de l'Homme, Commentaire article par article, Art. 6, 245.
144 CEDH, N°38695/97, Arrêt (15.02.2000), Affaire Garcìa Manibardo c. Espagne, par. 39.
145 Decaux/Imbert/Pettiti, La convention Européenne des Droits de l'Homme, Commentaire article par article, Art. 6, 245.
146 Marauhn/Merhof, Grundrechtseingriff und -schranken [interference in fundamental rights and their limitations], in: Grote/Marauhn (Publ.), EMRK/GG, 2. edition, Kap. 7, Rn. 6.
147 CEDH, N°17056/06, Arrêt (17.10.2009), Affaire Micallef c. Malte, par. 86.

foremost based on the fundamental guarantees in Art. 3 of the ECHR, namely the prohibition of torture and the prohibition of inhuman or degrading treatment and the guarantee in Art. 4 of the ECHR.[148] However, the procedural guarantee could be seen as an absolute right due to its particular role when it comes to the enforcement of the rule of law. Moreover, because of the obligation to adhere to the procedural guarantee in Art. 7 of the Charter, it is a dual obligation.

In the end, discretion is exercised when it comes to the right of access to courts or the right to an effective complaint. This is justified by considering the circumstances of the individual case. Contrary to this, the state's margin of discretion does not apply to procedural guarantees when it comes to the principle of fairness. During the assessment of the conduct of Member States regarding the procedural guarantee, the discretion, which normally relates to other substantive reprimands, does not apply in practice because the procedural guarantees can not be illusory and theoretical. Rather, procedural guarantees are effective and concrete guarantees.[149] Consequently, the signatory states must do everything in their power to meet the requirements of a fair trial as demanded by the Charter. When it comes to the procedural guarantee, the signatory states carry an obligation to achieve results. This is understandable when taking the special nature of the principle of fairness in a democratic state into account.[150] There is no pretence of a possible conflict with National interests. Therefore, the principle of fairness is a universally enforceable guarantee. A violation of the procedural guaranteesis, at the same time, an interference with the underlying human rights.[151] This demonstrates why, in case of a violation of the procedural guarantees, the signatory states should not be allowed to exercise discretion.

---

148 Marauhn/Merhof, in: Grundrechtseingriff und -schranken [interference in fundamental rights and their limitations], in: Grote/Marauhn (Publ.), EMRK/GG, 2. edition, Kap 7, Rn. 3; Greer, The margin of appreciation: interpretation and discretion under the European Convention on Human Rights, in: Human rights files No. 17, Council of Europe, 2000, 27.

149 CEDH, N°38695/97, Arrêt (15.02.2000), Affaire Garcìa Manibardo c. Espagne, par. 43.

150 CEDH, N°9024/80, Arrêt (12.02.1985), Affaire Colozza c. Italie, par. 32.

151 Dannemann, Haftung für die Verletzung von Verfahrensgarantien nach Art. 41 EMRK [Liability in case of a violation of procedural guarantees acc. to Art. 41 ECHR], in: Rabels Zeitschrift für ausländisches und Internationales Privatrecht [magazine for foreign and International civil law](1999), 452 (465).

B. Concluding Comment

Based on a judgment of the Togolese Constitutional Court contrary to international law and the resulting declaratory judgment of the ECOWAS Court of Justice, the present paper must answer several questions of both constitutional and international law. The examination primarily identifies a conflict of jurisdiction within the ECOWAS legal system. The source of the conflict of jurisdiction is the constitutional principles of procedure by the constitutional systems of the Member States and the introduction of an individual complaints procedure before the ECOWAS Court of Justice. At the centre is the core question of the position of the ECOWAS Court of Justice as a Constitutional Court in the West African constitutional order. Which obligations arise from its characterisation as a Constitutional Court, based on its judgments for the courts of the Member States and, in particular, for the Constitutional Courts?

It has been demonstrated in the first chapter that the ECOWAS Court of Justice, which primarily monitored the interpretation and application of the ECOWAS Community law, has developed into a Court of justice for Human Rights. The reason for this is an interaction of the security policy, the human rights situation and the awareness of the High ECOWAS States, which maintain a close relationship between the economic growth and the respect for principles of the rule of law in the West African countries.

The second chapter analysed the internal procedural binding force of constitutional decisions from a domestic and constitutional point of view. The consequences for the domestic Constitutional Courts and the parties to the proceedings stemming from this were shown. The principles of irrevocability and non-appealability must thereby be taken into consideration when it comes to Constitutional Court decisions that have acquired the status of res judicata. Following this, the fundamental *erga-omnes* binding effect is demonstrated based on the constitutional traditions of the Member States in the ECOWAS Community. *De lege lata, the* decisions by the Constitutional Courts of Member States develop an *erga-omnes* binding effect. Moreover, they are irrevocable and non-appealable. Therefore, there is no legal remedy available.[152] Subsequently, the decision of the decision by

152 See also: § 129 par. 2 Constitution of Ghana of 1992; Art. 106 Constitution of Togo of 14 October 1992; Art. 124 Constitution of Benin of 11 December 1991; Art. 94 Constitution of Mali of 25 February 1992; Art. 134 Constitution of Niger of 25 November 2010; Art. 99 Constitution of Guinea of 07 May 2010;

the Togolese Constitutional Court in the initial case was evaluated from a procedural point of view.

In the third chapter, the supra-National overcoming of the National legal force, as analysed in the second chapter, is shown. It should be emphasised that the operating principle of the ECOWAS Court of Justice resembles that of a Constitutional Court in many aspects. First of all, the questions the ECOWAS Court of Justice has to deal with in its human rights mandate are of a Constitutional litigation nature. There are, namely, the fundamental freedoms and individual human rights. Moreover, the decisions of this Court of Law are final judicial judgments. They are final and therefore non-appealable. Furthermore, the supra-National Court of justice has an exclusive competence regarding the interpretation and application of the African Charter on Human Rights at ECOWAS level.

From a possible viewpoint as a Constitutional Court of the Member States, the declaratory judgments of the ECOWAS Court of Justice trigger considerable consequences for the constitutional procedural principles of the Member States.[153] The extension of the ECOWAS Court of Justice's jurisdiction aims at securing the steering power and the effectiveness of regional human rights law. Declaratory judgments in principle do not develop a constitutive but rather a declarative effect. More precisely: the declaratory judgment of the Court of justice has no direct domestic force of application. However, the organisational structure, the position and the functioning of the Court of justice within the institutional framework of the Community shows all the features of a Constitutional Court. In addition, the scope of the decisions by this Court of justice has a constitutional function. The African Charter on Human Rights and Peoples' Rights are not at the National legal systems by the Member States' disposition. They must take the Charter into account.

Neither the domestic legislator nor the *Constitutional Courts* of the Member States may dispose of the Charter. The interpretation of the African

---

Art. 98 Constitution of Ivory Coast of 23 July 2000; Art. 159 Constitution of Burkina Faso of 02 June 1991; Art. 92 par. 2 Constitution of Senegal of 22 January 2001; Sect. 230, 232, 233, 235 Constitution of Nigeria of 29 May 1999; Art. 65 Constitution of Liberia of 06 January 1984; Art. 92 Constitution of Guinea Bissau of 16 January 1984; Sect. 126, 127 Constitution of The Gambia of 16 January 1997; Art. 229 par. 1 Constitution of Cape Verde of 23 November 1999; Art. 122 par. 1 Constitution of Sierra Leone of 03 September 1991.].

153 Szymczak, La Convention européenne des droits de l'homme et le juge constitutionnel national, 266.

Charter by the ECOWAS Court of Justice is an integral component of the Charter within the ECOWAS legal system.[154]

Although *res judicata* constitutes a procedural guarantee, it is nevertheless necessary to justify an exceptional relativisation of this procedural principle, because the legal force ensures the irrevocability of a judgment that has been issued on a fair basis. As soon as the conditions under which a judgment by a Member State has been issued represents an infringement of the principle of fairness, there is no longer a valid reason to protect the legal force against a challenge. It is well-known that a legal right must be protected as long as it requires protection. An unfair judgment does not constitute a legal right worthy of protection. As a result: the principle of fairness replaces the legal force. The thesis presented here, is based on the fundamental conflict between legal certainty (secured by the institution of legal force) and substantive justice (supported by the institution of the restitution in kind under International law). In case of a conflict between the jurisdiction of the ECOWAS Court of Justice and the domestic Constitutional Court, the answer is clearly that the ECOWAS Court of Justice has the last word. Otherwise there would not have been an individual human rights complaint at the ECOWAS level. Thus, the institution of the *restitutio in integrum* has more weight than that of *res judicata.* The result of the declaratory judgment is the obligation of reparation. The appropriate means of reparation is known to be the rescission of the judgment by the Constitutional Court causing the violation. Should the Court of justice order concrete corrective measures in the tenor of the judgment, such an order is legally binding for the convicted signatory state. Thus, there is no leeway left for the concerned signatory state. In such a case, the declaratory judgment constitutes de facto a judgment granting reparation.

Regarding the procedural guarantee, the declaratory judgment is purely a judgment granting reparation. In this regard, two fundamental problems of a procedural nature present themselves. On the one hand, the relationships between the Court of justice and the National courts with respect to areas of competence. Therefore, the question must be asked: would it be compatible with general International law if the Court of justice were allowed to overrule the decisions of National courts? This question would be answered in the affirmative if the ECOWAS Court of Justice had the competence of a "cassation court" under customary International law.Such a

154 CIJ, Demande en interprétation de l'arrêt du 31 mars 2004 en l'Affaire Avena et autres res- sortissants mexicains (Mexique c. Ètats-Unis d'Amérique), Arrêt du 19 janvier 2009, par. 8.

competence cannot be derived from the basis of the Court's jurisdiction.[155] However, this is followed by a substantive question, namely whether the Court of justice may, despite this, order the resumption of a judgment contrary to International law – irrespective of its legal force. With this question, the distinction between the formal legal force and the substantive legal force is legally relevant, because the ECOWAS Court of Justice cannot itself issue cassation judgments against National courts on the basis of its jurisdictional norms. However, in terms of legal consequence, a necessary material result is to be expected from the convicted state. This results is an implicit authorisation to reopen the initial domestic proceedings. Therefore, a power of the Court to annul the substantive legal force can be deduced from the substantive-legal perspective. In other words: the judgments by the ECOWAS Court of Justice do not have direct domestic force, however, there is an obligation by national courts including the National Constitutional Courts under International law to reopen the case and to take the jurisdiction of the ECOWAS Court of Justice into account. Thereby, the National courts are largely bound by the interpretation of the ECOWAS Court of Justice. Therefore, the judgments of the ECOWAS Court of Justice are, in fact, binding in substance. The view taken here is based on the basic idea that in the event of a Member States' court judgment being contrary to International law, responsibility under International law must necessarily lead to a rectification of the situation giving rise to the liability. This aspect has been discussed argumentatively through the material-legal relationship between the two legal systems as discussed in the fourth chapter. Moreover, the procedural guarantee is the basis to achieve this result for the signatory states. Subsequently, the consideration of the National-specific reality does not apply to a procedural guarantee. This is mainly the case if a violation of Art. 7 par. 1 of the African Charter is established. After all, the violation of the procedural guarantee creates a permanent situation contrary to International law in the National law of the convicted signatory state. The intervention of the Court of justice is therefore required to its greatest extent. The adoption of obligations under International law by the ECOWAS Member States resembles the limitation of sovereign state power in the area of human rights jurisdiction. Together with this, the signatory states have accepted a limitation of the legal force of their Constitutional Courts and equivalent judicial instances.

155 Protocole Additionnel A/SP.1/01/05 (19.01.2005) Portant Amendement du Protocole (A/P.1/7/91) Relatif à la Cour de Justice de la Communauté.

The prevailing regulation regarding the *erga-omnes* binding effect does not represent an insurmountable obstacle within the National law of the ECOWAS signatory states. In the area of human rights, this binding effect is to be viewed as provisional since the possibility of bringing a claim before the ECOWAS Court of Justice, based on the legally binding national constitutional judgment already triggers the relativisation of the binding effect. In case of a sustained declaratory judgment by the ECOWAS Court of Justice, the provisional character of the judgment by the National Constitutional Court is manifested. To express this metaphorically: the legal force of National Constitutional Court judgments is untouchable insofar as these judgments have been passed without errors. Should a misdirection be detected at the level of International law, an actual breach of the legal force is to be allowed. The corrective measure is the resumption of the initial domestic proceedings. Thus, the declaratory judgment by the ECOWAS Court of Justice develops a final judicial legal force under International law and the decision by the domestic Constitutional Courts a provisional National legal force. The resumption of the initial proceedings in terms of human rights alone confirms the last decision-making competence of the International Court of justice .

This results in the competence of the Court to order concrete corrective measures. The approach of ordering corrective measures does not violate the principle of the limited abatement of International courts. It is true that the International organisation in general and International courts, in particular, are only allowed to act within their assigned authority. Otherwise, there would be the risk of a transgression of competence. However, this principle is not contrary to the corresponding interpretation of International law. The development of the law through case law is needed especially in cases where the text in International law is unclear with regards to certain questions concerning the review competence regarding decisions by Constitutional Courts. The opinion of the ECOWAS Court of Justice, moreover, is not to be assumed since there are no norms of prohibition in the legal basis of the Court of justice with respect to the assessment of legally binding compensation by Constitutional Courts of Member States. Furthermore, there is the possibility of ordering concrete corrective measures in close connection with the area of competence of the Court of justice . This is, namely, a logical consequence of the power to establish a violation of human rights entrenched in the Charter. This results in an ancillary competence of the ECOWAS Court of Justice. This ancillary competence has been argumentatively justified in connection with the primary obligation of the signatory states to the African Charter on Human and

Peoples' Rights according to Art. 1 of the Charter. Due to the absence of a prohibition norm, the ECOWAS Court of Justice is ultimately entitled to draw the necessary consequences from its declaratory judgment, namely to order corrective measures in the concerned signatory state. The resumption by a Constitutional Court of a judgment, infringing International law shall not preclude that interpretation.[156] The Court of justice should accordingly refer to the standards of the International Court of Justice[157] In this context, Cohen-Jonathan detailed:

> « [E]n tant que juridiction Internationale des droits de l'homme, la Cour européenne pourrait atténuer ici la règle qu'elle s'est imposée de ne pas signaler aux États les conséquences de leur infraction à la Convention. Il nous semble que la cessation d'un acte illicite continu est une conséquence implicite mais inévitable du constat effectué par la Cour».[158]

The proposed solutions in the present study contribute to the prevention of a danger in the current protection system of the ECOWAS Court of Justice. The danger of creating a de facto obstacle at state level which opposes the obligation of implementation by the convicted signatory states. Therefore, it has been shown that judgments with National legal force are not an insurmountable obstacle regarding the review competence of the ECOWAS Court of Justice. If this were the case, Member States would be more likely to evade their obligations under International law (from the Charter, the Amendment Agreement and the associated Protocols). They would then have a legally binding judgment prematurely issued by their National Constitutional Courts in order to create the prerequisites for an inability to review such by International judicial bodies. This easy circumvention neither takes account of the purpose of the Charter nor that of the Additional Protocol of 2005.

---

156 Verdross/Simma, Universelles Völkerrecht [Universal International law], 3. edition, § 1295.

157 CIJ, Affaire relative au personnel diplomatique et consulaire des États-Unis à Téhéran (24.05.1980), États-Unis d'Amérique c. Téhéran, par. 3. Vgl. Breuer, Zur Anordnung konkreter Abhilfemaßnahmen durch den EGMR[Regarding the order of concrete corrective measures by the ECtHR], in: EuGRZ (2004), 268 (261).

158 Cohen-Jonathan, Quelques considerations sur la réparation accordée aux victimes d'une violation de la Convention Européenne des Droits de l'Homme, in: Les Droits de l'homme au seuil du troisiéme millénaire. Mélanges en hommage à Pierre Lambert, 109 (120).

Regarding the extent of the legal force of the declaratory judgment, the following has been shown: the elements of the tenor are significant. Nevertheless, the main reasons for the decision assist with the interpretation of the judgment. The relevant reasons for the decision by the ECOWAS Court of Justice are all those determining the facts from which the Court of justice gleans, by way of a necessary conclusion, the answer to the individual plaintiff's complaintsubmission.

Thus, the main reasons for the decision are closely linked to the scope of the procedural claim defining the object of dispute.

If ECOWAS case law is disregarded or not complied with, the concerned Member State must guarantee that a new complaint can be submitted to the ECOWAS Court of Justice against itself because the disregard of a declaratory judgment constitutes a permanent situation contrary to International law within the convicted signatory state. This state of offence constitutes an attack on International law in general and affects state responsibility.

The current loopholes within the ECOWAS Community can only be closed if procedural reforms are initiated on both sides: The reforms should be carried out in the Member States' constitutional procedure regulations and at the ECOWAS level.

At ECOWAS level: the Protocol as well as the procedural system of the ECOWAS Court of Justice should include the party-relatedness of the legal force, the extent of the binding force of the ECOWAS judgment in the decided case, the effectiveness of the judgments in the parallel-proceedings of those Member States not party to the proceedings, the authority of the Court of justice to order concrete corrective measures and, as a consequence, an obligation of implementation. As soon as the adherence to human rights and principles of the rule of law has become a legal tradition for the signatory states, the necessity of exhausting all National legal remedies as a prerequisite for the admissibility before the ECOWAS Court of Justice would become understandable.

Regarding the reforms at National level of the signatory states, an obligation to implement should be included in the constitutional procedure regulations of the Member Staes. It has been shown, with regard to the partiality, that the current content of Art. 15 par. 4 of the Amendment Agreement has a general binding effect of the decision of the ECOWAS Court of Justice. Based on the development of the law within the legal system of the Community and, in particular, the admissibility of an individual complaint before the Court of justice , an amendment of the regulation in Art. 15 par. 4 of the Amendment Agreement becomes necessary. *De lege ferenda* presumes a direct legal effect on the signatory state that is party to the proceedings. This does not mean that the declaratory judgments have no consequences for the signatory states not party to the proceedings. Rather, the decisions of the Court of justice constitute a normative basis for all Member States regarding their future behaviour, in order to prevent possible own convictions. Thus, the decisions by the Court of justice develop an orientation effect and have a guiding function atNational level. This means that the effects of the ECOWAS declaratory judgments can be observed in parallel proceedings by not directly involved Member States. Regarding the exceptional admissibility of individual complaints without prior exhaustion of all National legal remedies, a step by step solution within the ECOWAS Community should be found. Through the review of decisions of National Constitutional Courts, a culture of impartiality in the region can slowly be established because the independence of the justice system is confirmed on paper but the impartiality based on their subjective imprints can only be guaranteed through a culture of rule of law and responsibility. As the consolidation of the rule of law principles and the adherence to ECOWAS-standards within the signatory states is gradually completed, the requirement to exhaust all National legal remedies as a prerequisite for the proceedings before the ECOWAS Court of Justice should be required. This takes the notion of the need for legal protection and the subsidiary system of International law into account.

With regards to the Protocol, it must be clearly added that the interpretation of the Charter and the declaratory judgment by the ECOWAS Court of Justice have priority before those of the Constitutional Courts of Member States. In order to apply and implement the judgments by the regional Court uniformly, the Member States should amend their procedural law according to the ECOWAS-Protocol. A change in case law for these reasons seems necessary because the ambiguous wording that the Court of justice is not a cassation court further encourages the Member States to use the doctrine of res judicata to undermine the competence of the Court of justice .

In the fourth chapter, certain deficiencies regarding the reception of the legal force in the domestic legal system of the signatory states were identified. Even if a judgment of the ECOWAS Court of Justice is of a declarative character, it does not automatically have legal consequences for the convicted Member State. There is, namely, the obligation to comply with the judgment in the domestic legal system. There are, however, problems regarding the status of International law within the National law of the Member States, the strict *erga-omnes* effect of the judgments of domestic

Constitutional Courts and the question of implementation of ECOWAS declaratory judgments at National level. Subsequent to this, the question of the addressees of obligations of implementation under International law has been discussed. The position of International law in the hierarchy of norms within the National legal system of the signatory state does not play a role in terms of legal consequences. Should the ECOWAS Court of Justice establish a violation of the obligations adopted into the instruments of the Community, the concerned Member State is liable to enforcement, regardless of the position of International law within the domestic legal system.[159] When comparing the legal force of National judgments and that of the institution of restitution in kind, the latter has more weight. An order of restitution regarding the situation that is contrary to International law does not equal the direct annulment of the judgment by the Constitutional Court. How the state is to achieve the result of the declaratory judgment in conformity with International law judgment is left to its discretion. The annulment is not absolutely essential. The signatory state could take another domestic route in order to restore the legal status quo before the violation. From a comparative legal perspective, however, the resumption of the original initial proceedings should be considered as an appropriate means to restore a situation in accordance with International law. This can be derived from the practice of ECtHR case law and the Member States of the European Council. In this context, many Member States of the European Council have introduced the declaratory judgment of the ECtHR as a reason for a resumption in their respective domestic legal systems (Germany and France should be named here as examples).[160]

From a procedural perspective, all ECOWAS Member States should provide for the possibility of overcoming the legal force by way of exception in their rules of procedure. The declaratory judgment should be established as the constituent element of the resumption of the initial trial in

---

159 Comp.: ECJ, 26/62, Van Gend & Loos (05.02.1963), 25; ECJ, 6/64, Costa ENEL (15.07.1964).

160 Pettiti, Le réexamen d'une décision pénale française après un arrêt de la Cour Européenne des Droits de L'Homme: La loi française du 15 juin 2000, in: Revue Trimestrielle des Droits de l'Homme (2001), 3 (13); Hoffmann-Holland, Wiederaufnahme eines durch rechtskräftiges Urteil abgeschlossenen Verfahrens [resumption of a trial completed by a final judgment], in: Graf, Strafprozessordnung [Criminal Procedure Code], commentary, § 359, Rn. 35; Hart- mann, Die Restitutionsklage [restitution action], in: Baumbach/Lauterbach/Hartmann (Publ.), Zivilprozessordnung [Civil procedure Code, 71. edition, (2013), § 580, Rn. 27.

the rules of procedure of the Member States. For the parallel domestic proceedings the declaratory judgment should be applied as part of the facts of the case of a *question prio ritaire de conformité* corresponding with the prevailing *exception d'inconstituti onnalité*. For this purpose, the term *conformité* statt *constitutionnalité* is preferred because state acts are not examined in the light of the constitution but the African Charter and the associated case law of the ECOWAS Court of Justice. According to the current legal situation, the regulations of the legal force in National legal system are opposed to the obligation to comply with ECOWAS judgments because the implementation of declaratory judgments clearly constitute an infringement of opposing constitutional law of Member States.[161]Herewith, the respective regulations of the rules of procedure in the constitution of Member States should thus be adjusted. A fundamental non-appealability of constitutional court decisions should be maintained, but an exceptional deviation from the non-appealability based on ECOWAS-declaratory judgments should be provided for.[162]

The state powers of the Member States involved in the proceedings are not party to the trial before the ECOWAS Court of Justice. For this very reason, the signatory state alone is directly bound by the declaratory judg-

161 See also: § 129 par. 2 Constitution of Ghana of 1992; Art. 106 Constitution of Togo of 14 October 1992; Art. 124 Constitution of Benin of 11 December 1991; Art. 94 Constitution of Mali of 25 February 1992; Art. 134 Constitution of Niger of 25 November 2010; Art. 99 Constitution of Guinea of 07 May 2010; Art. 98 Constitution of Ivory Coast of 23 July 2000; Art. 159 Constitution of Burkina Faso of 02 June 1991; Art. 92 par. 2 Constitution of Senegal of 22 January 2001; Sect. 230, 232, 233, 235 Constitution of Nigeria of 29 May 1999; Art. 65 Constitution of Liberia of 06 January 1984; Art. 92 Constitution of Guinea Bissau of 16 January 1984; Sect. 126, 127 Constitution of The Gambia of 16 January 1997; Art. 229 par. 1 Constitution of Cape Verde of 23 November 1999; Art. 122 par. 1 Constitution of Sierra Leone of 03 September 1991.

162 Thus, the adjustment of the respective regulations seems advisable, namely: § 129 par. 2 Constitution of Ghana of 1992; Art. 106 Constitution of Togo of 14 October 1992; Art. 124 Constitution of Benin of 11 December 1991; Art. 94 Constitution of Mali of 25 February 1992; Art. 134 Constitution of Niger of 25 November 2010; Art. 99 Constitution of Guinea of 07 May 2010; Art. 98 Constitution of Ivory Coast of 23 July 2000; Art. 159 Constitution of Burkina Faso of 02 June 1991; Art. 92 par. 2 Constitution of Senegal of 22 January 2001; Sect. 230, 232, 233, 235 Constitution of Nigeria of 29 May 1999; Art. 65 Constitution of Liberia of 06 January 1984; Art. 92 Constitution of Guinea Bissau of 16 January 1984; Sect. 126, 127 Constitution of The Gambia of 16 January 1997; Art. 229 par. 1 Constitution of Cape Verde of 23 November 1999; Art. 122 par. 1 Constitution of Sierra Leone of 03 September 1991.

ment. However, the conviction of the Member State indirectly addresses the concerned National bodies.[163] Since domestic Constitutional Courts are state organs, they are indirectly bound by the declaratory judgment of the ECOWAS Court of Justice. The reason for this is: the signatory states cannot act by themselves as they are, without exception, bound by their organs. However, the actions of the state organs are ascribed to the signatory state. Every signatory state is liable for the misconduct of one of its organs and this is now an established rule of international state responsibility. The best way to correct misconduct is: to reverse the National misconduct which is in violation of human rights. Thus, the restitution in kind is to be deduced as a direct consequence from the declaratory judgment. In the case of a Constitutional Court decision, the resumption of a trial constitutes an appropriate means of reparation. This is logical. In their role as the highest guardians of the Charter, the Constitutional Courts and Supreme Courts of Member States and the associated judgments of the ECOWAS Court of Justice shall transfer an *erga-omnes*-commitment to the entire National legal system. The reason for this is that the other organs of the state are more open-minded towards the National Constitutional Court than towards the ECOWAS Court of Justice. For this reason, the national Constitutional Courts should play a jointly-responsible role for the implementation of the Charter at a National level. These proposed constitutional reforms are based on the fundamental finding of the contractual commitments in accordance with state responsibility under International law, as the ICJ has quite rightly explained.[164]

Both reforms should be able to contribute to the realisation of the purpose of the Additional Protocol A/SP.1/01/05. The signatory states have committed themselves to undertake such reforms. This is consistent: countries that commit themselves to International law, do not have any better means available to meet their obligation than to adjust their National legal systems to that of International law.[165] The current state of procedural rules oin the constitutions of Member States is an insurmountable obstacle

163 CIJ, Demande en interprétation de l'arrêt du 31 mars 2004 en l'Affaire Avena et autres res- sortissants mexicains (Mexique c. États-Unis d'Amerique), Arrêt du 19 janvier 2009, par. 61.

164 CIJ, Demande en interprétation de l'arrêt du 31 mars 2004 en l'Affaire Avena et autres res- sortissants mexicains (Mexique c. Ètats-Unis d'Amerique), Arrêt du 19 janvier 2009, par. 8.

165 Enabulele, Reflections on the ECOWAS-Community Court Protocol and the Constitutions of Member States, in: International Community Law Review 12 (2010), 111 (135).

for the implementation of ECOWAS-Court decisions. Reforming the procedural rules in the constitutions would be a preventive measure to prevent blocking the implementation of ECOWAS-Court decisions. This view is confirmed by the ICJ in its interpretation judgment regarding the Avena vs the United States case:

> « Un État qui a valablement contracté des obligations Internationales est tenu d'apporter à sa législation *les modifications nécessaires* pour assurer l'exécution des engagements pris ».[166]

The establishment of procedural regulations at domestic level would mean that the African Charter and the decisions of the Court of justice would always be present in the National organs of the Member States as a set of rules for the implementation of the ECOWAS rulings. Subsequently, the state organs would attribute great value to the judgments by the ECOWAS Court of Justice.[167] This is because the conviction of a Member State based on an infringement of the human rights guaranteed in the Charter has no effect if the *judgment* of the protective instance at regional level is seen by the National organs as non-binding. A reform of the National legal systems of Member States is necessary, in order to expressly clarify the question whether and to what extent the decisions by the ECOWAS Court of Justice develop their effects.[168] Such reforms are the only way to confirm Protocol A/SP.1/01/05 (19/01/2005) as an effective instrument of International law.[169] Without such reforms, plaintiffs must rely on the goodwill of the convicted signatory state after having endured long-winded proceedings before the ECOWAS Court of Justice.[170] The cooperation between both levels of law alone could guarantee the effective protection of

166 CIJ, Demande en interprétation de l'arrêt du 31 mars 2004 en l'Affaire Avena et autres res- sortissants mexicains (Mexique c. États-Unis d'Amérique), Arrêt du 19 janvier 2009, par. 8 (Her- vorhebung durch den Verfasser).

167 Mellech, Die Rezeption der EMRK sowie der Urteile des EGMR in der französischen und deutschen Rechtsprechung, 2. [The reception of the ECHR and the judgments of the ECtHR in the French and German jurisdiction, 2].

168 Oppong/Niro, Enforcing Judgments of International Court in National Court, in: Journal of International Dispute Settlement (2014), 1 (21); Enabulele, Reflections on the ECOWAS-Com- munity Court Protocol and the Constitutions of Member States, in: International Community Law Review 12 (2010), 111 (137).

169 Enabulele, Reflections on the ECOWAS-Community Court Protocol and the Constitutions of Member States, in: International Community Law Review 12 (2010), 111 (137).

170 Oppong/Niro, Enforcing Judgments of International Court in National Court, in: Journal of International Dispute Settlement (2014), 1 (4).

human rights.[171] In this context, the domestic procedural principles in the constitution should be amended in accordance with the guiding principles of regional International law. In established case law, the ICJ has, in this regard, emphasised that the argument of the obstacle to implementation must not be allowed to take effect in the light of the development of the state liability law. With this in mind, the ICJ recently stated in its interpretative judgment in the Avena case:

> « La Cour n'a cessé de réaffirmer dans sa jurisprudence qu'un État ne saurait invoquer son droit interne pour justifier de ne pas avoir exécuté une obligation Internationale. Ainsi, en prenant les mesures qui leur incombent en vertu de l'arrêt Avena, les États-Unis ne sauraient invoquer vis-à-vis d'un autre État leur propre Constitution pour se soustraire aux obligations que leur imposent le droit International ou les traités en vigueur».[172]

Two constellations have been analysed for parallel *National* proceedings. On the one hand, the transfer of an automatic *erga-omnes*-binding effect for parallel National proceedings, and on the other hand, the procedure of the *Exception d'Inconstitutionnalité* and the *Question Prioritiare de Conformité* (QPC) were referred to. The automatic erga-omnes-binding effect for parallel National proceedings means that in the case where a signatory state is concerned, the signatory state is obliged to make amends or terminate its obligation. However, this obligation should also apply for parallel proceedings at *National* level. Due to the generalisation of the binding effect, the convicted signatory state must prevent a new conviction. Thus, the declaratory judgment by the ECOWAS Court of Justice constitutes a de facto direct *erga-omnes* binding effect for *parallel* domestic *cases*. Furthermore, there would be doubts in parallel National proceedings regarding a legal question that is of substantial importance to the human rights jurisdiction before domestic Constitutional Courts. In this case, they are (as in case Art. 276 par. 3 TFEU) obliged to make a submission. The party to the dispute should also have the right to ask this legal question, to raise the question as a *Question Prioritaire de Conformité* before National courts as

171 Ebobrah, A critical Analysis of the human rights mandate of the ECOWAS Community Court of Justice, 25, available at: http://docs.escr-net.org/usr_doc/S_Ebobrah.pdf (last accessed on 16/05/2015).

172 CIJ, Demande en interprétation de l'arrêt du 31 mars 2004 en l'Affaire Avena et autres res- sortissants mexicains (Mexique c. États-Unis d'Amérique), Arrêt du 19 janvier 2009, par. 8.

well as the Constitutional Courts. This means the suspension of the main proceedings either on the initiative of the referring Constitutional Courts or by the concerned party to the dispute. The decision by the ECOWAS Court of Justice on this would then constitute a landmark decision for the entire legal system of the Community.

The study at hand should, after all, serve as a small contribution to the development of the National implementation of the judgments by the ECOWAS Court of Justice and the effective legal protection within the ECOWAS legal order. This can only be achieved if there is an improved interlocking of regional International law and national constitutional law. It is, therefore, necessary to maintain a constructive dialogue between both legal systems, which can lead to effective and operative legal protection. The joint participation of the National law of the Member States and the ECOWAS legal instruments create good conditions for implementation and at the same time lead to an optimal effectiveness of the African Charter within the legal order of the Community.[173] The reforms would help to eliminate the incompatibility of the National law and the Protocol.[174] Access to the International ECOWAS Court of Justice is illusory if the execution of final, legally-binding declaratory judgments is refused on National level. This would run counter to the idea behind Art. 7 par. 1 of the African Charter.

Moreover, the establishment of a monitoring body which is responsible for controlling the implementation of declaratory judgments by the Court of justice is necessary. In this regard, the creation of an independent executive body would assist in expediting the implementation of the judgments. Furthermore, the official status of implementation of the judgments by the ECOWAS Court of justice should be published at regular intervals in order to increase the attention of the public regarding the implementation of judgments. The current sanction mechanisms could do with some improvements.

---

173 Schaffarzik, Europäische Menschenrechte unter der Ägide des Bundesverfassungsgerichts [European human rights under the aegis of the Federal Constitutional Court], in: DÖV (2005), 860 (865).

174 Enabulele, Reflections on the ECOWAS-Community Court Protocol and the Constitutions of Member States, in: International Community Law Review 12 (2010), 111 (133).

Let us hope that the reform proposals will be heard so that Abuja, because of the ECOWAS Court of Justice stands for the West African constitutional order as "The Capital of Human Rights Protection".[175]

175 Kane, La Cour de justice de la CEDEAO à l'épreuve de la protection des droits de l'homme, Université Gaston Berger, Maitrise en Sciences Juridiques 2012, 50; Adjolohoun, The ECOWAS Court as a Human Rights Promoter? Assessing Five Years' Impact of Koraou Slavery Judgment, in: Netherlands Quarterly of Human Rights (2013), 342 (368).

Bibliography

Abebe, Adem Kassie: Towards more liberal standing rules to enforce constitutional rights in Ethiopia, in: African Human Rights Law (2010), 407–431.

Abebe, Adem Kassie/Vijoen, Frans: Amicus Curiae Participation Before Regional Human Rights Bodies in Africa, in: Journal of African Law (2014), 22–44.

Adeloui, Arséne-Joêl: L'autorité de la chose jugée par les juridictions constitutionnelles en Afrique, in: Revue Togolaise des Sciences Juridiques (2012), 54–75.

ders.[the same]: L'insertion des engagements internationaux en droit interne des Etats africains, in: Revue Béninoise des Sciences Juridiques et Administratives (2011), 51–95.

Adjolohoun, Horace S.: The ECOWAS Court as a human Right Promoter? Assessing Five Years' Impact of Koraou Slavery Judgment, in: Netherlands Quarterly of Human Rights (2013), 342–371.

ders.: Droits de l'homme et justice constitutionnelle en Afrique: le modèle béninois. À la lu mière de la Charte africaine des droits de l'homme et des peuples, Paris u. a. 2011.

Ahadzi-Nonou, Koffi: Droits de l'Homme et Développement: Théories et Réalités, in: Terri- toires et Liberté. Mélanges en Hommage au Doyen Yves Madiot, Brüssel 2000, 107–123.

ders.: Les nouvelles tendances du constitutionalisme africain, in: Afrique Juridique et Poli- tique (2002), 35–81.

Aivo, Fréderic Joél: Le juge constitutionnel et l'état de droit en Afrique. L'exemple du model béninois, Paris 2006.

Alter, Karen J./Helfer, Laurence R./McAllister, Jacqueline R.: A new International human rights court for West Africa: the ECOWAS Community Court of Justice, in: The American Journal of International Law (2013), 737–779.

Amselek, Paul: Une fausse idée claire: la Hiérarchie des Normes Juridiques, in: Renouveau du Droit constitutionnel. Mélanges en l'honneur de Louis Favoreu, Paris 2007, 983–1014.

Arangio-Ruiz, Gaetano: Second Report on State Responsibility, UN Doc. A/ CN.4/425 & Corr. 1 and Add. 1 & Corr. 1 (09.06.1989).

Badet, Gilles: Commentaire de l'arrêt dame Hadidjatou Mani Koraou contre la République du Niger, CJ CEDEAO, in: Revue Béninoise des Sciences Juridiques et Administratives (2010), 153–193.

ders.: Les Attributions originales de la Cour Constitutionnelle du Bénin, Cotonou 2013.

Bado, Kangnikoé: Verfassungsgerichtsbarkeit und Demokratisierung im frankophonen Westafrika, Länderstudie/Benin[Constitutional Jurisdiction and Democratisation in Francophone West Africa], available at: http://intlaw-sgiessen.de/filead min/ user_upload/bilder_und_dokumente/forschung/westafrikaprojekt/working papers/Draft_ WP_2014_benin.pdf.

Barsac, Tessa: La Cour africaine de Justice et des droits de l'homme, Paris 2012. *Barthelemy, Joseph/Duez, Paul*: Traité élémentaire de droit constitutionnel, Paris 1926. *Benda, Ernst/Klein, Eckart*: Verfassungsprozeßrecht [constitutional process law], 2. edition, Heidelberg 2001.

Benedek, Wolfgang: Durchsetzung von Rechten des Menschen und der Völker in Afrika auf regionaler und Nationaler Ebene [Enforcing the rights of the individual and the peoples in Africa on a regional and National level], in: Zeitschrift für ausländisches öffentliches Recht und Völkerrecht [Magazine for Public Law and Administrative Science, ZaöRV](1994), 150–181.

Bernabè, Boris/Cartier, Emmanuel: L'introduction d'un nouveau gène dans le procès, in: Emmanuel Cartier (Publ.): La QPC, le procès et ses juges: l'impact sur le procès et l'archi- tecture juridictionnelle, Paris 2013, 1–21.

Bernhardt, Rudolf: Internationaler Menschenrechtsschutz und Nationaler Gestaltungspiel- raum, in: Völkerrecht als Rechtsordnung [International protection of human rights and National margin of discretion, in International Law as the rule of law], Festschrift Hermann Mosler, Berlin 1983, 75- 88.

ders.: The Convention and Domestic Law, in: Ronald St. J. Macdonald/Franz Matscher/Her- bert Petzold (Publ.), The European System for the Protection of Human Rights, Dordrecht u. a. 1993, 25–40.

Bertele, Joachim: Souveränität und Verfahrensrecht. Eine Untersuchung der aus dem Völker- recht ableitbaren Grenzen staatlicher extraterritorialer Jurisdiktion im Verfahrensrecht [Sovereignty and procedural law. A study of the limitations of National extra-territorial jurisdiction in procedural law, deducible from International law], Tübingen 1998.

Bhoke, Chacha: Judgment in the First Case before the African Court of Human and Peoples' Rights a Missed Opportunity or a Mockery of International Law in Africa?, in: Journal of African and International Law (2010), 187–228.

Bimpong-Buta, Seth Yeboa: The role of the Supreme Court in the development of constituti- onal Law in Ghana (PhD), Pretoria 2005.

Bleckmann, Albert: Völkerrecht [International law], Baden-Baden 2001.

Bolle, Stéphane: La Cour de Justice de la CEDEAO: une cour (supra)constitutionelle?, available at: http://la-constitution-en-afrique.org/article-la-cour-de-justice-cedeano-une- cour-supra-constitutionelle-87092524.html.

ders.: Quand la Cour de Justice de la CEDEAO s'autolimite, in: La Constitution en Afrique (08.04.2012), abrufbar unter: www.la-constitution-en-afrique.org.

Boetticher, Eduard: Kritische Beiträge zur Lehre von der materiellen Rechtskraft im Zivil- prozeß [Critical contributions to the doctrine of substantive legal force in civil proceedings], Berlin 1930.

Boumakani, Benjamin: La prohibition de la « transhumance politique » des parlementaires. Étude de cas africains, in: Revue française de Droit constitutionnel (2008), 499–512.

Breuer, Marten: Staatshaftung für judikatives Unrecht. Eine Untersuchung zum deutschen Recht, zum Europa- und Völkerrecht [State liability in case of judicial injustice. A study regarding German law], Tübingen 2011.

ders.: Von Lyons zu Seydovic: Auf dem Weg zu einer Wiederaufnahme konventionswidrig zustande gekommener Nationaler Urteile?[On the way to a resumption of National judgments, issued in violation of the Convention], in: EuGRZ (2004), 782–786.

ders.: Zur Anordnung konkreter Abhilfemaßnahmen durch den EGMR, in: EuGRZ (2004), 257–262.

Bryde, Brun-Otto: Überseeische Verfassungsvergleichung nach 30 Jahren, in: Verfassung und Recht in Übersee [Overseas comparison of Constitutions after 30 years, in: Constitution and Law overseas] (1997), 452–464.

Burgorgue-Larsen, Laurence/Úbeda de Torres, Amaya: Les Grandes Décisions de la Cour Interaméricaine des Droits de l'Homme, Brüssel 2008.

Cabanis, André/Martin, Michel Louis: Les constitutions d'Afrique francophone. Évolutions recentes, Paris 1999.

Cadiet, Loïc: Leçons béninoises de théorie générale du procès, in: Revue Béninoise des Sciences Juridiques et Administratives. Numéro Spécial, 2014.

Cartier, Emmanuel: Le positionnement tactique et stratégique des acteurs du procès face à la QPC, in: ders. (Publ.), La QPC, le procès et ses juges: l'impact sur le procès et l'architecture juridictionnelle, Paris 2013, 53–62.

Cassesse, Antonio: International Law, Second edition, Oxford 2005.

Chantebout, Bernard: Droit constitutionnel, 27. éd., Paris 2010.

Chigara, Ben: What Should a Re-constituted Southern African Development Community (SADC) Tribunal Be Mindful of to succeed?, in: Nordic Journal of International Law (2012), 341–377.

Cohen-Jonathan, Gérard: La fonction quasi constitutionnelle de la Cour Européenne des Droits de l'Homme, in: Renouveau du Droit constitutionnel. Mélanges en l'honneur de Louis Favoreu, Paris 2007, 1127–1153.

ders.: Quelques considérations sur la réparation accordée aux victimes d'une violation de la Convention Européenne des Droits de l'Homme, in: Les Droits de l'Homme au seuil du troisième millénaire. Mélanges en hommage à Pierre Lambert, Brüssel [Brussels] 2000, 109–140.

Combacau, Jean/Sur, Serge: Droit International Public, 7. éd. Paris 2006.

Cowell, Frederick: The Death of the Southern African Development Community Tribunal's Human Rights Jurisdiction, in: Human Rights Law Review (2013), 153–165.

ders.: The impact of the protocol on good governance and democracy, in: African Journal of International and Comparative Law (2011), 331–342.

Creifelds, Carl/Weber, Klaus: Rechtswörterbuch [Legal Dictionary], 19. edition, München [Munich] 2007.

Cremer, Hans-Joachim: Entscheidung und Entscheidungswirkung [Decision-making and Effect of Decision-making], in: Oliver Dörr/Rainer Grote/Thilo Marauhn (Publ.), EMRK/GG, Konkordanzkommentar zum europäischen und deutschen Grundrechtsschutz [concordance commentary regarding the European and German protection of fundamental rights], 2. edition, part 2, chapter 32, Tübingen 2013, 2053–2147.

ders.: Zur Bindungswirkung von EGMR-Urteilen. Anmerkung zum Görgülü-Beschluß des BVerfG vom 14.10.2004[Regarding the binding effect of judgments by the ECtHR. Comment regarding the Görgülü judgment by the Federal Constitutional Court of 14/10/2004], in: EuGRZ (2004), 683–700.

Cross, Rupert/Bell, John: Statutory Interpretation, London 1987.

Dampha, Lang Fafa: Nationalism and Reparation in West Africa, Paris 2013.

Dannemann, Gerhard: Haftung für die Verletzung von Verfahrensgarantie nach Art. 41 EMRK. Zur Herausbildung europäischer Haftungsmaßstäbe [Liability in case of a violation of procedural guarantees acc. to Art. 41 ECHR. Regarding the development of European standards of liability], in: Rabels Zeitschrift für ausländisches und Internationales Privatrecht [magazine for foreign and International civil law] (1999), 452–470.

ders.: Schadensersatz bei Verletzung der Europäischen Menschenrechtskonvention [Compensation in Case of a Violation of the European Convention on Human Rights]. Eine rechtsvergleichende Untersuchung zur Haftung nach Art. 50 EMRK, Köln u. a. 1994 [A legal comparison regarding the liability acc. to Art. 50 ECHR, Cologne et al 1994].

De Bruyn, Donatienne: Le Droit à un recours effectif, in: Les Droits de l'Homme au seuil du troisième millénaire. Mélanges en hommage à Pierre Lambert, Brüssel 2000, 185–205.

Du Bois de Gaudusson, Jean: Défense et Illustration du constitutionnalisme en Afrique après quinze ans de pratique du pouvoir, in: Renouveau du droit constitutionnel. Mélanges en l'honneur de Louis Favoreu, Paris 2007, 609–611.

De Visscher, Charles: Problèmes d'interprétation des judicaires en Droit International Pub lic, Paris 1963.

Decaux, Emmanuel/Imbert, Pierre-Henri/Pettiti, Louis-Edmond: La convention Européenne des Droits de l'Homme, Commentaire article par article, Paris 1999.

Delanlssays, Thomas: La motivation des décisions juridictionnelles relatives à la QPC au prisme de l'efficience, in: Emmanuel Cartier (Publ.), La QPC, le procès et ses juges: l'im- pact sur le procès et l'architecture juridictionnelle, Paris 2013, 133–154.

Delmas-Marty, Mireille/Izorche, Marie-Laure: Marge Nationale d'appréciation et internatio- nalisation du droit: réflexions sur la validité formelle d'un droit commun pluraliste, in: McGill Law Journal (2000–2001), 923–954.

Detterbeck, Steffen: Streitgegenstand und Entscheidungswirkungen im öffentlichen Recht [The object of Dispute and the Effect of Legal Decisions in Public Law], Tübingen 1995.

Diop, El Hadji Omar: La justice constitutionnelle au Sénégal. Essai sur l'évolution, les enjeux et les réformes d'un contrepouvoir juridictionnel, Dakar 2013.

Djogbènou, Joseph: Procès équitable, in: Annuaire Béninoise de Justice constitutionnelle (2013), 587–617.

Doehring, Karl: Völkerrecht [International law], Heidelberg 1999.

ders.: Völkerrecht: ein Lehrbuch [International law: a textbook], 2. edition, Heidelberg 2004.

Dolzer, Rudolf: "Good governance": neues transNationales Leitbild der Staatlichkeit?["Good governance": a new transNational model of statehood], in: Zeitschrift für ausländisches öffentliches Recht und Völkerrecht [Magazine for Public Law and Administrative Science, ZaöRV] (2004), 535–546.

Dröge, Cordula: Positive Verpflichtungen der Staaten in der Europäischen Menschenrechts- konvention [Positive obligations of the states within the European Human Rights Convention], Berlin u. a. 2003.

Dujardin, Stéphanie: La Cour Africaine de Justice et des Droits de l'Homme: Un Projet de fusion opportune et progressiste des juridictions panafricaines par l'Union Africaine, in: Revue Juridique et Politique (2007), 511–533.

Dupuy, Pierre-Marie: Les juridictions Internationales face au procès équitable. Le point de vue de la Cour Internationale, in: Mireille Delmas-Marty u. a. (Publ): Variations autour d'un droit commun. Premières rencontres de l'UMR de droit comparé de Paris, Paris 2002, 239–244.

Ebobrah, Solomon Tamarabrakemi: A critical Analysis of the human rights mandate of the ECOWAS Community Court of Justice, 1–58, available at: http://docs.esc r-net.org/ usr_doc/S_Ebobrah.pdf.

ders.: A rights-protection goldmine or a waiting volcanic eruption? Competence of, and ac- cess to, the human rights jurisdiction of the ECOWAS Community Court of Justice, in: African Human Rights Law Journal (2007), 307–329.

ders.: Human Right Development in sub-regional court in Africa during 2008, in: African Human Right Law Journal (2009), 312–335.

ders.: Human rights developments in African sub-regional economic communities during 2009, in: African Human Right Law Journal (2010), 233–264.

ders.: Human rights development in African sub-regional economic communities during 2010, in: African Human Rights Law Journal (2011), 216–250.

ders.: Legitimacy and feasibility of human rights realisation through regional economic com- munities in Africa: the case of ECOWAS, Pretoria 2009.

ders.: Litigating Human Rights before Sub-Regional Court in Africa: Prospects and challen- ges, in: African Journal of International and Comparative Law (2009), 79–101.

Edi, Eric M.: Globalization and Politics in the Economic Community of West African States, Durham 2007.

Egede, Edwin: Bringing Human Rights Home: An Examination of the Domestication of Hu- man Rights Treaties in Nigeria, in: Journal of African Law (2007) 249–284.

Eissen, Marc-André: Le statut juridique interne de la Convention devant les juridictions ré- pressives, in: Gérard Cohen-Jonathan u. a. (Publ.), Droits de l'homme en France: 10 ans d'application de la Convention européenne des droits de l'homme devant les juridictions judiciaires françaises, Kehl u. a. 1985, 1–30.

Ekhator, Eghosa O.: Improving access to environmental justice under the African Charter on Human and Peoples' Rights: The role of NGOS in Nigeria, in: African Journal of Interna- tional and comparative Law (2014), 63–79.

Elsheikh, Ibrahim Ali: The future relationship between the African Court and the African Commission, in: African Human Rights Law Journal (2002), 252–260.

Enabulele, Amos O.: Reflections on the ECOWAS Community Court Protocol and the Cons- titutions of Member States, in: International Community Law Review (2010), 111–138.

Fall, Ismaïla Madior/Sall, Alioune: Une constitution régionale pour l'espace CEDEAO: le protocole sur la démocratie et la bonne gouvernance, available at: http://la-constituti- on-en-afrique.org/article-34239380.html.

Figari Layus, Rosario: Überblick über das interamerikanische Menschenrechtssystem. Do kumente und Kontrollmechanismen, [Overview of the Inter-American Human Rights System. Documents and control mechanisms] in: MenschenRechtsMagazin [in: HumanRightsMagazine] (2008), 56–61.

Flauss, Jean-François: L'effectivité de la Charte Africaine des Droits de l'Homme et des Peuples dans l'ordre juridiques des Etats Parties contractantes: Bilan et Perspectives, in: Jean-François Flauss/Elisabeth Lambert-Abdelgawad (Publ.), L'application Nationale de la Charte africaine des droits de l'homme et des peuples, Bruxelles 2004, 247–254.

Frowein, Jochen Abraham/Peukert, Wolfgang: Europäische Menschenrechtskonvention. EMRK-Kommentar [European Human Rights Convention. ECHR commentary], 3. edition, Kehl 2009.

Gambari, Ibrahim A.: Political and comparative dimensions of regional integration: the Case of ECOWAS, New Jersey und London 1991.

Gans, Christiane: Die ECOWAS. Wirtschaftsintegration in Westafrika [The ECOWAS. Economic integration in West Africa], Berlin and Münster 2006.

Germelmann, Peter Philipp: Das rechtliche Gehör vor Gericht im europäischen Recht. Die Gewährleistungen der Europäischen Menschenrechtskonvention und ihr Einfluss auf den prozessualen Grundrechtsschutz in der Europäischen Union[The legal hearing before a court in the European Law. The guarantees of the European Human Rights Convention and its influence on the procedural protection of the Constitution within the European Union], Baden-Baden 2014.

Gialdino, Rolando E.: Le Nouveau Règlement de la Cour Interaméricaine des Droits de l'Homme, in: Revue Trimestrielle des Droits de l'Homme (2005), 981–997.

Giegerich, Thomas: Wirkung und Rang der EMRK in den Rechtsordnungen der Mitglied- staaten[Effect and rank of the ECHR in the legal systems of Member States], in: Oliver Dörr/Rainer Grote/Thilo Marauhn (Publ.), EMRK/GG, Konkordanz- kommentar zum europäischen und deutschen Grundrechtsschutz[concordance commentary regarding the European and German protection of fundamental rights], 2. edition, Teil 1, Kapitel 2, Tübingen 2013, 57–97.

Gonidec, Pierre-François: Constitutionnalismes Africains, in: African journal of internatio- nal and comparative Law (1996), 23–43.

Grabenwarter, Christoph: Europäische Menschenrechtskonvention. Ein Studienbuch [European Human Rights Convention. A study guide], 4. edition, München et al. 2009.

Grabenwarter, Christoph/Pabel, Katharina: Europäische Menschenrechtskonvention. Ein Studienbuch [European Human Rights Convention. A study guide], 5. edition, München et al 2012.

Greer, Steven: The margin of appreciation: interpretation and discretion under the European Convention on Human Rights, in: Human Rights files No. 17, Council of Europe, 2000.

Grewe, Constance: Die Rezeption der EMRK in Deutschland, in: dies./Christoph Gusy (Publ.), Menschenrechte in der Bewährung. Die Rezeption der Europäischen Menschen rechtskonvention in Frankreich und Deutschland im Vergleich[The reception of the ECHR in Germany, in: dies./Christoph Gusy (Publ.), Human Rights on Probation. The reception of the European Human Rights Convention in France and in comparison in Germany], Baden-Baden 2005, 106-128, 106 (115); Sauve/Pauti, in: Thierry/Decaus, Droit International, 237 (240).

Grosche, Nils: Rechtfortbildung im Unionsrecht. Eine Untersuchung zum Phänomen richterlicher Rechtsfortbildung durch den Gerichtshof der Europäischen Union[Law development in Union Legislation. A sudy regarding the phenomenon of judicial legal further education through the Court of Justice of the European Union], Tübingen 2011. *Guinchard, Serge/Debard, Thierry (Publ.)*: Lexique des termes juridiques, 18. éd., Paris 2011.

Gumedze, Sabelo: Bringing communication before the African Commission on Human Rights and Peoples' Rights, in: African Human Rights Law Journal (2003), 118–148.

Gundel, Jörg: Verfahrensrechte[procedural rights], in: Rudolf Bernhardt/Detlev Merten (Publ.), Handbuch der Grundrechte in Deutschland und Europa, Band [Handbook on fundamental rights in Germany and Europe, volume] VI/1, Heidelberg and Hamburg 2010, § 146, 349–461.

Häberle, Peter: Europäische Verfassungslehre [European Constitutional Theory, 6th edition, 92], 6. edition, Baden-Baden 2009.

Hamuli-Kabumba, Yves: La répression Internationale de l'esclavage. Les leçons de l'arrêt de la cour de justice de la Communauté économique des États de l'Afrique de l'ouest dans l'Affaire Hadijatou Mani Koraou c. Niger (27 octobre 2008), in: R.Q.D.I (2008), 25–56.

Haratsch, Andreas: Die Solange-Rechtsprechung des Europäischen Gerichtshof für Menschenrechte, das Kooperationsverhältnis zwischen EGMR und EGH [The Solange-jurisdiction by the European Court of Human Rights, the relationship of cooperation between the ECtHR and ECJ], in: ZaöRV (2006), 927–947.

Hartmann, Christof: ECOWAS – Wirtschaftliche Gemeinschaft Westafrikas [ECOWAS – Economic Community of West Africa], in: Katja Frei- stein/Julia Leininger (Publ.), Handbuch Internationale Organisationen. Theoretische Grundlagen und Akteure [Handbook of International organisations. Theoretical bases and actor], München 2012, 85–93.

Hartmann, Peter: Die Restitutionsklage [action for restitution], in: Adolf Baumbach/Wolfgang Lauterbach/Peter Hartmann (Publ.), Zivilprozessordnung [Civil Procedure Code], 71st edition, München 2013, § 580, 1880–1912.

Heckötter, Ulrike: Die Bedeutung der Europäischen Menschenrechtskonvention und der Rechtsprechung des EGMR für die deutschen Gerichte[The meaning of the European Convention on Human Rights and the jurisdiction of the ECtHR for German courts],, Köln u. a. 2007.

Helfer, Laurence R.: Forum shopping for Human Rights, in: University of Pennsylvania Law Review (1999), 285–400.

Herdegen, Matthias: Verfassungsgericht als pouvoir neuter [The Constitutional Court as pouvoir neuter], in: ZaöRV (2009), 257–264.

Hillgruber, Christian: Parteienfreiheit [F reedom of assembly and political parties], in: Detlev Merten/Hans-Jürgen Papier (Publ.), Hand- buch der Grundrechte [Manual on Fundamental Rights], Bd. V [Vol. V], Heidelberg 2013, § 118.

Hillgruber, Christian/Goos, Christoph: Verfassungsprozessrecht [Constitutional Process Law], 4. edition, Heidelberg 2015.

Hilling, Carol: Le système interaméricain de protection des droits de l'homme: le modèle européen adapté aux réalités latino-américaines, in: R.Q.D.I (1991–1992), 210–217.

Hoffmann-Holland, Klaus: Wiederaufnahme eines durch rechtkräftiges Urteil abgeschlosse- nen Verfahrens[resumption of a trial completed by a final judgment],, in: Jürgen Peter Graf (Publ.), Strafprozessordnung [Criminal Procedure Code], commentary, Mün chen 2010, § 359 ff., 1628–1669.

Hopkins, Kevin: The effect of an African Court on the domestic legal orders of African states, in: Human Rights Law Journal (2002), 234–251.

Huneeus, Alexander: Court resisting Court, in: Cornell International Law Journal (2011), 101–155.

Huntington, Samuel P.: The Third Wave. Democratization in the late twentieth century, Nor man 1991.

Ipsen, Knut (Publ.): Völkerrecht. Ein Studienbuch[International Law. A Study Guide]], bearb. von [revised by] Knut Ipsen, Volker Epping, Wolff Heintschel von Heinegg, Ulrich Haltern, Hans-Joachim Heintze, 6. edition, München 2014.

Juma, Dan: Access to the African Court on Human and Peoples' Rights: A Case of the Poacher turned Gamekeeper, in: Essex Human Rights Review (2007), 1–21.

Kamanga, Khoti C.: 'Fast-Tracking' East African Integration and Treaty Law: *Pacta Sunt Servanda*, Betrayed?, in: Journal of African and International Law (2010), 697–718.

Kamto, Maurice: Charte africaine, instruments internationaux de protection des droits de l'homme, Constitutions Nationales: Articulation respectives, in: Jean-François Flauss/Eli- sabeth Lambert-Abdelgawad (Publ.), L'application Nationale de la Charte africaine des droits de l'homme et des peuples, Brüssel 2004, 11–31.

Kane, Thierno: La Cour de justice de la CEDEAO à l'épreuve de la protection des droits de l'homme, Mémoire de Maitrise, Université Gaston Berger (2012–2013).

Kanté, Babacar: Models of Constitutional Jurisdiction in Francophone West Africa, in: The Journal of Comparative Law (2008), 158–173.

Kau, Marcel: Der Staat und der Einzelne als Völkerrechtssubjekte [The State and the individual as subjects under International law], in: Wolfgang Graf Vitzthum/Alexander Proelß (Publ.), Völkerrecht, 6. edition, Berlin u. a. 2013, 131–235.

Kelsen, Hans: Die Einheit von Völkerrecht und staatlichem Recht [The unity of International law and state legislation], in: ZaöRV (1958), 234–248.

ders.: Allgemeine Staatslehre [General State Theory], Berlin 1925.

Kessougbo, Koffi: La Cour constitutionnelle togolaise et la régulation de la démocratie au Togo, in: Revue Béninoise des sciences juridiques et administratives (2005), 59–96.

Kilian, Dieter: Die Bindungswirkung der Entscheidungen des Europäischen Gerichtshof für Menschenrechte auf die nationalen Gerichte der Mitgliedstaaten der Konvention zum Schutze der Menschenrechte und Grundfreiheiten vom 4. November 1950[The Binding Effect of decisions taken by the European Court of Law for Human Rights with regards to the National Court of the Member States regarding the Convention on the Protection of Human Rights and Constitutional Freedoms of 4 November 1950],, Frankfurt am Main 1994.

Kindiki, Kithure: The Proposed Integration of the African Court of Justice and the African Court of Human and Peoples Rights: Legal difficulties and merits, in: African Journal of International and Comparative Law (2007–2009), 138–146.

Kirby, Michael: Domestic Court and International Human Rights Law – the Ongoing Judicial Conversation, in: Netherland Quarterly of Human Right (2009), 291–307.

Klabbers, Jan: An Introduction to International Organizations Law, 3. ed., Cambridge 2015.

Klatt, Matthias: Die praktische Konkordanz von Kompetenzen, entwickelt anhand der Jurisdiktionskonflikte im europäischen Grundrechtsschutz [The practical concordance of competences, developed on the basis of conflicts in jurisdiction within the European fundamental rights], Tübingen 2014.

Klein, Eckart: Should the binding effect of the judgments of the European Court of Human Rights be extended?, in: Paul Mahoney/Franz Matscher/Herbert Petzold/Luzius Wildha ber (Publ.), Protection des droits de l'homme: la perspective européenne. Mélanges à la mémoire de Rolv Ryssdal, Köln u. a. 2000, 705–713.

Knop, Daniel: Völker- und Europarechtsfreundlichkeit als Verfassungsgrundsätze [Openness toward International and European Law as constitutional principles], Tübingen 2013.

Köck, Heribert Franz: Die „implied powers" der Europäischen Gemeinschaften als Anwendungsfall der [of the European Unions as case of application]„implied powers" Internationaler Organisationen überhaupt [of International organisations in general], in: Karl-Heinz Böckstiegel u. a. (Publ.), Völkerrecht, Recht der Internationalen Organisationen, Weltwirt schaftrecht [International law, the law of International organization, Global economic law]. FS für Ignaz Seidl-Hohenveldern, Köln u. a. 1988, 279–288.

Kokoroko, Dodzi: L'apport de la Jurisprudence constitutionnelle africaine à la consolidation des acquis démocratiques, in: Revue Béninoise des sciences juridiques et administratives (2007), 85–128.

Kokott, Juliane: Der Interamerikanische Gerichtshof für Menschenrechte und seine bisherige Praxis [The Inter-American Court for Human Rights and its present practice, in: ZaöRV (1984), 806–839.

dies.: Souveräne Gleichheit und Demokratie im Völkerrecht [Sovereign Equality and Democracy in International Law], in: ZaöRV (2004), 517–533.

Koupokpa, Tikonimbé: La perte du mandat par un parlementaire pour cause de démission ou de l'exclusion de son parti en cours de législature en Afrique noire francophone, in: Revue Togolaise des Sciences Juridiques (2013), 65–80.

ders.: L'indépendance de la Cour de Justice de la CEDEAO, Communication donnée au col- loque International de Lomé, organisé par le Centre de Droit Public de Lomé et le départe- ment de Droit Administratif de la Faculté de droit de l'Université de Gand, tenu le 02 mars 2012 à Lomé, Lomé 2012.

Koussetogue Koude, Roger Magloire: Peut-on à bon droit parler d'une conception africaine des droits de l'homme?, in: Revue Trimestrielle des Droits de l'Homme (2005), 539–561.

Koussoulis, Stelios: Beiträge zur modernen Rechtskraftlehre [Contributions to a modern theory of legal force], Köln u. a. 1986.

Kpedu, Syvestre Yawovi: Réflexion sur la juridictionnalisation du droit International, in: Re vue Togolaise des Sciences Juridiques (2012), 41–53.

Kpodar, Adama: Commentaires des grands avis et décisions de la Cour constitutionnelle to- golaise, Lome 2007.

ders.: La communauté Internationale et le Togo: élément de réflexion sur l'extranéité de l'ordre constitutionnel, in: Revue Togolaise des Sciences Juridiques (2011), 38–44.

ders.: Les droits de l'homme saisis par le droit International, in: Revue Togolaise des Sciences Juridiques (2012), 22–40.

ders.: Réflexion sur la justice constitutionnelle à travers le contrôle de la constitutionnalité de la loi dans le nouveau constitutionnalisme: les cas du Benin, Mali, Sénégal et Togo, in: Revue Béninoise des sciences juridiques et politiques et administratives (2006), 124.

Lambert-Abdelgawad, Elisabeth: L'exécution des arrêts de la Cour européenne des Droits de l'Homme, in: Revue Trimestrielle des Droits de l'Homme (2011), 939–958.

Landauer, Carl: Things Fall Together: The Past and Future Africas of T.O. Elias's Africa and Development of International Law, in: Leiden Journal of International Law (2008), 351–375.

Lechner, Hans/Zuck, Rüdiger: Bundesverfassungsgesetz. Kommentar [Federal Constitutional Law. Commentary], 6. edition, München 2011.

Leibholz, Gerhard/Rupprecht, Reinhard: Bundesverfassungsgesetz [Federal Constitutional Law, Köln 1968.

Likibi, Romuald: La Charte africaine pour la démocratie, les élections et la gouvernance. Analyse et commentaires, Paris 2012.

Lindner, Josef Franz: Grundrechtsschutz in Europa – System einer Kollisionsdogmatik [Protection of Constitutional Rights in Europe – a System of Collision-Dogmatism], in: EuR (2007), 160–193.

Lock, Tobias: Das Verhältnis zwischen dem ECJ und Internationalen Gerichten [the relationship between the ECJ and International courts], Tübingen 2010.

Macdonald, Ronald St. J./Matscher, Franz/Petzold, Herbert (Publ.): The European System for Protection of Human Rights, Dordrecht 1993.

Mair, Stefan/Peters-Berries, Christian: Regionale Integration und Kooperation in Afrika südlich der Sahara: EAC, ECOWAS und SADAC im Vergleich [Regional Integration and Cooperation in Africa south of the Sahara: EAC, ECOWAS and SADC in comp.], Bonn und London 2001, 183–294.

Maman-Sani, Aboudou-Salami: Réflexion sur la politisation de l'administration publique togolaise, in: Revue Togolaise des Sciences Juridiques (2012), 89–107.

ders.: Vacance de la présidence de la République: la constitution togolaise à l'épreuve des faits, in: Revue nigérienne de droit (2006), 11–61.

Marauhn, Thilo/Merhof, Katrin: Grundrechtseingriff und –schranken [interference in fundamental rights and their limitations], in: Rainer Grote/Thi- lo Marauhn (Publ.), EMRK/GG. Konkordanzkommentar zum europäischen und deutschen Grundrechtsschutz [Concordance commentary regarding the European and German protection of fundamental rights], 2. edition, Teil 1, Kapitel 7, Tübingen 2013, 366–417.

Marsch, Nikolaus/Vilain, Yoan/Wendel, Matthias (Publ.): Französisches und Deutsches Ver fassungsrecht. Ein Rechtsvergleich [French and German Constitutional Law. A comparison of laws], Berlin und Heidelberg 2015.

Matscher, Franz: Der Gerichtsbegriff der EMRK[The concept of court by the ECHR], in: Hanns Prütting (Publ.), Festschrift for Gottfried Baumgärtel zum 70. Geburtstag, Köln u. a. 1990, 363–380.

ders.: Die Methoden der Auslegung der EMRK in der Rechtsprechung ihrer Organe [Methods of interpretation by the ECHR in the jurisdiction of its organs], in: Fritz Schwind (Publ.), Aktuelle Fragen zum Europarecht aus der Sicht in- und ausländischer Gelehrter[Current questions regarding the European Law from the viewpoint of domestic and foreign scholars], Wien 1986, 103–127.

Maurer, Hartmut: Staatsrecht I. Grundlagen, Verfassungsorgane, Staatsfunktionen[State Law I. Basics, Organs of the Constitution, Functions of the State], 4. edition, München 2005.

Mazzuoli, Valerio Oliveira: The Inter-American human rights protection system: Structure, functioning and effectiveness in Brazilian law, in: African Human Rights Law Journal (2011), 194–215.

McNair, Arnold Duncan: The Law of Treaties, Oxford 1961.

Mellech, Kathrin: Die Rezeption der EMRK sowie der Urteile des EGMR in der französischen und deutschen Rechtsprechung [The reception of the ECHR and the judgments of the ECtHR in the French and German jurisdiction], Tübingen 2012.

Meyer-Ladewig, Jens: Europäische Menschenrechtskonvention. Handkommentar [European Human Rights Convention. Hand commentary], 2. edition, Baden-Baden 2006.

Mole, Nuala/Harby, Catharina: Le droit à un procès équitable, un guide sur la mise de l'ar- ticle 6 de la Convention européenne des droits de l'homme, Strasbourg 2002.

Moyo, Admark: Defending human Rights and the rule of law by the SADC Tribunal: Campbell and beyond, in: African Human Right Law Journal (2009), 590–614.

Mubiala, Mutoy: L'accès de l'Individu à la Cour Africaine des Droits de l'Homme et des Peuples, in: Promoting Justice, Human Rights and Conflicts Resolution through internati onal Law (2007), 369–378.

Mückl, Stefan: Kooperation oder Konfrontation? – Das Verhältnis zwischen Bundesverfas sungsgericht und Europäischem Gerichtshof für Menschenrechte[Cooperation or confrontation? – the relationship between the Federal Constitutional Court and the European Court of Human Rights], in: Der Staat 44 (2005), 403–431.

Murray, Rachel: A comparison between the African and European Court of Human Rights, in: African Human Rights Law Journal (2002), 195–222.

Musungu, Sisule Fredrick: Economic Integration and Human Rights in Africa: A comment on conceptual linkages, in: African Human Rights Law Journal (2003), 88–96.

Ndiaye, Mouhamadou: La protection des droits de l'homme par la Cour de justice de la CEDEAO, Mémoire de Master II, Université Montesquieux Bordeaux IV, Bordeaux 2014. *Ndiaye, Papa Samba*: Les organisations Internationales Africaines et le maintien de la Paix: L'exemple de la CEDEAO, Paris 2014.

Neuman, Gerald L.: Import, Export, and Regional Consent in the Inter-American Court of Human Rights, in: European Journal of International Law (2008), 101–123.

Nicaise, Mede: Jurisprudence constitutionnelle, in: Afrilex N°4, abrufbar auf: http://cerdra- di.u-bordeaux4.fr/la-revue-afrilex.html, 353–372.

Nkhata, Mwiza Jo/Ebobrah, Salomon Tamarabrakemi: Is the SADC Tribunal under judicial siege in Zimbabwe? Reflections on Etheredge v Minister of State for National Security Responsible for Lands, Land Reform and Resettlement and Another, in: The Comparative and International Law Journal of Southern Africa (2010), 81–92.

Nolte, Georg: Art. 2 (7), in: Bruno Simma/Daniel-Erasmus Kahn/Georg Nolte / Andreas Pau- lus (Publ.), The Charter of the United Nations. A Commentary, 3. ed., Oxford 2012, 281- 333.

O'Shea, Andreas: A critical reflection on the proposed African Court on Human and Peoples' Rights, in: African Human Rights Law Journal (2001), 285–298.

Obi, Cyril I.: Economic Community of West African States on the Ground: Comparing Pea-cekeeping in Liberia, Sierra Leone, Guinea Bissau, and Cote d'Ivoire, in: Fredrik Söder- baum/Rodrigo Tavares (Publ.), Regional Organizations in African Security, London u. a. 2011, 51–67.

Okene, O.V.C/Eddie-Amadi, B.C.: Bringing Rights Home: The Status of International Legal Instruments in Nigeria, in: Journal of African and International Law (2010), 409–427.

Okresek, Wolf: Die Umsetzung der EGMR-Urteile und ihre Überwachung: Probleme der Vollstreckung und der Behandlung von Wiederholungsfällen [The implementation of ECtHR judgments and their supervision], in: Europäische Grundrechte-Zeitschrift (2003), 168–174.

Olinga, Alain Didier: La première décision, au fond de la Cour africaine des droits de l'homme et des peuples, in: La Revue des droits de l'Homme (2014), 2–19.

ders.: Les Droits de l'Homme peuvent-ils soustraire un ex-dictateur à la justice? L'affaire Hissène Habré devant la Cour de justice de la CEDEAO, in: Revue Trimestrielle des Droits de l'Homme (2011), 735–746.

ders.: Les Emprunts normatifs de la Commission Africaine Droits de l'Homme et des Peuples aux systèmes européens et Interaméricain de Garantie des Droits de l'Homme, in: Revue Trimestrielle des Droits de l'Homme (2005), 499–537.

ders.: Regard sur le Premier Arrêt de la Cour Africaine des Droits de l'Homme et des Peuples, Cour africaine des droits de l'homme et des peuples, Michelot Yogogombaye c. Sénégal, 15. décembre 2009, in: Revue Trimestrielle des Droits de l'Homme (2010), 749–768.

Onoria, Henry: The African Commission on Human and Peoples' Rights and the exhaustion of local remedies under the African Charter, in: African Human Rights Law (2003), 1–24. *ders.: The Locus Standi* of Individual and Non-State Entities before Regional Economic Integration Judicial Bodies in Africa, in: Journal of African and International Law (2010), 91–124.

Oppong, Richard Frimpong: Legal Aspects of Economic Integration in Africa, Cambridge 2011.

ders./Niro, C. Lisa: Enforcing Judgments of International Court in National Court, in: Journal of International Dispute Settlement (2014), 1–28.

Österdahl, Inger: Implementing Human Rights in Africa. The African Commission on Hu- man and Peoples' Rights and Individual Communications, Uppsala 2002.

Ouguergouz, Fatsah: L'application Nationale de la charte africaine des droits de l'homme par les autorités Nationales en Afrique occidentale, in: Jean-François Flauss/Elisabeth Lam- bert-Abdelgawad (Publ.), L'application Nationale de la Charte africaine des droits de l'homme et des peuples, Brüssel 2004, 163–205.

Ould Bouboutt, Ahmed Salem: Les Juridictions constitutionnelles en Afrique, évolutions et Enjeux, in: Annuaire International de Justice constitutionnelle (1997), 38–45.

Oumarou, Narey: La Cour constitutionnelle du Niger et le contrôle de conformité des traités et accords internationaux à la Constitution: Remarques sur la Jurisprudence CIMA, in: Revue Juridiques et Politiques (2008), 503–518.

Padilla, David: An African Human Rights Court: Reflections from the perspective of the Inter-American system, in: African Human Rights Law Journal (2002), 185–194.

Pache, Eckhard: Der Gerichtshof der Europäischen Union[Court of Justice of the European Union]. Art. 251–281 AEUV, Art. 340 AEUV, Art. 344 AEUV, in: Christoph Vedder/Heintschel von Heinegg (Publ.), Europäisches Unionsrecht [European Union Law], Baden-Baden 2012. TFEU

ders.: Die Europäische Menschenrechtskonvention und die deutsche Rechtsordnung [The European Convention on Human Rights and the German legal system], in: Europarecht (2004), 393–415.

Payandeh, Mehrdad: Internationales Gemeinschaftsrecht. Zur Herausbildung gemein- schaftsrechtlicher Strukturen im Völkerrecht der Globalisierung [International Community Law. Regarding the Development of community-law structures in International law], Heidelberg u. a. 2010

Pestalozza, Christian: Verfassungsprozeßrecht[Constitutional Process Law], 3. edition, München 1991.

Peters, Anne: Rechtsordnungen und Konstitutionalisierung: Zur Neubestimmung der Verhältnisse [Legal systems and constitutionalisation: regarding the new definition of relationships], in: Die öffentliche Verwaltung (2010), 3–63.

Pettiti, Christophe: Le réexamen d'une décision pénale française après un arrêt de la Cour Européenne des Droits de L'Homme: La loi française du 15 juin 2000, in: Revue Trimestrielle des Droits de l'Homme (2001), 3–13.

Peukert, Wolfgang, in: *Frowein, Jochen Abraham/Peukert, Wolfgang (Publ.)*, Europäische Menschenrechtskonvention. EMRK-Kommentar [European Human Rights Convention. ECHR commentary], 3. edition, Kehl 2009.

Polakiewicz, Jörg: Die Verpflichtung der Staaten aus den Urteilen des Europäischen Gerichtshofs für Menschenrechte, Berlin u. a. 1993. [The obligation of countries resulting from the judgments by the European Court of Human Rights, Berlin et al 1993.]

Preußler, Lukas: Question prioritaire de constitutionnalité. Perspektiven konkreter Normen- kontrolle in Frankreich, Frankfurt 2015.

Renoux, Thierry: Le Conseil Constitutionnel et l'autorité judiciaire, l'élaboration d'un droit constitutionnel juridictionnel, Paris 1984.

Ress, Georg: Aspekte der Entfaltung des Europäischen Menschenrechtsschutzes[Aspects of the development of the European protection of human rights], in: Jahrbuch der Juristischen Gesellschaft Bremen (2003), 17–39.

ders.: „Die Einzelfallbezogenheit" in der Rechtsprechung des Europäischen Gerichtshof für Menschenrechte, in: Völkerrecht als Rechtsordnung – Internationale Gerichtsbarkeit – Menschenrechte. [The relatedness of "the individual case" in the jurisdiction by the European Court of Human Rights, in: International law as a legal system – International jurisprudence – human rights] FS für Hermann Mosler (1983), Berlin 1983, 719–744.

ders.: Supranationaler Menschenrechtsschutz und der Wandel der Staatlichkeit[Supra-National Protection of Human Rights and the Change in Statehood], in: ZaöRV (2004), 621–639.

ders.: Wirkung und Beachtung der Urteile der Entscheidungen der Straßburger Konventionsorgane[Effect of and Compliance with the judgments of the Straßburg Convention organs], in: Europäische Grundrechte-Zeitschrift (1996), 350–353.

Rinsche, Karen: Die Welt nach Caroline – Rechtliche und faktische Umsetzung des EGMR-Urteils im Fall Hannover [The World after Caroline – legal and factual implementation of the ECtHR judgment in the case of Hanover], in: Roger Mann/Jörg F. Smid (Publ.), Festschrift für Renate Damm zum 70. Geburtstag, Baden-Baden 2005, 156–169.

Rohleder, Kristin: Grundrechtsschutz im europäischen Mehrebenen-System. Unter besonderer Berücksichtigung des Verhältnisses zwischen Bundesverfassung und Europäischem Gerichtshof für Menschenrechte[Protection of constitutional law in the European multi-level system. With particular consideration to the relationships between the Federal Constitution and the European Court of Human Rights], Baden-Baden 2009.

Rosenberg, Leo/Schwab, Karl Heinz/Gottwald, Peter (Publ.): Zivilprozessrecht [Rules of Civil Procedure], 13. edition, München 2010.

Rota, Marie: Chronique de jurisprudence de la Cour interaméricaine des Droits de l'Homme, in: Centre de Recherche pour les Droits Fondamentaux (2009), 189–198.

Rousseau, Charles: Droit International Public, Tome I, Paris 1970.

Ruffert, Matthias/Walter, Christian: Institutionalisiertes Völkerrecht [Institutionalised International law], 2. edition, München 2015.

Salami, Ibrahim David/Gandonou, Diane O. Melone: Droit Constitutionnel et Institutions du Bénin, Paris 2014.

Saliu, Hassan A.: Governance and development questions in west Africa, in: Lambert N'ga ladjo Bamba/John O. Igué/Kalilou Sylla (Publ.), Sortir du sous-développement, Quelles Nouvelles Pistes Pour l'Afrique de l'Ouest?, Paris 2011, 185–203.

Sall, Alioune: L'affaire Hissène Habré. Aspects judiciaires nationaux et internationaux, Paris 2013.

dies.: La Justice d'intégration, réflexions sur les institutions judiciaires de la CEDEAO et de l'UEMOA, Paris 2009.

dies.: Le Droit International dans les nouvelles constitutions africaines, in: Revue Juridique et Politique (1997), 339–352.

Sauer, Heiko: Jurisdiktionskonflikte in Mehrebenensystemen. Die Entwicklung eines Mo dells zur Lösung von Konflikten zwischen Gerichten unterschiedlicher Ebenen in vernetzten Rechtsordnungen[Conflicts of jurisdiction in multi-level-governance systems. The development of a solution model for conflicts between courts at different levels within a network of legal systems], Berlin u. a. 2008.

Schaffarzik, Bert: Europäische Menschenrechte unter der Ägide des Bundesverfassungsgerichts[European human rights under the aegis of the Federal Constitutional Court], in: Die öffentliche Verwaltung. Zeitschrift für öffentliches Recht und Verwaltungs- wissenschaft [Magazine for Public Law and Administrative Science, ZaöRV] (2005), 860- 868.

Schaffrin, Dora: Rechtskraft der Entscheidung[Legal Force of the Decision], in: Ulrich Karpenstein/Franz C. Mayer (Publ.), Konvention zum Schutz der Menschenrechte und Grundfreiheiten. Kommentar, 2. edition, München 2015, Art. 27 EMRK, 518–526.

Schilling, Jan Moritz: Deutscher Grundrechtsschutz zwischen staatlicher Souveränität und menschenrechtlicher Europäisierung. Zum Verhältnis zwischen Bundesverfassungsge- richt und Europäischem Gerichtshof für Menschenrechte [Protection of the German constitutional law between state sovereignty and Europeanisation of human rights. Reg. the relationship relationships between the Federal Constitution and the European Court of Human Rights], Tübingen 2010.

Schlaich, Klaus/Korioth, Stefan: Das Bundesverfassungsgericht. Stellung, Verfahren, Entscheidungen[The Federal Constitutional Court. Position, procedure, decisions], 8. edition, München 2010.

Schröder, Mainhard: Verantwortlichkeit, Völkerstrafrecht, Streitbeilegung und Sanktion [Responsibility, International criminal law, dispute settlement and sanction], in: Wolfgang Graf Vitzthum/Alexander Proelß (Publ.), Völkerrecht, 6. edition, Berlin u. a. 2013. *Simma, Bruno*: Das Reziprozitätselement in der Entstehung des Völkergewohnheitsrechts. Alfred Verdross zum 80. Geburtstag gewidmet, München u. a. 1970.

ders.: Charta der Vereinten Nationen. Kommentar, München 1991.

Sodan, Helge/Ziekow, Jan: Grundkurs Öffentliches Recht, 5. edition, München 2012.

Söderbaum, Fredrik/Tavares, Rodrigo: Problematizing Regional Organizations in African Security, in: Fredrik Söderbaum/Rodrigo Tavares (Publ.), Regional Organizations in African Security, London u. a. 2011, 1–13.

Somali, Kossi: L'indépendance de la Cour Africaine des droits de l'homme et des peuples, théories et réalités, in: Revue Togolaise des Sciences Juridiques (2013), 51–64.

Stern, Klaus: Das Staatsrecht der Bundesrepublik Deutschland, Bd. II: Staatsorgane, Staatsfunktionen, Finanz- und Haushaltsverfassung, Notstandsverfassung, München 1980.

Szymczak, David: La Convention européenne des droits de l'homme et le juge constitutionnel National, Brüssel 2006.

Tama, Jean-Nazaire: Droit International et africain des droits de l'homme, Paris 2012.

Tambedou, Malick: De l'indépendance du Pouvoir Judiciaire au Sénégal, in: Revue Juridique et Politique (2008), 271–314.

Tchapnga, Célestin Keutcha: Le juge constitutionnel, juge administratif au Bénin et au Ga- bon?, in: Revue française de Droit constitutionnel (2008), 551–583.

Tonnang, Edouard Gnimpieba/Fandjip, Olivier: La Cour de Justice de la CEMAC et les règles du Procès équitable, in: Recueil Penant (2010), 329–356.

Toufayan, Mark: When British Justice (in African Colonies) Point Two Ways: On Dualism, Hybridity and the Genealogy of Juridical Negritude in Taslim Olawale Elias, in: Leiden Journal of International Law (2008), 377–410.

Tsikrikas, Dimitrios: Die Wirkungen der Urteile des Europäischen Gerichtshof im Vertrags- verletzungsverfahren (Art. 169 ff. EWGV), Berlin 1990.

Twinomugisha, Ben Kiromba: The role of the judiciary in the promotion of democracy in Uganda, in: African Human Rights Law Journal (2009), 1–22.

Van den Boom, Dirk: Regionale Kooperation in Westafrika. Politik und Probleme der ECOWAS, Hamburg 1996.

Van Genugten, Willem: Avena ou le system juridique fédéral américain à l'épreuve, in: Hague Justice Journal (2008), 53–60.

Velu, Jacques: Considérations sur les arrêts de la Cour européenne des droits de l'homme relatifs au droit à un procès équitable dans les affaires mettant en cause la Belgique, Brüs- sel 2004.

ders./Ergec, Rusen: La Convention Européenne des Droits de l'Homme, Brüssel 1990.

Verdross, Alfred/Simma, Bruno: Universelles Völkerrecht. Theorie und Praxis [Universal International law. Theory and practice], 3. edition Berlin 1984.

Viljoen, Frans: International Human Rights Law in Africa, 2. ed., Oxford 2012.

Villiger, Mark E.: Handbuch der Europäischen Menschenrechtskonvention[Handbook on the European Human Rights Convention], 2. edition, Zürich 1999.

ders.: The principle of subsidiarity in the European Convention on Human Rights, in: Promo- ting Justice, Human Rights and Conflict Resolution through International law (2007), 623–637.

Vitzthum, Wolfgang Graf (Publ.): Völkerrecht [International law], 4. edition, Berlin 2007.

Wachira, George Mukundi: African Court on Human Rights and Peoples' Rights: Ten years on and still no justice, London 2008.

Wiethoff, Jan Heindrik: Das konzeptionelle Verhältnis von EuGH und EGMR unter besonde rer Berücksichtigung der aktuellen Verfassungsentwicklung der Europäischen Union [The conceptional relationship between ECJ and ECtHR with particular consideration to the current constitutional development in the European Union], Bochum 2007.

Wildhaber, Luzius: De l'évolution des idées sur les missions de la Cour Européenne des Droits de l'Homme, in: Promoting Justice, Human Rights and Conflict Resolution through International Law (2007), 639–653.

Wildhaber, Luzius: Eine verfassungsrechtliche Zukunft für den Europäischen Gerichtshof für Menschenrechte? [A constitutional future for the European Court of Law for Human Rights?], in: Europäische Grundrechte-Zeitschrift (2002), 569 ff.

Yebisi, Ebenzer Tunde: The constitutional power of review of Supreme Court of Ghana: Lesson for Nigeria, in: International Journal of Humanities and Social Science (2014), 39–49.

Zeuner, Albrecht: Die objektiven Grenzen der Rechtskraft im Rahmen rechtlicher Sinnzu sammenhänge. Zur Lehre über das Verhältnis von Rechtskraft und Entscheidungsgründen im Zivilprozeß [The objective limits of legal force within the framework of legal contexts. Reg. the theory on the relationship between legal force and reasons for decision-making in civil proceedings], Tübingen 1959.

Internet Sources

Community Court of Justice: www.courtecowas.org

Conseil Constitutionnel (France): www.conseil-constitutionnel.fr

Cour Africaine des Droits de l'Homme et des Peuples: www.african-court.org

Cour constitutionnelle du Togo: www.courconstitutionnelle.tg (last accessed on 22.06. 2015, zum Zeitpunkt der Veröffentlichung: www.legitogo.gouv.tg)

Cour de Justice de l'Union Européenne: www.curia.europa.eu Cour Internationale de Justice: www.icj-cij.org

East African Court of Justice: www.eacj.org

European Court of Human Rights: www.hudoc.ECtHR.coe.int Inter-American Court of Human Rights: www.corteidh.or.cr

International Institute for Democracy and Election Assistance: www.constitutionn et.org La Cour Constitutionnelle du Bénin: www.cour-constitutionnelle-benin.o rg

Revue d'étude et de Recherche sur le droit et l'administration dans les Pays d'Afrique: www. cerdradi.u-bordeaux4.fr/la-revue-afrilex

Southern African Development Community: www.sadc.int Supreme Court of Nigeria: www.supremecourt.gov.ng

The judicial service of Ghana: www.judicial.gov.gh